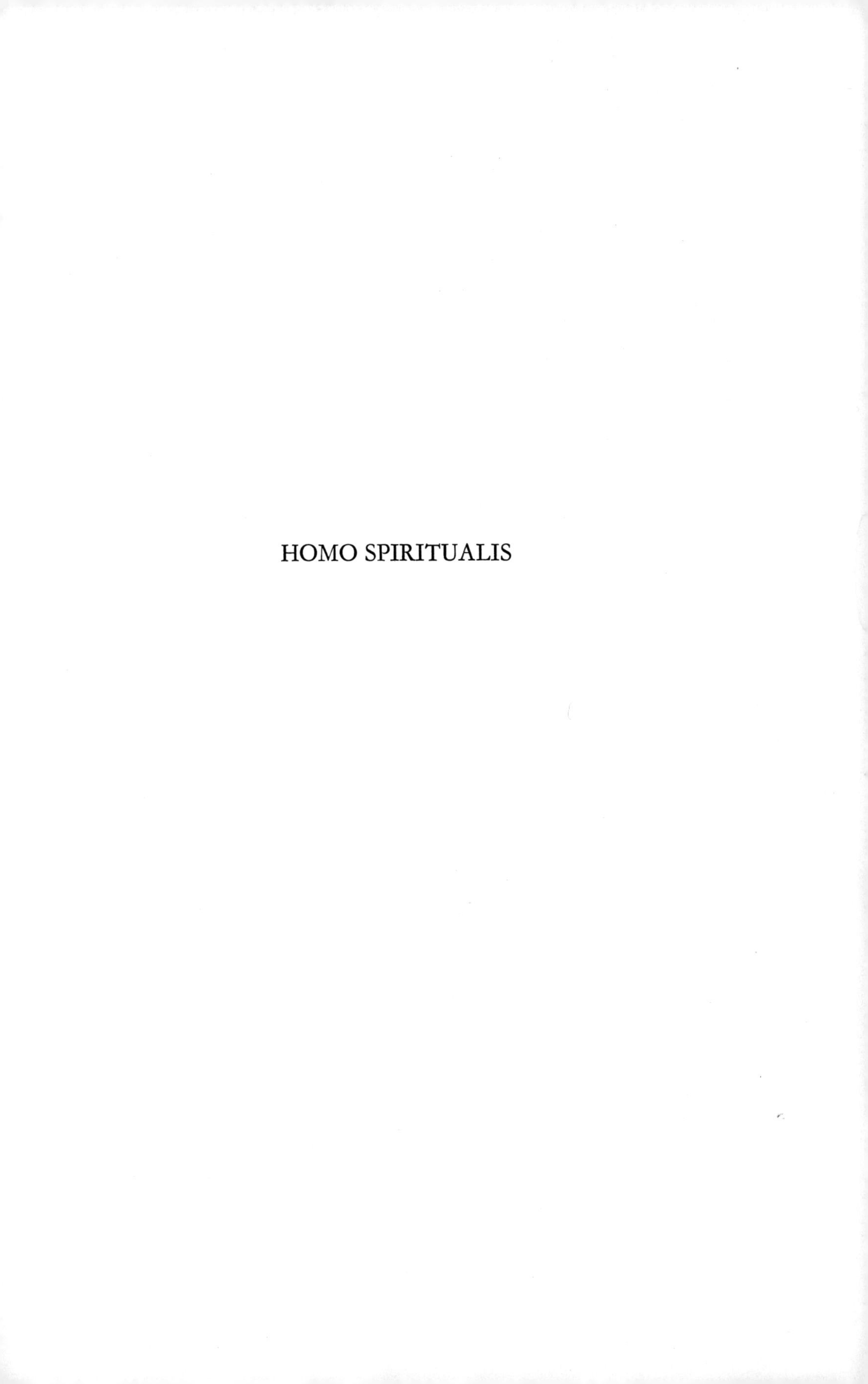

HOMO SPIRITUALIS

STUDIES IN MEDIEVAL AND REFORMATION THOUGHT

EDITED BY

HEIKO A. OBERMAN, Tübingen

IN COOPERATION WITH

E. JANE DEMPSEY DOUGLASS, Claremont, California
LEIF GRANE, Copenhagen
GUILLAUME H. M. POSTHUMUS MEYJES, Leiden
ANTON G. WEILER, Nijmegen

VOLUME VI

STEVEN E. OZMENT

HOMO SPIRITUALIS

LEIDEN
E. J. BRILL
1969

HOMO SPIRITUALIS

A COMPARATIVE STUDY OF THE ANTHROPOLOGY OF JOHANNES TAULER, JEAN GERSON AND MARTIN LUTHER (1509-16) IN THE CONTEXT OF THEIR THEOLOGICAL THOUGHT

BY

STEVEN E. OZMENT

LEIDEN
E. J. BRILL
1969

PRINTED IN THE NETHERLANDS

CONTENTS

Part Three

MARTIN LUTHER (1509-16)

PREFACE

If one desires to know what a particular author said, it suffices simply to read the works of this author. Should one, however, wish to go to the heart of the matter and understand why this author said what he said, then one must read what he read. This common-sensical hermeneutical principle is becoming normative today in Reformation Studies, especially with regard to the development of Martin Luther's thought. If there is 'newness' with the Reformation, it is not a newness *ex nihilo*. If there is a 'difference' with Luther, it is a difference from something. The Reformation demands interpretation within its systematic dialogue with the late medieval period. This study of Johannes Tauler, Jean Gerson and Martin Luther is an effort to fulfill this demand.

During the years in which this study was developed many scholarly debts have been accumulated. I am especially indebted to Professor Heiko A. Oberman of the University of Tübingen for the relentlessly searching analyses to which he subjected the manuscript. Without his critical persuasion the study would hardly have attained maturity. A special debt of gratitude is also due to Assistant Professor James S. Preus of Harvard Divinity School for his constant reminders that incommunicable profundity is really not so profound and Professor George H. Williams of Harvard Divinity School for his often embarrassingly pertinent questions. Lastly, deep appreciation must be extended to my colleagues and students at the University of Tübingen, who convinced me that German 'Gründlichkeit' and Anglo-Saxon 'style' can coexist with mutual profit.

Scholarly debts are not the only debts accumulated during the formation of this study. To my wife and children I extend the most appreciative affection for the understanding with which they permitted me occasionally to forget them and for the patient reminders that, *coram hominibus* if not *coram deo*, the *homo spiritualis* must also be *homo saecularis*.

University of Tübingen
March 18, 1968

Steven E. Ozment

ABBREVIATIONS

ARG	*Archiv für Reformationsgeschichte* (Berlin, 1904-)
FS	*Franziskanische Studien* (Münster i.W. und 1914-)
HTR	*Harvard Theological Review* (Cambridge, Mass., 1920-)
PL	*Patrologia Latina*, ed. J. P. Migne (Paris, 1844-90)
ThStK	*Theologische Studien und Kritiken* (Hamburg, 1828-)
WA	*D. Martin Luthers Werke: Kritische Gesamtausgabe* (Weimar, 1883-)
WA Br	*Weimarer Ausgabe, Briefe* (1930-)
ZKG	*Zeitschrift für Kirchengeschichte* (Gotha u.a., 1877-)
ZSTh	*Zeitschrift für systematische Theologie* (Gütersloh and Berlin, 1923-)
ZThK	*Zeitschrift für Theologie und Kirche* (Tübingen, 1891-)

INTRODUCTION

1. *HOMO SPIRITUALIS NITITUR FIDE*

One obviously does not enter upon an examination of Luther's scholarly activity in 1509-16 without taking his two most extensive works in this formative period into consideration: the tortuous *Dictata super psalterium* (1513-16) and the brisk lectures on Paul's letter to the Romans (1515-16). Indeed, it is generally accepted today that the major clues to Luther's Reformation theology are to be found in his engagement with the medieval exegetical and scholastic traditions in these two works.

The understandable hegemony of the *Dictata* and the lectures on Romans should not, however, lead one to overlook a much smaller work in this same period, which engages still another medieval tradition—the medieval mystical tradition. This work, which overlaps in time major portions of the *Dictata* and the lectures on Romans, is Luther's marginal notes on Johannes Tauler's Sermons (1515-16).[1] The brevity of these marginals and the paucity of scholarly curiosity about them belie their significance. For these notes contain a fresh perspective from which the development of Luther's Reformation theology can be interpreted with a heretofore unrecognized systematic cohesion.

Here it is made quite clear that, in his early period, Luther was neither a neurotic monk propounding riddles nor a charismatic visionary privy to paradoxes forbidden his all too medieval peers and predecessors. Here we find him as he no doubt was—a late medieval *doctor scripturae*, pouring over texts with pen in hand, scribbling affirmations and denials, questions and original reflections, on page after page of Tauler's book of sermons. And then, with the patience and precision

[1] *WA* 9,95-104. Johannes Ficker's analysis of Luther's handwriting leads him to argue that it is defensible to date the beginning of the notes on Tauler's Sermons in early 1515, i.e. before the conclusion of the *Dictata super psalterium* and during the early *scholia* (especially on chapter 8) of the lectures on Romans. "Zu den Bemerkungen Luthers in Taulers Sermones (Augsburg, 1508)," *ThStK*, 107 (1936), 56. This conclusion concurs with the position, based strictly on content considerations, of A. V. Müller, *Luther und Tauler auf ihrem theologischen Zusammenhang neu untersucht* (Bern, 1918), 22. We accept these findings as sufficient justification to interpret the notes on Tauler's Sermons both in the light of the development in the *Dictata* and in that of the lectures on Romans and *vice versa.*

fitting his vocation, Luther works his way to a perfect summary of what proved to be his 'master-idea': the spiritual man and true Christian lives by faith.

The appearance of Luther's 'master-idea' in the notes on Tauler's Sermons is significant because of the context in which it emerges. It results from two comments on Tauler's anthropology—the tripartite schema which distinguishes (a) an outward, animal, sensual man, (b) the rational man and (c) what Tauler describes as the *gemuete* or highest part of the soul.[1]

In one of these comments, Luther simply repeats and parallels the anthropological schema of Jean Gerson and refers the reader to the conclusions Gerson draws in his "Mystical Theology."[2] In the second comment, however, Luther refuses the cloak of another and presents his own anthropological schema, which follows both Tauler and Gerson save for one significant particular. Whereas Tauler defines the spiritual man with the term *gemuete* and Gerson with the term *synteresis*, Luther declares: "the spiritual man [is the man] who relies upon faith."[3]

This raises several questions. What happens to the theological systems of Tauler and Gerson when *fides* replaces the *gemuete* and the *synteresis* as the defining characteristic of the spiritual man? Does it have the polemical consequence of knocking the props out from under their understanding of the order of salvation and the nature of man's union with God in this life, or is it an innocuous adjustment? The first two parts of our study will show that the terms *gemuete* and *synteresis* are so basic to the full range of the theological reflection of Tauler and Gerson respectively, that their removal from a position of prominence threatens *in fundamento* the thrust of their entire thought. In this sense and to this extent the theological systems of Tauler and Gerson are Luther's earliest major conscious opponents.[4]

---

[1] *Die Predigten Taulers*, ed. Ferdinand Vetter (Berlin, 1910), 384.22ff, 21.7ff. See chapter I of our study of Tauler, *infra*, p. 15ff.

[2] *WA* 9,99.36-100.3: "Tria: sensus, ratio, mens vel apex mentis sive syntheresis. Vide Gerson in mystica theologia. Si in affectu tria: concupiscentia sensus seu appetitus sensus, appetitus intellectivus, synthe[re]sis." Note that Luther reads *synteresis* in parallel with "apex mentis" as well as with the highest affective power. For the former, Gerson reads "intelligentia simplex", not *synteresis*. Luther's reading is indicative of his awareness of and drawing upon the two-fold interpretation of the *synteresis* in the late medieval tradition. Cf. *infra*, p. 139, note 3.

[3] *WA* 9,103.40-104.3: "Homo sensualis qui nititur sensu; rationalis qui nititur ratione; spiritualis qui nititur fide. Hunc Apostolus videtur vocare [hominem] carnalem et hunc attingunt mundani tantum; animalem et hunc attingunt philosophi et heretici; spiritualem et hunc attingunt christiani veri."

[4] Cf. Wilhelm Link, *Das Ringen Luthers um die Freiheit der Theologie von der Philo-*

Similar questions can be raised in regard to the development of Luther's theological thought. What can it mean for Luther's theology when he writes that the spiritual man and true Christian relies upon faith? What changes are reflected in his understanding of the way to salvation and the nature of man's union with God in this life when *fides* and not an anthropological resource like Tauler's *gemuete* or Gerson's *synteresis* becomes definitive of the spiritual man? The final parts of our study will show that Luther's quest for the correlation between *fides* and *homo spiritualis* carries in its wake decisive clues to his understanding of law and gospel, the formation of his *simul iustus et peccator* doctrine, his acute appreciation for historical christology and his gradual overcoming of the Pelagian covenant theology of nominalism. Stated as forcefully as possible, we will argue that Luther's Reformation theology originates in and develops as a highly polemical answer to the anthropology of late medieval mystical theology.

2. THE SEARCH FOR THE DEMARCATION LINE

In the secondary literature which deals with Luther's relation to Tauler and Gerson, and, in the larger context, to the mystical traditions which Tauler and Gerson represent and to a rather large extent can be said to summarize systematically,[1] Luther's two comments on Tauler's anthropology have occasioned no major study. This is certainly not because fundamental differences between Luther and his medieval predecessors in the sphere of anthropology have gone un-

---

sophie (München, 1955), 315: "Die letzte und ganz entscheidende Begegnung des jungen Luthers ist die mit der deutschen Mystik." While we agree on the decisiveness of this encounter, we find, contrary to Link, that Luther's definition of his position over against Tauler is prior and not subsequent to the clarification of his major differences with late medieval nominalism.

[1] The typology of Erich Vogelsang distinguishes a Latin ("romanisch"), German ("germanisch") and Dionysian mysticism. Within this typology Gerson is classified as a representative of the Latin tradition together with Bernard of Clairvaux, Bonaventure and Hugo of St. Victor, whereas Tauler joins Wessel Gansfort, Johann Goch and the *Theologia Deutsch* within the German tradition. "Luther und die Mystik," *Luther Jahrbuch* (1937), 32ff. This classification is not uninfluenced by the research of Hermann Hering, who distinguished three periods in which Luther was under the influence of medieval mysticism, viz., 1509-12, under the tutelage of Staupitz, a "romanisch-mystische Periode" (1512-16), under the prestige of Bernard and Gerson, and a "germanisch-mystische Periode" (1516f), under the attraction of the Augustinianism of Tauler. *Die Mystik Luthers im Zusammenhange seiner Theologie und ihrem Verhältniss zur älteren Mystik* (Leipzig, 1879).

recognized. That Luther is 'Pauline' and not 'mystical' in his anthropology is generally accepted as a self-evident and thoroughly unassailable axiom of Luther scholarship to date. Erich Vogelsang speaks for generations past and present when he concludes that, with Luther, "the mystical-psychological consideration of man is overcome and replaced by a theological understanding."[1]

That there are major differences between Luther's theology and mysticism at the point of anthropology cannot, therefore, come as a revelation to Luther scholars. A historical and systematic specification of the centrality of these differences, however, is a rather unsightly chink in the armor of this otherwise formidable tradition of scholarship. Luther scholars have sought the line of demarcation between Luther's theology and mysticism within major doctrinal and confessional concerns, especially in the area of Christology, rather than within the sphere of anthropology. Moreover, it has often been extensive reporting of Luther's later evaluations, rather than intensive analysis of the documents in which the systematic encounter itself is developed, which has proven to be the more decisive criterion for interpretation. Criticism begs documentation. What are the main issues and conclusions presented in the secondary literature?

In 1918 A. V. Müller drew quite provocatively from the writings of Tauler and Luther to construct some thirteen points of agreement which he found to grow out of their common acceptance of the Augustinian conviction of "the powerlessness of the natural powers within the order of salvation and the so-called 'omnipotence of God'."[2] His effort, however, received a sharp confessional dismissal, which is generally accepted today, from Otto Scheel, who concluded: "the Catholic doctrine of grace underlies Tauler's mysticism, and this doctrine is the opposite of the Reformation doctrine of justification."[3]

The study by Bernd Moeller collects and analyzes twenty-five statements by Luther on Tauler. Moeller finds that Luther, by his own accounting, is especially appreciative of Tauler's "description of the

[1] Vogelsang, *Luther Jahrbuch* (1937), 48.

[2] Müller, *Luther und Tauler*, 168. At this point, Müller is followed by Horst Quiring, "Luther und die Mystik," *ZSTh*, 13 (1936), 210, 212, and Bengt Hägglund, "Luther's Doctrine of Justification in Late Medieval Theology," *Lutheran World*, 8 (1961), 25-26. Hägglund, further, finds the Augustinian elements in Tauler's mysticism to contain the theological antidote which Luther administers to the Pelagian *facere quod in se est* of nominalism. For an alternative interpretation, see our discussion *infra*, 30ff.

[3] Otto Scheel, "Taulers Mystik und Luthers reformatorische Entdeckung," *Festgabe für Julius Kaftan* (Tübingen, 1920), 311.

order of salvation," especially with its emphasis on resignation and spiritual temptation (*Anfechtung*). But he comes to the conclusion that Tauler has had no "formative influence" on Luther's theology.[1]

Friedrich Ruhland's study examines the influence of mystical vocabulary upon Luther, specifically the bridal imagery of Augustine, the *Glossa ordinaria*, Bernard and Tauler. He finds that Luther "reconstructs" this imagery so that no mystical content, inimical to his own theological position, remains present.[2] This position is shared by Johannes von Walter, who speaks of Luther's "misunderstanding" of mystical terminology, which issued in a salutary "reformatorische Umdeutung" of mystical terms.[3] In this line of interpretation Artur Rühl argues that it is not until 1522 that Luther finally discovers his basic differences with mysticism, a conclusion which our study will challenge.[4]

With the study of Olavi Tarvainen, the Christological differences between Luther's theology and mysticism come into the foreground. Tarvainen argues that the "deep, inward relationship to Christ" of the mystics is a common concern, but he reaches the conclusion that Luther's understanding of *conformitas Christi* is a religious, Christo-

---

[1] Bernd Moeller, "Tauler und Luther," *La mystique rhénane* (Paris, 1963), 158-59, 165f.

[2] Friedrich Ruhland, *Luther und die Brautmystik nach Luthers Schrifttum bis* 1521 (Gießen, 1938), 143, 145: "...die 'Brautmystik' Luthers [ist] Glied eines theologischen Gedankengefüges, das in seinem Zentrum nicht mystisch genannt werden kann."

[3] Johannes von Walter, *Mystik und Rechtfertigung beim jungen Luther* (Gütersloh, 1937), 32: "Indem er sich als Sünder bekennt, braucht [Luther] Ausdrücke wie nihil, nihileitas, die nach mystischer Entwerdung klingen. Hier liegt reformatorische Umdeutung, oder wie ich für den ganz frühen Luther lieber sagen möchte, Mißverständnis der mystischen Terminologie vor. Daher auch gerade an diesem Punkte die Vorliebe für mystische Schriften." See further von Walter's article "Meister Eckehart oder Luther?" (1935) in *Christentum und Frömmigkeit, Gesammelte Vorträge und Aufsätze* (Gütersloh, 1941), 288f.

[4] Artur Rühl, *Der Einfluss der Mystik auf Denken und Entwicklung des jungen Luthers* (Oberhessen, 1960), 110. Rühl summarizes his position: "Luther verstand den neuen Menschen paulinisch von der Sündenvergebung durch die reine schenkende Gnade Gottes her, denn darauf waren seine Einstellung und sein Interesse in erster Linie gerichtet. Der Mystiker dagegen versteht den neuen Menschen von der Vergottung her, denn sein Interesse zielt auf die 'unio mystica.' Diesen Unterschied sah Luther in seiner Frühzeit noch nicht, und er hat ihn bis 1522 nicht gesehen..." To the contrary, we will argue that there are decisive, irreconcilable differences between Luther and Tauler and Gerson in the period 1513-16. There is, to be sure, no outspoken attack by Luther on either in this period. There are, however, quite significant and conscious modifications directed against both, as for example, Luther's replacement of *synteresis* and *gemuete* with *fides*, a modification which, as we will see, inflicts considerable damage.

centric, evangelical and personal understanding which stands in stark contrast to the ethical, anthropocentric, legalistic and impersonal *imitatio Christi* to which mysticism leads.[1] Wilhelm Thimme,[2] Horst Quiring,[3] and Wilhelm Link[4] join Ruhland,[5] Vogelsang[6] and von Walter[7] to emphasize that it is ultimately Luther's focus on *Christus incarnatus*, rather than on the *Verbum increatum*, and, correlatively, Word and faith, rather than mystical *Schauen*, which decisively separates Luther from medieval mysticism. This Christological line of demarcation reaches its most extreme boundary in Johannes Ficker's suggestion that it is the title-page (reproduced by Ficker in full color!) of the edition of Tauler's Sermons read by Luther, with its moving portrait of Christ bearing His cross, that clarifies Luther's predilection for Tauler.[8]

In the only major effort to relate Luther and Gerson,[9] Walter Dress cites Gerson's concern for personal experience over against a dry intellectualism,[10] his recognition of spiritual temptation and his "af-

[1] Olavi Tarvainen, "Der Gedanke der conformitas Christi in Luthers Theologie," *ZSTh*, XXII (1953), 31, 34-35.

[2] Wilhelm Thimme, "Die 'Deutsche Theologie' und Luthers 'Freiheit eines Christenmenschen.' Ein Vergleich," *ZThK*, 3 (1932), 211, 215.

[3] Quiring, *ZSTh*, 13 (1936), 218, 221.

[4] Link, *Das Ringen Luthers*, 344: "Das sieht und betont Luther an den verschiedensten Stellen als den entscheidenden Verfall der mystischen Theologie: der Mystiker will an Christus vorbei zu Gott gehen, er will Gott nicht dort schauen, wo er sich uns zeigt."

[5] Ruhland, *Luther und die Brautmystik*, 93f.

[6] Vogelsang, *Luther Jahrbuch* (1937), 49. See further Vogelsang's later article in which he threatens the general unanimity of Luther scholarship by proposing to criticize the Ritschl-Holl view that Luther knows only a volitional, never a 'substantive' form of union, and that it is always "unio cum Christo," never "cum Deo," that Luther defends. "Die Unio Mystica bei Luther," *ARG*, 35 (1939), 64-65. The challenge, however, proves to be quite modest. Vogelsang concludes that in the passages which employ 'substantive' imagery, "dieses Einigwerden und Einswerden durch die Liebe ist natürlich nicht real und substantiell zu verstehen sondern geschieht im liebenden 'Affekt,' in Herz und Wille." *Ibid.*, 70. See our discussion of *substantia*, *memoria*, *intellectus* and *affectus*, *infra*, 105ff.

[7] Von Walter, *Mystik und Rechtfertigung beim jungen Luther*, 17. Von Walter appeals to the revealing and often-cited *scholion* on Romans 5:2. Here Luther opposes "per fidem" and "per Christum" ("per verbum incarnatum") to mystical rapture ("per anagogen") in the "verbum increatum" as the singular "accessus" to God. *WA* 56, 299.20ff.

[8] Ficker, *ThStK* (1936), 62f.

[9] Efforts prior to Dress' study are summarized by James L. Connolly, *John Gerson: Reformer and Mystic* (Louvain, 1928), 360ff.

[10] Walter Dress, *Die Theologie Gersons: Eine Untersuchung zur Verbindung von Nominalismus und Mystik im Spätmittelalter* (Gütersloh, 1931), 10-11, 69-70. This is considered important not only for Luther's concern to enhance the "pro nobis,"

fective transcendentalism" as formatively influencing the development of Luther's theology.[1] Dress agrees with Luther's own evaluation of Gerson as one who only "appeased the conscience" and failed to overcome the tyranny of the law through Christ and God's promise.[2] And he concludes that Gerson is a proponent of the neoplatonic "gradualistic, hierarchical form of thinking," typical of mysticism, which Luther's "thinking in terms of the whole" dismisses.[3] This last conclusion is indirectly and quite instructively challenged by Rühl. Rühl argues that, far from being an element which is foreign to Luther's theology, the non-scholastic, mystical "method of thinking," which is capable of reconciling opposites and firmly grounded in Paul, forms the most significant positive point of contact between Luther's theology and the medieval mystical traditions.[4]

As we have seen, the secondary literature presents a rich variety of

but also as the historical antecedent of his hermeneutic: "Man darf wohl sagen, daß für Luthers Auslegekunst, die immer nach dem Affekt suchte und nach dem Affekt zu urteilen trachtete, hier der geschichtliche Anknüpfungspunkt zu finden ist." *Ibid.*, 95. Related to Dress' stress on the importance of personal experience, is the study by Reinhold Seeberg, in which the connecting link between Luther and mysticism is described as "die durch geistliche Erfahrung gewonnene Überzeugung, daß der Mensch durch Glauben in Gott lebt, sofern er das, was Gott in ihm *will*, selbst *will*, und daß somit der Glaube nie eine bloße Vorstellung ist, sondern der Eindruck und Ausdruck einer Lebensvereinigung mit Gott." *Die religiösen Grundgedanken des jungen Luthers und ihr Verhältnis zu dem Ockamismus und der deutschen Mystik* (Berlin, 1931), 30. See our discussion of the nature of the *unio mystica* for Tauler and Gerson, *infra*, 35ff, 72ff.

[1] Dress, *Die Theologie Gersons*, 142f., 101; 69-70.

[2] *Ibid.*, 162, 168, with citation of *TR* II, Nr. 1351, 65. 2ff: "...non pervenit eo [Gerson], ut conscientias Christo et promissione consolaretur, sed tantum extenuatione legis dixit: 'Ah, es mus nicht alles so hart sundt sein': et ita solatur manente lege."

[3] Dress, *Die Theologie Gersons*, 79-85, 205.

[4] Rühl summarizes: "Mystik in einer nicht-mystischen Weltanschauung, so könnte man die Bedeutung des mystischen Denkens, sowohl für Paulus als auch für Luther charakterisieren." According to Rühl, this is a strictly non-Aristotelian form of thought which penetrates to unity "hinter dem Gegensatz." *Der Einfluss der Mystik auf Denken und Entwicklung des jungen Luthers*, 112, 114, 132-33. We take issue with this interpretation *infra*, p. 39, note 2, 180, note 1. In regard to the influence of Tauler's "Denkmethode" on Luther, see Moeller, *La mystique rhénane*, 166. Also relevant to this approach to the problem is the thesis of Reinhold Weier. Weier argues that through Faber Stapulensis' *Quincuplex Psalterium* (1509), Luther is decisively influenced by Nicholas of Cusa's understanding of the human word as both concealing and revealing as well as by Cusa's awareness of the importance of divine inner light *in intellectu* for true knowledge of God. "Der Einfluss des Nicolaus Cusanus auf das Denken Martin Luthers," *Das Cusanus-Jubiläum. Mitteilungen und Forschungsbeiträge der Cusanus-Gesellschaft*, 4 (Mainz, 1964), 214, 220. Now in book-form: *Das Thema vom verborgenen Gott von Nikolaus von Kues zu Martin Luther. Buchreihe der Cusanus-Gesellschaft*, II (Münster Westf., 1967), cf. 207-209.

major topics and problems. We find positive points of contact between Luther's theology and late medieval mysticism where this literature emphasizes the centrality of Augustinian motifs; the concern for self-resignation, humility and spiritual temptation; the significance of mystical vocabulary and imagery; the importance of inward, personal experience; and the role which theological methods of thought play. As the major line of demarcation, opposing interpretations of the significance of Christ within the order of salvation are underscored by this literature. The possibility that the hinge on which everything turns—including Christology—may be found in decisions made on the level of anthropology is not entertained. Our concern to give this possibility a hearing is the first exception we take to the research to date in this area.

A second exception is more methodological in nature. Our study dedicates separate and in large measure self-contained parts to an analysis of Tauler's Sermons, Gerson's understanding of mystical theology and the works of Luther in the period 1509-16. This is not done in order to conceal three different books under one cover. We adopt this procedure for both historical and systematic reasons.

First, there are problems and concerns which can only be clarified and appreciated as they are seen within the historical context of each man's thought. To abstract from these historical periods and to attempt systematic comparisons *above* these periods is a quite questionable undertaking, congenial perhaps to polemical (or reconciling 'ecumenical') concerns, but certainly not contributive to that degree of objectivity and comprehensiveness which historical understanding rightfully demands. This aspect of our method can be summarized quite simply: a historical figure must be fully interpreted within his own historical period before comparisons on any level with other figures in other historical periods are undertaken.

A second reason underlying the method of this study is strictly systematic. It lightens the task of the scholar when he can run through the works of several authors and cull and catalog selected paragraphs in which common words, phrases and themes appear in order to compare the results deductively. This 'part by part' method, however, runs the risk of ignoring the very different systematic contexts in which words, phrases and themes common to several authors may occur. *What* an author says is not fully understood until the *termini a quo* and *ad quem* of what he says are taken into account. To this extent the intelligibility of the parts must come through a grasp of the whole.

Parts abstracted from their systematic contexts, like historical figures abstracted from their historical contexts, remain quite questionable spokesmen. Our study, therefore, will compare the anthropology of Tauler, Gerson and Luther within the full systematic context of their thought. This aspect of our methodological procedure seeks to defend the following hermeneutical truth: authors may say very different things with the very same words, phrases and themes.

However obvious these two methodological points may appear to be, they are until this very day two of the most abused rules of scholarship, with particularly disastrous consequences in Luther research, where the question of the demarcation line between medieval and 'modern' is the touchstone by which all must ultimately be measured.[1]

---

[1] See my review of Reinhold Weier, *Das Thema vom verborgenen Gott von Nikolaus von Kues zu Martin Luther*, in *Journal of Ecclesiastical History*, XIX (April, 1968), 122-24.

PART ONE

JOHANNES TAULER

CHAPTER ONE

THE CONSTRUCTION OF A NATURAL 'COVENANT'

Our study of Tauler begins quite literally 'in the beginning.' The first section analyzes his interpretation of John 1:3-4—"what has been created was life in God." Tauler's understanding of man's pre-creaturely being in God manifests presuppositions which are not only foundational to his anthropology, especially his interpretation of the key concepts, *gemuete* and *grunt der selen* (section 2), but also exercise formative influence on his understanding of the order of salvation (chapter two) and the nature of man's union with God in this life (chapter three).

1. PRE-CREATURELY BEING: UNCREATEDNESS IN GOD

Interweaving neoplatonic imagery and content with the first chapter of John's Gospel, Tauler argues that before his flowing from God into createdness, man was "one essential being" (*ein istig wesen*)[1] with and in God. He writes, further, that until this pre-created purity is re-entered, man remains alien from his origin—"uncreatedness in God."[2]

We find the same picture drawn in the context of a discussion of Jesus' ascension (John 20:17). In this regard, Tauler writes:

> Beloved children, who may hinder us from steadfastly following our beloved Leader? Thus, Jesus spoke truly when he said: 'I go to your Father and my Father.' His original ground,[3] goal and blessedness and our blessedness are directly and rightfully[4] a blessedness in the Father.

[1] The important term, *wesen*, is translated consistently in this study as "being" when it is in the substantive form, as "substantive" or "substantially real" when it is in adjectival form, and as "is" when it is in verbal form. In all forms, it connotes an existential-ontological category, designating that which is fundamentally constitutive and definitive of the life of a particular.

[2] Vetter, 331.32-332.4: "Sant Johannes schribet: 'alles das gemacht ist, das was in im ein leben' [John 1:3-4]. Das selbe das der mensche nu ist in siner geschaffenheit, das ist er eweklich gewesen in Gotte in ungeschaffenheit, ein istig wesen mit im. Und als lange als der mensche nút in die luterkeit enkumet, als er us dem ursprunge geflossen ist in sin geschaffenheit us der ungeschaffenheit, so enkumet er niemer wider in Got..." All references to Tauler are to the Vetter edition.

[3] When Tauler uses, as he not infrequently does, the term *grunt* to indicate man's pre-created origin or ground, we employ the more comprehensive and

> For we have flowed from the same original ground, and we directly and rightfully belong, with all that we are, to the same goal and again in the same original ground.[1]

Since man's "inheritance" should be nothing else than the divine, unfathomable, formless, nameless and hidden being of God (*wesen Gotz*),[2] it is not surprising that Tauler depicts man's present life, in its createdness and in its fallenness, as standing between time and eternity and hanging between heaven and earth.[3] For with his highest powers, he is exalted above himself and over all temporal things, dwelling in God; with his lowest powers, he is subjugated to all temporal things; he is in the depths of lowliness and humiliation, completely as one who is only beginning.[4]

It is in reference to these highest powers and parts of the soul that Tauler describes the soul as a "material" in which divinity is implanted, giving the soul a "weight" as great as God's,[5] and argues that the Holy Spirit is the "life of the soul."[6]

---

specific phrase "original ground" in our translation. Otherwise, the *grunt* concerns the created ground of the soul, or the ground of the soul in createdness.

[4] In this passage, the context indicates that *rechte* has the force of a natural appropriateness which one dare not impede ("directly"), and which approaches the status of a just and legal claim ("rightfully"). Otherwise, we translate it with the normal connotation, "gerade."

[1] 81.9ff: "Ouch, minneclichen kinder, wer mag uns des hindern daz wir unserme minneclichen houbete nút on underlos envolgent? Wanne rehte also er ouch sprach: 'ich gan zu uwerme vatter und mime vatter,' sin grunt und sin ende und selikeit und unser selikeit ist rechte ein selikeit in ime; wir sint uz dem selben grunde heruzgeflossen, und mit allem dem daz wir sint, so gehoerent wir rechte in das selbe ende und wider in den selben grunt."

[2] 204.30ff: "...Die ensúllent enkein erbe haben denne das goetliche, wiselose, formlose, namlose verborgen wesen Gotz; das sol allein ir erbe sin."

[3] 202.12ff: "Kinder, von der vergiftikeit des ersten valles so ist die nature also nider gesunken in das niderste teil. Der mensche ist gemacht und stat enzwischent zwein enden, das ist zit und ewikeit. Die zit solte númme haben von uns, denne einen durgang zu dem ende. Und ewikeit solte unser wonunge, unser ende sin." 26.3f: "Die sele ist reht ein mittel zwúschent zit und ewikeit."

[4] 88.7ff: "Und alsus so hanget rechte der mensche enzwúschent himmel und erden: mit sinen úbersten kreften so ist er erhaben úber sich selber und úber alle ding und wonet in Gotte, aber mit sinen nidersten kreften so ist er verdunst under alle ding in den grunt der demuetekeit und ist rechte also ein anhabende mensche..."

[5] 143.1ff: "Diser phenning ["Der phenning ist die sele"—142.29] sol haben sin gewicht. Wissist: dis gewichte dis phennings das ist unwigelich; er wigt me denne himelrich und ertrich und alles das do inne beslossen ist. Wan Got ist in disem phenning, und dar umbe wigt er als vil als Got. // Die materie dis phennings ist die ingesunkene gotheit, die sich mit der úberweselicheit siner unsprechlicher minne in disen geist versenket hat und in herwiderumbe alzemole gar und gar in sich selber verslunden hat und versoeift hat." In regard to the interpretation of the *phenning* metaphor, see P. L. Reypens, "Der 'Goldene Pfenning' bei Tauler und

The specification of the God-bearing highest parts of the soul leads us to a consideration of Tauler's key anthropological-theological[1] terms: the *gemuete* and the *grunt* of the soul.

2. GEMUETE AND GRUNT

When Tauler speaks of the highest powers or parts of the soul, one thing he clearly has in mind is what he summarizes as the *gemuete*.[2] This is made explicit in the following presentation of his anthropological schema:

> Although he is one man, man exists as if he were three men. The first is the outward, animal, sensing man; the second, the rational man with his rational powers; and the third is the *gemuete*, the highest part of the soul. [And as there are various kinds of men in man] so there are various kinds of will in man, each according to its own manner.[3]

Before we turn to the issues raised in this passage and attempt to give precision to the term, *gemuete*, we place two further passages before the reader, each of which is an effort on Tauler's part to specify the nature and activity of the *gemuete*. First, he writes in reference to Luke 10:27:

> Now 'with all your *gemuete*' [latin: 'ex omni mente tua']. That in which everything else is enclosed is and is called the *gemuete*. It is named a measure, for it measures everything else, giving it its form, stability and weight. The *gemuete* embraces and penetrates all. [It is a] habit of the mind.[4]

Ruusbroec," *Altdeutsche und altniederländische Mystik*, ed. Kurt Ruh (Darmstadt, 1964), 353ff.

[6] 208.10ff: "...Als unser sele ist ein leben unsers lichamen und der licham lebt von der selen, also ist der heilig geist ein leben der selen und lebt die sele von dem heiligen geiste und ist unser selen leben." Cf. 307.5ff, 104.13ff, 61.3ff, 394,30ff.

[1] The descriptive phrase "anthropological-theological" is employed to indicate the inadequacy of attempting to interpret the *gemuete* and *grunt* as strictly anthropological terms. We feel it is a necessary qualification, and it is both clarified and justified in the subsequent discussion.

[2] Here, as elsewhere, we will retain Tauler's term without translating it immediately in order that the reader may consider it in its context. This procedure is adopted because a literal, dictionary rendering of Tauler's major terms is often inadequate if not misleading.

[3] 348.22ff: "...Der mensche ist rechte als ob er drú menschen si und ist doch ein mensche. Das eine das ist der uswendig vihelich sinneliche mensche; der ander das ist der vernúnftige mensche mit sinen vernúnftigen kreften; der dritte mensche das ist das gemuete, das oberste teil der selen. Dis alles ist ein mensche. Als ist och maniger kúnne wille in den menschen, ieklichs nach siner wise."

Tauler continues by calling attention to previous efforts to define the term:

> Now it is necessary for us to consider what the *gemuete* is. It is far higher and deeper than the powers of the soul; for these powers draw all their strength from it, are in it and have flowed from it. Still, the *gemuete*, though in all, is immeasureably higher. It is completely pure, substantive and constitutive. One master[1] speaks of this more than the others. The masters say that the *gemuete* of the soul is so noble that it is everywhere and always active, whether man is asleep or awake and whether he knows it or not. It has a God-formed and inexpressible, eternal orientation to God.[2] These masters say that it always sees, loves and enjoys God without interruption. How they understand this we ignore for the present. What is even more, this *gemuete* recognizes itself as God in God, and nevertheless it is created.[3]

Of the issues raised in these passages, we call attention to two. First, one detects a double accent in Tauler's description of the *gemuete*. On the one hand, it is described as a habit of the mind (*habitus mentis*), with the accent on its acquiredness, its substantiality, its 'grounding' the powers of the soul as a source and measure. On the other hand, it is described with an accent on its activity, penetrating the powers of the soul as a kind of will, as a power distinct from these powers. We do not consider these emphases contradictory—thus, the characterization of them as 'accents'—yet we are convinced that there is a distinction of importance here, which will require our attention.

Secondly, and related to this issue, there is the problem of specifying Tauler's sources—the *meister*—the identification of whom will facilitate our efforts to understand the nature and activity of the *gemuete*.

---

[4] 350.1ff: "Nu, 'von allem gemuete': in dem ist das ander alles beslossen, das ist und heisset das gemuete. Es wirt genant ein mosse, wan es misset das ander alles. Es git im sine forme, sine swere, sin gewicht. Es teilet al umbe und umbe. Habitus mentis."

[1] Meister Eckhart (c. 1260-1327). On Tauler's sources see *infra*, pp. 19-21.

[2] Here we translate *kaffen* (or *kapfen*) as "orientation," rather than literally as *schauen*—a "staring" or "gazing" back fixedly. The English word, "orientation," is broad enough to include both the intellective ("sees") and the affective ("loves" and "enjoys") dimensions, which Tauler emphasizes. The term is materially parallel with *meinen*, which we will render as "disposition."

[3] 350.9ff: "Nu súllen wir alhie merken was dis gemuete si. Das ist verre hoher und innerlicher wan die krefte; wan die krefte nement al ir vermúgen dannan us und sint do inne und dannan us geflossen und ist in allen doch ob sunder mosse. Es ist gar einvaltig und weselich und formelich. // Ein meister sprichet von disem und och me denne die meister. Die meister sprechent das dis gemuete der selen das si als edel, es si alwegent wúrkent, der mensche slaffe oder wache, er wisse es

An initial step toward the resolution of these two concerns is made when Tauler's other key anthropological-theological term, the *grunt der selen*, is brought into consideration. There is evidence that Tauler employs the terms, *gemuete* and *grunt*, interchangeably,[1] a fact that has led one interpreter of his Sermons to combine the two terms and speak of a "Gemütsgrund,"[2] and still another to conclude: "the *gemuete* is the ground of the soul itself."[3] The most profound intimacy between the *gemuete* and the *grunt* of the soul notwithstanding, such a merger of the two minimizes a distinction which is important. We must look more closely at their relationship.

In passages where the *grunt* is the sole subject of discussion, many of the same characterizations encountered in the above descriptions of the *gemuete* are present. But in the midst of these similarities, an emphasis which we do not find to be developed with noteworthy intensity in reference to the *gemuete* emerges. A primary representation of this situation is a passage from Tauler's sermon on John 1:7.

Here the *grunt* is described as beyond the reach of the powers of the soul and as exercising a directional, illuminating influence upon the powers of the soul, which inclines and excites both the highest and

---

oder enwisse es nút; es hat ein gotformig unzellich ewig wider kaffen in Got. Aber dise sprechent, es schouwe alwegen und minne und gebruche Gottes ane underlos. Wie das si, das lossen wir nu ligen; mer dis bekent sich Got in Gotte, und noch denne ist es geschaffen."

[1] He writes, for example: "Dis gemuet, diser grunt das ist als in pflanzet das die pflanze hat ein ewig reissen und ziehen nach ir, und das gemuete, der grunt der hat ein ewig neigen, ein grunt neigen wider in den ursprung. Dis neigen enverloeschet niemer och in der helle, und das ist ir meiste pin das in dis eweklich entbliben mus." 350.26ff.

[2] Ignaz Weilner argues that Tauler "gebraucht...vor allem seine beiden Herzworte 'grunt' und 'gemuete' häufig in einem Sinn, der die sittliche Verfaßtheit der Persontiefe im Menschen sowie dessen tätige Partnerschaft beim Zustandekommen dieses Habitus im Auge hat." *Johannes Taulers Bekehrungsweg. Die Erfahrungsgrundlagen seiner Mystik* (Regensburg, 1961), 124. In his sustained endeavor to interpret Tauler's thought as a "Psychologie der Tiefe" (*ibid.*, 58f), Weilner finds the integration of the terms to be more expressive of 'dynamic subjectivity,' i.e. the power of the *Seelengrund*-complex as an active subject directing man to his Origin, as well as an objective "ontologische Größe." "Er [der Seelengrund] wird also aktiv, und zwar in verantwortlicher Freiheit von der Wurzel her. Hier wird der Seelengrund zum Gemütsgrund. Dies ist wesenhaft Subjekt." *Ibid.*, 126; cf. 125.

[3] Paul Wyser, "Der Seelengrund in Taulers Predigten," *Lebendiges Mittelalter: Festgabe für Wolfgang Stammler* (Freiburg, 1958), 237. "Keinesweg darf man... 'Gemüt' als bloße seelische Kraft, die vom Seelengrund verschieden wäre, auffassen." *Ibid.*, 234. Wyser's article appears in abbreviated form in *Altdeutsche und altniederländische Mystik*, 324ff.

lowest powers back to their Origin. Also the purity and simplicity of the *grunt* is underscored. Each of these descriptions has been encountered in reference to the *gemuete*.

What we find to be a distinctive emphasis, although we consider it to be of one piece with the accent on the 'substantiality' of the *gemuete*, is the strong concern to point out that the *grunt* is the dwelling-place of God. Here God is present more than in heaven and in all other creatures. Here is a place from which God never separates Himself, for it is the place peculiar to God alone.[1]

The sources Tauler cites take us still a step further toward understanding not only the double accent in reference to the *gemuete*—which we now suggest is best understood as a reflection of a conscious distinction between the *gemuete* and the *grunt* of the soul—but also the precise meaning of the terms, *gemuete* and *grunt*.

We call attention, first, to the equation of the *gemuete* with the latin *mens*. Ephesians 4:23—"Renovamini autem spiritu mentis vestrae..."

[1] 331.1ff: "In disen grunt so enmúgent die krefte nút gelangen bi tusent milen nahe. Die wite die sich in dem grunde do wiset, die enhat weder bilde noch forme noch wise; es enhat weder hie noch do; denne es ist ein grundelos abgrúnde swebende in im selber sunder grunt, als die wasser wallent und flogierent: iezent sinkent si in ein abgrúnde und schinent als do kein wasser ensi; úber ein kleine stunde rúschet es her us als ob es alle ding ertrenken welle. Dis gat in ein abgrúnde; in disem ist eigenlich Gotz wonunge verre me denne in dem himel oder in allen creaturen; der har in gelangen koende, der fúnde do werlichen Got und fúnde sich in Gotte einvelteklich; wan Got enscheidet niemer von disem; im wer Got gegenwúrtig, und ewikeit wirt hie bevintlichen und smeklichen funden, und do enist weder fúr gondes noch nach komendes." And Tauler continues: "In disen grunt enmag kein geschaffen liecht nút gereichen noch gelúchten, wan allein Gotz wonunge und sin stat ist hie. Dis abgrúnde das enmúgent mit núte erfúllen noch gegrúnden alle creaturen; si enmúgent mit núte begnuegen noch gefriden, noch nieman wan Got mit aller siner unmosse. In dis abgrúnde gehoert allein das goettelich abgrúnde. 'Abyssus abyssum invocat.' [ps. 41:8] Diser grunt, der des mit flisse war neme, der lúchtet in die krefte under sich und neiget und reisset beide die obersten und die nidersten zu irem beginne und zu irem ursprunge, ob es der mensche war neme und bi im selber blibe und wer gehoerig der minneklichen stimme die in der wuestunge in disem grunde rueffet und leitet alles in bas in. In diser wuesti do ist also wuest das nie gedank in die in kan. Nein, nút: alle die vernúnftigen gedenke die ie mensche gedachte von der heiligen drivaltikeit, do etliche vil mit umbe gont, der enkan nie keiner her in. Nein nút; wan dis ist so innig, so verre und so verre; wan es enhat weder zit noch stat. Es ist einvaltig und sunder underscheit, und wer her in geratet recht, dem ist als er alhie eweklich gewesen si und als er ein mit dem selben si, noch denne das es nút enist denne ougenblike, und die selben blicke die vindent sich und zoeigent sich ein ewigkeit; dis lúchtet es us und git ein gezúg das das der mensche was eweklichen in Gotte in siner ungeschaffenheit. Do er in im was, do was der mensche Got in Gotte." For further associations of the *grunt* with the dwelling-place where God is substantively present, see 144.1ff, 266.7ff, 39.27ff, 342.22ff.

—is paraphrased by Tauler as: "werdent ernúwet in dem geiste úwers gemuetes."[1] Even more instructive is Tauler's paraphrase of Luke 10:27—"Diliges dominum deum tuum ex toto corde tuo et ex tota anima tua et ex omnibus viribus tuis et ex omni mente tua"—with the words: "du solt minnen dinen Got von allem herzen und diner selen und von allem dinem gemuete."[2]

Here the *gemuete* summarizes comprehensively the *mens* and the powers of the soul (*omnes vires*), and makes it clear that, although distinct from the powers of the soul, the *gemuete* comprehensively embraces and actively works in and through these powers. The parallel with *mens* should not lead to the assumption that only the intellective powers are so embraced, for the disposition of the heart is equally emphasized. Here a literal, dictionary definition is to the point: the *gemuete* is "the totality of the thoughts and feelings" of the soul.[3] Or, as Käte Grunewald has admirably summarized:

> Tauler comprehends the source of all power-to-life in general with the term *gemuete*. Here he finds the point at which the activities of the soul originate and find their unity. And here he sees the inexhaustible nature of the life of an individual soul in regard to every activity of which it is capable in its intellectual, affectual, volitional and religious operation.[4]

Whereas the *gemuete* finds its latin equivalent in the comprehensive term, *mens*, the latin equivalent for the *grunt der selen* is found in the less comprehensive, more specific and still more defiant of precise definition, Augustinian phrase "abditum mentis"—the hidden or secret place of the mind and heart. We find that Tauler equates the "inward man" and "invisible things" with "the ground that Saint Augustine named an *abditum mentis*."[5] And the "most inward ground where only true oneness is present," is equated with "what Saint Augustine called a hidden appetitive ground that has nothing to do

---

[1] 259.1

[2] 246.9f.

[3] *Matthias Lexers Mittelhochdeutsches Taschenwörterbuch*, 23rd edition (Stuttgart, 1966), 61.

[4] Käte Grunewald, *Studien zu Johannes Taulers Frömmigkeit* (Leipzig, 1930), 9.

[5] 357.23ff: "Nu die zwene nidersten menschen sol er úber tretten und under trucken. Her uf sprichet S. Bernhardus als hart: 'das ist das man den vihelichen menschen mit siner sinnelicher lust múge ab geziehen von den dingen die er mit minnen besessen hat.' Wie harte ein crútz das ist, das wissent ir wol: als swaer ist und nút minre, sprichet er, den uswendigen menschen ze ziehende in den innewendigen menschen und von den bildelichen dingen und gesichtlichen in die ungesichtlichen: das ist in dem grunde das S. Augustinus nemt: 'abditum mentis'."

with time or with the world."[1] And, finally, Tauler makes reference to the "inward ground" in order to explain Augustine's conviction that Proclus and Plato possessed knowledge of the gospel, even to the point of being aware that God sent His Son and that God was a holy trinity.[2] The ground of the soul is a source of revelation for Tauler.[3]

There is still another source for Tauler's doctrine of the ground of the soul. This source becomes evident in his summary of the conclusions of several immediate masters who sought to define "the inward dignity which lies concealed in the ground." These remarks demonstrate the influence of a contemporary *synteresis* tradition upon

---

[1] 101.25ff: "Man sprichet und meinet dis eigenliche on underlos in dem himmel dis wore gebet, das ein worer ufgang ist in Gotte, das treit rechte das gemuete zumole uf, also das Got in der worheit múge eigentliche ingon in daz luterste, in das innigeste, in daz edelste, in den innerlichesten grunt, do wore einikeit alleine ist, von dem sancte Augustinus sprichet das die sele habe in ir ein verborgen appetgrunde, daz enhabe mit der zit noch mit aller diser welte nút zu tuonde und es ist verre úberhaben úber das teil das dem licham leben und bewegunge git."

[2] 332.19ff: "Disem grunde woren die heiden heimlich und versmochten ze mole zergengkliche ding und giengen disem grunde nach. Aber do kamen die grossen meister als Proculus und Plato und gabent des ein klor underscheit den die dis underscheit als verre nút vinden enkonden. Sant Augustinus sprach das Plato das ewangelium 'In principio' al zemole hette vor gesprochen bis an das wort: 'fuit homo missus a Deo,' und das was doch mit verborgen bedekten worten, und dise fundent underscheit von der heiligen drivaltikeit. Kinder, dis kam alles us disem inwendigen grunde: dem lebtent si und wartent des."

[3] As concerns the influence of Augustine on Tauler's understanding of the *grunt*, see Weilner, who concludes, with reference to *De trinitate* I, 14.c 8: "Nimmt man hierzu noch des großen Afrikaners inniges Bemühen, den menschlichen Geist bereits 'in seinem eigenen Bestand, bevor er Gottes teilhaftig ist,' sowie in jener höheren Seinsweise des tatsächlichen, gnadenhaften Gottesbesitzes als *Abbild* des Höchsten zu erweisen, und dieses Abbild wiederum als 'Ort' und Formprinzip aller erfahrungsmäßigen Gottbegegnung, so haben wir alle wesentlichen Elemente der späteren Seelengrundtradition vor Augen." *Johannes Taulers Bekehrungsweg*, 90. See further where the Platonic doctrine of *Anamnesis*, which Weilner paraphrases as "metaphysiches Gedächtnis," is cited as an influential source. *Ibid.*, 87f. Wyser, with detailed comparisons with *De trinitate* and the *Confessiones*, concludes: "Taulers grunt entspricht sehr genau dem augustinischen *abditum mentis* nicht nur im Bilde, das in beiden Worten steckt, sondern vor allem in der Idee." *Lebendiges Mittelalter*, 228; cf. 232. On *mens* and *memoria* in Augustine, Michael Schmaus writes: "Die substanzielle Geistseele ist die mens schon durch ihr Sein, durch ihre Existenz, ohne daß sie die ihr immanenten Tätigkeiten des Denkens und Wollens setzt;" "...die memoria, eine Tätigkeitsrichtung der mens...." *Die psychologische Trinitätslehre des hl. Augustinus. Münsterische Beiträge zur Theologie*, 11 (Münster, 1927), 312f. Also in this regard see the study by Gottlieb Söhngen, where the conclusion is drawn: "Nur dann ragt das Gedächtnis in die religiöse Sphäre hinein, wenn es als der 'Ort' im Menschen bestimmt wird, wo dieser seines Gottes 'gedenkt'." "Der Aufbau der augustinischen Gedächtnislehre," *Die Einheit in der Theologie. Gesammelte Abhandlungen, Aufsätze, Vorträge* (München, 1952), 70.

Tauler's definition of the ground of the soul. He writes that these masters[1] spoke variously of a "spark of the soul" (*ein funke der selen*), a "floor" or "foundation" (*ein boden*), a "top" or "tower" (*ein tolden*), an "origin-ality" (*ein erstekeit*), and an image in which the holy trinity is formed and lodged. Choosing the expression "spark" as the more pertinent,[2] Tauler concludes that this spark never rests until it has returned to the uncreated ground out of which it has flowed.[3]

---

[1] Tauler's references (*infra*, note 3) are, first, to Albertus Magnus (1193-1280), in whose regard Joseph Bernhart writes: "[Albert] bemüht sich vergeblich, sie [*synteresis* and *conscientia*] auseinanderzuhalten, sieht ihre tragenden Subjekte bald in der *ratio*, bald in der *voluntas*, schließlich in beiden zugleich. Für die nachfolgende Mystik war es von Bedeutung, daß er eine von den übrigen Seelenkräften unabhängige, über Verstand und Willen regierende, von Natur schon mit den obersten sittlichen Prinzipien ausgestattete und auf Grund angeborener oder erworbener Erkenntnis zum Guten und Rechten bewegende Potenz annahm." *Die philosophische Mystik des Mittelalters von ihren antiken Ursprüngen bis zur Renaissance* (München, 1922), 148-49). A second reference is to Dietrich of Freiburg (d. 1310), a student of Albertus, and a German Dominican who interpreted Thomas as supporting a real distinction between essence and existence, and who criticized both Thomas and this distinction from a strong neoplatonic position. See further Martin Grabmann, *Mittelalterliches Geistesleben. Abhandlungen zur Geschichte der Scholastik und Mystik*, I (München, 1926), 147f, 330f. See also Gilson, who calls attention to Dietrich's explicit identification of the Plotinian active intellect with the Augustinian *abditum mentis*. *History of Christian Philosophy in the Middle Ages* (New York, 1955), 433-37. Also there is a monograph on Dietrich by Engelbert Krebs, *Meister Dietrich. Beiträge zur Geschichte der Philosophie des Mittelalters*, V (Münster, 1906). Tauler's final reference is to Meister Eckhart, in whose regard see Gilson's treatment of Eckhart's view of the soul as bearing a "spark" of the divine Intellect. *History of Christian Philosophy*, 438-442, esp. 441. The influence of Lombard's three-fold *scintilla* (*conscientiae*, *rationis*, *animae*) concept on Tauler is traced by Weilner, who comes to the conclusion that a "natürliche Komponente der Seelengrund-Dynamik" can be recognized as "eine lebendige Spielart jener unbeirrbaren Synderesis." *Johannes Taulers Bekehrungsweg*, 91-94, 160-161. Grunewald also comments on the influence of a *synteresis* tradition. *Studien zu Johannes Taulers Frömmigkeit*, 5-7. Finally, we call attention to the important study by Heinrich Appel, in which the distinction between the *synteresis* and *Seelengrund* traditions is summarized as follows: "Die Scholastiker und scholastischen Mystiker suchten das eigentliche Wesen der Seele in den obersten Habitus der Vernunft und des Willens. Die deutsche Mystik dagegen trennt den Wesensgrund der Seele scharf von den Kräften und betont ihn als einfach einen gegenüber der Mannigfaltigkeit jener. Dies hindert sie jedoch nicht, den Grund der Seele gleichsam als einen Habitus des Willens und der Vernunft zu betrachten." "Die Syntheresis in der mittelalterlichen Mystik," *ZKG*, XIII (1892), 542-43.

[2] For further explicit parallels of *funke* and *grunt*, see 137.1, 117.18, and 80.13.

[3] 347.9ff: "Von disem inwendigen adel der in dem grunde lit verborgen, hant vil meister gesprochen beide alte und núwe: bischof Albrecht, meister Dietrich, meister Eghart. Der eine heisset es ein funke der selen, der ander einen boden oder ein tolden, einer ein erstekeit, und bischof Albrecht nemmet es ein bilde in dem die heilige drivaltikeit gebildet ist und do inne gelegen ist. Und diser funke flúget als hoch, do im recht ist, das dem das verstentnisse nút gevolgen enmag,

3. CONCLUSIONS

The combined weight of these considerations leads us to our first major conclusion. Influenced by neoplatonic and Augustinian anthropological motifs and a distinguishable *synteresis* tradition which partakes of these speculations, Tauler specifies the highest parts of the soul, in distinction from the powers of the soul, with the closely related anthropological-theological terms, *gemuete* and *grunt*. Although these terms are occasionally presented as interchangeable, we have found the greater weight of textual evidence to suggest that Tauler consciously distinguishes (1) a naturally given and firmly established dwelling-place in the soul, where God is present and from which He neither can nor desires to separate Himself—the *grunt der selen*; and (2) an active power, grounded in and emerging from this 'ground,' which embraces and penetrates the powers of the soul (i.e. reason and will) and directs and excites the creature back to his origin in uncreatedness by first drawing him into the created and subsequently into the uncreated ground of the soul—the *gemuete*. The summarizing conclusion of Claire Champollion is most congenial to our own:

> One could attempt to schematize [the relationship between the *gemuete* and *grunt*] by saying that the *gemuete* is the spiritual energy of the innermost region of the soul, i.e. the *grunt*.[1]

This distinction is not without significance for Tauler's thought. For it establishes the fact—and much more strongly than the concept of a *synteresis voluntatis et rationis*—that above and beyond man's volitional and rational powers and activities, and regardless of the errant extremes to which these powers and activities might stray, God possesses and claims man's life and being in a natural, just and inalienable way: the soul is God's oyster.

At this point and in support of our conclusion, we make available to the English reader a concise, although quite lengthy statement by Tauler, which places in clear relief and cogent order the points we have considered in this chapter. The statement is from his sermon on Ephesians 4:23f: "Renovamini spiritu mentis vestrae..."

---

wan es enrastet nút, es enkome wider in den grunt do es us geflossen ist, das es was in siner ungeschaffenheit."

[1] Claire Champollion, "La place des termes 'gemuete' et 'grunt' dans le vocabuliare de Tauler," *La mystique rhénane*, 189. Miss Champollion summarizes further: "En face du dynamisme du gemuet, le grunt apparaît ici plutôt comme un lieu, une *stat* de l'âme." *Ibid.*

St. Paul says: 'you should be renewed in the spirit of your *gemuete*.' The spirit of man has many names in accordance with its operation and the perspectives from which it is considered. Sometimes the spirit means a soul; this is the case to the extent to which the spirit pours life into the body, and is thus in every member of the body, giving it movement and life. Sometimes the soul is called a spirit, and then it has so intimate a filial relationship *(sipschaft)* with God that it is immeasurably great. For God is a spirit and the soul is a spirit; whence the soul has an eternal inclination and orientation back to its original ground. As a result of this common spirituality *(gelicheit der geistlicheit)*,[1] the soul inclines and turns itself back again to the origin, to the likeness. This inclination is never extinguished, not even in those who are damned.

The spirit is also called the *gemuete*. This is rapture-inspiring! In it all the powers are assembled—reason, will. But in itself it is...and has more there.[2] It has an inward, substantive object above the activity of the powers, and when all is in order in the *gemuete* and it is properly turned and directed, everything is in order with all the other powers. And, conversely, when the *gemuete* is ill-turned and misdirected, so are all the powers, whether one is conscious of it or not.

Finally, the soul is called a man.

Children, that is the ground wherein the true image of the holy trinity is inwardly and secretly laid, and it is so noble that one can give it no proper name. Sometimes one calls it a foundation, sometimes a tower of the soul. For just as inadequately as one can give a proper name to God, so inadequate is the effort to name the ground. Should one see how God dwells in the ground, he would be truly blessed by what he beholds. The intimacy and filial relationship which God has there is so inexpressibly great that one can neither speak nor have spoken of it except from boldness.

Now St. Paul says: 'you should be renewed in the spirit of your *gemuete*.' When this *gemuete* is ordered, it has an inclination back to this ground, wherein, far above the powers of the soul, the image is present.

---

[1] In regard to the importance of the conviction in German mysticism that only like can know and love like, Theodor Steinbüchel writes: "Der christliche Mensch kann Gott nur darum erkennen, weil er von Gott ist und in der Gnade auch aus ihm. So ist dieses altgriechische Erkenntnisprinzip unlöslich verbunden mit der christlichen Mystik, Philosophie und Theologie." *Mensch und Gott in Frömmigkeit und Ethos der deutschen Mystik* (Düsseldorf, 1952), 188. Josef Quint concludes: "Das [die Einheitsspekulation]...heißt für den christlichen Mystiker des Mittelalters, daß er das innerste Wesen der Seele als irgendwie gleichgeartet mit dem innersten göttlichen Sein zu erfassen trachten muß, denn nicht nur kann Gleiches nur von Gleichem erkannt werden, sondern auch nur zwischen Gleichen ist eine Einswerdung möglich." "Mystik und Sprache: Ihr Verhältnis zueinander in der spekulativen Mystik Meister Eckeharts," *Altdeutsche und altniederländische Mystik*, 130. See also Rühl, *Der Einfluß der Mystik auf Denken und Entwicklung des jungen Luthers*, 106.

[2] The words are missing in the text.

And this returning operation of the *gemuete* is as noble and exalted above the powers of the soul as a full vat of wine is over one drop.

In this *gemuete* one should renew himself by constantly drawing himself back into the ground, and turning with an active love and disposition directly to God without any mediation. The *gemuete* certainly has the power to do this. It can well have a constant adherence to and an uninterrupted disposition toward the ground which is not within the capabilities of the powers of the soul.

This renewal should be in the spirit of the *gemuete*. Since God is a Spirit, the created spirit should unite itself, then direct itself to and sink itself into the uncreated Spirit of God with a permissive *gemuete*. Thus, as man was eternally God in God in his uncreatedness, so should he draw himself completely, with his createdness, back again.[1]

---

[1] 261.29-262.33: "Nu sprichet S. Paulus: 'ir súllent úch vernúwen in dem geiste úwers gemuetes.' Der geist des menschen der hat manigen namen, das ist nach der wúrklicheit und nach dem wider gesichte. Under wilen heisset der geist ein sele; das ist als verre als si dem libe leben in gússet, und also ist si in eime ieklichen gelide und git dem bewegunge und leben. Und etwenne heisset si ein geist, und denne hat si als nahe sipschaft mit Gotte, das ist úber alle mosse; wan Got ist ein geist und die sele ein geist, und dannan ab hat si ein ewig wider neigen und wider kaphen in den grunt irs ursprunges. Und do von der gelicheit der geistlicheit so neiget und wider búget sich der geist wider in den ursprung, in die gelicheit. Das wider neigen das enverloeschet niemer me och in den vertuemten. Denne heisset si ein gemuete. Das gemuete das ist ein wunneklich ding; in dem sint alle die krefte versament; vernunft, wille; aber es ist an im selber dar...und hat me dar zu. Es hat einen innigen weselichen fúrwurf úber die wúrklicheit der krefte, und wanne dem gemuete recht ist und es wol zu gekert ist, so ist allem dem andern recht, und wo das ab gekert ist, so ist es alles ab gekert, man wisse oder enwisse nút. // Nu heisset si och ein mensche. // Kinder, das ist der grunt do dis wore bilde der heiligen drivaltikeit inne lit verborgen, und das ist so edel das man dem enkeinen eigenen namen enmag gegeben. Under wilen heisset man es einen boden, under wilen ein dolten der selen. Und als wening als man Gotte einen eigenen namen mag gegeben, als mag man dem namen gegeben. Und der gesehen mochte wie Got in dem grunde wonet, der wúrde von dem gesichte selig. Die nehe die Got do hat, und die sipschaft, die ist so unsprechlich gros das man nút vil dannan ab getar sprechen noch enkan gesprechen. // Nu sprach S. Paulus: 'ir súllent úch vernúwen in dem geiste úwers gemuetes.' Dis gemuete, do dem recht ist, do hat es ein wider neigen in disen grunt, do dis bilde ist verre úber die krefte. Und ist dis werk dis gemuetz als edel und als gros úber die krefte, verre me denne ein fuder wins ist wider einem trahen. // In disem gemuete sol man sich ernúwen mit einem steten wider in tragende in den grunt und engegenkerende mit einer wúrklicher minne und meinunge Got sunder alles mitte. Dis vermúgen ist wol in dem gemuete, das einen steten anhang wol mag haben ane underlos und stete meinunge, ane die krefte die ein vermúgen des steten anhanges nút habent. // Alsus sol dise vernúwunge sin in dem geiste des gemuetes, wan Got ein geist ist: des sol der geschaffene geist sich vereinen und uf richten und sich in senken in den ungeschaffenen geist Gotz mit einem lidigem gemuete. Also als der mensche was eweklichen in Gotte Got in siner ungeschaffenheit, also sol er mit siner geschaffenheit sich al zemole wider in tragen."

A second major conclusion we draw is that Tauler's understanding of the ground of the soul establishes what we venture to describe as a *natural 'covenant'* between God and man. Here we introduce a technical term—'covenant'—in a context in which it is not normally placed: the order of creation and being.[1] We choose this phrase, rather than a more general description such as natural 'contact' or 'tie' or 'bond' between God and the soul, because it alone clarifies the radical content of Tauler's *Seelengrund* doctrine.

Tauler presupposes a 'commitment' of God—as we will shortly see, by "eternal ordination"—to the ground of man's soul, and an active faithfulness and subservience of the latter to its Origin even if man is unconscious of it. There is interaction and intercourse between the uncreated and created 'grounds' which is both prior and foundational to historical communion between God and man. Ultimately, it is in the ground of his soul that man must encounter God; the ground of the soul is the historical meeting- and dwelling-place of God. Historical communion subserves the realization of union on the level of being.[2] And, further, because the ground of the soul is an inalienable residence of God in human being, it gives man a natural, creational claim to salvation, which places God historically in man's debt.[3]

A primary passage which we cite in this regard and which in turn will initiate our consideration of Tauler's order of salvation, comes from a sermon on John 3:11. Commenting on the perfection of the *imago trinitatis*, Tauler writes:

> Other masters say—and this is an incomparably higher step—that the perfection lies in the utterly inward, hidden and deepest ground of the soul, the ground in which the soul has God substantively *(wesentlich)*, actively *(wúrklich)* and essentially *(isteklich)*, and where God works and is and enjoys Himself. One could so little separate God from this ground [of the soul] as he could separate himself. For it is by God's eternal ordination *(ewige ordenunge)* that He has established *(geordent hat)* that He neither *can* nor *desires* to separate Himself from this ground. Thus, in the ground [of the soul] this ground has all by grace that God

[1] This term appears literally with Johannes Cocceius (1603-1669). "Foedus operum, quatenus lege naturae nititur, foedus naturae appellari potest. Naturale enim est, hominem praeditum intelligentia et voluntate non sine imagine Dei creari." *De foedere et testamento Dei*, § 22. *Realencyklopädie für protestantische Theologie und Kirche*, IV (Leipzig, 1898), 189-90.

[2] See the conclusion of Walter Lehmann, quoted *infra*, 30, note 2, and our discussion *infra*, 40f.

[3] See *infra*, 33f.

has by nature. And should man permit, and turn himself to the ground, grace would be born. Apart from this turning, all other ways, even the highest, can accomplish nothing.[1]

---

[1] 300.17ff: "Aber nu sprechent ander meister, und daz ist unzellichen vil und verre harúber, und sprechent das es lige in dem allerinnigesten, in dem allerverborgensten tieffesten grunde der selen, do sú daz in dem grunde hat Got wesentlichen und wúrklich und isteklich, in dem wúrket und weset Got und gebruchet sin selbes in dem, und man moehte Got also wenig dannan abe gescheiden also von ime selber; daz ist von siner ewigen ordenunge, das er es also geordent hat das er sich nút gescheiden enmag noch wil, und do in dem grunde so hat diser grunt alles das von genaden daz Got von naturen hat. Also verre sich der mensche in den grunt liesse und kerte, do wúrt die genode geborn und anders nút eigenlich in der hoehsten wisen." Emphasis mine. Eckhart builds *necessity* into the Godhead. "Der vater gebirt sinen sun in der êwicheit im selber glîch. 'Daz wort was bî gote, und got was daz wort': ez was daz selbe in der selben natûre. Noch spriche ich mêr: er hât in geborn in mîner sêle. Niht aleine ist si bî im noch er bi ir glîch, sunder er ist in ir, und gebirt der vater sînen sun in der sêle in der selben wîse, als er in der êwicheit gebirt, und niht anders. *Er muoz es tuon, es sî im liep oder leit.* Der vater gebirt sînen sun âne underlâz, und ich spriche mêr: er gebirt mich sînen sun und den selben sun. Ich spriche mêr: er gebirt mich niht aleine sînen sun, mêr: er gebirt mich sich und sich mich und mich sîn wesen und sîn natûre. In dem innersten quelle dâ quille ich ûz in dem heiligen geiste, dâ ist ein leben und éin wesen und éin werk." *Meister Eckhart. Die deutschen und lateinischen Werke. Die deutschen Werke* [= *DW*], ed. Josef Quint, I (Stuttgart, 1958), 109, 2-11. Emphasis mine. Cf. Tauler's "must," *infra*, 32.

CHAPTER TWO

THE ORDER OF SALVATION

Man has flowed from uncreatedness into createdness. The primary obstacle to his return to the original state of uncreatedness is his involvement in nature, not only the nature into which he 'falls' when he assumes createdness, but also, and primarily, the fallen nature which he inherits from the first sinner. In our consideration of Tauler's order of salvation, we will argue that the overcoming of the effects of fallen nature and the recapitulation of the purity of created nature, form a foundation for an *historical approximation of uncreatedness*, the precise nature of which will be the concern of our final chapter. In this chapter, we wish to emphasize that it is not Adamic manhood, but original uncreatedness, which forms the ultimate historical goal of Tauler's order of salvation.

1. THE STRATEGIC WAY AND GOAL

Tauler draws a most severe portrait of man's fallen situation. Nature is poisoned by the original sin and so completely self-inverted in all things that man loves himself (his createdness) more than God, God's angels and all that God has ever made. The fault lies not with God's having made nature—a Thomistic thrust against Manichaeism. Nature is corrupted by the emaciating distortion it has incurred by turning away from God and to itself. Here a poisoning occurs and penetrates to the very ground of the soul, where it establishes a false ground in the spirit and in nature, a ground which becomes manifest when one thinks that he is completely God and that all he does is his own.[1]

[1] 94.9ff: "...Wanne von der vergiftekeite wegen die in die nature gevallen ist von der erbesúnde, so ist die nature alles uf sich selber nidergekeret in allen dingen; und sprichet meister Thomas das von der selben vergifte wegen so minne der mensche me sich selber denne Got oder sine engel oder alles daz Got ie geschuf. Das enist nút von dem das Got die nature gemaht het, sunder das sú also verdorben in der entmachunge ist von der wiederkerunge von Gotte. Nu ist dise vergiftekeit die ist so tief in den grunt gewurtzelt das alle kúnsteriche meister disem mit sinne nút enmogent nochgegon, und mit allem flisse múgent sú ime kume iemer getuon oder uzgerúten. Diser valsche grunt in geiste und in nature wonet dicke do man wenet das es Got si zumole, do ist do dicke dise vergiftige widerboegunge, und meinet der mensche alles daz sine in allem tuonde."

In more pastoral imagery, Tauler writes that there is now an "evil, hidden angel" in man, a distressingly unpleasant knave in his eye, causing him to grasp God and all created things as his own possessions.[1]

The strategy employed to outflank and ultimately destroy this 'knave' directs the attack upon the active manifestations of his corrupting presence.[2] The false ground is destroyed by a sustained and gradually intensified removal of the vegetation emerging from it. To use more *schulgemäß* language, it is by psychologically blunting and stripping away the self-affirming inclination of the will (*eigen willen*) and methodologically immobilizing its world-seeking activities, that a resurgence of the soteriological resources of the true ground of the soul to dominance is achieved. Thus, the repeated exhortations to "resignation" (*gelossenheit*) and "will-lessness" (*willeloskeit*).[3]

In this process all alien, external, temporal things must enter "forgetfulness."[4] The less nature and its joy live, the more God and

---

[1] 112.10ff: "...Ein boese verborgen angel ist in dem menschen, ein leit ougenschalk, das ist ein annemlicheit unde eine valsche nimlicheit, die alle ding an sich trucken wil, das sú begriffen mag an Gotte und an den creaturen, ie wil sú zuslahen mit eigenschaft und wil das sin; und duncket sú ie út von ir selber, so hat sú út geton; und so wil sú lust, trost, smacken und fuelen haben und wil also gros sin, also heilige, also selig, und bekennen und wissen, sú wil ie út sin und sich iemer nút verlieren." Cf. 246.23ff.

[2] Tauler stresses rigorous devotion and penitence: "Das heisset wore andaht alleine das dir nút ensmacket noch dich nút gelust denne dins Gottes mit minnen und meinen; daz ist der minnencliche ruf, darumb das uns der minnencliche Got alleine in disen heilgen orden geruffet hat, dem ruffe súllent wir volgen, und er hat uns erlost von der boesen valschen welte in daz heilge leben der woren penitencien, wanne wir von naturen sint kinder des zornes und des ewigen todes und wúrdig des ewigen verduempnisses von unsern wegen. // Sant Augustinus sprach: 'der mensche ist von einer fulen materien stinckende und verderbende, ein klotz und ein ful ertrich, des ende ist der ewige tod; daz überkummet man mit dem lebende der penitencien, und daz úch der minnencliche Got geladen und geruffet hat von siner frigen lutern minnen sunder alles verdienen'." 59.19ff. See 13.10ff, 26ff.

[3] 348.27ff: "Kinder, der wille der mus ab, als unser herre sprach: 'ich bin komen nút das ich tue minen willen, sunder mines vatter willen.' Als lange und alle die wile das du stest in dime eigen willen, so wissest das dir diser selikeit gebristet. Wan alle die gewore selikeit die gelit an rechter gelossenheit, willeloskeit; dis wirt alles geborn us dem grunde der kleinmuetikeit: do wirt der eigen wille verlorn..." Cf. 348.12ff, 357.8ff.

[4] 249.20ff: "Kinder, dise wise minne die zúhet des menschen gemuete verre von disen froemden usserlichen dingen, das er ir rechte kumet als mer als in ein vergessen. In der ersten suessen minne do kert er sich wol mit arbeit von den dingen. Aber hie in disem enpfallent im die ding und versmehet die ding und wirt in im geborn recht ein urdrutz und ein unwertikeit zu allem dem das unordenlich ist,

His will live; the more one wishes to live in the Spirit, so much more must he teach natural things to die.[1] He who would follow Christ must give nature its "walking papers."[2]

To express the situation positively, the sinners who are blessed and rich in love are those who, from the ground of their souls, turn away (*gruntliche abker*) from everything that is not purely and simply God. They have their heart and affection turned to God in such a way that, before and above all things, only God is loved, willed and thought (*in fúr alle minnent und meinet*). The turning from and forgetting of their sinful inclinations is reciprocated by God's turning away from and forgetting their sins:

> They have turned completely away [from their sins], and so God has turned away [from them]; they wish to know them no more, so God wishes also to know them no more.[3]

If resignation and will-lessness are the most comprehensive descriptions of the strategic way, the realization of a "divine form" is the ultimate goal of Tauler's order of salvation. He describes the third and final historical stage of the order of salvation as the

> passing over into a God-formed being, into the oneness of the created spirit in the essential spirit of God, which one may call a substantive conversion *(weseliche ker)*.[4]

---

und dis treit din gunst vil naher uf und von den dingen die zitlich sint, denne vil grosse uswendige uebunge."

[1] 130.25ff: "...Wanne ie me ir der naturen lebent und irme luste, ie me ir Gotte minre lebent und sinem willen; wie ir der naturen minre lebent und iren lusten, ie me ir Gotte lebent und sinem willen; ie me ir dem geiste wellent leben, ie me ir der naturen mussent leren sterben." Cf. 139.29ff.

[2] 83.8f: "...Kinder, wer Cristus nachvolgen wil, der mus der naturen urlop geben."

[3] 138.28ff: "[Selige minnekliche súnder] nohent sich zu unserm herren nu von grunde, und tuont oder hant geton einen waren gruntlichen abker von allem dem das Got nút luter und blos enist, oder do er nút inne enschint, und hant ir herze und iren gunst gekert zu Gotte in alsolicher wise das si in fúr alle minnent und meinent, und begerent von ganzem grunde das si in alleine minnen und meinen mussen fúr alle ding. In dem so lossent si sich Gotte ussen und innan in weler wise er wil. Von diser lúte súnden enwil Got niemer enkeine vorderunge getuon noch enwil ir nút wissen. Si hant sich gentzlichen dar ab gekert, so hat sich och Got dar ab gekert; enwellent si ir nút me wissen, so enwil ir och Got nút me wissen."

[4] 159.29-160.6: "Nu wellen wir sagen von drin greten, die mag der mensche haben in dem nidersten, in dem mittelsten oder in dem obersten grate. // Der erste grat eins inwendigen tugentlichen lebens die do die richten leitent in die hochste nacheit Gotz, ist das der mensche kere ze mole sich in die wunderlichen werk und bewisunge der unsprechelicher gaben und der usflússe der verborgener gutheit Gotz, und dannan us wirt geborn ein uebunge, die heisset *jubilacio*. // Der ander grat das ist ein armuete des geistes und ein sunderlich in ziehen Gotz, in einer

Here God is immediately—"one mittel"—one's life and being.[1] And here one is not concerned with the reacquisition of the *imago trinitatis* in its Adamic purity, nor with a fidelic, conformational union with the incarnate Christ, for one is at a stage beyond Adamic manhood and beyond historical Christology.[2] As Tauler summarizes the progression:

> The material in the body of the mother when she has become pregnant is first a formless material. Afterwards the material attains an animal form. But this form awaits and thirsts after a human form. When the material of man is thus prepared [i.e. the human form acquired], it thirsts after an eternal, rational and in-the-image-of-God-constructed form. And this form never attains eternal peace until it becomes transformed into the Form that bears in itself and perfects all forms—the uncreated, eternal Word of the heavenly Father.[3]

2. *SOLA GRATIA?*

Tauler has been heralded as a major proponent of an exclusive, Augustinian *sola gratia* in the late Middle Ages, and a forerunner, without serious qualification, of Luther's doctrine of justification by

qwelender beroubunge des geistes. // Das dritte das ist ein úbervart in ein gotformig wesen in einikeit des geschaffenen geistes in den istigen geist Gotz, das man einen weselichen ker mag heissen."

[1] 84.8f: "Liebes kint, du must sterben, sol der minnecliche Got din leben one mittel werden und din wesen werden."

[2] Although Tauler can eloquently describe the eschatological meaning of Christ's atonement (cf. *infra*, p. 31, n. 3), his focus on the historical, incarnate Christ s primarily upon a "picture" *(bild)*, the inward, spiritual imitation of which subserves one's progression to the point which is beyond all historical pictures. Historical Christology is a part of the way, the *praeparatio*, not of the goal of salvation. "Der ander wandel den wir súllen haben, der sol sin in biltlicher wise, das ist in dem minneklichen bilde unsers herren Jhesu Christi: die súllen wir fúr uns setzen in spiegellicher wise, als ein bildener, das wir alles unser tuon nach im súllen richten nach unserre macht." 209.22ff. "Die dritte wandelunge die ist unbiltlich sunder alle bilde. Kinder, dis ist gar ein behender, naher, vinster, unbekant, ellent weg..." 211.25ff; cf. 70.16ff, 240.27ff, 233.32ff. In regard to the a-historical concern of Tauler's soteriology, Walter Lehmann points out that it is "Gott in der Tiefe der menschlichen Seele... weder oben im Himmel, noch in der Geschichte, noch in der Kirche," which forms Tauler's burning focus. *Johannes Taulers Predigten*, I (Jena, 1923), xli.

[3] 136.29ff: "Die materie in der muter libe, als si swanger worden ist, zem erstem so ist es ein blosse materie. Dar nach gewint die materie ein tierliche forme. Die materie wartet und túrstet nach einer menschlichen forme. Als die materie des menschen bereit wirt, die túrstet nach einer ewiger, vernúnftiger, nach Got gebildeter formen. Die forme die engewint niemer ewekliche raste, si enwerde úber formet mit der forme die alle formen in ir treit und volmachet: das ist das ungeschaffene ewig wort des himelschen vatters." See 137.1f.

faith alone.[1] Frequent statements in his Sermons appear to lend confirmation to this distinction. Tauler writes that one should approach his salvation in complete disregard to his preparatory activity or worthiness, and that he should be as the heathen, who, unlike the Jews, had no holy ordinances or regulations on which to build, but received all as "grace for grace," as the "sheer mercy of God."[2] He argues, further, in reference to the reception of the Eucharist, that worthiness never in any way results from human works or merits but from the sheer grace and merit of Jesus Christ.[3] And we find that the activity of the Holy Spirit is credited with bringing man to the knowledge of his errors,[4] emptying him of his sins and making him receptive for God's presence.[5]

---

[1] A. V. Müller writes: "Durch die Folgerungen, die Tauler aus diesem Augustinismus gezogen hat, wurde Luther direkt auf die reformatorische Bahn gedrängt. Taulers Werktheologie bildet die Grundlage für Luthers so stark angefochtene Auffassung von den Werken. Taulers Kreuztheologie hat Luther den Ansporn zum Kampf gegen die mittelalterliche Busstheorie und gegen die Ablässe gegeben." *Luther und Tauler*, 25; cf. 164, 168. Bengt Hägglund concludes: "'Grace alone' and in a certain respect the basic understanding of righteousness and the denial of the idea of merit are nothing new when compared with mysticism, although the Reformers at these points expressed themselves with far greater and more decisive clarity." *Lutheran World* (1961), 45-46. For strong counterarguments to Müller's thesis see Otto Scheel, *Festgabe für Julius Kaftan*, 309-10.

[2] 64.11ff: "Und er sol dir geben die uebunge der heidenin, die enhettent enkeine wise noch heilikeite noch ewig, danne daz sú noment gnode umb gnode sunder alle ir verdienen; mer die juden die verliessent sich uf ir tuon, die hettent ir cerimonie und die gebot und den ewen und vil dinges; aber die heidenen die hettent enkeinen enhalt daruf sú buwetent, denne uf Gottes gnode bloeslichen in sine barmherzikeit. Sich, in der wisen sol ouch dine uebunge sin, daz du dich nút in enthaltest denne uf der blossen gnoden und barmherzikeit Gottes, und nemest und gist gnode von gnoden von Gottes guete alleine, und nút enwisse von keinre dinre bereitunge oder wirdikeit."

[3] 123.6ff: "Wanne die wúrdikeit enkummet niemer noch niemer von menschlichen werken noch von verdiende, sunder von luterre genaden und von dem verdiende unsers herren Jhesu Christi, und flússet zumole von Gotte an uns..." On the eschatological meaning of Christ's atonement, Tauler writes: "Dis bant [i.e. ewige tod] brach unser liber herre Jesus Christus an dem heiligen karfreitag, do er sich lies vahen und binden, und starb an dem krúze. Do machte er ein gantze suone zwischent dem menschen und sinem himelschen vatter. // Nu als hútte uf disen tag so ist die suone bestetiget und ist der edel túre schatz wider gegeben der ze mole verlorn was: das ist der minnekliche heilig geist, von des richeit und minne und der foelle die in im ist, do enkoendent alle herzen und alle verstentnisse nút zu komen." 304.19ff.

[4] 73.32-74.3: "...Wer der heilge geist do, so stroffete er diser lúte wise, wanne wo der heilige geist ist, do bekennet der mensche sine gebresten klerlich und lert gelossenheit und demuetikeit und alle ding."

[5] 305.20ff: "Der heilig geist hat zwei werk in dem menschen. Das ein ist: er itelt. // Das ander: das er fúllet das ital als verre und als vil als er ital vindet."

On the other hand, however, there are clear statements which make human preparatory activity an indispensable condition for divine presence. When the Holy Spirit finds that man has done his part, *then* He comes with His light, and pours in the supernatural virtues of faith, hope and love with His grace.[1] Without the achievement of a separation from all that is not God (*abgescheidenheit*) and a pure disposition to God in mind and will, the Holy Spirit and His gifts are not received.[2]

Several statements go so far as to place the acquisition of God's saving presence in the context of a good business deal. It is a "fair bargain" (*ein gelich kouf*): we draw the lower powers into and subordinate them to the higher powers of the soul, and God draws us into His highest and ultimate powers. "So much of our own, so much then of His own: it is a fair bargain."[3] Or the situation is described:

> When man has prepared the place—the ground [of the soul]—there is no doubt that God *must* completely replenish it. The heavens open and fill the empty place. God does not leave something empty; it would be against His whole nature and His righteousness...Should you become completely empty, God doubtlessly comes completely in. It is neither more nor less—as much out, so much in.[4]

Finally, we call attention to the placement of the order of salvation in the sphere of an "oath" to God. All of us have promised, Tauler tells his hearers, and all have sworn an oath to God that we would love and be disposed to Him, abjure and deny the world, and serve only Him until our death. This oath can be dissolved by neither priest nor bishop. It binds much more than any temporal oath one might

---

[1] 93.10ff: "Also der heilige geist danne vindet daz der mensche das sine getuot, so kummet er mit sime liehte danne und úberlúhtet daz natúrliche lieht und gússet darin úbernatúrliche tugende, also geloube, hoffenunge, goetteliche minne und sine genade."

[2] 92.16ff: "Dise abgescheidenheit mus man von not haben, so er dan heilgen geist und sine goben entpfohen sol, er sol Got meinen bloeslichen und sich abescheiden von allem dem das Got nút enist." See 235.8ff, 149.28ff.

[3] 231.14ff: "Die nidersten krefte die wil er ziehen in die obersten, mit den nidersten die obersten fueren in sich. Tuon wir das, so wil er uns och nach im ziehen in sin aller oberstes und in sin jungstes. Wan das mus von not sin: súllen wir dar in komen und do sin, so mus ich in von not hie nemen in das min. Nu als vil des minen, als vil denne des sinen: das ist ein gelich kouf." See 45.8ff.

[4] 10.8ff: "Wenne der mensche alsus die stat, den grunt bereitete, so ist kein zwifel do an, Got musse do alzumole erfúllen, der himel risse e und erfúlte daz itel, und Got lot nu vil minre die ding itel, es wer wider alle sin nature und wider sin gerehtikeit... Gest du nu alzumole uz, so Got er one allen zwifel zumole in, weder minre noch mere denne alse vil uz alse vil in." Emphasis mine.

swear, and the consequences of perjury are much greater here than in the breaking of a temporal oath.[1]

Why do we encounter two such series of statements, one which clearly exalts an exclusive *sola gratia*, another which clearly emphasizes that human preparatory activity has necessary, even decisive, soteriological value?

The fact that we are dealing with sermons preached to Christian congregations—often nuns—suggests that a pastoral concern for exhortation and clear-cut pragmatic directives may be a partial explanation. We discount it by no means. But we are convinced that the more telling explanation is less pastorally and more theoretically conditioned.

In this regard, one could argue that insofar as the ground of the soul is from God, is preserved by God, and in a certain definite sense "is" God, every activity which is significant for man's salvation does not and cannot escape the gracious initiative of God. And, on the other hand, insofar as the ground of the soul is created and its saving efficacy conditioned by the free exercise of the powers of the soul, every activity which is significant for salvation does not and cannot escape the conscious complicity of man. Were it not so lacking in power of clarification, we would find it defensible to conclude that, from this perspective, Tauler combines, simultaneously, almost pantheistic presuppositions, yet without the practical consequences of pantheism, and almost Pelagian practice, yet without the presuppositions of Pelagianism.

More clarifying and consistent with the textual evidence we have cited is the following solution. The absence of a clear and firm line between divine and human *activity* reflects the unclarity and tenuousness of the line between divine and human being (*wesen*). The ground of the soul, even *post peccatum Adae*, remains an anthropological-

[1] 58.8ff: "Lieben kint, dis hant wir alle Gote gelobet und mit eiden gesworn daz wir in minnen und meinen súllent, do wir die welt allererst verswuorent und verlobtent, und swuorent ime daz wir ime dienen soltent und in minnen und meinen soltent und ime dienen untz in den dot; von diseme eide enmoehtent uns alle pfaffen und bischoefe nút geloesen die ie geborn wurdent, und bindet vil me denne ob wir einen eit gesworen hettent under dem sale, und den brechent vil; me werdent wir hie meineidig wenne wir mit willen und mit beroteme muote unser hertze und unser meinunge einigen creaturen geben, daz wir Gotte hant gelobet, ouch hie mitte werdent wir me meineidig denne mit einigeme eide. Dis ist daz unser orden und alle unser gesetzede wisent und meinent." Tauler speaks in reference to ordination, but we interpret his remarks to extend to every baptised Christian.

theological repository of salutary resources which can never be extinguished, which is active even when man is sleeping, and from which God neither *can* (order of being) nor *desires* (order of history) to separate Himself.

The divine ordination—*sola gratia!*—which establishes this bond in the sphere of theological ontology and anthropology, underlies the establishment of an oath-conditioned, "fair bargain" policy in the sphere of the order of salvation. The God who is substantively bound to man is the God who is historically bound to respond to man's activity in the order of salvation: "so much out, so much in."

The scholastic parallel here is not so much the double perspective of nominalism, which, on the one hand, can view the order of salvation as *sola gratia*, and, on the other hand, as *solis operibus*,[1] as it is a Thomistic integration of primary and secondary causes from the perspective of an almost exclusively anthropological, rather than ecclesiological and sacramental, orientation and concern.[2]

---

[1] Heiko A. Oberman, *The Harvest of Medieval Theology: Gabriel Biel and Late Medieval Nominalism* (Cambridge, Mass., 1963), 176.

[2] See our comments, *infra*, p. 144, note 1.

CHAPTER THREE

THE *UNIO MYSTICA*

1. DISCIPLE OF BERNARD OF CLAIRVAUX?

It has been convincingly argued by Etienne Gilson that Bernard of Clairvaux understands the *unio mystica* as the reattainment of a true "likeness" to God in the precise sense of a volitional conformity (*voluntas communis*) between the divine and human wills. This conformity results from the penitential elimination of a false *proprium hominis*, which is described by Bernard as a state of volitional (*voluntas propria*) and intellective (*consilium proprium*) disorientation from and "unlikeness" with the will of God.[1] The reattainment of likeness with God, Gilson concludes, respects the "real distinction" between divine will and substance and human will and substance. He writes in summary:

> The mystical union integrally respects this real distinction between the divine substance and the human substance; between the will of God and the will of man; it is neither a confusion of the two substances in general, nor a confusion of the substances of the two wills in particular; but it is their perfect accord, the coincidence of two willings. Two distinct spiritual substances—two substances even *infinitely* distinct as far as concerns the existential order, but in which intention and object coincide to such an extent that the one is perfect image of the other. There we have the mystical union and unity as St. Bernard conceived them.[2]

The conclusions drawn in recent secondary literature on Tauler's understanding of the *unio mystica* converge toward a similar picture. It is argued variously that Tauler ultimately is not an exponent of a "substantive" (*wesentlich*) union between God and man, i.e. following Gilson's definition, a union in which the distinction between the created and the uncreated, the human will and substance and the divine will and substance, is confused to the point of disappearing.

---

[1] Etienne Gilson, *The Mystical Theology of Saint Bernard*, trans. A. H. C. Downes (London, 1940), 53-59, 93, 115-116.

[2] *Ibid.*, 123; cf. 129, 141. See further Aimé Forest, "Das Erlebnis des consensus voluntatis beim heiligen Bernhard," *Bernhard von Clairvaux: Mönch und Mystiker. Internationaler Bernhardkongress Mainz* 1953, ed. Joseph Lortz (Wiesbaden, 1955), 120-27; Joseph Bernhart, *Bernhardische und Eckhartische Mystik in ihren Beziehungen und Gegensätzen* (Kempton, 1912), 51ff.

Rather, it is argued, Tauler understands man's union with God to consist in a conscious, volitional (a power of the soul for Tauler!) and faithful union with or conformity to the will of God, which gradually embraces the whole life and activity of man.[1]

2. *GELICHEIT* AND *MEINEN*

Of primary importance for the evaluation of the cogency of this interpretation, is a clarification of what Tauler means when he speaks of "likeness" (*gelicheit*) with God and an inward and pure "disposition" of mind and will (*meinen*) to God. The position we will argue is that such *gelicheit* and *meinen* concern a union with the divine will which is not the *unio mystica* itself, but rather the final preparatory stage for a still higher, historical level of union: unity in the divine being.

Tauler writes that man has "likeness" with God in the sense that he and God can be actively and beneficially with one another, when the inward man has an unchanging and inward adherence to God,

---

[1] Sr. M. Engratis Kihm writes: "Der Geist [des Menschen] wird, sofern er umgestaltet ist, ein Wesen, ein Sein mit Gott durch Teilnahme, aber nicht wesentlich eins mit ihm, darin liegt ein Unterschied; letzteres hiesse Gott werden von Natur, nicht von Gnaden." "Die Drei-Wege-Lehre bei Tauler," *Johannes Tauler: Ein Deutscher Mystiker. Gedenkschrift zum* 600 *Todestag*, ed. E. Filthaut O.P. (Essen, 1961), 295. P. Pourrat concludes: "We are not...transformed...into the divine being, for the soul which possesses [the divine image] in its depths always remains distinct from God." *Christian Spirituality in the Middle Ages*, II (Westminster, Md., 1953), 241. Weilner makes faith the key term in the union: "Wohl spricht er oft... davon, daß Gott im Seelengrund gegenwärtig oder an ihm handelnd erfahren wird. Aber er ist sich darüber im klaren, daß dies alles letztlich doch eine *Glaubens*-Erfahrung bleibt." *Johannes Taulers Bekehrungsweg*, 204. For Wyser, it is a matter of "Bewußtsein": "Wie er sich Gott in Gott erkennt, ist uns...klar geworden: sein ganzes Bewußtsein ist ganz und gar in Gottes Erkenntnis und Liebe absorbiert. Aber er ist und bleibt Kreatur auch in dieser mystischen Rückkehr zu Gott..." *Lebendiges Mittelalter*, 281. The most eloquent and forcefully argued presentation of this position is found in Grunewald: "Der menschliche Wille versinkt 'tieffer und tieffer' in den 'clarificierten Willen Gotz.' Gottes Wille selbst kommt in den Menschen. Aber das geschieht nicht durch ein naturhaftes Hineinsinken des göttlichen Willens in den menschlichen, sondern so, daß der neue Wille des Menschen in 'Einförmigkeit' mit Gottes Willen handelt. Das ist die wahre Freiheit des Willens, die will, was Gott will. 'In Gottes Willen gebilt' werden, 'mit Gotte einen Willen' haben und 'einförmig' sein heißt Willensbefreiung als Willenserneuerung, heißt gehorsam sein. Wir haben es hier mit Taulers eigenster Form einer 'unio' zu tun." *Studien zu Johannes Taulers Frömmigkeit*, 40-41. Grunewald's recognition of the distinction between a "naturhaft" and a "wesentlich" union is fundamentally correct. The question remains, however, whether "Einförmigkeit" is exhaustive of the "wesentlich" union between God and man which Tauler clearly supports. See our discussion, *infra*, p. 41ff.

which is an inward, perfect and pure disposition to God *(inwendig, volkomen luter Got meinen)*.[1] To follow God in *gelicheit* means to be turned to God with one's highest and lowest powers, an orientation which is in accordance with man's being formed in the image of God in his powers and "like" God according to his being.[2] Tauler can argue, in Bernardian fashion, that all the inward and outward powers should, each in its own sphere, be solidly fixed and prepared so that neither sense nor will nor any power is free, but all bound and girdled together in direct and uncompromising regulation and subjection to what God has eternally willed.[3]

In these three passages, a distinction between divine will and substance and human will and substance is maintained. Such adherence and dependence on God, however, is not the ultimate historical union for which one strives. It is a true and pure devotion[4] which is preparatory to a still more intimate union. The ultimate goal is not union with God, but oneness in God: "not united, but completely one."[5] It

[1] 158.1ff: "Die gelicheit hat der mensche mit Gotte das er mag sin wirklich und gebruchlich mit ein ander, das ist das der inwendige mensche habe ein unwandelberig anhangen an Gotte innerlichen in eime inwendigem, volkomenem, luterm Got meinent. Das meinen ist als ungelich dem das man nach uswendiger wise heisset Got meinen, als louffen und sitzen. Dis ist ein engegenwúrtig inwendig ansehent meinen..." See 116.13ff.

[2] 156.30ff: "Alsus hat Got alle creaturen gemacht wirklich im selber gelich: den himel, die sunne, die sternen und denne úber alle ding verre den engel, den menschen ieklichs nach siner wise...Solte denne der edel nach Gotte gebildet werde mensche nút wúrklich sin nach Gotte in Gotte gebilt an sinen kreften und ime gelich nach sinem wesende? Die edele creature die mus vil adellicher wirklich sin wan die unvernúnftigen creaturen, als der himel. Und dise súllent ime in einer gelicheit nach volgen an wúrkende und schouwende, in weler wise der mensche mit allen sinen kreften, den obersten und den nidersten, gekert ist. So ist der mensche wirklich, und iekliche in irem fúrwurf ze wúrkende, dar nach ir fúrwurf ist, es si goetlich oder creaturlich fúrwurf, dar in wúrkent si dar nach das in engegen getragen wirt."

[3] 32.8ff: "Och wan alle dise krefte, innewendig und ussewendig, sinnelich und begirlich und vernúnftige krefte, so die alzumole werdent gegúrtet ein iegeliche uf ir stat, daz noch die sinne noch der wille noch enkein kraft fri werde, dan gebunden und ufgegúrtet ston in rehter ordenunge under dem goettelichen willen, daz Got ewiclich gewellet hat in sime ewiclichen willen." Cf. 30.5ff, 28.3ff.

[4] 84.13ff: "Kinder, uf disem berge Oliveti do wahsset das oley uffe. Bi dem oleije verstat man wore andaht. Kinder, wesenliche andaht das ist ein gemuetlich anhangen Gottes mit einem bereiten gemuete, minnen und meinen alles daz Gotte zugehoeret, und das man sich innerlich Gotte verbunden habe und welle und meinen..."

[5] 47.18ff: "Also er ouch bat sinen vatter: 'daz sú mit uns eins sint also wir eins sint, ich in dir und du in mir, nút vereiniget, sunder zumole eins, das sú also eins sint mit uns, doch nút von naturen, mer von genaden noch unbegriffenlicher wisen'."

is a "fusion" with the divine abyss, in which the created spirit neither knows nor feels nor senses itself, but only a single, pure, sheer and simple God.[1]

Tauler argues explicitly that this is a goal beyond "likeness":

> In this conversion, the purified and clarified spirit sinks completely into the divine darkness, into a still silence and an inconceivable and inexpressible unity. In this absorption all like *(gelich)* and unlike *(ungelich)* is lost. In this abyss the spirit loses itself and knows neither God nor itself, neither like nor unlike. It knows nothing, for it is engulfed in the oneness of God and has lost all differences.[2]

In this unity, the created spirit not only loses all its weakness, naturalness and unlikeness to God, but also all its likeness to God, as it flows into the divine unity, just as wood, when it burns, loses finally both its unlikeness and likeness to fire.[3]

In contradistinction to the conversion which concerns the pure disposition of the spirit to God, this higher conversion concerns an inward and formless presence of God, in which a trans-substantial entrance of the created spirit into the uncreated Spirit of God occurs.

---

[1] 88.1ff: "Der geist enweis es selber nút, wanne er ist also versmoltzen in das goetteliche abgrunde das er nút enweis, enfuelet noch ensmacket dan einen einigen lutern blossen einvaltigen Got."

[2] 117.30-118.2: "In diseme [ker] versinket der geluterte verklerte geist in daz goetteliche vinsternisse, in ein stille swigen und in ein unbegriffenlicheme und unsprechenlicheme vereinen, und in diseme insinkende wurt verlorn alles gelich und ungelich, und in diseme abegrunde verlúret der geist sich selber und enweis von Gotte noch von ime selber noch gelich noch ungelich noch von núte nút, wan er ist gesuncken in Gottes einikeit und hat verlorn alle underscheide."

[3] 120.24-121.3: "Hie in diser vereinunge wurt der geist gezogen und erhaben úber alle sine krangheit und natúrlicheit und ungelicheit, und wurt do gelutert und verklert und erhaben úber alle sine kraft und úber sich selber und sine wise, und alles sin wurken und sin wesen wurt mit Gotte durchgangen und wurt in eine goetteliche wise gewiset und úberfuert, und do wurt die geburt in der worheit geborn, und do verlúret der geist alle gelicheit und verflússet in goetteliche einikeit, gelicher wise also das fúr wúrcket in das holtz und benimmet ime die fúchtekeit, die gruenekeit und die grobekeit und machet es warmer und hitziger und gelicher. Also danne das holtz also lange der gelicheit neher kummet, so die ungelicheit me und me flúhet, so in einer sneller stunden so zúhet daz fúr die materie des holtzes abe und wurt ouch fúr und verlúret die materie beide ungelich und gelich und ist fúr worden und ist nút me gelich, sunder ist eins mit dem fúre worden. In einikeit verlúret man gelicheit. Also rechte zúhet dise minnecliche spise den geist usser aller ungelicheit in gelicheit und den us gelicheit in ein goetteliche einikeit. Daz geschiht dem verklerten geist, der verlúrt ungelich und gelich." For further parallels with the Eucharist, see 295.25ff, 294.3ff, 56.13ff. See 251.20ff, where the image of a drop of water in the sea is used, 55.15ff, where the image of a drop of water absorbed by the earth is employed, and 33.20ff, where the image of a drop of water in a bottle of wine is expressed.

Here there is an inward inversion of the spirit, from the ground of the soul, into the Spirit of God. Tauler concludes that this inversion is a truly substantive conversion *(ein weselich ker)*, in which a substantially real reward and God *must* simultaneously correspond with one another *(disem mus alwegen antwúrten weselich lon und Got mit im selber)*.[1] In the higher conversion, the natural and historical indebtedness of God to man embrace: the created spirit receives a "substantially real reward."

The distinction between (a) the volitional and intellective union with God *(anhangen* and *meinen)* on the level of the powers of the soul, and (b) the substantive conversion *(weseliche ker)* and union with the being of God in the ground of the soul, is further supported by Tauler's insistence upon the impossibility of the simultaneous coexistence of two forms.[2] He argues that if man is to be transformed into the trans-substantial being of God, then *all* "forms" which he has ever received in all his powers must be removed—perception, knowledge, volitional desire, activity, orientation to temporal objects, feeling and his self-defining peculiarity.[3] No two forms can stand together. Should

[1] 169.5ff: "Hin ab schribt S. Thomas das grosse uswendig werk, wie gros die sint, als verre als si werk sint, den enantwúrt nút denne zuvallender lon. Aber in dem inkere des geistes inwendig zu Gottes geiste us dem grunde sunder allen zu val, denne alleine suchet Got blos und luter und úber alle werk oder wise und úber allen gedant oder vernunft,—ja sprach S. Dyonisius: 'es ist unvernúnftig, es ist ein unsinnig minne.' Dis ist ein recht weselich ker; disem mus alwegen antwúrten weselich lon und God mit im selber. // Ein ander ker mag och wol in einer gemeiner usserlicher wise weselich heissen, das ist in allen den keren do der mensche Got luterlichen und bloslichen meint und nút anders, noch enkein warumbe, denne Got durch sich selber in im selber. // Aber der erste ker der ist in einer inwendiger unformlicher unwislicher engegenwúrtkeit in einem úber substentklichen intragende des geschaffenen geistes in den ungeschaffenen geist Gotz. Und koende der mensch alles sin leben der ker einen getreffen, so were im wol geschehen."

[2] A sound Aristotelian principle; cf. *Categoriae* (McKeon edition), ch. 6, 5b.40-6a.3. Insofar as Tauler is representative of the mystical *Denkmethode*, we do not agree with Rühl that this method is strictly non-Aristotelian. The Aristotelian principle of the impossibility of the simultaneous coexistence of two forms is fundamental for Tauler. See *supra*, p. 7, note 4.

[3] 257.13ff: "Wan also schribent die meister: wenne ein núwe forme sol gewerden, so mus von not die alte gar verderben, und sprechent: wenne das kint wirt enphangen in der muter libe, zem ersten so ist ein blosse materie. Dar nach wirt der materie ein tierliche materie in gegossen, der lebet als ein tier. Dar nach, nach der vorgeordenter zit, so schoephet Got ein vernúnftiger sele und gússet die in die. Denne so vergat alle die erste forme: in der solicheit die gescheftlicheit, die gedenklicheit, die grosse, die varwe. Dis mus alles gar dannan, denne ein luter blosse materie blibet do. Also sprich ich: hie sol der mensche úber formet werden mit disem úber weselichen wesende; so mussen alle die formen von not dannan die

fire be present, then wood must be "destroyed;" should there be a tree, then the seed must be destroyed. And should God enter us with the accomplishment of His birth, then the created and natural in us must be destroyed.[1]

3. SUSPENSION OF THE *POTENTIA DEI ORDINATA*[2]

When one reaches the point where he stands on the brink of the mystical union itself, Tauler calls for a thorough-going suspension of God's historical means of grace. Here all that has helped one in the past—the body of Christ, the Word of God and one's own exercises—becomes a hindrance.[3] Now

> one takes the sacraments away from [the poor nature] for the sake of God's ordination. Before, when [the poor nature] came, I had given it the body of God daily. Now I do so in no way. For it must go another way now which is higher than this way, where the spirit should rest in God's Spirit, in a hidden silence in the divine being.[4]

When one is found by God to be turned in purity and poverty to Him, the divine abyss inclines to and sinks into the purified ground of the soul. It transforms *(úberformet)* the created ground and draws

---

man in allen kreften ie enphieng: das kennen, das wissen, das wellen, die wúrklicheit, die fúrwúrflicheit, die bevintlicheit, die eigenscheftlicheit."

[1] 222.19ff: "Wan als die meister sprechent das enkeine zwo formen enmúgen mit einander ston: sol fúr werden, das holtz mus verwerden; sol der boum gewerden, der kerne mus verwerden; sol Gotz fúrgang in uns gewerden mit der erfúllung siner geburt, so mus die creature in uns verwerden." Cf. 314.7ff.

[2] The caption comes from Oberman's discussion of nominalist mysticism, in which such a suspension is a primary feature of the mysticism rejected by nominalism. *The Harvest of Medieval Theology*, 330, 338. As F-W Wentzlaff-Eggebert emphasizes, the ordained means of grace have exhausted their function once the mystic has reached the brink of the *unio mystica*. "Der Mystiker fühlt sich nicht mehr gebunden an äußerliche Mittler der Offenbarung göttlichen Lebens, wie Schrift, Sakrament, Kirche, sondern er erlebt unmittelbar in seinem Innern das Wirken einer höheren Macht." *Deutsche Mystik zwischen Mittelalter und Neuzeit* (Berlin, 1944), 15.

[3] 315.2ff: "In diseme grote hinderent dich drú ding der du in diseme enberen must: das ist unsers herren lichame und das Gottes wort und din eigene uebunge; wan alle behelfunge die ist in disem dir ein hindernisse." Cf. 315.35ff, 313.35ff, 432.22ff.

[4] 411.27ff: "Hie wurt die arme nature einen ander weg gefuert in ein bekorunge, ja innewendig nút alleine, sunder ouch ussewendig alles enthaltes und trostes; man entzúhet ir die sacramente von Gottes ordenunge wegen; hie vormoles e sú herzu keme, so het ich ir alle tage Gotz licham geben, sunder nu keine wise also; sú mus nu einen andern weg der úber sú ist, do sol der geist rasten in Gottes geiste in einer verborgenen stillen in dem goettelichen wesen."

it by this transformation into uncreatedness, so that the spirit becomes "as one" with it.[1] Here one is beyond the mediation and assistance of the sacraments, the Word of God, and all historical aids and activities. The historical order is transcended for the sake of an even higher ordination of God, the ordination on the level of being. Leaving the historical order, the created spirit enters its uncreatedness and recognizes itself as God in God, although it is, in itself, a creature and created.[2]

4. *WESELICH* UNION WITH GOD

There are several qualifications which Tauler expresses and which one might turn into objections to the position we have presented. First, it is possible to argue that Tauler considers the mystical union to be a "foretaste" of eternal life, which at best is only "momentary."[3] Is this not a significant qualification?

In response, it must be recognized that the fact that the union is a momentary foretaste of eternal life does not alter another fact, viz., that it is qualitatively identical with the eschatological significance of eternal life, and it is a *de facto* possibility capable of historical realization. Indeed, it is the very historical goal of the order of salvation. The distinction between a momentary foretaste of eternal life—a return to uncreatedness despite createdness—and this life itself, is quantitative. The time to which the spirit of man is privy can bear and momentarily be eternity.

Secondly, it can be argued that Tauler himself insists that it is only dumb and stupid people who understand the union with God in a carnal way, and say that they should be changed into the divine nature *(in goetteliche nature)*. This position, he concludes, is heresy, for even in the highest and most intimate union with God, divine nature and

[1] 363.11ff: "Denne als Got den menschen also vindet in der luterkeit und in der blosheit zu gekert, so neiget sich das goetlich abgrúnde und sinket in den luteren zu gekerten grunt und úberformet den geschaffen grunt und zúhet in in die ungeschaffenheit mit der úberformunge, das der geist als ein mit dem wirt." See 80.11ff.

[2] 358.10ff: "In der verborgenheit wirt der geschaffen geist wider getragen in sin ungeschaffenheit, do er eweklichen gewesen ist e er geschaffen wúrde, und bekent sich Got in Gotte und doch an im selber creatur und geschaffen."

[3] 56.3ff: "...waz sú do vint, daz ist úber alle sinne, vernunft kan es nút erlangen, nieman mag es begriffen noch verston, es ist ein war fúrsmag des ewigen lebendes." 46.22f: "...wer in disem ein púntelin gelebet nútzer dan viertzig jor in eigen ufsetzen."

being are higher than all heights, in a divine abyss that never was and never becomes a creature.[1] Is this not a significant qualification?

Again, in response, we must insist that what Tauler here denies is the identity of divine nature and being with human existence *(fleisch)*. We do not dispute this distinction. Tauler does not deny here, however, as he never denies in his Sermons, that divine being *(wesen)* and human being *(wesen)* can be one in history. In this regard, only a quantitative impossibility *(hoch und hoch úber alle hoehi)* is expressed. But even in man's eternal status in uncreatedness this was true; he was "God in God," spiritual being with and in spiritual Being, not the divine nature and being themselves. And it is precisely the historical approximation of "Godness in God" which Tauler argues consistently and frequently is the *unio mystica*. The fact, then, that divine Spirit is not subject to the conditions of created existence, does not alter the fact that the human spirit is capable of attaining divine form and being.

The "likeness" of created and uncreated spirit, of created and uncreated 'grounds,' is an established presupposition in Tauler's thought. And the oneness of created and uncreated spirit in a "substantive" *(weselich)* and "formful" *(formelich)* unity beyond unlikeness and likeness, is an equally well established conclusion. As time can bear and momentarily be eternity, created being (the *grunt der selen)* can bear and momentarily be divine being.

Finally, Tauler juxtaposes the phrases "von gnaden" and "von naturen," when he speaks of man's "deification." This juxtaposition is considered by at least one interpreter of his Sermons to be the decisive argument against a "wesentlich" union with God.[2] Let us look closely at the context of these phrases in several representative passages before attempting to measure the seriousness of this qualification. First, Tauler writes:

> Man is so completely deified that everything he is and does, God does and is in him. He is so completely lifted out of his natural way [of life] that he becomes *von gnaden* what God substantively is *von naturen*. Here

---

[1] 121.23ff: "Vil minre ist daz zu begriffende und nachzugonde wie der geist verwurt in goettelicher einikeit, do er sich also verlúret das enkeine vernunft darbi kan kummen obe ie creature wart. Dis nemment tumbe affehte lúte fleischlichen und sprechent, sú súllent gewandelt werden in goetteliche nature, und das ist zumole boese valsche ketzerige. Von der allerhoehster innigester nehster einunge mit Gotte so ist noch goetteliche nature und sin wesen hoch und hoch úber alle hoehi, daz get in ein goetteliche abgrunde das nimmer keine creature und och keine enwurt."

[2] See *supra*, p. 36, note 1.

he feels and experiences himself as lost; he neither knows, experiences nor feels himself anywhere. He knows nothing except one simple being.[1]

And a second passage:

> The spirit loses itself in the abyss so deeply and in so groundless a way that it knows nothing of itself. It knows neither word nor way, neither taste nor feeling, neither perception nor love, for everything is one, pure, sheer and simple God, one inexpressible abyss, one being, one spirit. *Von genade*, God gives the spirit what He is *von naturen*; there God has united His nameless, formless, mannerless being with the spirit.[2]

And a final passage:

> Here the soul becomes completely God-colored, divine and godly. It becomes everything *von gnaden* that God is *von naturen* in the union with God, in the absorption in God. It is held above itself in God. Thus, it becomes God-colored there. Should it then see itself, it would see itself completely as God. And whoever should see it would see it in the clothes, color, manner and being of God *von gnaden*. And who so sees would be blessed in his beholding, for God and the soul are one in this union *von gnaden*, not *von naturen*.[3]

In these passages, the juxtaposition of "by grace" and "by nature" does not argue against a substantive union between God and man. "By means of grace," man *becomes that which God substantively is* "by nature." "By means of grace," God gives the created spirit *what He is* "by nature." "By means of grace," the soul *becomes everything that God is* "by nature." The juxtaposition of grace and nature in the last sentence of the third passage cited here underscores the fact that God does not become a created, fleshly nature in the *unio mystica*, but it does

[1] 162.8ff: "...Wirt do der mensche als vergottet das alles das der mensche ist und wúrket, das wúrket und ist Got in ime, und wirt als verre uf erhaben úber sin natúrlich wise das er recht wirt von gnaden das Got weslichen ist von naturen. Hie inne voelt und bevint sich der mensche selber verlorn haben und enweis noch enbevint noch engevoellet sich niergen; er enweis nút denne ein einvaltig wesen."

[2] 109.20ff: "In dem abgrunde verlúret sich der geist so tief und in so grundeloser wisen das er von ime selber nút enweis, er enweis do noch wort noch wise, noch smacken noch fuelen, bekennen noch minnen, danne es ist alles ein luter blos einvaltig Got, ein unsprechenliches abgrunde, ein wesen, ein geist; von genade git Got dem geiste daz das er ist von naturen, und hat dem geiste do geeiniget das namelose formelose wiselose wesen..."

[3] 146.21ff: "In disem wirt die sele alzemole gotvar, gotlich, gottig. Si wirt alles das von gnaden das Got ist von naturen, in der vereinunge mit Gotte, in dem inversinkende in Got, und wirt geholt úber sich in Got. Also gotvar wirt si do: were das si sich selber sehe, si sehe sich zemole fúr Got. Oder wer si sehe, der sehe si in dem kleide, in der varwe, in der wise, in dem wesende Gotz von gnaden, und wer selig in dem gesichte, wan Gott und si sint ein in diser vereinunge von gnaden und nút von naturen."

not significantly qualify the argument that by means of grace the created ground and spirit of man are qualitatively identical with the uncreated Ground and Spirit.

5. THE RECONCILIATION OF DIVINE MERCY AND JUDGMENT: TAULER AND LUTHER

A concluding commentary on the *weselich* union of man with God is forthcoming when one takes into consideration two senses in which Tauler parallels God and *wesen*. On one level, Tauler has the neoplatonic-Augustinian identification of being and God in mind. God is the being of all being *(das aller wesen wesen ist)*, yet He can be contained by no thing *(doch enist er aller dinge in keines)*: "all that is and is being and has being and is good, therein is God."[1] Here Tauler has the ontological and anthropological basis for a substantive presence of God in the ground of the soul even *post peccatum Adae*.

In another sense God and *wesen* are paralleled in terms of the absolute simplicity and unity of all that God is. When man enters the being of God with his own multiplicity, then he too is 'simplified' and unified. Oppositions within himself as well as the opposition between him and God are completely overcome. Here is the theological basis for the historical approximation of uncreatedness under and in spite of the conditions of created existence. In this regard Tauler writes:

> [God's] being is His acting, knowing, rewarding, loving, judging—all one, His mercy, His righteousness. Go therein and take your incomprehensibly great diversity, so that He may simplify and unify it in His pure and unified being.[2]

Although this passage is strictly theocentric, rather than Christocentric, and lacks the 'Worthaftigkeit' which contemporary research ascribes to Luther's understanding of divine and human union in and through faith, still the unity of divine mercy and righteousness in a

[1] 277.2f: "Alles das ist und das wesen ist und wesen hat und gut ist, da inne ist Got."

[2] 277.14ff: "Denne sehe der mensche an die eigenschaft der einiger einikeit des wesens, wan Got ist an dem lesten ende der einvaltikeit und in ime wirt alle manigvaltikeit geeiniget und einvaltig in dem einigen ein wesende. Sin wesen ist sin wúrken, sin bekennen, sin lonen, sin minnen, sin richten alles ein, sin barmherzikeit, sin gerechtekeit: dar in gang und trage din unbegriffenlichen grosse manigvaltikeit, das er die einvaltige in sinem ein valtigen wesende." See the parallels in the thought of Nicholas of Cusa, *Cusanus-Konkordanz. Unter Zugrundelegung der philosophischen und der bedeutendsten theologischen Werke*, ed. Eduard Zellinger (München, 1960), 92,§45; 91,§45.

present and existentially realizable possibility of self-being and self-understanding, which this same research argues is decisive in Luther's Reformation discovery ('Turmerlebnis'),[1] is theoretically present. Is Tauler Luther's 'forerunner' at this point? Are they simply saying the same thing by different means and in different words?

The absence of historical Christology and of the importance of the Word of God from this passage are indications that these questions cannot be answered with an unqualified 'yes'. The secondary literature has justifiably exalted these points as crucial factors in the definition of Luther's relation to Tauler. Just how important they are, however, is not comprehensively established and appreciated until the differences between Luther and Tauler on the level of anthropology are manifest. Luther writes that the spiritual man relies on faith—not on his *gemuete* or a ground of the soul. Only as we have probed the pre-history and systematic implications of this statement (Part Three) can we define with confidence the relation between Tauler's and Luther's theological thought.

6. SUMMARY

1. Tauler's understanding of man's pre-creaturely status as "one essential being" with God is a major presupposition behind his definition of the *gemuete* and *grunt* of the soul. The latter, *post peccatum Adae*, are anthropological-theological resources to which God is ontologically committed. He neither *can* (order of being) nor *desires* (order of history) to separate Himself from them. A natural 'covenant,' a

[1] Especially striking is the statement by Albert Brandenburg: "Im 'gläubigen Selbstverständnis' kommt das göttliche Tat-Wort des Evangeliums zur Realisierung *(impletio!)*, und es geschieht das Heilswerk. Nichts wird gesagt von einer Repräsentation eines einmaligen Faktums. Christus und die fides verschmelzen (fast) zu einer Einheit: Christus tunc *ist* in der fides Christi nunc. Es geschieht Gericht und Gerechtigkeit im existentiellen Jetzt des Wortes." *Gericht und Evangelium: zur Worttheologie in Luthers erster Psalmenvorlesung* (Paderborn, 1960), 141. Regin Prenter writes less ecstatically: "Luther sagt: Gott sendet diese Gerechtigkeit und zugleich mit ihr auch den Frieden." *Der barmherzige Richter: Iustitia dei passiva in Luthers Dictata super psalterium* 1513-1515 (København, 1961), 73. Reinhard Schwarz argues against Ernst Bizer that *Evangelium* is the "Wort von Christus" as *iudicium* and *iustitia*. *Fides, Spes und Caritas beim jungen Luther* (Berlin, 1962), 171. Heiko A. Oberman concludes: "One can summarize...Luther's discovery in the following sentence: the heart of the Gospel is that the *iustitia Christi* and the *iustitia Dei* coincide and are granted simultaneously." "'Iustitia Christi' and 'Iustitia Dei': Luther and the Scholastic Doctrines of Justification," *HTR*, 59 (1966), 19. B. A. Gerrish speaks of Luther's "realized eschatology."

commitment of God to the ground of the soul and of this ground to its Origin, exists on the level of being. Like cannot deny like.

2. Tauler can speak of man's salvation by grace alone and still emphasize the decisive importance of human preparatory activity. One can find passages in which both the Spirit of God and the spirit of man hold the initiative in the order of salvation. The tenuousness of this line between divine and human initiative and activity in the historical order of salvation, reflects the tenuousness of the line between divine and human being in the a-historical order of being. While Tauler's understanding of the order of salvation cannot be described unqualifiedly as Pelagian, it is certainly not possible to consider him to be a major representative of an exclusive, Augustinian *sola gratia*. Pushed to its (illogical) extreme, Tauler's system of thought avoids Pelagianism only at the expense of pantheism, and pantheism only at the price of Pelagianism.

3. The effort to interpret Tauler's understanding of the *unio mystica* as a *conformitas voluntatis*, which does not intend a substantive union with God, overlooks the fact that such conformity, expressed in the terms, *gelicheit* and *meinen*, is preparatory to a still higher union with God: absorption in the being of God, in which all unlikeness and likeness between divine and human spirit are transcended. At this level, God's *potentia ordinata*, and that means not only all historical aids, including the passion of Christ, the Word of God, and the sacraments, but also the *historicity of man*, is suspended. The significance of human life, for Tauler, lies ultimately in its becoming divine life. Historical man is an organ *en route* to his a-historical Origin: the being of God.

Grace and Reason: A Study in the Theology of Luther (Oxford, 1962), 126. Each of these interpretations are variations of the theme sounded in 1929 by Erich Vogelsang, who, through an analysis of the *scholia* on psalm 70, emphasized the importance of Luther's discovery of the reconciliation of the *iustitia Dei* and the *iudicium Dei literaliter* in Christ and *tropologice* in faith—faith by which man's life is judged and justified simultaneously. *Die Anfänge von Luthers Christologie nach der ersten Psalmenvorlesung* (Berlin, 1929), 55f, 64, 103, 119ff.

PART TWO
JEAN GÉRSON

CHAPTER FOUR

THE PROJECT OF A MYSTICAL THEOLOGY[1]

In undertaking the endeavor to develop a distinctive "mystical theology," Jean Gerson is concerned to specify the better way to the attainment of a "clear and savory understanding" of those things which are believed in the gospel. Or, alternatively expressed, he seeks the better way in which God is known in this life. The concluding statement of his lecture, *Contra curiositatem studentium* (November, 1402), which deals with the abuses and vanities of speculative theology,[2] and which forms the immediate historical point of departure for *De mystica theologia speculativa* (1402-03), projects both the goal he seeks and the means he will employ to reach it.

> The clear and savory understanding of those things which are believed in the gospel is called mystical theology, and it is to be acquired more through penitence than through human investigation alone. In this regard, the question will be treated, whether it is through penitential affection more than through intellective investigation that God is known in this life.[3]

---

[1] Oriented by Luther's reference to Gerson's anthropological schema in "Mystica Theologia" (see *supra*, p. 2), we will be concerned primarily with a detailed consideration of Gerson's *De mystica theologia speculativa* [= *De myst. theol. spec.*] and *De mystica theologia practica* [= *De myst. theol. pract.*] in *Ioannis Carlerii de Gerson*: *De mystica theologia*, ed. André Combes (Lugano, [1958]). In drawing upon other works in close historical proximity with the double treatment of mystical theology, we are guided by the research of Combes, especially the evaluative analyses and conclusions drawn in *Essai sur la critique de Ruysbroeck par Gerson* [= *Essai...*], III (Paris, 1959), 98-317.

[2] Gerson's ability to speak of the "caligatio philosophorum" and the "claritas theologorum" (*De myst. theol. spec.*, *cons.* 34,87.1f) should not lead us to think immediately of Gregory of Rimini and Luther. Gerson is explicit in his insistence that the "articulos fidei nullo modo esse contra philosophiam naturalem." His concern is not to censure the intrusion of philosophical method and subject matter into theology, but to encourage philosophy to be respectful of its limits: "Porro si philosophi se inter hos limites coarctassent, et Deum sic cognitum ut dignum fuerat, glorificassent, bene erat cum eis; sed pergere ultra volentes defecerunt scrutantes scrutinio." *Contra curiositatem studentium* [= *Contra...*], *Oeuvres complètes*, ed. P. Glorieux, III (Paris, 1962), 231.

[3] *Contra...*, 249: "Intelligentia clara et sapida eorum quae creduntur ex Evangelio, quae vocatur theologia mystica, conquirenda est per poenitentiam magis quam per solam humanam investigationem. Et circa hoc pertractabitur ista quaestio an magis per poenitentem affectum quam per investigantem intellectum Deus in via cognos-

The material on which Gerson draws is the experiential knowledge of those who are learned in the subject of mystical theology. For just as symbolic and systematic or speculative theology draws upon natural analogies and extrinsic effects and data to make its affirmations and compose its doctrines, so the doctrines of mystical theology are drawn from internal experiences in the hearts of the devout.[1] And just as the principles of symbolic and speculative theology are acquired through a trusting acceptance of the authority of the *doctores ecclesiae*, so the principles of mystical theology are acquired in a like manner:

> If knowledge of the principles in our case is to be attained, it is done so through faith and belief alone, by which we agree with the narrators and experts in the subject.[2]

Fidelic knowledge and rational treatment of first principles are just as possible and meaningful in mystical theology as they are in symbolic and speculative theology.[3]

Gerson is most emphatic about the distinctiveness and integrity of the cognitive content of mystical theology. He registers disagreement with Dionysius the Areopagite to the extent that the "negative way" of the latter implies the forfeiture of a positive, experiential knowledge of God. "Who," Gerson asks, "would say that mystical theology pursues only a negative way, relinguishing all positive knowledge and

---

catur." The prologue to *De myst. theol. spec.* makes explicit appeal to this statement. *Prol.* 1.9ff.

[1] *De myst. theol. spec., cons.* 2,8.4ff: "Theologia mistica innititur ad sui doctrinam experientiis habitis ad intra in cordibus animorum devotorum, sicut alia duplex theologia [theologia simbolica et theologia propria] ex hiis procedit, que extrinsecus operantur." Cf. *cons.* 3,11.4ff; 2,10.23f. Cf. Bonaventura: "...per symbolicam [theologiam] recte utamur sensibilibus, per propriam [theologiam] recte utamur intelligibilibus, per mysticam [theologiam] rapiamur ad supermentales excessus." *Itinerarium mentis in deum* in *Bonaventura. Itinerarium mentis in deum. De reductione artium ad theologiam* [= *Itin.*] (München, 1961), I, 7, 62.

[2] *De myst. theol. spec., cons.* 4,13.13ff: "Cognitio autem principiorum in casu nostro si habetur, habetur per solam fidem et credulitatem, per quam narrantibus et expertis consentimus." See *cons.* 4,12.3ff and *cons.* 8,21.40f, where Augustine, Hugo of St. Victor, Bonaventure, William of Paris and Thomas are listed among the learned. For comprehensive treatments of Gerson's sources, see André Combes, *Jean Gerson commentateur dionysien: les Notulae super quaedam verba Dionysii de caelesti hierarchia* (Paris, 1940), 422-472; Connolly, *John Gerson*, 330ff; Johann Stelzenberger, *Die Mystik des Johannes Gerson. Breslauer Studium zur historischen Theologie*, X (Breslau, 1928).

[3] On the 'scientific' character of Gerson's mystical theology, see Walter Dress, who concludes: "Die mystische Theologie ist die gelehrte Form der Mystik, sie ist ein Versuch, das mystische Erlebnis zu systematisieren." *Die Theologie Gersons*, 49.

experience of God?"[1] And, further, he argues that if philosophy is defined as all knowledge proceeding from experience, then mystical theology will be 'philosophy,' and all who are experienced therein, even though to the technically skilled they may appear to be ignorant, are not to be denied the title, 'philosophers.'[2]

Gerson is not, however, concerned simply to argue for the equality of mystical with symbolic and speculative theology. He is convinced of the superiority of the former over the latter. As love excels knowledge, will the intellect and the virtue of love the virtue of faith, so the knowledge of God attained in mystical theology through penitential affection is more desirable and perfect than the knowledge which is attained *solely* through the intellective investigation and contemplation of symbolic and speculative theology.[3]

In this regard, he sketches several contrasts between the school of

---

[1] *De myst. theol. spec., cons.* 2,9.10ff: "Quis autem diceret quod theologia mistica solam abnegationem consectetur, nichil reliquens de Deo positive cognitum vel expertum?" André Combes considers the "quis" to be a clear reference to Dionysius: "...contrairement à la pensée de Denys, la pensée de Gerson tend invinciblement vers un contenu positif." Combes, further, sees this departure from Dionysius to lie (1) in Gerson's acceptance of "une faculté supérieure que ne souffre pas des limites de l'intellect," viz., the *synteresis*, and (2) the influence of the "spiritual Dionysians," Hugh of Balma and Thomas Gallus. The latter were much less obsessed with the unknowability of God than was their namesake: "Avec eux, et c'est la révolution dont ils assument la responsabilité, la théologie mystique change de sens: d'essentiellement négative chez Denys, elle devient essentiellement positive," although not in the sense of an intuitive vision. *La thèologie mystique de Gerson: profil de son évolution*, I (Rome, 1963), 86, 95-96, 98-99.

[2] *De myst. theol. spec., cons.* 3,11.16-12.20: "...si phylosophia dicatur scientia omnis procedens ex experientiis, mistica theologia erit phylosophia, eruditique in ea, quantumlibet aliunde ydiote sint, phylosophi recta ratione nominantur."

[3] *Ibid., cons.* 28,70.5ff: "Cognitio Dei per theologiam misticam melius acquiritur per penitentem affectum, quam per investigantem intellectum, ipsa quoque ceteris paribus eligibilior est et perfectior quam theologia symbolica vel propria de qua est contemplatio, sicut dilectio perfectior est cognitione, et voluntas intellectu, et caritas fide." We emphasize the "solely" in order to make clear that Gerson's criticism of the intellective powers and their activities is not a criticism *per se*. They are criticized in the important context of their attempting to attain knowledge of God in complete disregard to the affective powers. As Gerson writes: "Contemplatio namque, si nude consideretur sine dilectione vel affectu subsequente, iam arida est, inquieta est, curiosa est, ingrata est, inflata est..." *De myst. theol. spec., cons.* 44,120.8ff. Compare Tauler's insistence upon the superiority of love (*minne*) to knowledge (*bekentnis*): "Von diser minne hant die meister vil tisputacie, weder bekentnissin hoher si oder die minne. Das lossen wir nu ligen. Aber do enist kein zwivel an, die minne ensi hie vil verdienlicher und nútzer wan bekentnisse. Wan die minne die get do in do das bekentnisse mus husse bliben. Die minne die enbedarf keins grossen subtilen bekentnisse, denne eins luteren lebenden glouben in cristenlichen wisen." Vetter, 349.1ff.

religion or love, in which the affective powers and mystical theology are active, and the school of knowledge and speculative investigation,[1] in which the intellective powers and contemplation rule.

The first and most fundamental difference between mystical and speculative theology is drawn from their different subjects or powers, speculative theology being located in the intellective power and mystical theology reposing in the affective power. Closely allied with this difference is the difference which results from the objects to which the two theologies are oriented, speculative theology finding its object in the "true," mystical theology in the "good."[2]

A third difference results from the fact that, in mystical theology, understanding may rise beyond itself. For the mind, heated by love, may boil over, ascending where rational contemplation alone cannot take it.[3] Fourthly, mystical theology is the more democratic way; even young girls and simpletons can become proficient in it, since logical and metaphysical acumen is not requisite to its attainment.[4]

A fifth difference results from mystical theology's ability to exist complete in itself without the complementary aid of speculative theology, whereas the reverse is never possible.[5] Sixthly, speculative theology is prone toward becoming the servant of injurious pursuits, while mystical theology intrinsically lacks the neutrality which makes such subservience possible, notwithstanding the fact that "accidentally," when it is coerced into abusing hope and faith, it may lend itself to such pursuits.[6]

---

[1] Cf. *De myst. theol. spec.*, *cons.* 30,77.22ff.

[2] *Ibid.*, *cons.* 29,73.7ff: "Prima et principalis differentia sumitur ex subiecto vel potentia, quoniam licet utraque sit in anima rationali, nichilominus distinguendo potentias anime secundum rationes suas, ut supra dictum est [*cons.* 9,24.51f], speculativa igitur theologia est in potentia intellectiva, cuius obiectum est verum, misticam vero reponimus in potentia affectiva, cui pro obiecto bonum assignamus."

[3] *Ibid.*, *cons.* 29,75.51-76.54: "...mens nondum amore calescens intra seipsam se continet, sed spiritu fervoris amore concepto, supergreditur quodammodo semetipsam, quasi extra se saltitans atque volitans." "Sic intelligentia nostra illustrata contemplatione serena celestium quandoque quidem remanet intra seipsam non incalescens neque ardens, quandoque vero tantus amoris ardor concursu radiorum celestium exoritur, ut in affectum se erigat nec se capiat neque contineat, sed iubilat et exultat, ex quibus tertia concluditur differentia." *Ibid.*, *cons.* 29,76.58ff.

[4] *Ibid.*, *cons.* 30,78.33ff: "Ex quo illam concludimus differentiam, quoniam theologia mistica, licet sit suprema atque perfectissima notitia, ipsa tamen potest haberi a quolibet fideli, etiam si sit muliercula vel ydiota."

[5] *Ibid.*, *cons.* 30,79.45ff: "Ex premissis concludimus... quod theologia speculativa numquam in aliquo perfecta est sine mistica, sed bene e contra."

[6] *Ibid.*, *cons.* 32,82.4ff: "Theologia speculativa vel litteratoria per hoc vel maxime a mistica secernitur, quod prima servire potest vitiis, secunda nequaquam nisi per accidens valde, sicut si contingeret abuti spe vel fide."

A seventh difference is that speculative theology may be present without actively conforming to what it knows.[1] Mystical theology, on the other hand, has consistent allegiance to the Aristotelian principle that only by working well does one become good.[2] And, finally, in mystical theology there is an attainment and stabilizing of one's relation with God, while speculative theology alone leaves one restless and unsettled.[3]

The arguments for the superiority, or more precisely stated, the greater depth and comprehensiveness, of mystical theology should not be interpreted as a minimization of the importance of the intellective powers and *scientia*.[4] For fundamental to Gerson's project of a mystical theology is his conviction of the mutually supporting relation between *devotio* and *scientia*. This conviction reflects one of the strongest, clearest, most common sensical, and yet most overlooked motifs in Gerson's mystical theology, viz., the naturally correlative and reciprocal character and operation of the affective and intellective powers.[5] Gerson is convinced that the only *devotio* worthy of the Christian is that which is *secundum scientiam*, and the only *scientia* worthy of the Christian that which is *secundum devotionem*. Thus, on the one hand, he warns against the heretical implications of affective experiences which are not regulated by the norm of Christ's law—the Beghards and Turlupins being the most obvious historical cases in point.[6] On the other hand, he emphasizes the value and appropri-

[1] *Ibid.*, *cons.* 33, 86.17ff: "Hec similitudo respicit eum, qui de divinis scit artificiosa disserere, qui de moribus similiter et virtutibus regulas habet et speculativum plurimum sermonem, sed nondum vult ad ea que cognoscit conformiter operari."

[2] *Ibid.*, *cons.* 33,87.32ff: "Porro ita pueri magis sine arte paulatim extendendo deambulationem discunt recte ambulare quam iacendo...; sic fabricando fabri fimus, quia similiter inquirimus quid est virtus, non ut tantummodo sciamus sed ut bene operando boni efficiamur, ait Aristotiles."

[3] *Ibid.*, *cons.* 34, 87.5ff: "Per theologiam misticam sumus in Deo, hoc est in eo stabilimur et a mari turbido sensualium desideriorum ad litus solidum eternitatis adducimur. // In hac consideratione, differentia etiam inter duas theologias speculativam et misticam edocetur. Speculativa quippe si sola est, numquam quietat, inquietat potius..."

[4] Schwarz presents a one-sided, incorrect picture of Gerson when he writes: "Diese Einsicht in die Relevanz des intellectus zeichnet Luther speziell gegenüber allgemeinen Tendenzen in der franziskanischen Mystik aus. Die *Theologia Mystica* Gersons gründet sich ganz auf den Affekt; sie setzt nur einen einfältigen, positiv-kirchlichen Autoritätsglauben voraus und vermittelt im übrigen eine cognitio experimentalis, eine affective Erfahrungserkenntnis." *Fides, Spes und Caritas beim jungen Luther*, 133.

[5] See our discussion *infra*, p. 64ff.

[6] *De myst. theol. spec.*, *cons.* 8,20.19ff, 33ff.

ateness of the study of mystical theology for scholastic theologians, since from increased intellectual familiarity may come the experiential confirmation of what one must meanwhile hold by faith.[1]

Our study of Gerson is now oriented. The project of a mystical theology is a quest for the better way to knowledge of God in this life. It is a project which will engage the whole man, intellectively and affectively, and avoid the extremes of contemplation or affection alone. The affective way will be exalted as the more effective way, but the realization of the potentialities of the intellective powers is intrinsic to Gerson's goal. Indeed, it is the 'final cause' of his project. In our subsequent chapters, we will follow this quest in detail, turning first to his anthropology and finally to his understanding of the *unio mystica.*

---

[1] *Ibid., cons.* 8,19.4ff: "Expedit scholasticos viros etiam devotionis expertes in scripturis devotis theologie mistice diligenter exerceri, dummodo credant eis. // Hoc ideo dicitur primum quia quis novit si tandem ipsis ex familiari talium collocutione aggenerabitur, ut solet, amor et ardor quidem experiendi ea, que sola interim fide tenent et que docta ratiocinatione conferunt ad invicem."

CHAPTER FIVE

A DEO EXIVIT: THE ASSUMPTION OF A NATURAL 'COVENANT'

In his sermon, *A deo exivit* (March, 1402),[1] Gerson presents, to borrow the apt descriptive phrase of André Combes, "une fresque métaphysico-theologique,"[2] in which the nature of the soul in its pre-created and created status is considered. In regard to the former, the pre-created status of the soul, Gerson is critical of the position, which he ascribes to the Manichaeans, in which John 1:3-4.—"what has been created was [prior to its creation] life in God"—is interpreted as implying a real and essential identity *(identitas realis et essentialis)* between what was to be created and the Creator. Against this interpretation Gerson, presupposing a distinction between divine essence and divine will and understanding, locates pre-created reality in God's cognitive and volitional creative power—not in His essence.

> Life was [in God] in the sense of an ideational, vivific exemplar or architypal concept [i.e. in the divine intelligence] and through the most efficacious power to create [i.e. in the divine will]. [This form of pre-existence] is far more excellent and ineffable than [the way in which] a house which is to be built or an image which is to be painted 'exists' and in its fashion 'lives' in the mind of the craftsman.[3]

---

[1] Combes considers *A deo exivit* (dated March, 1399 viś à viś Glorieux's dating, March, 1402) to be the second member of a Maundy Thursday trilogy "consacrée à la souveraineté du Chretien entant que tel," which begins with *Omnia dedit ei pater* (March, 1398 viś à viś Glorieux, March, 1401) and concludes with *Ad deum vadit* (March, 1401 viś à viś Glorieux, April, 1403). While the entire trilogy is viewed as a theological and philosophical background for *De mystica theologia speculativa*, the latter member of the trilogy is considered to mark "la prémiere pénétration de la mystique proprement gersonienne dans le cycle du Jeudi-Saint." *Essai...*, III, 196, 138. We share Combes' insistence upon the importance of these works as background to *De mystica theologia speculativa*, but here, as throughout our study, the later research of Glorieux, which places these works in closer historical proximity to *De mystica theologia speculativa*, is followed as far as dating is concerned.

[2] *Essai...*, III, 201.

[3] *A deo exivit*, *Oeuvres*, V, 13f: "Dicit itaque divinus theologus Johannes: 'quod factum est in Deo vita erat.' Vita erat non quidem per identitatem realem et essentialem rei factae ad factorem, ut Manichaei blasphemant dicentes animam esse partem a Deo decisam per actionem principis tenebrarum; sed vita erat per idealem et vivificam exemplarem seu architypam cognitionem et virtutem producendi efficacissimam, longe praecellentius, longe ineffabilius quam in ipsa mentis artificis

The life that was in God before its creation was in God in an ideational and volitional mode; it was not an indistinguishable oneness of being with God. In its created status, this life is *esse realis* and it is quite other than its pre-creaturely *esse idealis*.[1] As Combes summarizes, while "a certain presence of the creature in his ideational being remains," the creation entails a "separation," which distinguishes the creature *(esse realis)* from his ideational being in God *(esse idealis)*.[2]

As created, the soul is the connecting link between the spiritual (because of a certain presence still of its *esse idealis)* and corporeal (because it is now created, *esse realis*) worlds.[3] Inasmuch as it alone is made capable of communion with God and is a participant in God through intelligence and reason, it is to the soul only that the power

---

domus fabricanda vel imago pingenda existat et suo modo vivat." Graphically represented, the situation is as follows:

"per idealem et vivificam exemplarem seu architypam cognitionem"

"per virtutem producendi efficacissimam"

Gerson does not deny the simplicity and unity of God. But he does endeavor here to interject a distinction between divine essence and divine intelligence and will which overcomes the 'Manichaean' interpretation of John 1:3-4. This unity-in-distinction is indicated by the broken lines in the graphic representation. See Tauler's very different interpretation of John 1:3-4, *supra*, p. 13, note 2. Tauler's defense of a form of pre-existence in which pre-created reality is "ein istig wesen" with God stands in stark contrast to Gerson's denial of an "identitas realis et essentialis."

[1] *Ibid.*, 14.

[2] *Essai...*, III, 269-70. "Les choses ont donc, par Gerson, un être double. Un être ideále, dans la connaissance que Dieu a de son œuvre avant de la projeter hors de lui. Un être réel, par le jeu des éléments constitutifs qui situent cette œuvre hors de la pensée créatrice." *Ibid.*, 220. Combes argues further, and we think correctly but too strongly, that Gerson's metaphysical presuppositions place him outside Occam's fold: "Nous en sommes d'autant plus assurés, que la créature tient tout son être réel de son être idéale, et retourne vers cet être idéale même. Dans une telle doctrine, la distinction ockhamiste entre intelligence et essence disparaît en tant que telle. L'intelligence divine se confond avec l'essence, source et fin des créatures." *Ibid.*, 222-23. Combes does soften this statement by pointing out the corrective influence of Occam on Gerson against the essential immanence of the created in the Creator which Ruysbroeck maintained in his *De ornatu spiritualium nuptiarum*. *Ibid.*, 217: "une petite cure d'ockhamisme;" cf. 271.

[3] *A deo exivit*, 14f: "Ceterum anima humana praecipue illa est inter omnes rationales spiritus quae non solum regredi ad Deum sed omnia alia in eum referre debet. Propterea enim ipsa corpori conjuncta est et nervis certis ligata secundum Platonicos; propterea nexum duplicis mundi tam spiritualis quam corporalis operatur, quasi duas illas catenas causarum, auream et argenteam, nectens."

to return to God, "through knowledge and love," is granted.[1] And, in this connection, the soul becomes the agent through which the corporeal world returns to God.[2] The consequences of sin notwithstanding, the ontological structure and goal of the soul remain so firmly established for Gerson that he can argue for the "necessity" of a future resurrection:

> As theological divines and learned metaphysicians have taught, the face of the soul is situated on the horizon of two worlds, so that through it all things are borne back to God by its knowing and using what has gone forth from Him when He created. Hence, Aristotle in Book I of the *Politics* and the Platonists said that all things are made for the sake of man and man for the sake of God. And, therefore, the necessity of a future resurrection *(necessitas resurrectionis futurae)* is concluded. Otherwise a naturally established end would be in vain...[3]

Gerson supports a mode of pre-creaturely being which is much more cautiously defined than that presented by Tauler. Both speak of the most intimate union conceivable, but for Gerson the phrase, "identitas realis et essentialis" (Tauler: "ein istig wesen," cf. *supra*, p. 13), is inappropriate. Man was in and with God as an idea is in and with the mind of an artist, i.e. not in essential unity, but in ideational participation. This will not be without consequences for Gerson's understanding of the *unio mystica.*

This difference between Tauler and Gerson notwithstanding, *A deo exivit* presents and defends a natural 'covenant,' as the remarks about the *necessitas* of a future resurrection place in clear relief. And, precisely

---

[1] *Ibid.*, 14: "Tu nempe, rationalis spiritus, sicut capax et particeps Dei solus factus es per intelligentiam atque rationem, hinc ad imaginem Dei et similitudinem factus affirmaris Gen. 1[:26]. Sic soli tibi ad Deum regredi concessum est per cognitionem et amorem."

[2] See *supra*, p. 56, n. 3. The soul's agency in returning the corporeal world to God becomes manifest in the *unio mystica*: "...Spiritus noster tractus a Deo trahit consequenter ea, que corporis sunt, ac proinde resultat unio mirabilis spiritus ad Deum et corporis ad spiritum." *De myst. theol. spec., cons.* 41,112.116ff. Combes summarizes: "Son [Gerson's] univers revient à Dieu, non point par une défection ontologique quelconque, mais par l'exercise même des activités propres à chacun des êtres qui le composent et en dernière analyse, par l'operation reductrice qu'accomplit l'âme humaine grâce a sa conjonction avec son corps. De plus, le retour à Dieu ainsi conçu est l'une dès deux moments constitutifs de l'univers." *Essai...*, III, 251-52.

[3] *A deo exivit*, 15: "Deinde in horizonte duplicis mundi statuitur facies sua, prout divini theologi et elevati metaphysici docuerunt, quatenus per ipsam ea omnia referrentur in Deum, cognoscendo et utendo quae ab eo egressa sunt in creando. Hinc dixerunt Aristotles I Politicorum et Platonici, omnia propter hominem, ipsum vero propter Deum factum esse. Hinc resurrectionis futurae necessitas concluditur; alioquin naturalis instituti finis frustra esset..."

as with Tauler, this natural bond in the sphere of theological ontology and anthropology finds a correlate in the historical bondage of God to the humiliational activity of man within the ordained order of salvation. Specifically, the necessity of a future resurrection in order to preserve the "naturally established end" finds its historical correlate in Gerson's acceptance of the nominalist conviction that "facientibus quod in se est deus non denegat gratiam." Gerson concludes the first part of *A deo exivit* with the argument that, although only Christ can empower the soul's return to God, "the gift [of this return] is presented to those—and only to those—who strive for it, in accordance with the common law."[1] Schematically summarized, the situation is as follows:

Natural 'Covenant':	Historical Covenant:
Finis naturalis instituti	*Lex communis*
Necessitas resurrectionis futurae	*Exercentibus dat deus donum regressus*[2]

[1] *Ibid.*, 16: "Hoc solo auctore sicut anima a Deo exivit, sic ad Deum vadit; quamquam donum hoc exercentibus se ad ipsum et nonnisi talibus de lege communi praestetur." Gerson's "exercentibus se ad donum [regressus]" parallels the nominalist "facientibus quod in se est," and his appeal to the "lex communis" parallels the nominalist understanding of the "potentia Dei ordinata." Further, the juxtaposition of a *sola gratia* ("hoc solo auctore") with a "nonnisi exercentibus" profiles the nominalist doctrine of justification. Cf. Oberman, *The Harvest of Medieval Theology*, 175ff, 30ff. See further Gerson's summary of his project in the second part of *A deo exivit*, which argues that the humble have a "right" (*ius*) to all things governed by divine law: "Recte quidem de beato humilitatis exitu totum huius collationis reliquum contexetur, ut alias pollicitus sum ostensurum ex titulo humilitatis jus tradi humilibus ad omnia quae dominantur possidenda, non quidem civili lege sed divina." *A deo exivit*, 17. See still further the discussion in *Omnia dedit ei pater*, which grants the Christian a *de iure* claim to lordship with Christ through the sacramental grace of baptism, penance and the Eucharist. *Oeuvres*, V, 408-09.

[2] See the convergence of the *synteresis*, *facere quod in se est* and *meritum (de congruo)* in Gerson's 1416 Pentecostal sermon, *Spiritus Domini replevit (Sap.* 1:7*)*. Having urged a retreat "in apicem mentis", and spoken of God's assistance, he writes: "Ipsam nihilominus animam cohortantur Scripturae Sacrae ut se praeparet, ut se disponat, ut faciat quod in se est...orando, lacrimando, gemendo vel ut aliquid operetur ad Spiritus Sancti susceptionem. Nam et Dei nos coadjutores esse tradit Apostolus [1 Cor. 3:9]. Et certe si nihil prorsus agit arbitrium, unde meritum?" *Oeuvres*, V, 527-28. Compare Tauler, *supra*, 30-34 and Luther, *infra*, 174-183.

CHAPTER SIX

THE ANATOMY OF THE SOUL

1. THE QUEST FOR THE PURER POWER

A primary motive behind Gerson's extensive and detailed anthropological analyses in *De mystica theologia speculativa* is to discover the "purer" power of the soul. For with this power mystical theology and man's historical *regressus ad deum in via* will find its anthropological foundation. He writes:

> Among the six powers..., however much some one should [be found to be] purer and more luminous [than the others], and such as much from itself as from an added illumination, to that extent it becomes more fitted for mystical theology.[1]

Gerson is emphatic about the unity of the soul and its simplicity *(simplex animae substantia)*.[2] Critical of the Scotist formal distinction, he argues that, while the powers of the soul may be distinguished in accordance with a variety of offices and operations, these distinctions are "in name," not "really" in the soul itself.[3] This is an important consideration and will influence the insistence upon a correlative, reciprocal operation among the powers of the soul.

As the subjects of his analysis, Gerson presents three cognitive powers and three affective powers in a paralleled, hierarchical[4] arrangement. These can be schematically outlined as follows:

Vires Cognitivae:	*Vires Affectivae:*
intelligentia simplex	*synderesis*
ratio	*appetitus rationalis*
sensualitas	*appetitus sensualis*[5]

---

[1] *De myst. theol. spec., cons.* 9,46.4ff: "Inter sex potentias...quanto aliqua fuerit purior et luminosior tam ex se quam ex adiuncta illuminatione, tanto fit ad theologiam misticam aptior." Cf. *cons.* 9,22.14ff.

[2] *Ibid., cons.* 9,23.22.

[3] *Ibid., cons.* 9,24.51ff: "Dicamus ergo de anima rationali, quod ipsa pro diversitate officiorum et agibilium distinctas vires habet, distinctas inquam non re, sed nomine."

[4] Cf. *ibid., cons.* 17,40.43ff; 11,30.27ff.

[5] *Ibid., cons.* 9,25.63ff. In our subsequent discussion of Gerson's anthropology, we use the form, "synderesis," rather than "synteresis," in accordance with the edited texts of Gerson. See *infra*, p. 139, note 2.

2. *INTELLIGENTIA SIMPLEX*

Pure intelligence is formally defined as

> the cognitive power of the soul which receives a certain natural light immediately from God, in and through which first principles, with the apprehension of the terms, are known to be true and unquestionably certain.[1]

It is a disposition naturally established in the soul,[2] drawn from the infinite light of the Original Understanding,[3] and in accordance with John 1:9—"that was true light illuminating every man coming into this world"—and Psalm 4:7—"the light of your face is manifest over us, O Lord." This disposition is privy not only to such logically immutable axioms as the law of contradiction,[4] but also receives nature, grace and glory immediately from God.[5]

Finally, Gerson reminds the reader that there is a variety of names with which this reality has been described, sometimes being called mind *(mens)*, the highest heaven *(caelum supremum)*, spirit *(spiritus)*, the light of intelligence *(lux intelligentiae)*, the shadow of angelic understanding *(umbra intellectus angelici)*, divine light in which truth immutably shines *(lux divina in qua veritas incommutabiliter lucet)*, and the spark *(scintilla)* or peak of reason *(apex rationis)*.[6]

3. *RATIO*

Reason is formally defined as a

> cognitive power of the soul which deduces conclusions from premisses, elects nonsensory from sensory data and abstracts from quiddities, requiring no [physical] organ for its operation.[7]

[1] *De myst. theol. spec.*, *cons.* 10,26.4ff: "Intelligentia simplex est vis anime cognitiva suscipiens immediate a Deo naturalem quamdam lucem, in qua et per quam principia prima cognoscuntur esse vera et certissima, terminis apprehensis."

[2] *Ibid.*, *cons.* 10,27.15f: "...aliqua dispositio connaturalis et concreata anime."

[3] *Ibid.*, *cons.* 10,27.19: "...derivata ab infinita luce prime intelligentie, que Deus est."

[4] *Ibid.*, *cons.* 10,26.8ff: "Principia huiusmodi nominantur aliquando dignitates, aliquando communes animi conceptiones, aliquando regule prime incommutabiles, et impossibiles aliter se habere: ut quod de quolibet affirmatio vel negatio, quod totum est maius sua parte, quod intellectivum perfectius est non intellectivo, quod spirituale corporali ceteris paribus, quod si homo intelligit homo vivit, et similes."

[5] *Ibid.*, *cons.* 10,28,34ff: "Attamen quis negaverit angelum eo modo recte dici superiorem anima nostra et Deo proximiorem, quo perfectior est? Nullus utique. Dicamus idcirco quod uterque a Deo eque immediate tria suscipit, que sunt natura, gratia et gloria."

[6] *Ibid.*, *cons.* 10,28.42ff.

[7] *Ibid.*, *cons.* 11,29.4ff: "Ratio est vis anime cognoscitiva deductiva conclusionum

Whereas pure intelligence is exclusively concerned with the reception of pure and simple knowledge from the superior light of God, the operation of reason attends to the deduction of conclusions from principles which are either proper to itself, taken (by deduction and abstraction) from sensory experience, or received directly from the data which pure intelligence makes available to it.[1]

The double operation of reason, i.e. its turning to and drawing upon both the superior principles of pure intelligence and the inferior principles of sensory experience, leads Gerson to speak of its having superior and inferior parts or faces. It is reason which manifests the soul's existence on the horizon of the spiritual and corporeal worlds.[2] It is the "middle heaven in the soul" *(caelum medium in anima)*, dwelling in the shadow of pure intelligence just as pure intelligence dwells in the shadow of the angels, who, in turn, climax the hierarchy, as they dwell in the shadow of God.[3]

4. *SENSUALITAS*

Sensibility, the lowest in the hierarchy of cognitive powers, is formally defined as a

> power of the soul which uses a corporeal organ, as much outwardly as inwardly, in order to know things which, either in themselves or accidentally, are sensible.[4]

Here, in accordance with Thomist anthropology, Gerson locates the five senses, the common sense, which judges among the receptions of

---

ex premissis, elicitiva quoque insensatorum ex sensatis et abstractiva quidditatum, nullo organo in sua egens operatione."

[1] *Ibid., cons.* 11,29.9ff: "Hec descriptio per ultimam particulam notat differre rationem a sensualitate, que utitur organo, per alias autem ab intelligentia simplici secernitur, cuius operatio magis attenditur in receptione cognitionis simplicis a superiore luce Deo, quam attendatur in deductione conclusionum ex principiis, quod est proprium rationis, sive principia sumpta sint ab experientiis per sensus, sive illa sibi ex alto presentaverit simplex intelligentia."

[2] *Ibid., cons.* 11,29.15-30.23: "Ex hoc vero duplici usu rationis, nunc a superioribus principiis per se notis in lumine intelligentie simplicis, nunc ab inferioribus, que per experientiam acquiruntur, ut quod ignis est calidus, sortitur ratio duplex nomen, ut dicatur portio rationis superior et portio inferior; ut preterea dicatur habere duas facies, unam ad superiora, ad inferiora alteram; immo et ex hoc ponitur constitui velut in orizonte duorum mundorum, spiritualis scilicet et corporalis."

[3] *Ibid., cons.* 11,30.27ff.

[4] *Ibid., cons.* 12,30.4-31.1; "Vis cognoscitiva sensualis est vis anime utens in sua operatione organo corporeo, tam exteriori quam interiori, ad ea, que sensibilia sunt per se vel per accidens cognoscenda."

the five senses, and the powers capable of retaining species which are not immediately present, viz., imagination and estimation or memory.[1] This power also is described by other names, being called soul, animality *(animalitas)*, the earthly or lowest heaven *(caelum terreum vel infirmum)*, and the shadow of reason *(umbra rationis)*.[2]

In Gerson's schema, every cognitive power has a corresponding affective power.[3] This is contingent upon the fact that the soul spontaneously and affectively either applauds or takes offense at the objects presented to it by the cognitive powers.[4] We turn now to these affective powers.

5. *SYNDERESIS*

The *synderesis* of the soul is formally defined as

> an appetitive power of the soul which receives a certain natural inclination to good immediately from God, through which it is led to follow a good motion presented to it from the apprehension of pure intelligence.[5]

Just as pure intelligence is related to truth or to the first and certain truths, so the *synderesis* is related to final good. And just as little as pure intelligence can dissent from the acknowledgement of the truths to which it is privy, so little can the *synderesis* refuse the first principles of morality, when they are presented to it through pure intelligence.[6]

[1] *Ibid., cons.* 12,31.9ff: "Nam cum accipit immediate motiones obiectales rerum exteriorum, sic dicitur sensus exterior, in quinque distinctus, qui sunt visus, auditus, gustus, olfactus et tactus. Aut recipit immediate sensationes factas in hiis quinque sensibus iudicans inter eas, sic est sensus communis. Aut consequenter ex iudiciis vel sensationibus factis in sensu communi componit et dividit, et sic dicitur imaginatio vel fantasia vel virtus formativa. Et si ex sensatis elicit insensata, hanc estimativam nominamus, que de proficuo vel nocivo diiudicat. Due preterea sunt vires retentive specierum in absentia, una imaginatio, que pro sensu communi quandoque nominatur, altera pro estimativa, cui memorie nomen inditum est."

[2] *Ibid., cons.* 12,31.23-32.28.

[3] *Ibid., cons.* 13, 32.3f: "...correspondet proportionalis virtus affectiva."

[4] *Ibid., cons.* 13,32.5-33.9: "Cum enim apprehenditur aliquid a potentia cognitiva, quod est conveniens sibi vel disconveniens, et sub tali aliqua ratione sibi obicitur, experimur animam applaudere quodammodo hanc apprehensionem si sit conveniens velut convenientis, et horrere si sit ut disconvenientis."

[5] *Ibid., cons.* 14,33.4ff: "Synderesis est vis anime appetitiva immediate a Deo suscipiens naturalem quamdam inclinationem ad bonum, per quam trahitur insequi motionem boni ex apprehensione simplicis intelligentie sibi presentati." Cf. Bonaventure: "...synderesis dicit potentiam affectivam, in quantum naturaliter habilis est ad bonum et ad bonum tendit..." II *Sent.* d. 39, a. 2, q. 1, ad 1.

[6] *De myst. theol. spec., cons.* 14,33.8ff: "Nam quemadmodum se habet intelligentia respectu veritatis sive veri primi et certi, ita synderesis respectu boni finalis sine

Further, just as with pure intelligence, the *synderesis* may be considered as a power, an act, or a habit resultant from acts.[1] Here is an integration of 'substantive' and 'active' dimensions, which is not unlike that which we have seen Tauler belabor in reference to the definition of the *gemuete* and *grunt* of the soul (cf. *supra*, p. 15ff).

The *synderesis* also goes by other names, variously described as a practical habit of principles *(habitus practicus principiorum)*, the spark of intelligence *(scintilla intelligentiae)*, a virginal part of the soul *(portio virginalis animae)*, a natural stimulus to good *(stimulus naturalis ad bonum)*, the peak of the mind *(apex mentis)*, an indelible instinct *(instinctus indelibilis)* and the first heaven among the affective powers.[2]

6. *APPETITUS RATIONALIS*

Rational desire is formally defined as "the affective power of the soul adapted so as to be moved immediately by the cognitive apprehension of reason."[3] When it is considered in regard to what is possible and impossible it is called will *(voluntas)*, and in regard to acts which are self-elected, freedom *(libertas)*. But when it is considered in regard to objects irrespective of their finality or possibility, it is described as choice *(electio)* or elective desire *(appetitus electivus)*, and in regard to its directing the acts of the soul, a sovereign or executive desire *(appetitus dominativus vel executivus)*. When it is viewed as the will in pursuance of what is chosen, it is called resolution *(propositio)*, and as the inclination to such pursuance, conscience *(conscientia)*; for conscience brings forth both judgment and a concomitant affection.[4]

Finally, Gerson points out that the moving passions of rational desire are described generally as rational affection, although in respect to good and evil they are known as desirous *(concupiscibilis)* affections, and in respect to good and evil which are both high and difficult, as irascible *(irascibilis)* affections.[5]

---

mixtione malitie simpliciter presentati, quoniam simplex intelligentia sicut non potest dissentire talibus veritatibus agnitione habita quid termini significent, ita non potest synderesis nolle positive principia prima moralium, dum sibi per intelligentiam monstrata sunt."

[1] *Ibid.*, *cons.* 14,34.22ff.

[2] *Ibid.*, *cons.* 14,34.24-35.31.

[3] *Ibid.*, *cons.* 15,35.4f: "Appetitus rationalis est vis anime affectiva apta moveri immediate ab apprehensione cognoscitiva rationis."

[4] *Ibid.*, *cons.* 15,35.6-36.15.

[5] *Ibid.*, *cons.* 15,36.15ff.

7. *APPETITUS SENSUALIS*

Animal or sensory desire, the lowest in the hierarchy of affective powers, is formally defined as the "appetitive power of the soul adapted to be moved immediately by sensory apprehension alone."[1] Here is a natural sense, a law of nature, inerrantly promoting a movement toward self-preservation and self-realization.[2]

8. THE CORRELATIVE AND RECIPROCAL OPERATION OF THE POWERS OF THE SOUL

Our tedious trek through the soul is completed. In his definitions of the affective powers, we have seen Gerson make it quite clear that their operation is contingent upon and conditioned by (*ab* and *ex*) the activity and data of the intellective powers. The two powers are paralleled in their operation, but it is with the intellective powers that the initiative lies.

One of the most important adjustments which occurs in *De mystica theologia speculativa*, and which is the single most decisive factor for an adequate understanding of the nature of Gerson's mystical theology and his interpretation of the *unio mystica*, is the development in *consideratio* 17 in which it becomes clear that the operations of the two powers of the soul are not only in a parallel relationship, but in a *correlative* and *reciprocal* relationship. This is an important emphasis. It will mean that the affective as well as the intellective powers can initiate movements which naturally evoke a reaction from the other set of powers. The most definitive statement in this regard is the following.

> Every effect, especially immanent effect, produced by this rational nature is said to acquire some light either in the form of clarity in the cognitive powers or of heat in the affective powers, *or to acquire both simultaneously*. For it is difficult to find a cognition which is not formally or virtually a certain affect, just as it seems quite impossible to find an

---

[1] *Ibid., cons.* 16,36.3f: "Appetitus animalis vel sensualis est vis anime affectiva apta moveri immediate solum ab apprehensione sensitiva."

[2] *Ibid., cons.* 16,37.19-38.29: "Quid vero mirandum, si corpora animalium ducantur secretis instinctibus vel pulsibus ad suos fines, quando in corporibus aliis minus perfectis minusque organizatis tot mirabiles ad suos fines consequendos naturales tractus invenimus? Immo plurimi sunt rerum variarum ad invicem tales tractus, quorum finem ignoramus, ut est tractus ferri ad magnetem et maris ad lunam et aliorum ad alia. Hunc autem sensum nature iam in omni re posuimus, qui alio vocabulo lex nature vel inclinatio naturalis vel directio intelligentie non errantis potest nominari. Et nichil ab hac positione dissentimus."

affect which is not a certain experiential knowledge. Indeed, neither power causes its effect without the other, since an affective power concurs in the emergence of a cognition just as a cognitive power concurs in the generation of an affect.[1]

In light of several earlier works, it is not surprising to find Gerson stating this position. In his *Epistola prima ad fratrem bartholomaeum* (1398-99), the predilection for the affective powers is clearly manifest; but with equal clarity it is insisted that true wisdom consists in the unity of affective contemplation, which "flavors," and intellective contemplation, which "illumines," so that "wisdom" or a "savory knowledge" is resultant.[2]

In *Ad deum vadit* (March, 1401), although the step of love appears to be associated exclusively with mystical theology, it is clear that the greater reach of the *pes amoris* has the intention of bringing the *pes cognitionis* where the highest things might be known in a clearer light. We are exhorted to "taste and see" (Ps. 34:8).[3]

---

[1] *Ibid.*, *cons.* 17,39.17ff: "Omnis preterea effectus, presertim immanens, productus a tali natura rationali dici meretur lumen aliquod, aut ratione claritatis in cognitiva, aut caliditatis in affectiva, aut simul utriusque. Non enim forte contingit reperire cognitionem, que non sit formaliter aut virtualiter quedam affectio, sicut affectio non videtur posse discerni quin sit quedam experimentalis cognitio. Quippe neutra potentia effectum suum causat sine altera, quoniam ad cognitionis causationem affectiva potentia, sicut ad affectionem generandam cognitiva concurrit." Emphasis mine. Combes recognizes a "parallélisme des puissances cognitives et affectives," but not the issuance of this parallelism in a correlative and reciprocal operation. *La thèologie mystique de Gerson*, I, 105. This oversight accounts in large measure for the problems he has in reaching a clear statement on the status of the cognitive content of mystical theology in *De mystica theologia practica*. See our discussion, *infra*, p. 79ff. Nearer to the point are Dress' remarks: "Wenn wir nun... auf das Ganze der Theologie Gersons zurückblicken, so ergibt sich, daß Gerson mit der Forderung der *devotio secundum scientiam* letzten Endes ein Prinzip des Nominalismus wieder aufnimmt, das Prinzip der Einheit der Seele und ihrer Kräfte. Und zwar wird es angewandt auf die Einheit von intellektueller und affektiver Bewegung." *Die Theologie Gersons*, 132f. Dress relates the nominalist unity of the soul to Luther's *totus homo* concept. *Ibid.*, 136.

[2] *Epistola prima ad fratrem bartholomaeum*, ed. André Combes, *Essai sur la critique de Ruysbroeck par Gerson*, I (Paris, 1945), [= *Epistola prima...*], 631.9ff: "Vult ergo aliquis esse et dici vere sapiens? Habeat utramque contemplationis speciem, illam videlicet affectus quae saporem dat, et illam intellectus quae scientiae luminositatem praestat, ut constituatur sapientia, id est sapida scientia. Quod si altera carendum esset, eligibilius judicarem communicare in prima quam in secunda, sicut optabilius est habere pium affectum humilem et devotum ad Deum quam intellectum frigidum solo studio illuminatum."

[3] *Ad deum vadit*, *Oeuvres*, V, 7f: "Pes amoris in via hac Dei saepe intrat ubi cognitionis pes foris stat; quamvis itaque ambulando in via Dei modo praetacto, dum pede fidei praeposito subsequitur pes dilectionis, trahi possit consequenter

In *De comparatione vitae contemplativae ad activam* (December, 1401), the inhabitants of the land of Judea, i.e. the land of glorification, confession and the vision of peace beyond the desert, are "holy thoughts" and "devout affections."[1]

Finally, we find in *A deo exivit* that the end in accordance with which Adamic humanity is defined is the possibility of returning to God "through contemplation and love."[2]

In each of these works the full realization of the possibilities of the intellective powers is just as much a primary concern as the realization of the possibilities of the affective powers. And this ideal both motivates and receives theoretical and anthropological justification and confirmation in Gerson's insistence upon the correlative, reciprocal operation of the intellective and affective powers in *De mystica theologia speculativa.*

---

pes cognitionis ad ulteriora, propinquiori luce cognoscenda, eundo sic pede post pedem; attamen pes amoris dexter sublimius semper extendi potest pro hac via quam sinister. Haec est theologia mystica, id est occulta. Haec scientia propria catholicorum, hoc manna absconditum, hic calculus in quo est nomen novum quod nemo novit nisi qui accipit [Apoc. 2:17]; haec ambulatio ad Deum exemplo Moysi in monte et divina caligine, quae ambulatio magis potest suaderi quam doceri; ita enim monuit propheta: gustate ac videte [Ps. 33:9], ac si pro re nostra diceretur: vadite et videte, nam quorsum et quousque valeat attingere pes amoris solo eundi experimento cognoscitur." Combes offers the following interpretation of *Ad deum vadit*: "Pour le prédicateur d'*Ad deum vadit*, la théologie mystique ne doit donc nullement être confondue avec une èlimination radicale de connaissance, même intellectuelle. En soi, elle est purement amour. Mais cet amour même ne peut être tenu pour exclusif de toute connaissance. Il est une connaissance *sui generis*, à savoir expérimentale. Il est autre chose: une exigence de connaissance intellectuelle. Le propre du pied droit est d'entraîner le gauche. Si l'amour transcende l'intellect, c'est pour permettre à l'intellect de se dépasser." *Essai...*, III, 309. Compare Dress' conclusion: "Der leere Raum, den der (rein intellektualistisch verstandene) Glaube durch sein Urteil von der Unfaßlichkeit und Unerkennbarkeit Gottes und die Philosophie durch die Betonung ihrer negativen Methode zwischen dem ewigen Schöpfer und der ins Zeit-Räumliche hinein geschaffenen Welt aufgezeigt haben, wird überwunden und ausgefüllt durch die Bewegung der Affekte, die hin und her spielt." *Die Theologie Gersons*, 99.

[1] *De comparatione vitae contemplativae ad activam*, *Oeuvres*, III, 69. "At vero ubi Johannes est in deserto mentis praedicto solitarius in contemplatione, ubi comedit manna absconditum, adjacet circumquaque regio Judeae, regio scilicet glorificationis cuiusdam et decorae confessionis, regio insuper Jerosolymae, regio visionis pacis; sic enim Judea et Jerusalem interpretantur. Huius regionis speciosissimae et uberrimae habitatores sunt cogitationes sanctae et affectiones piae, quae sunt revera Jerosolymitae, id est pacificae, et propter confessionem laudis et glorificationem Judae regionem inhabitare merentur."

[2] *A deo exivit*, *Oeuvres*, V, 15: "Ad hunc finem olim egressus fuerat Adam in sui primaria creatione ut ad Deum regrederetur per speculationem et amorem."

9. THE EFFECTS OF ORIGINAL SIN

Prior to his consideration of the functions or activities of the six powers of the soul, Gerson considers the effects of sin upon the soul. He writes that deformity and operational immobility penetrate into the six powers of the soul,[1] a fact attested by experience[2] and ultimately explained only in terms of original sin. He summarizes:

> Such a general and unavoidable defilement arises from the original fault, which drew our soul, with all its powers, into this miserable oppression so that, turned from heavenly to earthly and from intelligible to brutish things and now immersed in the earthly and brutish, our soul weeps bitterly.[3]

Why does Gerson undertake his discussion of sin prior to the discussion of the activities of the six powers and subsequent to the discussion of the correlative, reciprocal operation of these powers? The most obvious reason is that he wishes to remind the reader that his quest is for the purer power, which, as he earlier pointed out, will be the anthropological base of mystical theology. This is affirmed in the *consideratio* itself, as he concludes with a reminder of the inimitable reformational possibilities of mystical theology.[4]

In addition to this reason, it should be noted that by treating the discussion of sin after the establishment of the reciprocity of the soul's powers, Gerson has both preserved his concern to engage the 'whole man' (intellective and affective powers) in the project of mystical theology and increased his options for the location of the purer power. Should the effects of sin prove to be more incapacitating with one set of powers than with the other, the reciprocal operation of the powers

---

[1] *De myst. theol. spec.*, *cons.* 20,49.6ff: "...non minus incidit difformitas et infectio in speculis spiritualibus sex potentiarum, quarum tres sunt cognitive, affective pari numero."

[2] *Ibid.*, *cons.* 20,49.10ff: "Experientia etiam sine similitudine docet nos quam sepe turpia fantasmata et errores et fede representationes obiectales, concupiscentie preterea et passiones sordide, tetre et horride tamquam fumi quidam caliginosi vel infecti et venenosi animas nostras obnubilant, fedant atque commaculant presertim in primaria et novella talium apprehensione, velut in pueris." See Luther's insistence that our sinfulness is not obvious to us, *infra*, p. 146; 214, note 2.

[2] *Ibid.*, *cons.* 20,49.16-50.20: "Denique generalis et inelicibilis sordidatio talis provenit ab originali macula, que animam nostram cum omnibus potentiis suis ad hanc miserabilem traduxit aggravationem ut e celestibus ad terrena et ab intelligibilitate ad brutalitatem deploret mersa."

[4] *Ibid.*, *cons.* 20,50.29ff: "In hoc [the reformation of the powers of the soul] precipue versatur ipsa, cuius naturam inquirimus, theologia mistica, quam per penitentiam et credulitatem evangelii adipisci, et non aliter phas habemus..."

of the soul will guarantee the location of the initiative for the reformation of the whole man with the less affected powers.

10. THE *ACTIONES* OF THE SIX POWERS OF THE SOUL

As the powers of the soul are hierarchically arranged, so too are their functions or modes of activity. The lowest intellective function is simply cogitation *(cogitatio)*, a spontaneous reaction to the reception of actual sensations and intermittent phantasms.[1] The intermediate level of cognitive operation is the much more difficult level of meditation *(meditatio)*, where the attempt is made to reach a level above sensations and phantasms, and to stand fixedly with some one thing.[2] At this level there is a passing over from sensitive cogitation to an attentive consideration, which overcomes the diverting influences of the lower level,[3] and strips away the accidents of time and place which accompany purely sensitive cogitation.[4]

The highest level of intellective activity is contemplation *(contemplatio)*, which occurs through the purification of intelligence.[5] Here, again, there is a *transitus*, as meditation passes over into a contemplative exercise which purifies what the lower activities have made available to pure intelligence. This exercise is accomplished either through abstraction and separation of intelligence from sensible things, or, more frequently, through the illumination of divine grace which raises it to the sight of divine things.[6] Schematically summarized, the situation is as follows:

---

[1] *Ibid., cons.* 22,54.3ff: "Cogitatio facilis est, quia formatur immediate vel ex sensationibus actualibus, vel ex fantasmatibus passim occurentibus, et ultra non nititur."

[2] *Ibid., cons.* 23,55.4ff: "Meditatio difficultatem sortitur ex eo quod ultra sensationes actuales vel fantasmata passim occurrentia, ipsa nititur ultra pertingere vel in aliquo fixa stare."

[3] *Ibid., cons.* 23,55.7ff: "Experitur in se crebro quilibet studiosus difficultatem, que est in sistendo ad aliquid attente considerandum cogitationem sine diverticulis ad alia; et hoc dum fit, cogitatio iam transit in meditationem, non ut cogitatio desinat esse, sed ut desinat esse cogitatio."

[4] *Ibid., cons.* 23,56.20ff: "At vero difficultas hec augetur et fit labor insuspicabilis, dum animus denudare nititur cogitationem suam ab involucro accidentium, hoc est a circumstantiis loci et temporis et aliorum, que presentat sensus, ut absolute et nude quidditates rerum appareant, quasi non convolute tempori et loco."

[5] *Ibid., cons.* 25,65.28ff: "Et hoc est, quod reddit multos ex eis qui dicuntur formalizantes [Scotists] in fabulam et risum, immo in insaniam, quia per solam imaginationem et rationem querunt illud, quod per intelligentie depurationem erat inveniendum."

[6] *Ibid., cons.* 24,60.4ff: "Contemplatio facilitatem habet tum ex habitibus per

Vires:	*Actiones:*
ntelligentia simplex	*contemplatio*
ratio	*meditatio*
sensualitas	*cogitatio*[1]

At this point, Gerson turns to a consideration of the effects of original sin upon the intellective powers. Before the fall of Adam, he points out, the eye of contemplation, with its undistracted view from the top of the mountain of God,[2] was most lively, pure and efficacious in its operation.[3] Now, however, *post peccatum Adae*, it is practically totally extinct, just as the rational eye is almost totally blind,[4] and the sensitive eye almost totally corrupt.[5]

What is important to observe in this consideration of the impact of sin is the severity with which Gerson speaks of this impact in reference to each of the intellective powers and activities. This severity suggests that it will not be among the intellective powers that he finds the purest anthropological base for mystical theology; for here, through the deformity of sin, no pure resource for the *regressus ad deum in via* remains. Is the situation otherwise with the affective powers?

Gerson outlines three modes of affective activity, viz., passionate desire *(cupido, libido, concupiscentia)*, prayerful, remorseful contrition *(contritio, compunctio, oratio)* and ecstatic and transcendental love *(dilectio extatica et anagogica)*,[6] parallel to sensitive cogitation,[7] medita-

---

meditationem acquisitis, tum propter abstractionem et separationem intelligentie a sensibilibus, tum sepius propter divine gratie collustrationem in divina spectacula sublevantem." See *ibid., cons.* 24,60,8ff, *cons.* 25,64.5ff, *cons.* 26,66.17ff.

[1] Cf. *ibid., cons.* 26,66.6ff: "Tres cognoscendi modi sunt, quorum unus animalis dicitur, utens maxime oculo carnis; alius rationalis, utens plus oculo rationis; tertius spiritualis, utens oculo contemplationis, sicut distinxerunt divini homines tres oculos et tres videndi modos." For roots of these descriptions in the Victorian school, see Dress, *Die Theologie Gersons*, 72f.

[2] *De myst. theol. spec., cons.* 24,61.36-62.40: "Inveniemus quod si anima stare possit in arce intelligentie sine dilapsu ad inferiora, ipsa poterit libero intuitu circumquaque semet diffundere, nunc sursum, nunc deorsum, nunc ante, nunc retro, nunc dextrorsum, nunc sinistrorsum."

[3] *Ibid., cons.* 24,62.40ff: "Et hic est oculus contemplationis, qui in Adam ante lapsum vivacissimus, purissimus et expeditissimus fuerat."

[4] Gerson writes in reference to reason: "...quia peccante primo homine rupta est concordia, scissum fedus legis indite inter rationem gubernatricem et obsequentem sensualitatem..." *Ibid., cons.* 34,90.63ff.

[5] *Ibid., cons.* 24,62.42ff: "Nunc, ve nobis, totus fere extinctus est, sicut oculus rationis obtenebratus et oculus sensualitatis fere corruptus."

[6] *Ibid., cons.* 27,67.4-68.9.

[7] *Ibid., cons.* 27,68.12ff: "...sicut cogitatio est improvidus animi obtutus ad evagationem pronus, ita consequenter ad talem cogitationem, si sit de obiecto

tion,[1] and contemplation.[2] And it is now made explicit beyond question that it is in ecstatic and joyful love that mystical theology is to be found[3].

With this development, we can now bring our schematic outline to completion:

Vires Cognitivae:	*Actiones:*	*Vires Affectivae:*	*Actiones:*
intelligentia simplex	*contemplatio*	*synderesis*	*dilectio extatica*
ratio	*meditatio*	*appetitus rationalis*	*contritio, compunctio, oratio*
sensualitas	*cogitatio*	*appetitus sensualis*	*cupido, libido, concupiscentia*

Two facts are especially noteworthy in Gerson's treatment of the activities of the affective powers. First, there is no detailed treatment of the incapacitating effects of sin upon these activities. This is striking in light of Gerson's forceful insistence upon the incapacitating effects of sin upon the activities of the intellective powers. For Gerson, the effects of sin are not considered to be as profound in the affective as they are in the intellective powers.

Secondly, an implicit consequence of the reciprocity which Gerson establishes between the intellective and affective faculties and activities is that the operation of the affective powers will not be unaffected by the deformity present in the intellective powers. The positive point, however, which Gerson intends to emphasize, is the reverse

delectabili, sequitur affectio improvida et vaga sine utilitate et fructu, et hec satis michi congrue videtur appellari libido seu cupido vel concupiscentia."

[1] *Ibid., cons.* 27,68.18ff: "Porro ad meditationem, que est providus anime obtutus in veritatis inquisitione et celestium rerum inventione vehementer occupatus, consequitur quedam affectio alia a priori ad res taliter quesitas et inventas, si non sit in dispositio anime, et hec affectio est provida et non vaga, cum difficultate et fructu, et hec interim vocetur devotio vel compunctio aut oratio, id est affectus pius et humilis vehementer et fortiter tendens et nitens in amorem prime veritatis et bonitatis."

[2] *Ibid., cons.* 27,69.26ff: "Denique contemplatio, que est libera et expedita consideratio eorum, que meditatio cum ingenti difficultate perquirit, habet suam affectionem in anima disposita suamque dilectionem similiter liberam, puram, expeditam et abstractam, et hec ratione vocari potest extatica dilectio vel iubilatio, que ultra devotionem addit facilitatem et iocunditatem inestimabilem et indescriptibilem, inexpressibilem et exsuperantem omnem sensum."

[3] *Ibid., cons.* 27,69.33ff: "Et hec [extatica dilectio] est sapientia Dei in misterio abscondita; hec est mistica theologia, quam querimus, que ad anagogicos et supermentales excessus deducit..."

side of the coin. This reciprocity implies that the greater purity and soteriological possibilities of the affective powers will not be without significance for the reformation and salutary fulfilment of the intellective powers. To put our point concisely, the major consequence, which Gerson will theologically exploit, of the establishment of a reciprocal relation between the intellective and affective powers, is the retention of the possibility of interjecting cognitive content into the *unio mystica*. This content will be in an experiential mode *(experimentalis)*, but it will also be knowledge *(cognitio)*.[1] Some hint of this is already present in his insistence that contemplation—the supreme activity and self-fulfilment of the intellective powers—is not worthy of its name if it is without love.[2] The possibilities which, *post peccatum Adae*, remain within the reach of the affective powers, specifically the *synderesis*,[3] contain also the possibility of the reformation and fulfilment of the intellective powers, specifically *intelligentia simplex*.

These considerations account for Gerson's conviction that the penitential-affective way to *cognitio Dei in via* is superior to the speculative-intellective way alone. Further, these considerations make clear the reason why Gerson locates the first and most fundamental difference between mystical theology and speculative theology (i.e. the intellective powers viewed *nude*) in their subjects or powers, i.e. in their different anthropological substrata.[4] The greater purity of the affective powers *post peccatum Adae*, which grants them soteriological resources for the *regressus ad deum in via*—although not in disunion with sacramental mediation[5]—entitles them to be the locus of mystical theology.

---

[1] See our discussion, *infra*, p. 78ff.

[2] *De myst. theol. spec.*, *cons.* 27,69.38f: "...non fallitur, qui dicit contemplationem sine dilectione nomen contemplationis non mereri."

[3] In regard to the foundational role of the *synderesis*, Combes writes: "Rien n'est plus important, pour l'auteur de la *Mystica*, qu'une definition correcte de la *syndérèse*. C'est en effect pour lui la piece maîtresse du système. Homologue de l'intelligence pure, ce sommet de la puissance affective est le lieu même de la théologie mystique." *Essai...*, III, 118. Cf. Connolly: "Mystical theology is the act of the *synderesis*." *John Gerson*, 289.

[4] Cf. *supra*, 52.

[5] We call attention to the statement in *Ad deum vadit*, which has reference to the Eucharist: "Quotidianus usus huius sacramenti, si digne fiat, miro modo promovet in via Dei pedum utrumque, cognitionis simul et amoris." *Oeuvres*, V, 10. See our discussion *infra*, 76ff.

CHAPTER SEVEN

THE *UNIO MYSTICA*

Gerson's anatomy of the soul both clarifies and confirms his conviction that the penitential, affective and amorous way of mystical theology is the more certain and efficacious way to saving knowledge of God in this life. Specification is given to this conviction and the sphere of the *unio mystica* is entered, when he turns to a detailed treatment of the three properties of love. These are: (1) rapture which lifts one to the Beloved, drawing him out of himself; (2) union which unites one with the Beloved, making both "as if one;" and (3) a sufficiency which intrinsically satisfies, neither requiring nor seeking anything beyond the Beloved.[1]

1. RAPTURE

The rapture which occurs only through love and is accomplished by affective rather than cognitive power and activity,[2] is a rapture in the superior parts of the soul. It concerns the highest intellective *(intelligentia simplex)* as well as the highest affective *(synderesis)* power, with salutary repercussions upon the lower intellective and affective powers.[3] Gerson underscores this comprehensiveness of rapture with special considerations of the rapture of imagination *(raptus imaginationis)* over its inferior activities through the affection of love *(per amoris affectionem)*;[4] the rapture of reason *(raptus rationis)* over the

[1] *De myst. theol. spec.*, *cons.* 35,95.21ff: "Amor enim rapit, unit, satisfacit. Primo quidem amor rapit ad amatum et inde extasim facit. Secundo amor iungit cum amato et quasi unum efficit. Tertio amor sibi sufficit, nec aliud preter amare querit." The third property of love—*amor sibi sufficit*—can be viewed as a parallel to Luther's 'certitude of salvation' by faith.

[2] *Ibid.*, *cons.* 36,98.48f: "...affectio potius quam cognitio raptum agat."

[3] *Ibid.*, *cons.* 36,96.12ff: "Porro extasim dicimus speciem quamdam raptus, que fit appropriatius in superiori portione anime rationalis, que spiritus vel mens vel intelligentia nominatur, dum mens ita in suo actu suspensa est quod potentie inferiores cessant ab actibus, sic quod nec ratio nec imaginatio nec sensus exteriores, immo quandoque nec potentie naturales nutritive et augmentative et motive possint exire in suas proprias operationes."

[4] Cf. *ibid.*, *cons.* 37,99.4ff.

inferior powers through the love of the will *(per voluntatis amorem)*;[1] and the rapture of the mind *(raptus mentis)* above the inferior powers "through the spark of affection, which is kindred with and actually appropriated by the mind, and which is called ecstatic love or the ascension of the mind."[2]

What we witness in these remarks are the practical consequences of the correlation and reciprocity between the affective and intellective faculties and activities. In his initial anthropological analyses, before the consideration of the consequences of sin, the emphasis, as we have seen,[3] was on the initiating priority of the intellective to the affective powers. The consideration of the debilitating effects of sin, however, and Gerson's conviction that these effects were greater with the intellective than with the affective powers, drew the importance of the reciprocal operation of the powers into sharp focus. Here the theological fruit is harvested, as the affective powers make possible the rapture also of the intellective powers, in accordance with their greater purity and operational efficacy.

There is no question here of an exclusive focus on the affective powers. The ultimate goal remains the reformation and realization of the possibilities of the whole soul, and this means the intellective powers—*COGNITIO Dei*—as well as the affective powers—*cognitio Dei EXPERIMENTALIS. Post peccatum Adae*, the affective way is exalted not in order to denigrate or to exclude the intellective powers *per se*, but because it is the more effective way to the salutary *regressus ad Deum in via*.

2. UNION

The second property of love is the union of the one who loves with the Beloved, and in such a way that he stands firmly with Him.[4] It is a spiritual, not a corporeal union,[5] and it is in accordance with the Aristotelian definition of friendship: "among friends there is a conformity of will." As Gerson summarizes, when man's spirit adheres to

[1] Cf. *ibid., cons.* 38,100.3ff.

[2] *Ibid., cons.* 39,101.3ff: "Raptus mentis supra potentias inferiores fit per affectionis scintillam menti cognatam vel appropriatam, que amor extaticus vel excessus mentis nominatur."

[3] Cf. *supra*, 64.

[4] *De myst. theol. spec., cons.* 40,103.6f: "Amor unit amantem cum amato, ac proinde hunc stabilire ac sistere facit cum illo."

[5] *Ibid., cons.* 40,103.10f: "...hec unio...non corporalis sed spiritualis est."

God through intimate love, it is one spirit with Him through conformity of will.[1]

At this point, Gerson attacks erroneous interpretations of the union with God, as he endeavors to clarify his own position on the nature of the soul's transformation into God.[2] He continues his criticism of Jan van Ruysbroeck's *De ornatu spiritualium nuptiarum*,[3] as he censures those who have argued that perfect love brings the spirit of man into God in such a way that it is completely removed from its (creaturely) self and returns to the ideal being which it had immutably and eternally in God prior to its creation.[4] Here the soul is viewed as losing its own being and receiving the being of God, so that it is no longer a creature, nor sees and loves God in creatureliness.[5]

In this regard, we call attention to Gerson's criticism of those who have used the similes of a drop of water in a bottle of wine[6] and Eucharistic transubstantiation[7] to interpret the union of the soul with God—an attack which, as our study in Part I has made clear, would not be exclusive of Tauler, who frequently employed such images.

The position Gerson is prepared to support is revealed in his acceptance of a later, revised position of Ruysbroeck. He writes:

> In other writings he [Ruysbroeck] appears to have corrected this error by maintaining that such a soul always remains in its own being, which it has according to its own species, and is said to be transformed only

[1] *Ibid., cons.* 40,104.19ff: "Hec vero unio amantis cum amato ab Aristotile in Ethicis tangitur ubi ait: 'Amicus est alter ego,' cuius unionis ratio exprimi videtur cum ab eodem dicitur: 'Amicorum est idem velle et idem nolle.' Spiritus ergo noster, cum Deo adheret per intimum amorem, unus spiritus est cum eo per voluntatis conformitatem." Cf. Thomas, III *Sent.* d. xxvii, q. 1, art. 1, resp.: "...Amor nihil aliud est quam quaedam transformatio affectus in rem amatam." *S. Thomae Aquinatis, Scriptum super sententiis magistri Petri Lombardi*, III, ed. M. F. Moos O.P. (Paris, 1933), 855.

[2] *De myst. theol. spec., cons.* 41,105.1ff.

[3] *Ibid., cons.* 41,106.20ff. Cf. the earlier attack in *Epistola prima...*, 618.15ff.

[4] *De myst. theol. spec., cons.* 41,105.8ff: "Fuerunt enim, qui dicerent spiritum rationalem dum perfecto amore fertur in Deum deficere penitus a se, ac reverti in ideam propriam, quam habuit immutabiliter ac eternaliter in Deo, iuxta illud Iohannis: 'Quod factum est, in ipso vita erat' [John 1:3f]."

[5] *Ibid., cons.* 41,105.12ff: "Dicunt ergo quod talis anima perdit se et esse suum et accipit verum esse divinum, sic quod iam non est creatura nec per creaturam videt aut amat Deum, sed est ipse Deus qui videtur aut amatur."

[6] *Ibid., cons.* 41,107.38ff. Cf. Bernard of Clairvaux, *De diligendo Deo, PL* 182, 991 A-B: "Quomodo stilla aquae modica, multo infusa vino, deficere a se tota videtur, num et saporem vini induit et colorem... Sic omnem tunc in sanctis humanam affectionem quodam ineffabili modo necesse erit a semetipsa liquescere, atque in Dei penitus transfundi voluntatem."

[7] *De myst. theol. spec., cons.* 41,108.62ff. Cf. Eckhart, *DW* I, 328,6ff.

> in the sense of being made 'like' *(tantummodo similitudinarie transformari)* [its ideal being], as we say that those who love one another are of 'one heart and soul.' And this position we certainly grant.[1]

In an earlier work Gerson had spoken of an "imperfect similarity" of the soul with God.[2] We can specify the meaning of these descriptive phrases for Gerson by looking more closely into his interpretation of the way in which divine life is present in the unitive soul, and the sense in which the soul can be said to become 'like' God. Having rejected a series of dangerous analogies, Gerson accepts the simile of the union of form and matter as a legitimate clarification of the soul's transformation in the *unio mystica*.

> It is indisputably established that before the reception of form a material is imperfect and without beauty, power and activity. When form is given to it, however, it attains a perfection which is characteristic of the form united to it. Thus, the soul, before it is united with God through vivifying love, remains in a certain spiritual death, without beauty and power to perform vivifying [meritorious] acts; it is dead to eternal life. If, however, the soul is joined to God as to the original fount of all life, a certain divine life is given to it. This does not occur through a formal inherence of God in the soul—that is incompatible with the divine perfection—but through a certain more intimate and spiritual infusion which excludes every possible imperfection.[3]

---

[1] *De myst. theol. spec., cons.* 41,106.23ff: "...in aliis scriptis eius hunc errorem correxisse videatur, ponendo quod anima talis semper remanet in esse suo proprio, quod habet in suo genere, sed dicitur tantummodo similitudinarie transformari, sicut amatorum dicimus esse 'cor unum et animam unam': quod utique concedimus."

[2] *Epistola prima...*, 618.11ff: "Et si hoc ita est in beatitudine consummata, quod Deus non est visio et claritas nostra essentialis, sed tantum objectalis, quantomagis hoc erit alienum in beatitudinis quadam assimilatione imperfecta quam fas haberemus degustare hic in via."

[3] *De myst. theol. spec., cons.* 41,110.79ff: "Constat nimirum quod materia ante susceptionem forme imperfecta est et sine decore, sine virtute, sine actione. Detur ei forma, mox venit ad perfectionem iuxta forme sibi unite proprietatem. Sic anima, priusquam uniatur Deo per vivificum amorem manet in quadam morte spirituali, sine decore, sine virtute ad actus vivificos, mortua vite eterne. Si autem Deo coniungatur tamquam fontali totius vite principio, datur sibi vita quedam divina, non quidem per formalem inhesionem Dei ad animam, hoc enim repugnat divine perfectioni, sed per illapsum quemdam intimiorem et spiritualem seclusa imperfectione qualibet." Cf. the alternative readings by Glorieux, *Oeuvres*, III, 287. Cf. Thomas, III *Sent.* d. xxvii, q. 1, art. 1, resp. ad 5: "Alia est unio quae facit unum simpliciter, sicut unio continuorum et formae et materiae; et talis est unio amoris, quia amor facit amatum esse formam amantis..." *Scriptum super sententiis*, 858. The dangerous analogies rejected by Gerson are: a drop of water in a bottle of wine; the transformation of food into bodily nourishment; Eucharistic transubstantiation; burning iron; the solar illumination of the atmosphere; magnetized iron; and vaporized air. *De myst. theol. spec., cons.* 41,107.38ff.

If the criticism of Ruysbroeck made it unequivocally clear that the integrity of the created soul is preserved in the most intimate union with God, then this passage makes it just as clear that the divine perfection is not threatened as a "certain divine life" is infused into the soul. Despite the most intimate and efficacious presence possible, God does not assume the form of man in the souls of those united with Him. As form destroys neither itself nor the matter to which it is joined, so divine life removes neither itself nor the soul in which it is infused. The integrity and distinctiveness of both divine and human nature are preserved.

The position taken by Gerson is within the theological-philosophical framework of the Thomistic understanding of a *forma accidentalis* as the living mode of God's gracious presence to and in the soul.[1] This means that Gerson invokes and inserts the necessity of sacramentally sanctifying and ecclesiastically administered grace *(gratia gratum faciens)* into the achievement and definition of the union of the soul with God.[2] If the anthropological resources of the *synderesis* and humiliational, penitential activity[3] form the *conditio sine qua non* for the achievement of this union, no less imperative is the complementing purification achieved through sacramental grace.[4]

---

[1] Cf. *Summa Theologiae* (Ottawa, 1941), I-II^{ae}, q. 110, art. 2, 1365^{a}: "Quia gratia est supra naturam humanam, non potest esse quod sit substantia aut forma substantialis; sed est forma accidentalis ipsius animae. Id enim quod substantialiter est in Deo, accidentaliter fit in anima participante divinam bonitatem..."

[2] In *Ad deum vadit*, friendship and union with God are achieved through faithful reception of the Eucharist: "Quisquis ad Deum vadit utatur viatico hoc, non deficiet, non oberrabit, non peribit sed pertinget. Omnia quippe serviunt ei qui fruitur hoc alimento; angeli etiam obsequuntur ne forte offendat ad lapidem pedem suam. Nam cum ex vetere proverbio, 'amicorum omnia sunt communia,' et omnis utens hoc viatico, utens inquam non abutens, sit amicus Dei, immo una cum ipso caro et spiritus, nam in eo manet et Deus in eo, quid consequentius quam omnia esse subdita sub pedibus eius...?" *Oeuvres*, V, 3. The importance of God's ordained means of grace—*potentia ordinata*—is stressed by Oberman as a central feature of "nominalistic mysticism," of which he finds Gerson to be a major representative. *The Harvest of Medieval Theology*, 330. In this regard, see also Connolly, who lists among the "chief characteristics" of Gerson's mystical teaching, a "perfect harmony with the doctrines and sacramental dispensation of the Church." *John Gerson*, 317.

[3] The importance of man's "assistantship" with God (*coadiutores Dei*), given divine aid and inspiration (*presupposito primo afflatu divino*), is especially stressed in Gerson's discussion of the twelve activities conducive to the attainment of mystical theology in the *De mystica theologia practica*, *Prol.* 127.34ff. See in this regard the treatment of the "tria praeconia humilitatis" in accordance with Prov. 29:23 ("humilem in spiritu suscipiet gloria"), Prov. 11:2 ("ubi humilitas, ibi sapientia") and James 4:6 ("Deus superbis resistit, humilibus autem dat gratiam"), *A deo exivit*, *Oeuvres*, V, 18.

[4] A point Tauler can emphasize also, as P. Adolf Hoffman points out: "Tatsäch-

This fact is clarified and confirmed by the passage immediately following Gerson's statement on spiritual infusion.[1] Here, man's likeness with God through sacramental purification and the causal connection between this likeness and the union with God are emphasized.

> Let us say...that love, like heat, has the nature of gathering together or uniting things which are of the same kind *(homogenea)*, and, therefore, it separates and divides those things which are not of this kind *(heterogenea)*. It is clear that spiritual things have a certain homogeneity, i.e. likeness *(similitudo)*. They mutually serve one another, and they are things which are unlike corporeal and terrestrial things. Therefore, everything in man which is found to be spiritual or divine is placed apart, through living love, from all that which is terrestrial and corporeal. Thus, there is a division of spirit and life, i.e. of spiritual and animal and sensible things; and the precious is separated from that which is of lesser worth. And because God is spirit and likeness is the cause of union *(causa unionis)*, it is clear why the rational spirit, so purified and cleansed, is united with the divine Spirit, for quite obviously it is made like *(similis)* Him.[2]

He who is spiritually "like" God through the purifying effects of faithful, self-humiliating activity and sacramental grace (sacraments of penance and the Eucharist)[3] can become one with God. A form

---

lich nennt Tauler den Empfang der Eucharistie den kürzesten Weg zur Vollkommenheit: es gibt keine bessere Zubereitung für diesen Zustand..." "Die Christus-Gestalt bei Tauler," *Johannes Tauler: Ein Deutscher Mystiker*, 248.

[1] Quoted *supra*, p. 75.

[2] *De myst. theol. spec., cons.* 41,110.93-111.106: "...Dicamus... quod amor, sicut calor, naturam habet congregandi seu uniendi homogenea, et heterogenea sic etiam separat et dividit. Constat autem quod spiritualia cum spiritualibus homogeneitatem quamdam, id est similitudinem, servant ad invicem, et a corporalibus seu a terrestribus sunt dissimilia. Omne igitur, quod in homine reperitur spirituale vel divinum segregatur quodammodo per amorem vivificum ab omni eo, quod terrestre est atque corporeum. Sic fit ibi divisio spiritus et anime, id est spiritualitatis et animalitatis et sensualitatis, et separatur preciosum a vili. Et quia Deus spiritus est et similitudo est causa unionis, perspicuum est cur spiritus rationalis sic depuratus et defecatus unitur spiritui divino, quia videlicet similis efficitur cum eo."

[3] We disagree with André Combes' suggestion that Gerson's location of the "magisterium theologie mistice" with Jesus Christ alone (*De myst. theol. pract., Prol.* 126.24f) in *De mystica theologia practica* is a thesis with which *De mystica theologia speculativa* is apparently unconcerned. *La théologie mystique de Gerson*, I, 138. Within the order of salvation, Gerson's Christological concern is two-fold. First, he focuses on the historical, incarnate Christ, as did Tauler, as an exemplary life, the imitation of which serves the achievement of humility: "Nam et mysterium, non dicam diei huius solius sed totius passionis dominicae quid aliud principalius eloquitur quam imitandi humilitatis exemplum." *A deo exivit*, *Oeuvres*, V, 17-18.

of generic similitude grounds, empowers and entitles one to volitional conformity.

The final property of love is that it quiets, satisfies and stabilizes the soul.[1] Since the material has acquired the form which joins and unites it to God, and is, therefore, now coupled with its good, its center, its end and its full perfection, "what else," Gerson asks, "should it require, or what further thing should it desire?"[2]

3. THE *DUPLEX* CHARACTER OF MYSTICAL THEOLOGY

Our quest is not yet sated. We must pursue more deeply the nature of the cognitive content interjected into mystical theology by Gerson's discussion of the rapture of the intellective powers through the affect of love. Such pursuance will complete our consideration of *De mystica theologia speculativa* and lead us into what André Combes considers the most important issue for a final evaluation of the mystical theology of Gerson, viz., whether the position outlined in *De mystica theologia practica* indicates a major shift in Gerson's thought in which the *formalizantes* (Scotists), consistently the opponents in Gerson's earlier works, have now become his allies and to the extent that mystical theology culminates in "une doctrine d'esprit scotiste."[3]

We begin by calling attention to Gerson's summarizing definitions of mystical theology. He writes that mystical theology is (1) an extension of the soul *(extensio animi)* to God through the desire of love *(per amoris desiderium)*,[4] or (2) a transcendental movement *(motio ana-*

Secondly, he is concerned with the sacramental significance and presence of Christ as the *conditio sine qua non* for the purifying efficacy of the sacraments. In these two senses, Jesus Christ holds the *magisterium* in the *Speculativa* every bit as much as in the *Practica.*

[1] *De myst. theol. spec., cons.* 42,113.5ff: "Per predictam amorosam unionem, in qua mistica theologia consistere videtur, anima quietatur, satiatur, et stabilitur."

[2] *Ibid., cons.* 42,113.12-114.18: "Sic materia in forma habita, sic lapis in centro positus, sic res quelibet in adepto fine suo quietatur. Anima quippe rationalis dum coniungitur et unitur Deo, copulatur suo summo bono: est enim Deus summe bonum eius, est centrum, est finis, totaque ipsius perfectio; quid ergo aliud ipsa requireret, aut ad quid aliud ulterius inhiaret?"

[3] *La théologie mystique de Gerson*, 174f. See *infra*, p. 79ff.

[4] Oberman breaks the reciprocal operation of the intellective and affective powers of the soul by focusing on this summarizing definition alone. This leads him to establish the affective powers and the good over against the intellective powers and the true, a separation which climaxes in a typology in which an affective, penitential mysticism is set "versus" a speculative, transformational mysticism, the former characteristic of Gerson and nominalistic mysticism, the latter of the Eckhartian school. *The Harvest of Medieval Theology*, 331, 339. We find the failure

gogica) to God through fervent and pure love *(per amorem fervidum et purum)*. Or, it can be described as (3) experiential knowledge of God *(cognitio experimentalis habita de Deo)*, acquired through the embrace of unitive love *(per amoris unitivi complexum)*. And, finally, it is characterized as (4) wisdom, a savory knowledge *(sapida notitia)* of God, achieved when the highest affective power (the *synderesis*) is joined and united to Him through love *(per amorem coniungitur et unitur)*.[1]

In these summarizing definitions, an activity *(extensio animi, motio anagogica)* together with an achieved cognitive content *(cognitio experimentalis, sapida notitia)* receive primary emphasis. There is volitional *and* intellective communion with the will *and* understanding of God. Further, it is clear that, in reference to both, love—as a human activity *(facere quod in se est)* and as a sacramentally received reality *(caritas infusa)*—is consistently considered to be the instrumental way *(per)* to their achievement.

Mystical theology is not exhausted by the unitive embrace of love, nor is it limited to the anthropologically resourceful and sacramentally assisted affective powers. These powers subserve, by grounding and embracing, the possibility of an extension and transcendental movement of the soul into God, where a strictly defined knowledge of God *(cognitio experimentalis, affectus mentalis aut intellectualis supremus*[2]*)* becomes a factual possibility.

4. *COGNITIO DEI EXPERIMENTALIS:* "UNE DOCTRINE D'ESPRIT SCOTISTE?"

Two passages in *De mystica theologia practica*, a later (1407) companion piece to the *Speculativa*, lead Combes to the strong suspicion that there

to see the correlative, reciprocal operation of the intellective and affective powers and Gerson's overriding concern to retain and develop this reciprocity at the highest level of union with God to leave Oberman with only a part of Gerson's mystical theology. In emphasizing the *cognitio* as well as the *experimentalis* in Gerson's summarizing phrase, "cognitio dei experimentalis," our interpretation is a step toward a more comprehensive picture of Gerson's thought, and to this extent is allied with the continuing supererogatory efforts of Combes.

[1] *De myst. theol. spec., cons.* 28,72.34ff: "...theologiam misticam sic possumus describere: Theologia mistica est extensio animi in Deum per amoris desiderium. Vel sic: Theologia mistica est motio anagogica, hoc est sursum ductiva in Deum, per amorem fervidum et purum. Aliter sic: Theologia mistica est cognitio experimentalis habita de Deo per amoris unitivi complexum. Aliter sic: Theologia mistica est sapientia, id est sapida notitia habita de Deo, dum ei supremus apex affective potentie rationalis per amorem coniungitur et unitur."

[2] *Ibid., cons.* 43,118.31f.

is a major shift in Gerson's thought. This shift is indicated by Gerson's apparant attraction to "une doctrine d'esprit scotiste," in which, surprisingly, "une connaissance intellectuelle" now not only is compatible with but, indeed, included by mystical theology.[1] The first passage is the following, which we translate in its full context.

> It is fitting here for us to recall those things which we have said about the nature of mystical theology. We maintained, accordingly, that mystical theology is ecstatic love which accompanies understanding in the spirit [of man], an understanding which certainly has no dense clouds of phantasy. Therefore, it is necessary for one who wishes to commit himself to mystical theology to strive after this pure understanding. Otherwise how may he order[2] the love immediately following?[3]

The explicit appeal to what has already been discussed in the *Speculativa* is significant; it means that Gerson does not consider his remarks a new frontier of thought. The *effort* to attain *pura intelligentia* is an indication of an intellective *facere quod in se est*, which is not sur-

[1] Combes writes: "Au moment de conclure sa *practica*, de façon tout à la fois technique et efficace, Gerson tient donc à ouvrir son texte à une thèse théologique qui, si on l'adopte assez intégralement pour lui permettre de porter tous ses fruits, rompt de façon éclantante avec la pure tradition dionysienne et s'épanouit dans la spéculation des *formalizantes.*" "S'atténuer, il faut l'avouer, au point de paraître concevoir, désormais, comme légitime une théologie mystique où l'union suprême d'amour, loin d'être incompatible avec une connaissance intellectuelle, l'inclurait; et non pas seulement à titre de préparation immédiate, mais comme la connaissance même à laquelle l'élimination de toutes les imperfections conduirait." *La théologie mystique de Gerson*, I, 175; 177; cf. 172ff.

[2] We render "comparare" as 'order' and not 'attain'; *intelligentia* functions to structure the knowledge of God which one reaches only in and through *amor extaticus*. Cf. *infra*, 81ff. In this regard, we call attention to Gerson's earlier image of honey (the savor of devotion) and the honeycomb (the light of erudition), which, although occurring in not inconsiderable historical distance and a quite general statement, still adumbrates an ideal of rich affective experience which is structured and ordered (honeycomb) intellectively: "...bonum est mel cum favo, sapor scilicet devotionis cum lumine eruditionis." *Epistola prima...* (1398-99), 634.6f. For the influence of the (Greek-Augustinian) ideal of ordered affection on Gerson, see Dress, *Die Theologie Gersons*, 119.

[3] *De myst. theol. pract.*, *cons.* 12,208.5ff: "Oportet nos hic eorum meminisse, que de quidditate mistice theologie tractavimus. Posuimus itaque theologiam misticam esse amorem extaticum, qui consequitur ad intelligentiam ipsius spiritus, que intelligentia utique caret nubibus fantasmatum. Propterea necesse est eum, qui vult mistice theologie se tradere conari ad hanc puram intelligentiam; alioquin amorem inde subsequentem qua ratione compararet?" To the extent that *consequi* and *subsequi* suggest a priority of *intelligentia pura* to *amor extaticus*, this priority is to be understood logically and not temporally. Companionship—correlation and reciprocity—is the systematic point of this passage. For an alternative and, in our opinion, unconvincing exegesis, see Combes, *La théologie mystique de Gerson*, I, 173.

prisingly inconsistent with his earlier position.[1] Because of his understanding of the correlative, reciprocal operation of the powers of the soul, Gerson can formulate "une doctrine anti-dionysienne" without drawing "une doctrine d'esprit scotiste" as the necessary consequence. If anything, the consequence is one which stands between and against Dionysius and Scotus; it takes the form of a "cognitio experimentalis," quite harmonious with the definitions of mystical theology in the *Speculativa*.[2] But let us go a step further.

A second passage on which Combes draws is the following:

> In a fashion similar [to the way in which a sculptor removes wood or stone to form an image], the spirit, removing by negation all things which it is able to know here, i.e. things which doubtlessly bear with them the soul's imperfection, either of potentiality, dependence, privation or mutability, comes finally—all these things having been removed—to an image of God. This is knowledge *(notitia)* of what is most actualized without any potentiality, what is supreme without dependence, what is purest without privation, and what is most necessary without mutability. And *if that knowledge is experiential only* and in the highest affective union with God through love, and if it is able to be called 'intellectual,' not indeed as intuitive but as abstractive and dimly grasped knowledge *(cognitio)*, and not simply as connotative but as absolute knowledge, then it would be most worthy of consideration and investigation.[3]

Granting the possible parallels with and influence from the Scotistic *conceptus perfectissimus*, or even the Occamistic *notitia abstractiva deitatis*,[4] the qualifying "solum experimentalis in affectu supremo unito

[1] Cf. *supra*, 58, 68ff, 76, note 3.

[2] Cf. *supra*, 78ff. The reciprocity between *intellectus* and *affectus* on the level of the *unio mystica*, which makes it possible for Gerson to interject cognitive content into this union, is a major point of distinction between Gerson and Bonaventure. The latter writes: "In hoc autem transitu, si sit perfectus, oportet quod relinquantur omnes intellectuales operationes, et apex affectus totus transferatur et transformetur in Deum." *Itin.* VII, 4.150. See *supra*, p. 78, n. 4.

[3] *De myst. theol. pract.*, *cons.* 12,210.44-211.55: "Conformiter spiritus removens omnia per abnegationem qualia potest hic cognoscere, que utique suam gerunt secum imperfectionem vel potentialitatis vel dependentie vel privationis vel mutabilitatis, invenit tandem omnibus hiis ablatis agalma Dei, hoc est notitiam tamquam rei actualissime sine potentialitate, supreme sine dependentia, pure sine privatione, necessarie sine mutabilitate. At vero si notitia illa sit solum experimentalis in affectu supremo unito Deo per amorem, vel si possit dici intellectualis, non quidem intuitiva sed abstractiva seu cognitione vespertina, nec solum connotativa cognitione sed absoluta, dignissimum esset consideratione et inquisitione." Emphasis mine.

[4] In addition to Combes, we call attention to Paul Vignaux's comments on Scotus in this regard. "The metaphysical quest (*inquisitio metaphysica*), by proving the existence of an infinite in being, furnishes Scotus with the highest concept

Deo per amorem," makes it quite clear that we are not confronted with a cognitive content which is sought and capable of attainment apart from the affective way and the union of love.[1] This conclusion, further, is indicative of the effort, already clearly established in the anthropological analyses of the *Speculativa*, to maintain and develop the correlative, reciprocal operation of the intellective and affective powers at the highest level of their possibilities. Against Combes, we must insist that mystical theology has consistently been defined by Gerson with sufficient latitude to include, "une connaissance intellectuelle," both as 'preparatory' to and 'consequent' upon *amor extaticus*, but only in and with affective activity: *cognitio dei experimentalis*. The cognitive content of mystical theology is not resultant from an enigmatic Scotistic inspiration, but from the anthropological analyses of the *Speculativa*.

At the peak of mystical experience there is a historical approximation of *Adamic manhood* as the unitive soul returns to God through love and knowledge, and, in this approximation and return, achieves "similitude" with its pre-created status—*esse idealis*—in the divine Mind. There is no question here of losing one's *esse realis*. One knows in the company of another *(con-scia mens)*, and loves in the embrace of another *(in amplexu sponsi)*.[2]

---

conceptus perfectissimus) which any human understanding, seeking His very essence, can form of God—that of an infinite being." *Philosophy in the Middle Ages: An Introduction*, trans. E. C. Hall (Cleveland, 1962), 153. Cf. Effrem Bettoni, *Duns Scotus: The Basic Principles of His Philosophy* (Washington, 1961), 38, 44. In reference to Occam, see Dress, *Die Theologie Gersons*, 59, and P. Boehner, "Zu Ockhams Beweis der Existenz Gottes," *Collected Articles on Ockham* (St. Bonaventure, N.Y., 1958), 419. Also relevant are Boehner's articles on "The Notitia Intuitiva of Non-existents According to William Ockham," *Ibid.*, 268ff, and "The Realistic Conceptualism of William Ockham," *Ibid.*, 156ff.

[1] This is forcefully expressed when Gerson concludes: "Loquamur tamen pro minus eruditis in metaphisica seu theologia, et dicamus si possumus quo pacto quove observationis studio poterit se spiritus a fantasmatibus avertere, dum anagogicos aut supermentales querit excessus. Et fortassis hoc poterit fieri, si in omni cogitatione et meditatione sua de Deo nequaquam sistat homo in cognitione, sed aspiret per vim affectivam quasi ore cordis inhyante in suam potentiam, in suam sapientiam, in suam bonitatem saporandam et gustandam..." *De myst. theol. pract.*, *cons.* 12,213.86ff.

[2] *Ibid.*, *cons.* 12,216.122ff: "At vero dum eo usque pervenerit bene conscia mens et munda ut neque gaudia neque aliud omnino vel servile vel mercennarium recogitet, neque preterea de Deo quicquam durum, asperum, negotiosum penset vel turbulentum, sicut de iudice retributore vel vindice, sed hoc unicum in mentem venerit quod sit totus desiderabilis, 'suavis et mitis' [Ps. 85:5], totus amari, 'etiam si occiderit' [Job. 13:15], dignissimus, dum ita solum placuerit amoris negotium, tunc vola securus in amplexus sponsi, stringe pectus illud divinum amicitie purissi-

5. SUMMARY

1. Gerson's project of a mystical theology centers upon a quest for the more effective way to knowledge of God in this life. Foundational to the implementation of this project is the discernment of the purer anthropological power. This purer power is found to be in the affective powers, specifically the *synderesis voluntatis*. The conviction that the *synderesis* is the purer power is a major clue to understanding why the affective, penitential way is the more effective way to saving knowledge of God for Gerson.

2. A second conviction of equal significance is the correlative, reciprocal operation of the affective and intellective powers. This reciprocity enables Gerson to interject the cognitive content into the *unio mystica* which realizes his goal. Through the affective way, a reformation and fulfilment of the intellective powers is achieved: *cognitio dei experimentalis*.

3. The union with God in this life is an approximation of Adamic manhood. Through anthropological resources, humiliational activity and sacramental grace, the faithful man reaches a form of generic similitude with his *esse idealis* in the divine Mind. He who is 'like' *(homogeneus)* God becomes one with God and lives in His embrace.

4. There is no removal of man's *esse realis* in the *unio mystica*. He is 'like' God through an approximation of Adamic, not pre-creaturely, manhood; or, stated another way, he is like his *esse idealis* as Adam was like his *esse idealis* before the Fall. Thus, while both Tauler and Gerson, *mutatis mutandis*, conceive the union with God as the point of maximum similitude and intimacy with God, Gerson cautiously removes language which would suggest a substantive union.

5. Gerson, then, preserves the distance between God and man in the mystical union. But it is a distance and otherness of two generic 'likes.' The radical opposition between a righteous God and a sinful man disappears in the union of likes.

---

mis brachiis, fige oscula castissima pacis exsuperantis 'omnen sensum' [Phil. 4:7], ut et dicere subinde possis, gratulabunda et amorosa devotione: 'Dilectus meus michi, et ego illi' [Cant. 2:16]."

PART THREE

MARTIN LUTHER (1509-16)

CHAPTER EIGHT

THE DUALISM IN THE *DICTATA SUPER PSALTERIUM*

1. A. W. HUNZINGER AND GERHARD EBELING

Drawing upon passages from the *scholia* on psalm 121[1] as primary sources for his thesis, A. W. Hunzinger drew the conclusion, in 1906, that the dualism which one encounters in a variety of oppositions in Luther's *Dictata super psalterium* is ultimately anchored in the ontological presuppositions of Neoplatonism.[2] Hunzinger states his position concisely when he writes:

> It is clear from this distinction [*WA* 4,400.35ff] that an ontological element underlies Luther's normative contrast between *visibilia* and

[1] The primary loci to which Hunzinger appeals are *WA* 4,400.35-401.16. We consider these comments *infra*, p. 90ff. Luther's first lectures on the psalms began in August, 1513. By Autumn, 1514, he was in the vicinity of psalm 69; by March and April, 1515, he was to psalm 108. With additional material on psalms 1,4 and 18 prepared between March and October, 1516, the lectures were ready for publication in Autumn, 1516. Our dating follows the research of Erich Vogelsang, "Zur Datierung der frühesten Lutherpredigten," *ZKG*, 50 (1931), 112f; see esp. 118,137; *Unbekannte Fragmente aus Luthers zweiter Psalmenvorlesung 1518* (Berlin, 1940), 8-30.

[2] When Neoplatonism is mentioned in this study, it has reference not only to the metaphysical dualism of a visible, sensible world of multiplicity and flux and an intelligible, invisible world of unity and stability, but especially to the distinction on the level of anthropology between two opposed parts of the soul. In addition to Hunzinger, the following illuminating summary by Robert W. Mulligan is definitive for our purposes: "The upper part of the human soul, which Plotinus asserts to be sinless, is conceived as being in constant but unconscious contact with the realm of the intelligibles. When the soul turns consciously away from the world of sense and gazes upon the intelligibles, it then finds true happiness and wisdom; for its objects are now eternal and unchanging. In short, the soul has two phases, 'one inner, intent upon the Intellect-Principle, the other outside it and facing to the external.' The virtues proper to the inner phase of the soul are wisdom and contemplation (the virtues of St. Augustine's *ratio sublimior*); the function of the external phase is action (the function also of the lower part of the reason in St. Augustine's theory)." "*Ratio Superior* and *Ratio Inferior*: the Historical Background," *The New Scholasticism*, 29 (1955), 11-12. See further Mulligan's instructive demonstration of a direct line between this dualism and the movement of a *syntheresis* tradition, *via* Jerome, into the late Middle Ages. *Ibid.*, 24f. For a summary of Neoplatonism in Luther's time, see Frederick Copleston's chapter on "The Revival of Platonism," *A History of Philosophy*, III[2], *Late Mediaeval and Renaissance Philosophy* (New York, 1963), 11ff.

invisibilia. This ontological element is a Platonic, or more precisely put, neoplatonic concept of being, according to which the measure of all true being is found in the principle of universality, unity, simplicity, indivisibility and unchangeability.[1]

Contemporary Luther research, keenly aware of the theological relevance of the hermeneutical and philosophical conclusions of Existentialist Philosophy, has presented a quite different picture of the dualism in the *Dictata*. As this picture is presented by Gerhard Ebeling, the dualism one finds has reference to opposing possibilities of living before God and not to a metaphysical opposition between an intelligible, invisible world and a visible, sensible world. It is a "contrast between two possible ways of living *(Existenzmöglichkeiten)* available to one and the same whole man," or a contrast between "two quite different, opposed and exclusive possibilities of (self-)perception and (self-)understanding."[2]

Ebeling makes reference to some thirty passages in the *Dictata* in order to expose the problematic—one could almost say simplistic—character of Hunzinger's position.[3] Ebeling's brief but penetrating effort in this regard is quite convincing. What is not quite convincing, however, is his alternative—a dualism of existential possibilities. Granted its relevance, does this existentialist solution so accent particular aspects of Luther's thought that major, even decisive, areas of his early theology are threatened with permanent concealment?

This, then, will be the polemical concern of our discussion in the first part of our study of Luther. By critically reviving the Hunzinger-Ebeling 'debate,' we seek nothing less than the formation of a new

---

[1] A. W. Hunzinger, *Lutherstudien*, I, *Luthers Neuplatonismus in der Psalmenvorlesung von 1513-16* (Leipzig, 1906), 7. For the same judgment in reference to Luther's doctrine of God and his doctrine of justification, see *Ibid.*, 7-15, 15-20. In contemporary research, Hunzinger's position finds a proponent in the study by U. Saarnivaara, *Luther Discovers the Gospel* (St. Louis, 1951). See especially his (quite unconvincing) conclusions on Luther's Christology and his doctrine of justification in the *Dictata*. *Ibid.*, 61ff, 65ff.

[2] Gerhard Ebeling, "Die Anfänge von Luthers Hermeneutik," *ZThK*, 48 (1951), 195, 198. See the larger summary: "Was ergibt sich daraus? Daß in der Tat sein [Luther's] theologisches Denken in ungewöhnlicher Weise existenzbezogenes Denken ist und daß der *Dualismus*, von dem die Psalmenvorlesung beherrscht ist, ein solcher ist, *der das Verhältnis zwischen Gott und Mensch betrifft*, also nicht einfach statisch Gott und Mensch in Gegensatz zueinander stellt, sondern zwei entgegengesetzte Weisen des Verhältnisses zwischen Gott und Mensch aufdeckt." *Ibid.*, 194. Ebeling is followed quite closely by Schwarz, *Fides, Spes und Caritas beim jungen Luther*, 150.

[3] Ebeling, *ZThK* (1951), 189-191.

interpretive framework for Luther's thought in the period 1509-16. Without excluding still further options for understanding the dualism in the *Dictata*,[1] we will turn first to a consideration of the neoplatonic and existentialist solutions. The consideration of the former (section 2) will introduce our investigation of Luther's anthropological concepts, *anima*, *cor*, *spiritus* and *conscientia* (section 3); the consideration of the latter (section 4) our discussion of the concepts, *substantia*, *memoria*, *intellectus* and *affectus* (sections 5-7). With the more comprehensive interpretive horizon attained in these sections, we will be in a position to specify the nature of the opposition between *superbia* and *fides* (section 8). We will then endeavor to deepen and clarify our conclusions by showing their importance in understanding the relation of law and gospel in the *Dictata* (section 9). Only then, in a final section, will we attempt to state our position on Luther's 'ontological' presuppositions and the nature of the dualism with which the *Dictata* is really concerned.

Moving passage by passage, concept by concept, our study in this first chapter will demonstrate the rich complexity of Luther's anthropological terms and the impossibility of fitting them exclusively into either neoplatonic or existentialist categories. We will argue that what Luther initially places in suspension and gradually denies altogether in the neoplatonic world-view are the natural, soteriological resources with which it endows the soul of man. What he retains and theologically exploits from the neoplatonic world-view is the importance of the 'objective reference.' Neither of these major points, we will argue further, is fully carried by the categories of Existentialist Philosophy. We will, therefore, introduce fresh categories, which come historically and systematically from Luther's own texts, so that justice can be done to the full range of his thought.

As we proceed in this programmatic first chapter, we work in the full awareness that the *Dictata super psalterium* is the first major 'voyage' of the Reformer. It is a work in which theses are being tested. Tensions are both broken and left unbroken; issues are left dangling, pursued and dropped and then pursued again in new contexts. Words

[1] See *WA* 4,189.11ff (*Schol.* to Ps. 103:13): "duplex est mundus seu creatura." Here one finds a dualism which has nothing to do with either the neoplatonic contrast between *transitoria* and *permanentia*, or the existentialist "contrast of Existenzmöglichkeiten." Here, rather, we find a dualism without opposition, concerned with the two-fold character of God's creation, viz., a visible, physical world, providentially created and directed, and an invisible, intelligible *nova terra*, the Church.

and concepts clash, and often the compass of consistency appears to have been misplaced. This should not, however, be interpreted as an indication that a "Halbwisser" is at the helm. Because he listens so intently and imaginatively to the psalmist, Luther is led to travel the rough and 'uncharted' as well as the smooth and 'charted' theological waters. For this reason, new 'navigational methods' and a new concept of theological 'seamanship' emerge. Only old salts, who find comfort in the safe, well-charted waters and the seamanship of their fathers, would stand hesitatingly before this challenging adventure. But we do not write as old salts; our study shall not shrink from the uncharted waters. For to do so would be to prevent the reader from sharing the both painful and exhilarating excitement of a truly maiden voyage in the history of ideas.

2. THE NEOPLATONIC THESIS: A CLOSER LOOK

In the *scholia* on psalm 121:3 cited by Hunzinger, we find Luther contrasting life in and outside faith. As he develops the differences, Luther argues that it is the nature of temporal things that one person cannot, at the same time, possess, use and enjoy what another possesses, uses and enjoys. One man cannot eat what another eats, nor can he wear the clothes another wears. This fundamentally unshareable character of *temporalia*, it is concluded, underlies temporal discord. In contrast to this state of affairs, the faithful have one bread, one cup, one faith, one lord; temporally diverse and spatially divided, they are nonetheless united, eating, wearing and possessing the same "good things." This unity, rooted in the *nature of the good things* which sustain the life of the faithful, makes possible their concord, friendship and other distinguishing characteristics. "What possible harm can it do me," Luther asks, "if you have the same faith in Christ that I have? But it does infinite harm if you have the same money, wife and dwelling!"

It is in the sense of a contrast between the understanding and 'objects' of faith and the realities of sixteenth century daily life, that Luther here insists, as he not infrequently does in the *Dictata*,[1] that spiritual things are "the very opposite" of temporal things.[2] The

[1] Cf. *WA* 3,151.36ff,252.27ff,361.26ff,4,108.26ff,239.36ff.

[2] *WA* 4,400.35-401.16: "Sic enim est natura temporalium, quod uno eodemque non possint duo simul uti vel frui. Quod enim tu comedis, ego non comedo, licet simile, sed aliud. Et quod tu induis, ego non possum induere. Et hinc fit causa

spiritual things of which he speaks are summarized as "Christ, our common good," the "cause of union, concord, association and friendship" among the faithful in this life.[1]

What catches the attention in these statements is not, as Hunzinger argued, a latent neoplatonic ontology, but a combination of rare teutonic common sense and a theological understanding of the *alibi* and *contraria* character of the *bona fidei*. The presuppositions underlying this 'dualism' are not to be found in Neoplatonism or in any other strictly philosophical ontology, but, as we will see, in Luther's distinctively theological definition of *substantia*.[2]

This is not to suggest that Hunzinger's thesis is without serious merit. We do think, however, that he could have more profitably instanced other passages as his "main sources" for a latent neoplatonic ontology. There is, for example, the argument in the *scholia* on psalm 63 that all the works of creation are "transitory things, things signifying what is eternal and permanent," and that Christ is the "end and center of all things,"[3] the one "who is," and we mortals are those "who are not, but only signify."[4] And, further, there is the lamentation

---

discordiarum, bellorum, inimicitiarum, cedium, furtorum, rapinarum et omnium peccatorum et malorum. Nos autem si cives sumus huius civitatis, ecce unus panis, unus calix, una fides, unus dominus, omniaque sunt nobis unum. Omnia autem Christus in nobis. Quia spiritualia habent hanc naturam, ut non possint dividi in diversa, sed diversos et divisos colligunt in unum. Cum enim Christus omnibus sufficiat, ipse idipsum et unum nostrum omnes ad se trahit et unum facit. Ita quod tu comedis, induis, habes, idem ego comedo, bibo, habeo. Et hinc fit causa omnis concordie, pacis, amicitie, vite, communionis sanctorum et omnium bonorum... Patet itaque, quod spiritualia habent contrariam conditionem temporalibus: hec enim eos, qui sunt unum, dividunt in multos et diversos, quia ipsa sunt necessario dividenda, cum non possint eadem eisdem sufficere, illa autem eos, qui sunt divisi, colligunt in unum, quia non possunt dividi et singulis sufficiunt. Quid enim mihi deperit, si eandem fidem habes quam ego in Christum? Sed deperit totum, si eandem pecuniam, uxorem, domum habeas quam ego. Ergo 'participatio eius in idipsum,' sed participatio illius in diversa."

[1] *WA* 4,401,18ff (*Schol.* to Ps. 121:3): "Et ne quis non intelligat, quo modo dixi, quod Christus est nostrum idipsum, in quo omnes participamus, quod si participamus, eo ipso assotiamur omnes simul, id est in unum, ei id est Christo. Hec enim assotiatio omnium fit per participationem eius. Quia dixi, quod istud idipsum causa est unionis, concordie, assotiationis, amicitie, etc."

[2] Here we alert the reader to our discussion *infra*, p. 105ff.

[3] See Fritz Hahn, "Faber Stapulensis und Luther," *ZKG*, 57 (1938), 364, 367f. What Hahn describes as a neoplatonic metaphysics influencing the theology and Christology of Faber through Nicholas of Cusa, parallels in many respects the Christological picture drawn by Luther in these passages.

[4] *WA* 3,368.18ff (*Schol.* to Ps. 63:10): "Quia omnia opera creationis et veteris legis signa sunt operum dei, que in Christo et suis sanctis facit et faciet, et ideo in Christo illa [preterita] tanquam signa omnia implentur: nam omnia illa sunt tran-

in the *scholia* on psalm 80 that the body *(corpus)*, i.e. the flesh *(caro)* as quite literally the dwelling-place of the soul *(tabernaculum animae)*,[1] is a "basket which weighs down the soul," and which is filled with "sins and many pollutions."[2]

While the most imaginative contextualizing efforts cannot explain away the not-so-latent neoplatonic influence here, it is not insignificant that in other passages of the same *genre*, the derogation of the body or the flesh concerns its inability to "support" the heart,[3] and to serve as a 'spiritual home.'[4] And we find the 'significatory' character of created things dealt with in a similar context.[5] Most of all, it should not be forgotten that the old man is a 'whole man;' divine judgment falls upon the soul as well as upon the flesh,[6] and the "soul and its understanding," as well as the body, are objects of *odium* for those

sitoria, significantia [earum], que sunt eterna et permanentia; et hec sunt opera veritatis, illa autem omnia umbra et opera figurationis. Ideo Christus finis omnium et centrum, in quem omnia respiciunt et monstrant, ac si dicerent: ecce iste est, qui est, nos autem non sumus, sed significamus tantum." We read *preterita* for *pacta*. See further *WA* 3, 561.1ff,375.29ff.

[1] *WA* 3,336.22ff,338.22ff,337.37ff.

[2] *WA* 3,617.15f (*Schol.* to Ps. 80:7): "Cophinus autem corpus est, quod aggravat animam. Hoc enim impletur peccatis et pollutionibus multis."

[3] *WA* 3,355.22ff (*Schol.* to Ps. 61:4): "...paries est corpus nostrum, et idem maceria, utrunque ad mortem semper inclinata et semper ruinam minans. Quare super ipsum niti et cor suum super eum ponere, est horribile. Quia cadente isto pariete per mortem, necesse est ut anima ruat in perditionem. Si autem sursum heret in coelestibus et non nititur super carnem, tunc non potest ruere, etiam si corpus ruat. Sed sursum herebit in deo."

[4] *WA* 3,580.34-581.2 (*Schol.* to Ps. 77:28): "Sed manna evangelicum cogit exire corpus peccati et exuere hominem, exire de terra sua cum Abraham et oblivisci domum patris sui: alioquin colligi non potest. Unde usque hodie ad literam seorsum sunt Ecclesie a domibus constructe, in quas populus convenit ad verbum audiendum et manna colligendum: ubi docentur, quod sicut domum suam foris reliquunt, ita et spiritualiter domum, carnem inquam, reliquere debere."

[5] *WA* 3,561.1ff (*Schol.* to Ps. 77:2): "Omnisque creatura dei verbum dei est: 'quia ipse dixit et facta sunt' [Ps. 33:9]. Ergo creaturas inspicere oportet tanquam locutiones dei. Atque ideo ponere cor in res creatas est in signum et non rem ponere, que est deus solus." This passage is also significant because it emphasizes creation through the Word, not a neoplatonic doctrine of emanation. The absence of this neoplatonic *Grundgedanke* from the *Dictata* is stressed by Ebeling against Hunzinger. *ZThK* (1951), 189f.

[6] *WA* 4,461.3f (*Gl.* to Ps. 149:9): "*Ut faciant in eis iudicium*, i.e. condemnationem veteris hominis cum sensu, voluntate et omnibus viribus eius..." 4,376.37-377.3 (*Schol.* to Ps. 118:149): "Ideo secundum iudicium tuum vivificabis me, ut mihi amplius 'non occide me,' quaeso, sed 'ut tibi vivam, vivifica me.' Sic enim oportet animam meam occidi et carnem crucifigi ut vivam spiritu. Hoc salutare consilium et iudicium tuum: sed hoc horrent amatores sui, inimici crucis, et dissuadent sibi et mihi, et potius volunt misericordia tua carere spiritum vivificante, quam iudicium tuum portare in carne mortificativum."

who are aware of their sins.[1] There is, apparently, for Luther, no *terra immacula* in the life of man.

These concluding statements require a more detailed consideration of Luther's anthropology. Only as we come to grips with the complexity of his view of man in this life do we reach a vantage point from which the inadequacy of the neoplatonic world-view as the interpretative framework for his thought is fully appreciated.

3. *HOMO SECUNDUM ANIMAM*

In this section, we guide our consideration with a polemical question: do Luther's descriptions of the soul indicate, as Hunzinger argued, a picture of man divided into two 'parts,' one part of his nature completely limited to the sensible world, the other exclusively related to an 'intelligible' world?[2]

Luther states clearly that there is nothing so near to man, nothing more intimate to him, and nothing for which he should have greater diligence than his own soul.[3] He writes, further, that the soul is not a part of man independent from the activities of his other powers, but is such that it comprehensively embraces the 'whole man.'

> The whole soul is in every part. Therefore, when the soul employs one member the whole is in that member; indeed, all powers cooperate in what the soul is busy doing. Thus, all members become in a certain sense one member. As a result, the whole man becomes as one member in doing that to which the soul directs itself; for when it applies itself to something, the soul takes with it all the powers.[4]

---

[1] *WA* 4,387.27f (*Schol.* to Ps. 118:165): "Omnis enim hereticus inde fit, quia non odit animam suam et sensum suum, ac per hoc odit et crucem domini et suam accipere."

[2] "Ein Doppelleben zu führen scheint der Mensch verurteilt. Mit dem einen Teile seines Wesens sieht er sich ganz und gar auf die Sinnenwelt beschränkt, auf den Verkehr mit ihr angewiesen, ja unlöslich an sie gebunden, mit dem anderen steht er ausschließlich in Beziehung zu der intelligiblen Welt." Hunzinger, *Lutherstudien*, I, 18. This description may be more appropriate to Bernard of Clairvaux, in regard to whom Walter Hiss concludes: "Der anthropologisch-metaphysische Dualismus ist die Grundlage für Bernards Theologie." *Die Anthropologie Bernhards von Clairvaux* (Berlin, 1964), 65.

[3] *WA* 3,579.14f (*Schol.* to Ps. 77:25): "Cum autem nobis nihil propius, nihil intimius sit quam anima nostra, nihil ita timere, nil ita suspectum habere debemus quam animam nostram..."

[4] *WA* 3,296.2ff (*Schol.* to Ps. 51:4): "...Anima tota est in qualibet parte. Et ideo quando uno membro utitur, tunc tota in illo est: immo omnes vires ad illud tunc cooperantur. Et sic omnia membra quodammodo fiunt unum membrum, et

We find that Luther employs other terms, and without the precision which would permit us to speak of anthropological 'categories,' in parallel, if not in synonomy, with *anima*. He speaks, for example, of "my mind or spirit" *(mens mea vel spiritus)*,[1] of "spirit or soul" *(spiritus vel anima)*,[2] and of "my heart, conscience or soul" *(cor meum, conscientia mea vel anima)*.[3]

These parallels indicate that *spiritus*, *mens*, *cor* and *conscientia* are not independent parts of the soul for Luther. Rather they are concepts correlative with *anima* which he uses to designate as comprehensively as possible the life and activity of human being.

Our interpretation of *spiritus* as a distinctively anthropological reality runs counter to the treatment of this term in contemporary Luther scholarship. Here *spiritus* is interpreted as a divine-human principle of 'Spiritual being.' Ebeling argues that Luther's understanding of *spiritus* intertwines divine and human dimensions so that the most consistent meaning is "the spirit of man as it is enlightened by the Spirit of God, i.e. the God-directed self-understanding of man."[4] Reinhard Schwarz comes to a similar conclusion: *spiritus* is not a "neutral faculty in man," but rather "the principle of spiritual being which stands in contrast to *caro*, the principle of fleshly being."[5] And the catholic theologian, Albert Brandenburg, locates *spiritus* within the same divine-human twilight-zone, as he helpfully makes clear the

---

per consequens totus homo fit velut unum membrum illud, ad quod anima sese transfert et sic transferendo omnia secum sumit."

[1] *WA* 3,140.8 (*Gl.* to Ps. 22:5). Cf. 4,165.9 (*Gl.* to Ps. 102:16): "...spiritus, anima corporis vita et motrix..."

[2] *WA* 3,148.27 (*Gl.* to Ps. 26:6).

[3] *WA* 3,350.30 (*Gl.* to Ps. 60:3). Cf. 3,180.8 (*Gl.* to Ps. 32:15): "...*corda eorum* animas..." 4,323.31 (*Schol.* to Ps. 118:44): "...ex animo, de corde puro et conscientia..." See still further the parallel with *homo interior*, *infra* p. 95, n. 2. In the Augustinian tradition both the affirmation of the unity of the soul and the insistence upon its ability to be described with various names (i.e. *distinctiones in nomine* and not *in re*) are present. "Anima est spiritus intellectualis, rationalis, semper vivens, semper in motu, bonae malaeque voluntatis capax: secundum benignitatem creatoris atque secundum sui operis officium variis nuncupatur nominibus. Dicitur namque anima, dum vegetat; spiritus, dum contemplatur; dum discernit, ratio; dum recordatur, memoria; dum consensit, voluntas. Ista tamen non different substantia, quemadmodum in nominibus; quoniam omnia ista una anima est: proprietates quidem diversae sed essentia una." *De spiritu et anima*, XIII, *PL* 40, 789. Cf. Ephraem Hendrikx O.E.S.A., *Augustins Verhältnis zur Mystik* (Theol. Diss., Würzburg, 1936), in *Zum Augustin-Gespräch der Gegenwart. Wege der Forschung*, V (Darmstadt, 1962), 290f.

[4] Ebeling, *ZThK* (1951), 206.

[5] Schwarz, *Fides, Spes und Caritas beim jungen Luther*, 79.

contemporary inspiration and apologetic concern behind this definition:

> Luther conceives *spiritus* primarily as a grace-filled power, i.e. a power which grants a new way of life. This power is effective in the new law, illumining as a Light and beckoning as a Voice. It is an entirely inward operation. (Bultmann would express it so today: the power of understanding and proclamation of the Word.)[1]

The danger of this 'Spiritualizing' interpretation is that, by excessively intertwining the theological and anthropological dimensions, one overlooks the distinctively down-to-earth anthropological meaning this concept has for Luther. And, further, with this interpretation one has difficulty distinguishing Luther's definition of *spiritus* from Tauler's definition of the *Seelengrund-Gemüt*.

Luther can and does, of course, bring *homo interior* and *Spiritus Sanctus* together.[2] But in the *Dictata* the term *spiritus* also has its own integrity, together with the sister terms *anima*, *cor*, *mens* and *conscientia*, as an anthropological designation of human being *qua* human being in clear distinction from *Spiritus Sanctus*.[3]

Luther showers a multitude of dignifying titles and attributes upon the soul. Man, he points out, is "heaven" by virtue of his soul.[4] His soul is directly created by God *ex nihilo*, without human seed,[5] and it is by its nature immortal.[6] It is a "temple of God," a dwelling-place

---

[1] Brandenburg, *Gericht und Evangelium*, 144-45.

[2] *WA* 3,474.23: "...anima in [sancto] spiritu erudita et homo interior..." See the marginal gloss on Romans 8:5 in reference to Galatians 5:19-22: "'Spiritus' proprie accipitur pro interiore homine, quod patet ex antithesi illa scil. 'caro' et 'spiritus.' Et infra: 'Spiritus vivit propter iustitiam' [Rom. 8:10]. Verumtamen 'Spiritus' i.e. homo interior non est, nisi spiritum sanctum habeat..." *WA* 56,75. 24ff.

[3] There is good support in the Augustinian tradition for a clearly anthropological application of the term *spiritus*. Cf. *De spiritu et anima*, IX, PL 40, 784. On the distinction between *spiritus hominis* and *Spiritus Dei* in Augustine's anthropology, see the discussion by Erich Dinkler, *Die Anthropologie Augustins* (Stuttgart, 1934), 153f.

[4] *WA* 3,139.28f(*Gl.* to Ps. 21:30): "...terrena regere est hominem, qui ad celum creatus est, descendere ad sese inferiora, cum ipse terra non sit sed celum secundum animam."

[5] *WA* 3,387.27: "...sine semine hominum nata est..." 4,290.19f: "*Manus tuae... fecerunt* ex nihilo secundum animam *me*..."

[6] *WA* 4,323.27f (*Schol.* to Ps. 118:44). Although the passage is in the context of a discussion of the *lex spiritualis*, this point is clearly made: "Spiritualis autem lex, que animam coram deo dirigit, quia est in immortali anima, que nunquam mutatur de esse suo, ideo semper durat ineternum."

where God is "immediately" present,[1] and a "womb" in which the words of God are conceived.[2]

What is even more striking than these titles of honor, however, are the qualifications which frequently accompany them. We call attention to three such qualifications.

First, Luther joins the 'celestial' nature of the soul to the imperative, *debere*. "The soul ought to seek heavenly goods;"[3] the interior man "ought to be spiritual through faith."[4] That the soul is 'heavenly' and 'spiritual' is not a conclusion deduced automatically from its intrinsic nature. It is a conclusion drawn in reference to the soul's purpose, not an achieved, ontological status. Indeed, the "wisdom of the flesh" is as near to the soul as the "wisdom of the Holy Spirit."[5] Further, the *debere* is fulfilled only from without. Only as the soul is trained in the Holy Spirit "through the Gospel or Scripture,"[6] and only as it is "cudgelled" and "refined" by the Word of God, is it prepared to be a vessel of the Holy Spirit and a "house of Christ."[7]

Another noteworthy qualification is the association of the dignity and immortality of the soul with a *promise* of God.[8] That God finds a 'dwelling-place' in the soul is not resultant simply from the excellence

[1] *WA* 3,148.19. Cf. 3,401.18ff (*Schol.* to Ps. 67:18): "Quia *Dominus in eis* per fidem *in Sina*. Non Sina quecunque, sed que est *in sancto*. In ipsis est dominus, ipsi autem in Sina, sed Sina est in sancto. Hec sunt tria tabernacula, anima, corpus et Ecclesia. Quia Deus immediate est in anima: et sequenter cum anima in corpore et cum utroque in communitate Ecclesie, que est sanctum."

[2] *WA* 4,376.27f (*Schol.* to Ps. 118:147): "Hoc est semen, quod ait: 'Ut meditarer eloquia tua,' id est ut conciperem semen tuum in utero anime mee..."

[3] *WA* 3,147.32 (*Gl.* to Ps. 25:10): "...anima, que celestia debet bona querere..."

[4] *WA* 4,447.18f (*Gl.* to Ps. 143:8): "...*dextera eorum*, homo interior et qui spiritualis esse per fidem debuit..." Note 3,258.21ff (*Schol.* to Ps. 44:3), where *homo interior* and *homo spiritualis* are paralleled in reference to a "per gratiam": "...Homo interior habeat pulchros oculos, pulchras aures, labia, genas, dentes, totam faciem, manus, pedes, ventrem etc, que omnia sunt in homine spirituali per gratiam et virtutes."

[5] *WA* 4,175.14ff (*Schol.* to Ps. 103:3): "Spiritus enim est superius, caro autem inferius hominis in hac vita. Et sic homo prout rationalis vel secundum animam est 'firmamentum inter aquas et aquas' (id est inter sapientiam carnis et spiritus). Si autem sese vertit ad sapientiam spiritus iam superiora eius teguntur aquis, quia non inferiora, sed superiora eius tegit aquis."

[6] *WA* 3,474.22ff (*Gl.* to Ps. 72:17): "Sic sanctuarium dei est illud, quod fit per Evangelium seu scripturam (i.e. anima in spiritu erudita et homo interior)."

[7] *WA* 3,261.4f (*Schol.* to Ps. 44:9): "Sicut quando anima expolitur et dolatur per verbum dei, paratur in vas unguentarium spiritus sancti et domum Christi."

[8] *WA* 3,302.13ff (*Schol.* to Ps. 53:6): "...Christus et Christiani licet secundum carnem patiantur et occidantur, tamen anima eorum semper salva evadit et nunquam comprehenditur, secundum quod dominus promisit: 'Nolite timere eos, qui occidunt corpus, animam autem non possunt occidere' [Matt. 10:28]."

it can claim for itself, but is within the context of a promise by God to dwell there.

> The sanctuary of God is nothing else than the soul spiritually turned to God. Since the soul is the seat of wisdom and in the middle of the people (i.e. in their hearts), He promises to dwell there.[1]

A final qualification comes as Luther points out that the soul's survival of the *nihileitas* to which the nature of the creature runs[2] occurs through "faith in Christ."[3] The soul is a womb in which the

[1] *WA* 3,479.21ff (*Schol.* to Ps. 72:17): "Sanctuarium enim Dei est non nisi anima spiritualiter ad deum conversa. Quia anima est sedes sapientie et in medio populi (id est corde eorum) habitare sese promittit." 4.347.3ff (*Schol.* to Ps. 118:83): "Propheta...vult, quod populus Israel a domino velut uter ["id est spiritus seu anima et voluntas hominis" 4.347.14f] paratus et per verbum promissionis in spe dilatatus, ut vinum Evangelicum in Christo futuro susciperet." See 3,399.29ff (*Schol.* to Ps. 67:14), where it is God's imputation that values the soul: "Quia [fideles anime] ornate auro et argento describuntur: non que homines querunt, sed spiritualibus, que deus pro auro et argento reputat ac sic nobis indicat per ea, que preciosissima sunt apud nos."

[2] *WA* 3,378.27f (*Schol.* to Ps. 65:3): "...auferendo quod dei est residuum quod nostrum est nihil est." 3,384.23f (*Gl.* 67:5): "...*qui* [Christus] *ascendit super occasum* super omnem creaturam, que ex natura sua ad occasum et nihil tendit." 4,453.31f (*Gl.* to Ps. 145:4): "Ergo cum seipsos non possint salvare, quomodo salvabunt in se confidentes? q.d. anima recedit et corpus in terram redit, quomodo ergo te salvabit?" These statements may admit interpretation within the framework of the neoplatonic distinction between the transitoriness of the creature ("ex natura sua ad occasum et nihil tendit"), and the permanence of the uncreated (God as "esse"). To counter this, we call attention to the following statements. "Infirmata est, i.e. agnoscit se infirmam, stultam et nihil: ideo tu robur, sapientia et entitas eius es. Quoniam qui se humiliat, infatuat, annihilat, exaltabitur, sapiens fit." 3,392.18ff (*Schol.* to Ps. 67:11). "Nam cum singulis diebus et horis beneficia dei acceperis, scil. vitam, esse, sensum, intellectum, insuper victum et amictum et ministerium solis, coeli et terre et omnium elementorum multis nimis varietatibus, manifestum est quod acceptis gratias debes." 3,429.19ff (*Schol.* to Ps. 68:17). In these statements *esse* and *entitas* concern the *beneficia dei*, and have reference to God's daily, providential and saving presence. They are not indicative of a grand metaphysical scheme. Also relevant to the discernment of the dividing line between neoplatonic vocabulary and neoplatonic content is Luther's interpretation of Exodus 3:14f, the traditional *locus classicus* for the definition of God as the '*esse*' sought by the philosophers. (In this regard, cf. Etienne Gilson, *Philosophie et incarnation selon Saint Augustin* (Montreal, 1947).) Luther finds in Exodus 3:14f an occasion to interrelate hearing, faith and the 'name'—not the *esse*—of God, in order to make a Christological point. "Unde in Evangelio dicit: 'Et manifestabo ei meipsum' [Joh. 14:21], q.d. iam nomen meum habetis, sed nondum meipsum. Denique nomen ex auditu cognoscitur, sed ipse per visionem. Auditus autem fidem, visio speciem habet. Et ita potest illud Exo. 3 [14-15, 6:3] intelligi, ubi dominus dicit, quod patribus Abraham, Isaac et Iacob non manifestavit nomen suum, sed nomen nominis. Quia fidem revelatam non habuerunt, sed credebant revelandam in nomine Ihesu Christi." 4,403.20ff (*Schol.* to Ps. 121:4).

[3] *WA* 4,408.29ff (*Gl.* to Ps. 123:3): "Sicut enim Christus proper immortalem

words of God are conceived, but "through faith."[1] And Christ sits in the souls of the faithful, but "upon faith."[2]

These qualifications of the excellence of the soul—(1) the imperative character of its 'heavenly' and 'spiritual' nature, and (2) the placement of its immortality and saving relationship to God within the historical context of (a) a promise made by God and (b) faith in Christ—find parallels in Luther's descriptions of the heart, spirit and conscience. The heart is described as a sanctuary of God,[3] where only God is able to speak[4] and exercise judgment.[5] But it is only by faith and hope that the heart is directed to God.[6] The promises of the law and prophets and the affectual responses of the people to these promises have reference to the spirit of man, and they should be understood as spiritual and not corporeal in nature.[7] Conscience is described as "our

---

divinitatem, licet mortuus esset secundum humanitatem, tamen semper fuit persona viva: ita quilibet Christianus, licet moriatur et occidatur, tamen propter fidem Christi in ipso semper vivit." 4,200.23 (*Gl.* to Ps. 105:20) "...gloria sua, i.e. fides anime..."

[1] *WA* 4,376.16f (*Schol.* to Ps. 118:147): "...habens verba per fidem habet omnia, licet abscondite."

[2] *WA* 4,126.17f (*Schol.* to Ps. 98:1): "Super fidem autem sedet Christus in animabus fidelium." Cf. 3,141.36ff (*Gl.* to Ps. 23:7): "Non enim intravit Christus ut rex glorie, nisi in celum ascendendo, et in animam, que est spirituale coelum, per fidem ingrediendo."

[3] *WA* 3,479.30f.

[4] *WA* 3,348.10ff (*Schol.* to Ps. 59:8): "Quare autem 'cor'? Quia deus non ad aures sicut homo, sed tantummodo ad cor loquitur. Ideo cum vox hominis ad cor loqui nequeat, sed tantum ad aures, sequitur quod solum eructet verbum et non loquatur, quia Deus ipsum loquitur solus, qui solus ad cor loquitur." In regard to this 'devaluation' of the *vox humana*, cf. 3,262.6ff, 30ff, where of the three modes of revelation discussed, the *last*, and in a valuative sense, is that "per verbum externum et linguam ad aures hominum." Over against both these passages, however, see 4,229.37ff, where the *vox humana* is described as the *only* "*pes*" for truth (*veritas*).

[5] *WA* 3,319.21ff.

[6] *WA* 3.567.3ff (*Schol.* to Ps. 77:8): "Dirigitur enim cor, quando a se ad dominum tenditur: que est vera directio: que fit per fidem et spem. Non potest cor in dominum dirigi nisi fide..."

[7] *WA* 4,160.16ff (*Schol.* to Ps. 101:12): "Ideo secundum spiritum necesse est eam [misericordia] accipere, ut nos accipimus. Eodem modo de omnibus promissionibus legis et prophetarum, ubi semper assumuntur nomina de rebus temporalibus. Et in hoc Iudei occiduntur litera, et tamen sub illis spiritualia intelligi vult. Sic veritas, iustitia, iudicium, sapientia, bonitas, potentia, virtus, fortitudo..." 3,583.19ff (*Schol.* to Ps. 77:37): "Igitur timor, amor, spes, odium, gaudium, tristitia, omnia nunc sunt aliter quam olim, scilicet spiritualium: tunc autem corporalium." Also Luther speaks of a "sensibilitas in spiritu," having reference to a seeing, hearing and sensing God's omnipresence: "...impius est insensibilis ad timorem dei, quia prophanus et immundus... Quanto autem purior et sanctior est, tanto maioris est sensibilitatis in spiritu. Talis enim ubique videt, audit et sensit

place, where we ought to dwell with God as a bride with her bridegroom;" but it is a conscience burnished by the yoke of compunction,[1] and dwelling in the house that faith builds for the soul, that attains such distinction: "fides est locus animae, quia domus conscientiae nostrae."[2]

Finally, we call attention to the fact that the soul, heart, spirit and conscience are not only, *mutatis mutandis*, subjects of dignifying titles and attributes, but also places where the *enemies of God* are at home. Not only are good things in the soul, but also sins, miseries and evils.[3]

---

deum presentem." 4,246.30ff (*Schol.* to Ps. 110:9). In light of Schwarz's discernment of an "absoluter Gegensatz" between the *intelligere* of faith and the *sentire* of philosophical understanding and Jewish self-understanding *(Fides, Spes und Caritas beim jungen Luther*, 136), we call attention to Luther's ability to speak of a *sentire of faith* in contrast to the *insensibilitas* of the impious.

[1] *WA* 3,593.27ff (*Schol.* to Ps. 77:46): "Unde et Iohannes baptista locustas comedebat. Et debet noster cibus esse locusta, ut locus noster, in quo nos cum deo, sponsus cum sponsa, habitare debet (id est conscientia), ustus sit et absumptus per iugem iram compunctionis, secundum ps. 4 [5]: 'Irascimini et nolite peccare'."

[2] *WA* 3,651.2f (*Schol.* to Ps. 83:7). See further 3,603.11ff (*Schol.* to Ps. 78:7): "Locus sane est fides in conscientia seu conscientia in fide: que est locus, in quo edificantur bona doctrinarum, scientie, sapientie, intellectus..."; and 3,504.11ff (*Schol.* to Ps. 73:11): "Quia sicut homo in sinu corporali; ita Christus per fidem requiescit in sinu cordis, in memoria et conscientia quieta... Et sic sinus Abrahe dicitur conscientia fidei Abrahe: in quo recipiuntur omnes fideles et membra Christi." Hans M. Müller's statement is thus straight to the point: "Weder die Seele noch das Gewissen, sondern der Glaube an Christus hat Gottes Verheissung." *Erfahrung und Glaube bei Luther* (Leipzig, 1929), 127. In his study of Luther's understanding of conscience, Emmanuel Hirsch draws conclusions with another concern. "Nun ist das Gewissen nach Luther der Kern, die Mitte der ganzen lebendigen menschlichen Innerlichkeit und Persönlichkeit." "Eben das ist der eigentümliche Nerv seiner Anschauung vom Menschen, daß er *das Gewissen als Messer der Lebensführung und das Gewissen als Träger des Gottesverhältnisses als eine durch nichts zu zerschneidende Einheit ansieht*." *Lutherstudien*, I (Gütersloh, 1954), 150, 166. To the extent that Luther parallels or synonomizes *anima*, *cor*, *mens* and *spiritus* with *conscientia*, Hirsch's remarks say nothing about the latter which is not also applicable to the former. The very flexibility of Luther's use of these terms as synonomous ways in which man's life before God can be summarized comprehensively, indicates that *fides* and *spes*, not an anthropological "Kern", will carry man's relationship to God. See our discussion *infra*, 118ff. A fundamental problem with Hirsch's approach to Luther's anthropology is his quidditative focus. This is further indicated when he interprets the *spiritus hominis* (with reference to *WA* 3,478.5ff, 638.23ff, 4,286.15ff) as the *synteresis*. *Ibid.*, 111. See our criticism, *infra*, p. 197, note 1, and our discussion of Karl Holl's interpretation of Luther's "Religion" as "Gewissensreligion," *infra*, p. 198, note 2.

[3] *WA* 3,233.28ff (*Gl.* to Ps. 41:5): "Magnum verbum est effundere animam, i.e. coram deo, ubi deus videt, quia est omnia que in anima sunt, scil. peccata, miserias, bona malaque Deo confiteri et nihil abscondere et negare. Item adhuc est se humiliare, i.e. se confiteri esse effusum et nihil habere." See in reference to the doctrine of original sin, 4,55.6ff, 392.21ff, 354.23ff.

Pride appears in the spirit, in the heart and in the mind.[1] Flesh and its understanding are not only the enemies of the interior man, but "members of his very household!"[2] Conscience is a "basket of sins,"[3] a "bed of suffering"—"suffering from its sins."[4] And it is in the heart and conscience that righteousness and truth find, engage and accuse iniquity and impiety.[5]

In these various descriptions of the soul, heart, spirit and conscience of man, we do not find a clear picture of human life as a 'double life,' divided into two parts, one naturally limited to the sensible world, the other naturally oriented to an intelligible order. We find a much more complex picture, lacking the terminological precision and consistency which we have encountered in Tauler and Gerson. It is a picture of a man who is operationally united *(totus homo velut unum membrum)*, endowed with dignifying titles which are not infrequently neoplatonic

---

[1] *WA* 4,128.38-129.29-31 (*Gl.* to Ps. 100:5): "Totus psalmus [100] loquitur contra hypocrisim illam scilicet spiritualem superbiam, que est de bonis spiritualibus superbire et confidere: que est multo peior quam corporalis superbia, ut in Iudeis, hereticis et nostro tempore religiosis multis. Ergo humiliatum spiritum et non corpus requirit Dominus." 4,420.29 (*Gl.* to 130:2): "Ex superbia enim cordis oritur superbia mentis." In reference to the soul: "...dicit: *libera animam meam.* Quia perfidia et superbus sensus non corpus, sed animam querit occidere." 4,394. 9f (*Schol.* to Ps. 30:10).

[2] *WA* 3,167.30f (*Schol.* to Ps. 119:2): "...caro et sensus sunt domestici hominis interioris et ideo inimici eius sicut Iudei Christo."

[3] *WA* 3,617.14f (*Schol.* to Ps. 80:7): "Cophinus ergo est conscientia peccatorum: immo dorsum est conscientia, que portat onera."

[4] *WA* 3,231.13ff (*Schol.* to Ps. 40:3-4): "*Dominus conservet eum* etc. 'Lectus doloris' primo est conscientia pre peccatis suis dolens, quia in sola conscientia quiescit anima vel inquietatur, per gratiam vel culpam. Non enim est dolor super dolorem conscientie, ideo est lectus doloris, in quo cogitur iacere peccator post peccatum. Et deberet quidem esse lectus ad quietem. Sed nunc per peccatum est lectus doloris; non enim potest fugere a conscientia sua propria: ideo est lectus. Et tamen non quiescere in ea: ideo est doloris." See 3,309.25ff, 4.67.29ff.

[5] *WA* 3,624.29ff (*Schol.* to Ps. 81:8): "...Christus dixit: 'Videbitis filium hominis in nubibus etc' [Matt. 26:64]. Ita veritas illis loquitur occulte: quia non sunt tam mali, quin audiant intus synteresim et suspicentur atque timeant, ne forte palam fiat eorum iniquitas tandem et prevaleat veritas contra eos. Hic timor, hec suspitio est admonitio illa, quam Christus tunc illis verbis significavit et eis dedit. Hoc est quod dicit: 'in medio autem deos diiudicat.' In medio scilicet eorum, id est in corde eorum verberat conscientias. Hec omnia faciunt, quia noverunt veritatem qualis quantaque est et suam voluntatem preferunt ei." 3,625.4ff (*Schol.* to Ps. 81:1): "In medio autem iudicemus eos: quia spiritualis omnia iudicat et ipse a nemine iudicatur. Non enim potest fieri, ut impius visa constantia iusti apud se non confundatur et iudicetur a propria conscientia: hoc autem iudicium quis agit, nisi iustitia iusti? que contra impiorum in corde dicit: 'usquequo iudicas iniquitatem?'..." Note that the censure comes from without; an 'objective reference' awakens conscience. In regard to its importance for the *synteresis*, see *infra*, p. 149ff.

in terminology, yet sufficiently qualified so as to leave no serious doubt that he possesses no 'natural' claim on things divine. The attainment of the latter is a possibility *de facto* contingent upon the promises of God and faith in Christ.

From the foregoing, it is clear that Luther is not primarily concerned with an evaluation of the *quidditates animae*—an enterprise he is apparently content to concede to the philosophers.[1] His concern is with the *vita animae*, and that means *vita totius hominis* in its subjection to the power of sin and the power of God's promises and faith in Christ. He speaks of man *secundum animam* primarily, but not simply, because the philosophical, theological and ecclesiological traditions out of which he thinks, dispose him to do so. He also speaks of man in this way because the terms *anima*, *cor*, *spiritus* and *conscientia* provide him with a kind of anthropological 'shorthand' which he can flexibly employ to speak of his overriding concern: the theoretical and existential understanding of the *vita fidei*.

4. THE EXISTENTIALIST THESIS: ITS RELEVANCE AND ITS WEAKNESS

From our foregoing discussion, it would appear that the existentialist approach is the more fruitful way to an understanding of the 'dualism' that pervades the *Dictata*. Indeed, Luther can make it quite clear that the "interior and hidden man" is not a soteriologically potent higher part of the soul, but a way of living for the whole life of man: "...man is called an interior and hidden man when he does not live in a secular, carnal way."[2] And Luther can leave no doubt that "adherence to the flesh" does not concern the proclivities of a lower part of human nature, but the lively migration of the interior into the old and exterior man.[3] Here the categories of Existentialist Philosophy present a much clearer picture of Luther's intention than do those of Neoplatonism.

[1] *WA* 4,188.12f (*Schol.* to Ps. 103:24): "...philosophia et humana sapientia, que solum quidditates querit..." Cf. 3,419.25ff, where the same judgment is expressed in the concern to interpret *fides* as *substantia* in Holy Scripture. We consider this passage, *infra*, p. 105ff. Also relevant in this regard are the *scholia* on Romans 8:19, considered *infra*, 202ff.

[2] *WA* 3,150.19ff (*Schol.* to Ps. 26:5): "...omnis gloria eius sit in sola anima sed sic quia homo dicitur interior et absconditus eo quod non vivit seculariter et carnaliter."

[3] *WA* 4,174.5f (*Schol.* to Ps. 103:3): "Carni autem adherere est hominem interiorem in veterem et exteriorem nimis migrasse..."

But let us go deeper. In the *glossa* and *scholia* on psalm 26, two passages reveal the demarcation line between the relevance of the neoplatonic and existentialist theses. They suggest, further, that the latter may ultimately be just as inadequate as the former in penetrating the full range of Luther's thought. The first passage is a marginal gloss on verse 8. Luther writes:

> Our [higher powers of] understanding *(mens)* form our 'face;' [our lower powers of] sensation *(sensus)* our 'back.' For through our sensitive powers we are turned to creatures, and through our powers of understanding to God. If we turn the latter also to creatures, then we turn our face away from God and turn our back to Him.[1]

In this passage, Luther is in agreement with the traditional interpretation of *ratio superior* and *ratio inferior*, as this was understood in the neoplatonic-Augustinian tradition. He makes no mention of faith and unbelief; he speaks of two parts of the soul (*mens* and *sensus*) and their appropriate *natural* orientations. Although he does appeal to divine illumination for the constitution of *mens* as *facies*,[2] he has said nothing that advances beyond the anthropology of Tauler or Gerson.

Let us look, however, at the *scholion* on verse 9. Here it is clear that Luther's use of the terms, "nostra facies" and "nostrum dorsum," concerns an intellective and affective conversion to God through true faith *(per veram fidem)* and an intellective and affective turning elsewhere through unbelief *(per incredulitatem)*.[3] Reference is made to Gerson in this passage precisely at that point which we found to be most decisive in his anthropology, viz., the reciprocal operation of *intellectus* and *affectus*. Luther's appeal to faith and unbelief, however, is his own insertion. It is a fundamental exception from Gerson and may be closely paralleled with the exception he will later (1515-16) take in his notes on Tauler's Sermons, where *fides*—not the *synteresis*—is definitive of the spiritual man.[4]

In this *scholion*, Luther is not speaking of something that can be

---

[1] *WA* 3,149.28ff (*Gl.* to Ps. 26:8): "Mens nostra est facies nostra, sensus autem est dorsum nostrum. Quia per sensum vertimur ad creaturas, per mentem ad deum. Si autem mentem etiam ad creaturas vertimus, tunc avertimus faciem a deo et dorsum ei vertimus." See Gerson, *supra*, p. 61, n. 2.

[2] *WA* 3,149.34f (*Gl.* to Ps. 26:8): "Immo mens non dicitur facies, nisi quando est illustrata et noscibilis deo facta, quod fit per cognitionem dei."

[3] *WA* 3,151.5ff (*Schol.* to Ps. 26:9): "Facies nostra est mens nostra, id est secundum Ioh. Gerson anima per intellectum et affectum ad deum conversa (quod fit proprie per fidem veram...). Econtra dorsum nostrum est anima per intellectum et affectum a deo aversa, quod fit per incredulitatem."

[4] See *supra*, p. 2f.

interpreted exhaustively by the thesis of Hunzinger. But can it be so interpreted in terms of "Existenzmöglichkeiten?" We think not. What Luther retains and theologically re-interprets from the neo-platonic world-view is the central importance of the objective reference. The existential dimension of 'turning' is there. But it is a turning to something, to a 'place' and a 'reality' which can support one's *intellectus* and *affectus*.

In order to bring this point to greater precision, we call attention to several other important passages. In the *scholia* on psalm 67, Luther contrasts two forms of sleep:[1] the "sleep of the world," which characterizes the carnal man, and the "sleep of the Church," which is appropriate to the spiritual man. The former is a sleep in the spirit of man. It is without vigilance to God. Here one finds all those who, before God and in their spirit, have set aside eternal things and seek and find their joy, hope, fear and suffering in transitory things.[2]

On the other hand, the sleep of the Church is a sleep with regard to the flesh and the world. It exhibits the spirit's alertness to God. Here one finds the *sancti*, who use the things of the world as though they did not use them, i.e. they are "always somewhere else in their heart," locating their concerns "in heaven."[3]

What is the primary focus of these passages? Is it two opposed "Existenzmöglichkeiten" available to one and the same man, or is it something both deeper and more comprehensive? We find the latter clearly to be the case and consider the language of Existentialist Philosophy too weak to carry it. For Luther's primary focus here is

[1] *WA* 3,397.35ff (*Schol.* to Ps. 67:14): "Ubi sciendum, quod preter corporalem somnum et mortem corporalem, que etiam somnus in Scripturis dicitur, est duplex somnus, unus Ecclesie, alter mundi. Quia sicut alter alteri est mutuo crucifixus, stultus, infirmus, homo spiritualis et homo carnalis, unde oritur duplex sapientia, crux, infirmitas, fortitudo, stultitia..."

[2] *WA* 3,398.5ff (*Schol.* to Ps. 67:14): "Mundi est dormire in spiritu, non vigilare deo. Hoc est ludere in rerum affectu et omnino involvi. Quia sicut dormiens non veris rebus gaudet, tristatur, sed phantasmatibus et rerum imaginibus fallitur: ita coram deo et in spiritu omnes, qui in rebus transitoriis, posthabitis eternis, gaudent, sperant, timent, dolent, in imaginibus falluntur..."

[3] *WA* 3,398.27ff (*Schol.* to Ps. 67:14): "Ecclesie est dormire secundum carnem et mundo: vigilare autem deo, sicut illi vigilant mundo.//Quia sicut dormiens non videt res foris, que sunt in mundo: ita sancti sic utuntur rebus, quasi non utantur (utentes hoc mundo tanquam non utentes) [I Cor. 7:31]. Et semper alibi sunt in corde. Quia in coelis est conversatio eorum." Note that among the 'worldly' things that divert the "via ad coelum" are indulgences: "...Putamus nos aliquid esse et sufficienter agere: ac sic nihil conamur et nullum violentiam adhibemus et multum facilitamus viam ad coelum, per indulgentias, per faciles doctrinas, quod unus gemitus satis est." 3,416.20ff (*Schol.* to Ps. 68:1).

upon two opposed objective references, two opposed 'objective contexts,' two opposed 'places' to which and in which the heart of man directs and locates its hope and fear, and from which it receives its joy and suffering: *in rebus transitoriis—in coelis*.

When this 'objective context,' in which not only man's possibilities but also the realities which empower them are emphatically exalted, is short-circuited by a short-sighted focus upon man's existential possibilities, then we come very close to interpreting Luther with a refined version of the neoplatonic-Augustinian doctrine of two opposed and exclusive parts of the soul. Obedience to *ratio superior* and subservience to *ratio inferior* are also "Existenzmöglichkeiten."

If the relevance of existentialist terminology is to be fully exploited, its insights must be placed within a more extentive interpretive framework, one that can carry the *extra nos* as well as the *pro nobis* and can speak meaningfully of the *remembered* past and *promised* future works of God as well as dismiss an objectifying *fides historica*. A salutary first step is taken when we see that, for Luther, the primary incompatibility and mutual exclusivity concern objective 'goods': "the goods of the flesh and the goods of the Spirit are not compatible, and they mutually exclude and impede one another."[1] The reaction *in* the "land of promise," where no reality is present except the Word of God, is the decisive factor in the definition of *homo spiritualis* and *homo carnalis*.[2]

We have taken only the first step in our effort to formulate a more extensive interpretive horizon for Luther's thought. Throughout the remainder of this chapter, we will be concerned to clarify and deepen the importance of what we have described as an 'objective context.' We turn first to a consideration of Luther's attempt to specify the terms, *substantia*, *memoria*, *intellectus* and *affectus*, as these become his controlling concepts for the interpretation of the *vita fidei*.

---

[1] *WA* 4,377.26ff (*Schol.* to Ps. 118:151): "Cum ergo horum [i.e. bona carnalia] contraria in sanctis Christi et in viis eius videant, scilicet paupertatem, contemptum et mala carnalia, ignorantes et scire nolentes, quod per illa bona figurata sunt meliora, quibus venientibus figuralia cessare oportuit, eo maxime quod non sunt compatibilia bona carnis et spiritus et mutuo sese excludunt et impediunt."

[2] *WA* 4,382.3ff (*Schol.* to Ps. 118:162): "Ut figura filiorum Israel, quibus omnia deesse videbantur in deserto, ut etiam manna eis nausea esset, querulantibus quod in deserto essent sterilitatis; ita verbum dei audituros necesse est in desertum duci, ubi nihil sit, quod caro postulat. Sed crucifixa ipsa omnibus ablatis, que sunt carnis, solummodo spiritus pasci et duci debet in terram promissionis, id est spiritualis homo. Ideo necesse est carnalis homo hic murmuret, quia nihil invenit, quod sibi placitum est. Sic quanto carnalior et mundanior homo, tanto plura habet, que causetur in verbum dei."

5. *SUBSTANTIA*

In the *scholia* to psalm 68, Luther presents a threefold consideration of "substance in Scripture." This is undertaken in explicit contradistinction to what he describes as a philosophical understanding of substance. Although we find these comments to form a unified statement, we will guide the reader's eye alphabetically in accordance with what we consider to be Luther's theoretical division.

(a) In Scripture, "substance" is a metaphor. It concerns a 'place' where one can stand firm and settle down *(substaculum seu subsidentia)*,[1] a place where he can set his 'feet' *(affectus* and *intellectus)*,[2] confident that he will not sink and become engulfed "in the depths," i.e. in the abyss of sin and death.

(b) Thus, substance concerns all that by means of which one subsists and sustains his life, as is exemplified when one speaks of the rich subsisting through riches, the healthy through health, the honored through the honor bestowed on him, the pleasure-seeker through something pleasurable. It is obvious, therefore, that substance has reference to an outwardly received qualification of human life. It concerns "qualities," not "quiddities of things." 'Where' one lives and 'how' one lives constitutes his 'substance' in this life. In the absence of riches, one lives 'as' a pauper and 'in' poverty; only 'in' riches is he rich.

(c) The *sancti* do not subsist and flourish by means of the goods of the world. Rather, they support their lives in and through a better and more permanent substance. This is the substance of things which are not yet visibly present, i.e. things which are still future and in which they can only believe and for which they can only hope (Heb. 10:34, 11:1).

(d) In Scripture, then, 'substance' is what supports and embraces

1 Luther's definition of *substantia* as a "substaculum seu subsidentia in qua pedibus stari potest" (cf. *infra*, p. 106, note 1) and the non-quidditative interpretation of *qualitates* and *accidens* which it clearly calls for, separates him *in fundamento* from Thomas and the *habitus* speculation of the late Middle Ages. As Ebeling points out: "Es ist eine unerhörte Umkehrung des Substanzbegriffes." *ZThK* (1951), 192. For possible sources in the medieval exegetical and systematic traditions for Luther's interpretation of *substantia*, see Schwarz, *Fides, Spes und Caritas beim jungen Luther*, 162.

2 Luther speaks of the *pedes animae* as simply "affectiones" (*WA* 3,145.4, 332.32), as "affectus et voluntas" (3,147.16), and as "voluntates et desyderia" (3,117.24). But most consistently he means both: *intellectus and affectus* (cf. 4,259.23). This will be further documented as the study proceeds.

one's whole life; it includes all the accidental, i.e. extrinsically received, qualifications in body and soul.[1]

A similar presentation is found in a second *scholion* on the same psalm. Here Luther points out that the substance of the ambitious is glory, the rich, riches, the gluttonous, food and their belly, the prodigal, sensual pleasure. Christ destroyed these forms of substance; they are now not objects to which one can turn with confidence, nor places in which one can locate and live his life. Christ's death and that of the martyrs are witnesses to the fact that to trust and flourish "in oneself and in the world" is to attempt to ground one's life in a bottomless pit. Honor, riches and pleasure are not constitutive of the sphere in which Christ and the martyrs subsisted. They point to a life without these forms of substance, a life turned and grounded elsewhere: in the "substance of God" and the "substance of faith."[2] As Luther ex-

---

[1] *WA* 3,419.25-420.11 (*Schol.* to Ps. 68:2): "Substantia in Scriptura metaphorice accipitur tam ex grammaticali quam physicali significatione. Et proprie, non ut philosophi de ea loquuntur, hic accipienda est. Sed pro substaculo seu subsidentia, in qua pedibus stari potest, ut non in profundum labantur et mergantur. Et sic Christus non habuit tale substaculum vite, quin caderet omnino in mortem. Si autem passus solum, non usque in mortem fuisset, substantiam utique habuisset et in quo constitisset. Secundo potest hic accipi, sicut Sapient. ait: 'De substantia tua honora deum' [Prov. 3:9]. Et Apostolus: 'In hac substantia glorie' [2 Cor. 11:17]... Sic enim dicitur omne illud, per quod quisque (in sua vita) subsistit: ut dives subsistit per divitias, sanus per sanitatem, honoratus per honorem, voluptarii per voluptatem. Quia tam diu sunt tales, quam diu ista durant. Et sic substantia proprie magis est qualitas vel extrinsecum quam ipsa essentia rei. Quia Scriptura nihil curat quidditates rerum, sed qualitates tantum. Et sic qualiter unusquisque est et agit, secundum hoc habet substantiam: qua si caret, iam non subsistit. Quare pauper, abiectus, afflictor sui sunt sine substantia. Denique substantia magis de bonis mundi dicitur. Quare breviter quicquid est in mundo, quo aliquis potest secundum hanc vitam subsistere et florere, substantia dicitur. Sed sancti talem non habent. Heb. 10[:34]: 'Consyderantes vos habere meliorem et permanentem substantiam.' Et 'fides est substantia rerum sperandarum' [Heb. 11:1], id est possessio et facultas rerum, non mundanarum (que est visio vel sensus), sed futurarum. Credo autem, quod spiritus sanctus dedita opera contrario modo philosophis substantia utatur, scilicet pro accidentibus bonis fortune, corporis et anime et pro tota duratione existentie, non prout contra accidens distinguitur, sed propter accidentia, etiam ea includens."

[2] *WA* 3,440.34-441.10 (*Schol.* to Ps. 68:1f): "Substantia...ambitiosorum est gloria, divitum divitie, gulosorum esca et venter, luxuriosorum voluptas. Has autem substantias Christus per suam non substantiam omnes destruxit: ut fideles in illis non subsistant nec confidant, sed sint sine substantia, habeant autem fidem pro eis, que est substantia alia, scil. substantia dei. Sicut mors Christi destruxit vitam glorie, divitiarum, ut in ea non vivant neque subsistant. Et sic nomen substantie similiter quadrupliciter potest accipi. Primo ad literam de Christi naturali vita. Secundo martyrum similiter. Tercio quod agnoscunt sese non habere substantiam fidei, vel timeant et videant, quoniam omnia que sunt in se et mundo, sunt non substantia, sed limus profundi. O felix, qui hoc videre potest, quia talis

presses it elsewhere, the world is no "stable foundation for confidence;"[1] God is the only "firmament" "on which [one] can stand and abide."[2]

This understanding of *fides* and *spes* as the 'substance' of Christian life is the major ingredient in Luther's statements that faith is the "substance, foundation, origin, source, beginning and first principle of all spiritual graces, gifts, powers, merits and works;"[3] a "rock, substance [and] ground;"[4] the "work and power of God;"[5] and the "cornerstone of the whole of salvation."[6] It is the major theological presupposition behind the insistence that the "wisdom of faith" is the instrument Christ employs to create Christians;[7] that only the "salvation," "redemption" and "righteousness of faith" are eternal;[8] that

---

facile contemnit ea omnia et aliam substantiam querit. Cui enim honor et divitie et voluptas non est substantia, et tamen se in eis videt, sine dubio contritus est spiritus eius et anxius. Et fit contemptor glorie, pauper et afflictus. Quarto prophetice, quod pre abundantia iniquitatis substantia fidei peribit sicut dominus predixit: 'putas inveniet fidem in terra?' [Luke 18:8]." In reference to *spes*, see 4,352.5ff (*Schol.* to Ps. 118:96): "Qui autem spe vivit in mandato et verbo dei, nihil possidens in hoc mundo, nihil de istis angustis rebus cupiens, ipse utique vivit in latitudine spiritus."

[1] *WA* 4,453.7ff (*Gl.* to Ps. 145:2): "*Nolite confidere*, quia non sunt stabile fundamentum confidentie...*in principibus*, ergo multo minus in aliquod aliud in mundo; in filiis hominum, talibus inquam, qui sunt filii hominum, q.d. sunt caro et homines, non deus, *in quibus...non est salus* vera."

[2] *WA* 3,453.40ff (*Schol.* to Ps. 70:3): "Et...ratio datur petitionis, q.d. mea conditio et salus ita sese habet, ut solum in te possit solida permanere, quia non ex carne eam habeo. Ideo aliis quidem firmamentum est mammon, honor, quia quam diu illa sunt, ipsi honorati, divites sunt. Sed meum (id est ego qui tuis divitiis inhio) non potest esse aliud firmamentum, in quo consistam et permaneam, nisi tu solus."

[3] *WA* 3,649.17ff (*Schol.* to Ps. 83:7): "...substantia, fundamentum, fons, origo, principium, primogenitum omnium spiritualium gratiarium, donorum, virtutum, meritorum, operum." Cf. 4,166.23ff, 167,4ff, 13ff.

[4] *WA* 3,641.27 (*Gl.* to Ps. 83:7).

[5] *WA* 3,532.13ff (*Schol.* to Ps. 76:12-13): "Opus dei et virtus eius est fides: ipsa enim facit iustos et operatur omnes virtutes, castigat et crucifigit et infirmat carnem: ut ipsa non habeat opus suum nec virtutem, sed ut opus dei in illa. Et sic salvat et roborat spiritum." Cf. 4,40.5ff.

[6] *WA* 4,215.23ff (*Gl.* to Ps. 107:2): "...Quidquid de Christo intelligi potest ut capite, etiam de ecclesia et fide eius intelligi potest. Fides enim est caput virtutum sicut Christus sanctorum, et lapis a multis reprobatus, sed tamen fundamentum angulare totius salutis."

[7] *WA* 4,428.10f (*Gl.* to Ps. 135:5).

[8] *WA* 4,246.18ff (*Schol.* to Ps. 110:9): "*Mandavit ineternum testamentum suum.* Testamentum novum eternum est, quia eternam salutem et redemptionem operatur. Sicut iustitia fidei est eterna, cum tamen fides non sit eterna, sed iustitia, quam dat fides: ita testamentum Christi non est eternum, sed salus et redemptio et remissio, quam dat testamentum eius."

it is faith in which every good thing is contained;[1] and that *credere* and *sperare* are the proper correlates of *habere*.[2] It is the major factor in the description of faith as our "shield,"[3] and hope as our "refuge" in this life.[4] And it makes clear Luther's conviction that all *fideles* (and Jesus) live "by sheer hope alone"[5] "in God's Word alone," '*res*-less' before men.[6] Thus, he concludes that "all our joy is in the hope of future things,"[7] and "all our goods are only in words and promises."[8]

From our consideration of Luther's interpretation of *substantia*, we draw the following conclusions, which will be tested and developed further in our sections on *memoria* and *intellectus* and *affectus*.

1. Luther consciously outlines a distinctively theological definition of *substantia*. He will be understood as speaking of a reality which only theological concepts *(in Scriptura)* can express. This is hardly surprising since from his earliest work he has insisted upon the

[1] *WA* 4,266.26f (*Gl.* to Ps. 115:11): "...solum qui credunt, sunt veraces, quia fides est veritas. Sed hec fides in qua omne bonum tenetur, donum dei est."

[2] *WA* 3,180.24ff (*Gl.* to Ps. 32:22): "*Fiat misericordia* gratia *tua domine super nos: quemadmodum speravimus in te*, quia tantum habemus, quantum credimus et speramus. Credenti enim omnia possibilia sunt..." 3,450.35 (*Gl.* to Ps. 70:7): "...omnia mea in fide et spe habeo..." 4,150.10ff (*Schol.* to Ps. 101:3): "Et hunc [Jesus Christ] scire est omnia scire et habere. Facies enim notitia est domini, que nunc per fidem in nobis est, tunc autem per speciem." Compare Luther's earlier interpretation of *facies*, *supra*, 102.

[3] *WA* 4,62.12ff, 62.1ff.

[4] *WA* 4,98.20f.

[5] *WA* 3,410.16ff (*Gl.* to Ps. 68:4): "...*Spero in deum meum*, quia non est substantia sed sola spes: q.d. nuda spe adhuc sum superstes, ceteris omnibus destitutis a me, q.d. nihil factus sum, nisi quod spero reparari a deo et resuscitari." 4,266.24ff (*Schol.* to Ps. 115:10): "Quia Christus negatur fidem habuisse, eo quod fuit simul et comprehensor. Si tamen velimus dicere, quod sicut spem habuit, ita et fidem: sine dubio enim speravit sui corporis glorificationem, quam tamen nondum vidit in presentia: ergo et credidit, non obstante, quod eam clarius vidit in verbo, quam nunc videt in proprio genere."

[6] *WA* 4,355.29f (*Schol.* to Ps. 118:103): "Sancti enim in conspectu hominum nihil habent nisi spem; ideo despiciuntur ab illis, qui habent rem in conspectu hominum." 4,381.38ff (*Schol.* to Ps. 118:161): "...ille consolatur virtute eloquiorum. Mira permutatio, ut verba prevaleant rebus et rebus contrariis atque fortissimis! Sicut promisit Isaie: 'Dominus dedit mihi linguam eruditam, ut sciam sustentare eum qui lassus est, verbo [Isa. 50:4].' Verbo inquit, scilicet nudo sine re exhibita, sed non sine re exhibenda." 4,390.3ff (*Schol.* to Ps. 118:168): "Sed in paupertate, ignominia, cruce servat nudus nuda verba. Quia scilicet non vivit hominibus in re, sed deo in spe. Et omnes vie eius coram deo."

[7] *WA* 4,380.35ff (*Schol.* to Ps. 118:162): "Omnis nostra letitia est in spe futurorum et non in re presentium. Ideo enim gaudemus, quia promissionibus divinis credimus, et que promittit, speramus atque diligimus. Quia non ait 'letabor ego super divitias mundi,' sed 'super eloquia tua'."

[8] *WA* 4,272.16f (*Schol.* to Ps. 115:10): "...Omnia nostra bona sunt tantum in verbis et promissis."

integrity and distinctiveness of theological language and subject matter.[1]

2. The substance which constitutes the Christian is a 'place' where he can stand with all his intellective and affective powers, confidently 'subsisting' and 'flourishing' in the face of a death which destroys all temporal 'ground' on which he might attempt to stand. This substance is not present and visible to him; still, his faithful and hopeful orientation to it and expectation of it 'substantiate' his life before God and in the face of sin and death.

3. Luther emphatically accents the *extra nos* of this substance: *substantia rerum sperandarum*. To engage his thought on this score an extensive interpretive horizon is imperative, an horizon which is broad enough to take into account not only the 'subsistence' of faith as an existential possibility, but also the 'objective context' which empowers this possibility. The *substaculum* and *subsidentia* as well as the *subsistere* and *florere* must be embraced.

Ebeling has taught us well that, for Luther, "the meaning of substance is decided in human existence."[2] It is an existential, not a theoretical definition. But seen soteriologically, this existence has quite specific and indispensable *termini* for Luther. It 'remembers' past works of God and 'hopes' in future works of God. And these *termini*, *extra nos* (i.e. accessible in memory and hope), compose the objective context without which the 'subsistence' of faith could never occur. Memory and hope form the contextual *conditio sine qua non* for the emergence and persistence of the existential possibility of faith.

---

[1] In the commentary on Lombard (1509-10), we find the statement: "Sicut nemo potest sine fundamento aedificare, ita sine fide nemo sperare et bene agere. Ex hoc autem, quod dicit: 'sperandarum rerum,' sequitur quasi corolarium quod fides sit 'argumentum non apparentium,' quia 'spes quae videtur non est spes' [Heb. 11:1; Rom. 8:24]. Non est itaque determinatio phisica vel logica, sed theologica. Sicut quasi diceretur: Quid est Christus? Respondet logicus: est persona, etc. Theologus autem: est 'petra', 'lapis angularis', etc. Sic fides est argumentum i.e. signum etc, est merum accidens relativum, sicut quid est homo? Respondetur: est filius dei." *Luthers Werke in Auswahl*, 5, *Der junge Luther*, ed. Erich Vogelsang (Berlin, 1955), 17.4ff (=*WA* 9,91.18ff). The "determinatio phisica vel logica," which Luther mentions, reflects his nominalist training. See Occam, *Expositio in Librum Porphyrii de Praedicabilibus*, ch. II, §10, in *Gulielmi Ockham*, *Expositionis in Libros Artis Logicae Prooemium et Expositio in Librum Porphyrii de Praedicabilibus*, ed. Ernest A. Moody (St. Bonaventure, N.Y., 1965), 31f.

[2] Ebeling, *ZThK* (1951), 192.

6. *MEMORIA*

Writing in explicit contradistinction to the analysis of "parts of the soul," which Luther clearly considers to be standard in philosophical procedure, he argues that memory is not to be understood as a "distinct part of the soul." Rather, it is the most comprehensive description for the persistence of each and every power of the soul in praise of God. "To remember" and "be mindful" means always to praise, give thanks, narrate and bless "the works of the Lord" with one's whole heart, tongue and life.

In this sense, it is possible to say that when the intellective powers meditatively reside in the works of God, intellective activity is 'remembering;' or when the volitional powers affectively and with constancy direct themselves to the works of God, volitional activity is 'remembering;' or when the hand labors in the works of God, manual labor is 'remembering.'[1]

As the orientation of the 'feet' of the soul *(intellectus* and *affectus)* to, and their grounding meditatively and affectively *(meditatio, amor, oratio)* in the works of God, memory or remembering can be understood as the 'substance' of the soul.[2] As Luther emphasizes, to forget

[1] *WA* 3,531.8ff (*Schol.* to Ps. 76:12): "...Non debet accipi memoria ut in philosophia pro parte anime distincta. Sed amplissima significatione pro cuiuslibet potentie perseverantia...in dei laude. Sic enim memorari est semper laudare, gratias agere, aliis narrare, benedicere, non tantum lingua, sicut carnalis synagoga, sed toto corde, lingua et tota vita. Sic enim intellectus memor est, quando assidue meditatur in illis, voluntas memor, quando iugiter amat et orat, manus memor, quando iugiter operatur...Atque ut hoc disceremus esse memoriam, dicit psalmo precedente, 'Memor fui operum domini: quia memor ero ab initio mirabilium tuorum. Et meditabor in omnibus operibus tuis; et in adinventionibus tuis exercebor.' Ecce exposuit, quid sit memorem esse, scilicet meditari et exerceri utique tota vita."

[2] Luther employs the traditional parallel of *memoria* and *substantia animae* in the *scholia* to psalm 4 in conjunction with an analysis of the *dilatatio* of the three powers of the soul *(intellectus, memoria* and *voluntas)* "per eruditionem et intelligentiam," "per virtutem et robur gratie" and "per letitiam et consolationem." *WA* 55,II.60.1ff, 59.5ff. Cf. 4,206.26 and 4.153.6f for the same trinitarian structure of the soul discussed in reference to the debilitation of its powers "per peccatum" —a debilitation also noted in this passage, 55,II.60.2f. See further the editors' citation of the tradition—Augustine, Lombard, Bonaventure, Gerson, and Biel—especially where *memoria* is described as a "Zeugungsgrund der Seelentätigkeit." 55,II.60.33ff. If our interpretation of *substantia* and *memoria* may serve as a guideline, then *memoria* is not taken by Luther as a 'quidditative' ground of the powers of the soul (any more than *cor* or *conscientia*), but as a comprehensive description of the *perseverantia* of the whole man as he lives meditatively *(intellectus)* and affectively *(voluntas)* in and from the *opera dei*, i.e. in and from a "Zeugungsgrund" which is outside himself. See our discussion *infra*, p. 111ff.

the manifest past works of God *(praeterita exhibita)* is simultaneously to forfeit confidence and trust in the promised future works of God *(certitudo futurorum)*.[1] Oriented neither to the past nor to the future works of God, oblivious to what God has done and promises to do, one's 'stability' in the present is threatened. For concurrent with the failure of memory is the failure of *intellectus* and *voluntas*, and vice versa.[2]

The works of God exhibited in the past and promised in the future form the indispensable objective context in which a *substaculum vitae*, i.e. a 'place' in which the whole man can stand with assurance, is made possible. As Luther serializes for purposes of emphasis, we are *in conspectu dei*, *coram deo*, *apud deum* and *ante deum* when we know and love "what God chooses."[3] One's conformity with God consists in his intellective and affective orientation to and 'grounding' in common 'objects'—"what God chooses." It is living with the 'feet of the soul' solidly fixed on those 'places'—the remembered past and the hoped for future works of God—which can 'substantiate' one's life in the present.

7. *INTELLECTUS* AND *AFFECTUS*

Luther's definition of *memoria* as the most comprehensive description of the persistence of all the powers of the soul in praise of God does not have the consequence of exalting *memoria* to a major and frequently employed interpretive term. Indeed, he speaks with much greater frequency of a duality *(intellectus* and *affectus)* rather than a trinity *(intellectus*, *affectus*, *memoria)* of powers in the soul.

[1] *WA* 3,585.10ff (*Schol.* to Ps. 77:41): "Si enim preteritorum exhibitio est certitudo futurorum: ergo qui preterita exhibita obliviscitur vel non curat, simul certitudinem futurorum amittit ac sic dubitat de promissis: quia oblitus est exhibita, ut patet in miserrima experientia."

[2] *WA* 4,153.9ff (*Schol.* to Ps. 101:5): "Verum tamen memoria deficiente etiam intellectus et voluntas defecit, quia iam aliud novit et vult quam prius, quando memoria stetit. Ideo in omni peccato omnes tres concurrunt."

[3] *WA* 3,479.1ff (*Schol.* to Ps. 72:16): "Differunt 'ante me' et 'ante deum': non secundum spacium loci, cum ubique simus ante deum et omnia ante eum et ante nos. Sed secundum cognitionem et affectum... Sic ante deum sunt omnia, que secundum spiritum reputabilia sunt, seu que deus reputat. (Unde ista videre hoc est ante deum esse. Sic econtra ante hominem et mundum sunt ea, que mundus putat vel habet: ista videre hoc est ante hominem esse.) Nam que ipse reprobat, non sunt ante eum. Unde frequens est verbum istud in Scriptura 'in conspectu dei,' 'coram deo,' 'apud deum,' et 'ante deum.' Et nos enim ante deum sumus, quando ea cognoscimus et amamus, que deus eligit. Sic enim anima est ante deum et ante faciem eius." See 3,524.4ff.

We consider the explanation for this hegemony of *intellectus* and *affectus* to result from the fact that, inasmuch as intellective and affective orientation to and grounding in the works of God is what "being mindful of" and "remembering" God is concerned with, the active correlation of intellective and affective activity,[1] which clearly finds a historical parallel in Gerson's *De mystica theologia*, appropriates, and in this sense becomes synonomous with, "memory." Luther can speak of a "revealing in memory and intellect"[2] and say that "affection remembers."[3] We must, therefore, turn to a consideration of *intellectus* and *affectus*, with especial regard to the importance of the objective context in which they are empowered and sustained.

Once again we find Luther writing in contradistinction to a philosophical definition, this time in reference to the term, *intellectus*. He argues that, "in Holy Scripture," this term derives its name "from an object" *(ab obiecto)* rather than from its status as a power of the soul. He points out that if sensible, visible things are the objects with which one is concerned, then the understanding of man is to be described as "sensibility." For sensation and reason, in Holy Scripture, do not merit the designation, *intellectus*. This is because they are incapable of establishing a relationship with the 'objects' requisite to that understanding with which Scripture is concerned.

These objects are "spiritual things"—the events constituting salvation, 'soteriological' rather than 'epistemological' objects. "Understanding in Holy Scripture," therefore, means a "recognition, knowledge or understanding of Christ;" the "wisdom of the cross of Christ;" the "understanding that the Son of God is incarnate, crucified, dead and resurrected for our salvation;" the "acknowledgement of the spiritual and hidden things of salvation and of the grace of God."[4]

---

[1] Often the correlation is expressed as one of apparently natural reciprocity, the presence of an object *in intellectu* automatically triggering or embracing an affective response, and vice versa. *WA* 3,223.2: "Dicit 'ut sciam,' scilicet affectuali cognitione." 3,280.3: "*Intelligite* i.e. corde seu intellectu attendite." 4,104.19f: "Vicium ergo affectus vestri hoc est simul et intellectus." On the other hand, the correlation is expressed as if further effort was required to bring what is *in intellectu* into the *affectus*, suggesting that an object may be *in intellectu* without repercussions on the *affectus*. Cf. 3,423.8ff. The more consistent picture conforms to Luther's conviction of the operational unity of the soul. Cf. 4,282.8f,11f, where the *cor totum* is pitted against "solum...intellectu sine affectu".

[2] *WA* 55,II.81.3f (*Schol.* to Ps. 4:7): "...ostensio in memoria et intellectu."

[3] *WA* 3,534.24f (*Schol.* to Ps. 76:12-13): "Affectus meminit et agnoscit confiteturque domino opus suum."

[4] *WA* 3,176.3ff (*Schol.* to Ps. 31:8): "'Intellectus' in scripturis sanctis potius ab obiecto quam potentia nomen habet, contrario quam in philosophia. Est enim

Such understanding is realized only through faith. For it is through faith only that these 'objects' enter one's presence.[1] We can summarize by saying that sensation and reason are forms of knowing *(cognoscere)* in correlation with what is visible and apparent, or accessible to extrapolation (abstraction) from what is visible and apparent—objects originating and supporting sensitive perception, objects presupposed by sensation and reason. On the other hand, the understanding made possible through faith[2]—*intellectus theologicus et gratuitus*—[3] is also a

intellectus cognitio vel notitia sensus Christi, de quo Apostolus I Corinth. 1 et 2 [2:7-8] excellenter docet, quoniam 'Sapientiam loquimur inquit absconditam in mysterio, quam nemo principum huius seculi cognovit.' Et est breviter nihil aliud nisi sapientia crucis Christi, que gentibus stultitia et Iudeis scandalum est, scilicet intelligere, quod filius dei est incarnatus et crucifixus et mortuus et suscitatus propter nostram salutem... Sed quia totum hoc est in fide et non in sensu neque ratione, ideo etiam intellectus hominum in scriptura dicitur sensualitas, eo quod non nisi sensibilia capiat, quantumcunque sit subtilis et acutus et prudens. Sic Apostolus ait, 'Prudentia carnis' id est carnalis hominis, qui utique habet intellectum, in quo sit prudentia, 'mors est' [Rom. 8:6]... Intelligere itaque est spiritualia et mysteria salutis et gratie dei agnoscere, unde usus loquendi obtinuit dicere 'mysteria' redemptionis et incarnationis, eo quod non nisi mysticis pateant et spiritualibus, non autem hominibus, quibus est potius stultitia, quia ipsi sunt stulti equi et muli: ideo primum illos oportet mutari, ut sic mysteria, que sunt eterna, cognoscant." See the parallel statements at 3,230.19ff, 507.34ff, 515.12ff.

[1] *WA* 3,548.2ff (*Schol.* to Ps. 76:21): "Sed nunc, cum spiritum illius manifeste litere occultum facturus es: erunt opera tua ita occulta, opera tua adeo abscondita, ut nisi fide percipiantur, nullo modo cognoscantur. Immo nisi fides doceat, quod passio tua tanta opera faciat, videbitur quod sint opera infirmissimi hominis cuiusque. Quid enim est pati? Nunquid est hoc opus dei? Igitur diabolum esse victum, mortem occisam, celum apertum, fides intelligit: ratio autem non cognoscit. Velavit enim ea opera sub infirmitate passionis, ut deitatem sub humanitate, ut fide quoque velaret rationem et stultam faceret sapientiam mundi." See the important statement on "cognoscere," which makes it clear that the concern for the 'objective' is not in the context of a *fides historica*: "Quamdiu enim non cognoscitur aliquid esse factum, nondum ei vel apud eum factum est, fit autem apud eum, quando cognoscitur factum esse." 3,435.37ff (*Schol.* to Ps. 68:26). See further the statement in reference to "agnoscere": "Sed quid prodesset si nullus agnosceret aut sciret tantam bonitatem [viz. the fulfilment of the "promissiones dei"]." 4, 337.4f (*Schol.* to Ps. 118:65)

[2] Schwarz concludes: "In der Identifikation von fides und intellectus erhebt Luther das intelligere zu einer unerläßlichen Funktion des Glaubens, ohne sich dabei von der habitus-Lehre beeinflussen zu lassen." *Fides, Spes und Caritas beim jungen Luther*, 139-40. The *per fidem* and *ex fide* in reference to *intellectus* do not argue for an "identification" of *fides* and *intellectus*. Rather they suggest (*per* and *ex*) that *fides* and, we would add, *spes*, are the 'ground' and possibility of understanding and affection *coram deo*. Luther associates *fides* and *spes* with *substantia*, *substantia* in the strictly theological sense presented above (*supra*, p. 105ff). As the orientation of the 'feet of the soul' to the *opera*, *promissiones* and *testimonia Dei*, *fides* and *spes* embrace and empower *intellectus*, *affectus* and *memoria*. But this presupposes a distinctively theological 'objective context;' to identify *fides* and *intellectus* is to abstract from this context. Schwarz, who is aware of the passages

form of knowing, but in correlation with what is neither visible nor apparent—the Son of God incarnate-crucified-dead-resurrected-for-man's-salvation. This is the 'object' which originates and supports faith, and it is the 'object' presupposed by faith.[1]

A similar emphasis can be found in Luther's description of *affectus*. Luther writes that it is customary in Holy Scripture—as with poets—to speak of an object of affection by means of a description of the affection. Poets speak of the beloved as "my fire" or "my love;" by naming the affection which is engendered by an object one names the object. The reason cited for this manner of expression is that the reverse is also and primarily the case: it is from such an object that such an affection originates and is preserved.[2]

As with *intellectus* so too with *affectus* "according to the custom of Scripture": it is 'from the object' that grammatical and existential definition originate. When the soul directs its affection to temporal objects, it is qualified as vain and carnal. When it turns to the testimonies of God, it is qualified as spiritual.[3] Such qualifications do not

---

which underscore the importance of the "obiectum" (*ibid.*, 182), fails at this point to recognize fully their theological implication.

[3] *WA* 4,324.3. See the instructive summary by G. K. Metzger: "Luthers Begriff der Glaubenserkenntnis verweist von vornherein auf die Offenbarung Gottes in Christus, er trägt soteriologisches Gepräge. Die Eigenart des theologischen Erkenntnisobjektes schafft einen neuen Begriff des Verstehens, dem gegenüber das natürliche, philosophische Erkennen mit dem animalischen sentire in dieselbe Dimension zusammenrückt. Das Eigenartige besteht in dem passivischen Vorbehalt. Der Mensch wird erkannt: so erkennt er." *Gelebter Glaube: Die Formierung reformatorischen Denkens in Luthers erster Psalmenvorlesung, dargestellt am Begriff des Affekts* (Göttingen, 1964), 108.

[1] See *WA* 3,171.32-172.19ff (*Gl.* to Ps. 31:1): "Ista...intellectificatio non est secundum humanam sapientiam, sed secundum spiritum et sensum Christi, de quo apostolus I Cor. 2 [8f] pulchre disputat, quoniam solum spirituales et credentes hunc intellectum habent. Et breviter est: non nisi celestia, eterna et spiritualia et invisibilia intelligere, quod fit per solam fidem, scil. ea que oculus non vidit, nec auris audivit, nec in cor hominis ascenderunt, que nullus philosophus et nullus hominum, nullus principum huius seculi cognovit. Quia hec est sapientia abscondita in mysterio et in velamento fidei occulta... Scire ergo filium dei esse incarnatum pro salute nostra et extra eum omnes esse in peccatis, hec est eruditio ista, intellectus iste: quod nemo nisi per sanctum spiritum cognovit." 3,474.14f (*Gl.* to Ps. 72:16): "Fides enim, que est non sensitiva nec ex sensitiva procedens cognitio, sed desursum solum intellectualis..." See 3,507.34f, 173.11.

[2] *WA* 4,199.33ff (*Gl.* to Ps. 105:14): "Sic enim mos est scripture, obiectum cuiusque affectionis nomine affectionis appellare, quod et poetis usitatum est, ut 'ignis meus', i.e. amatus meus, 'amor meus', i.e. amore meo amatus. Et hac ratione, quia tali obiecto pascitur et oritur talis affectus." See *infra*, p. 212f.

[3] *WA* 4,284.1f (*Gl.* to Ps. 118:25): "*Adhaesit* affectu carnali *pavimento* carni, que est terra, hebr. 'pulveri', *anima mea...*" 4,250.18f (*Schol.* to Ps. 111:1): "Et hec est tota vanitas, quod amorem et timorem ponunt in temporalia, que amari et timeri

occur outside or irrespective of an objective context: 'where' one is with the feet of his soul is fundamental to 'how' he is *coram deo*.

The importance of this objective context for the formation and preservation of a distinctive intellective and affective state is present in the *scholion* on psalm 118:105. In contradistinction to the "word of the letter and human wisdom," which grants comprehension and sighting of what is spoken, Luther interprets the nature of faith for this life in terms of an affective following of the Word of God, which illumines in a 'practical' way.

> 'Your word is a lantern to my feet and a light to my paths.' An astonishing statement! Why does he not rather say, 'a lantern to my eyes and a light to my vision?' For how can feet be illumined and how is it possible for paths see! He speaks in this way because the nature of faith in this life is expressed here. The eyes should be made subservient to Christ, and led by the Word alone, which is perceived by the ears, not seen with the eyes. We believe invisible, but not *inaudible* things. For this reason, as little as the Word illumines the eyes, so little does it illumine the ears. And still the Word is a lantern because it directs the feet: faith needs affection, not understanding. What is of primary importance is that you are willing; not that you understand and know, but only that you do those things which you have heard. You will not err if, although you do not see, you believe and you go. Just walk secure in what is heard, because His Word will be a lantern to your feet and a light to your paths. Nothing is required except that you do the very things you do not understand, and go forth into the unknown, following the directive of the Word, becoming foolish and dismissing your own understanding. It is just as if you were following a leader in darkness on a way unknown to you, and you were to say to him, and quite rightly: 'You are the light of my feet, not of my eyes, for I see nothing whatsoever, and yet I walk straightly as if I could see. I err, and I know not where I am, yet my feet, as if seeing light, go securely on the right path.' So does faith illumine the affects; it does not illumine the understanding; indeed, it blinds it! Through the hearing of the Word, faith leads the affects to the place where salvation occurs. Hearing the Word, the affects begin to go after it, not knowing where they are going, but going nevertheless. The Word of God is truly marvelous, for it illumines the feet and the paths on which they walk. This is not so with the word of the letter and of human wisdom. It voids faith because it causes the comprehension of what it says, extending itself as a lantern to the eyes. But the Word of God does not void faith, for it does not say, 'a lantern to your paths and a light to your feet.' The Word of God includes light as a lantern encloses a candle, and this light is for the feet. But light for the paths is not so included. Why is this? For no other reason than that at first the faith of the one beginning

non debent." 4,285.1f (*Gl.* to Ps. 118:31): "*Adhaesi* affectu spirituali *testimoniis tuis* evangelicis *domine*..."

> is less clear, enclosed in the mind as the light of a lantern. But when you have undertaken the journey and are occupied in doing what you believe, already the way is more clearly known than it was before the journey began, so that you have clearer light from your activity than from believing with the affects alone. For when you believe you have light enclosed in the affects. But when you are engaged in the journey, going forth on the basis of this light, then, just as if you were drawing forth light through experience, you are led in the right way. Those who have greater light dwell in practical rather than in speculative faith. For, as even the Philosopher recognizes in the *Metaphysics* [I,1. 981a.13ff], the experienced conduct themselves with more assurance than the inexperienced.[1]

Two comments are in order in regard to this passage. First, we are not within the traditional *fides informis*, *infusa*, *formata* framework. Luther does not speak of an *assensus* to the articles of revelation, as these are defined by ecclesiastical authority and presented by the priest *(fides informis)*, and an accidental quality of the soul *(fides infusa)* mediated through the sacraments of the Church *(gratia gratum faciens)*, establishing and consequently being enhanced by acts of love *(fides*

[1] *WA* 4,356.7ff: "*Lucerna pedibus meis verbum tuum et lumen semitis meis*. Mira sententia. Cur non lucerna oculis meis et lumen visus? Nunquid pedes possunt illuminari aut semite videre? Sed natura fidei expressa est pro ista vita. Nam oculos oportet captivari in obsequium Christi et solo verbo duci, quod auribus percipitur, oculis non videtur. Quia invisibilia credimus, sed non inaudibilia. Quare verbum quidem non illuminat oculos, sed nec aures. Et tamen est lucerna, quia pedes dirigit et affectum, non intellectum requirit fides. Non ut intelligas, sed ut velis oportet, non ut scias, sed ut facias ea que audiuntur. Et non errabis, si credideris et iveris, licet non videris. Tantum securus vade in audita, quia lucerna erit pedibus tuis verbum eius et lumen semitis tuis. Non requiritur, nisi ut facias que nescis, opereris que non intelligis, evadas quo ignoras, ducatum sequens verbi, et stultus fias, tuum sensum amittens. Tanquam si in tenebris ducem sequaris viam quam ignoras, optime dicis ad ducem: tu quidem es lumen pedum meorum, sed non oculorum, quia nihil video et tamen recte gradior, ac si viderem. Ego quidem erro et nescio, ubi sim, et tamen pedes mei quasi viderent lumen, ita certo eunt rectam viam. Sic enim fides non intellectum illuminat, immo excecat, sed affectum: hunc enim ducit quo salvetur, et hoc per auditum verbi. Audiens enim affectus verbum incipit ire post ipsum nesciens quo. Igitur mirabile est verbum dei, quod lucet pedibus et semitis. Non sic verbum litere et humane sapientie, quod evacuat fidem, quia comprehendere facit quod dicit et lucernam oculis sese ostentat. Deinde nec hoc vacat, quod non ait 'Lucerna semitis et lumen pedibus'. Quia verbum includit lumen sicut lucerna candelam, et hoc pedibus. Sed semitis est lumen non ita clausum. Cur hoc? Nisi quod primo fides incipientis est minus clara et magis clausa menti ac velut lucerna. Sed ubi ire ceperis et facere quod credis, iam via clarius cognoscitur quam pedes tui, ita ut clarius lumen habeas ex operando, quam solo affectu credendo. Quia dum credis, clausum habes lumen in affectu, sed dum operaris, iam velut educto lumine per experientiam duceris in via recte. Multo enim illuminatiores sunt in fide practici quam speculativi, ut etiam philosophus dicit in metaphisicis, quod expertus certius operatur."

caritate/operando formata).[1] His appeal to doing what one does not comprehend, secure only in what is heard, concerns an abiding posture of the *vita fidei* and cannot be reduced to an initial trusting acceptance of ecclesiastical authority. And the "clarification" that comes by going and working has reference to an existential verification of the 'substantiating' power of the way one walks *ex auditu verbi dei* and *per affectum*, not to a *fides operando formata* in the sense in which the traditional *ordo salutis* understood it.

Secondly, and here one can find definite parallels with Gerson,[2] although Luther censures comprehension and speculative faith, this passage is not primarily concerned with an exaltation of *affectus* against the danger of "Intellektualismus," as Brandenburg argues.[3] At this point, not only is Luther's active correlation of *affectus* and *intellectus* to be remembered, but also the nature of faith's 'object.' Faith is concerned with what is "invisible" but not "inaudible," i.e. with what is incapable of rational comprehension and speculative grasp but not incapable of being heard, believed, trusted and followed: *the verbum dei*. And hearing, believing, trusting and following the Word of God do not exclude "understanding"—*fides practica* "illumines"—but places it in this peculiar dimension demanded by the nature of the 'object' of faith. What is primary in this *scholion* is a comprehensive 'objective context': the Word of God (the objective *substaculum*) originating, preserving and embracing a distinctive affective and intellective state (the 'subsistence' and 'confidence' of faith).

---

[1] In the *Dictata*, one can call attention to Luther's description of the state of sin as being "extra fidem informem/formatam," and *iniquitas* as the establishment of one's own *iustitia* "contra fidem informem/formatam." *WA* 4,441.26ff. Also there is the interpretation of faith, in accordance with I Cor. 13:8, as destined to pass away, while *charitas*, "que est plentitudo et spiritus fidei et iustitia spiritualis," endures "in aeternum." 4,353.29ff. Thus, the conclusion of Friedrich Kropatscheck: "Es liegt hier einfach ein Rest des katholischen Ethicismus vor. Die infusio gratiae beherrscht den Gedankengang. Die Psalmenglosse, und die Scholien dazu, sind noch völlig von diesen Gedanken beherrscht." *Die natürlichen Kräfte des Menschen in Luthers vorreformatorischer Theologie* (Greifswald, 1898), 8-9. We call attention, however, to the characterization of the *antiqui iusti* as righteous "ex fide informi" (4,117.12f, 16f), whereas earlier Luther had spoken of "fides informis et mortua." 3,490.25f. This is one example of the freedom and material revision with which he can employ traditional terminology in the *Dictata*.

[2] We have reference to Gerson's understanding of the correlative, reciprocal operation of *affectus* and *intellectus*. Cf. *supra*, p. 64ff. This parallel notwithstanding, it is significant that when Luther exalts *affectus*, it is *fides* and *verbum dei* and not the natural orientation of the synteretically informed *spiritus rationalis*, that comes to the fore. See Gerson, *A deo exivit*, *Oeuvres*, V, 14.

[3] Brandenburg, *Gericht und Evangelium*, 74-75.

8. *SUPERBIA* AND *SENSUS PROPRIUS* VERSUS *FIDES* AND *SPES*

One can subsist and confide in the creations of his own understanding *(sensus)*, will, counsel *(consilium)* and reason. He can himself institute the 'objects'—the "spiritual things"—to which he is oriented and on which his life is established.[1] His own understanding and will can create the place where he finds his 'substance' in this life.

For this reason, Luther uses the same metaphors to describe *sensus proprius* and *superbia* that he employed to describe faith and hope. They form the "support" for the old man,[2] the "source" and "mother" of error and heresy, and "originate" the works of the flesh.[3] They are the "cause" of disbelief and the "beginning" of all evils,[4] contesting faith not only for hermeneutical primacy in the understanding of Scripture,[5] but also for the definition of the spirit[6]—the whole man *in intellectu, affectu,* and *memoria.*[7] All these things they attempt to be in spite of the

[1] *WA* 3,331.17ff (*Schol.* to Ps. 58:2): "...Tamen proprie iniquitas per excellentiam dicitur, quando sensus proprius et voluntas propria statuitur contra sensum domini et voluntatem eius. Hoc est enim consilium impiorum et via peccatorum. Consilium propter sensum proprium, via propter voluntatem et iustitiam propriam. Et ratio est, quia inter omnia, que deo debemus et propter eum dimittere, est intellectus et voluntas nobilissimum: ideo ad hanc converti est maxima et summa iniquitas, reiecto sensu et voluntate dei. Et ideo talis iniquitas fere non habet locum, nisi in rebus spiritualibus, quia intellectus et voluntas proprie invisibilium est. Quare est ipsum demonium meridianum [ps. 91:6], quo aliquis suam iustitiam statuit et aversus a spiritualibus rebus, quas deus statuit (sicut lex, verbum dei, gratia, salus), convertitur ad spirituales res, quas ipse statuit; sicut sue ceremonie, sue doctrine, suus sensus. Et iste error valde facilis et subtilis est, quia spiritualis." 3,331.37: "Rationalia deo preferre est iniquitas maxima," "spiritualis idolatria." See 4,420.24ff.

[2] *WA* 4,363.13ff (*Schol.* to Ps. 118:121): "Nam et heretici gloriantur se iustitiam et iudicium docere, sed et facere. Verum cum ipsi proprio sensu sint inflati, et iudicium sit mortificatio hominis veteris, qui nititur sensu proprio, patet quod mentiuntur et non faciunt iudicium, quia non humiliant, iudicant, damnant sensum suum, quod est iudicium facere, sed extollunt, salvant atque defendunt, quod est ex vetere homine vivere et nondum cum Christo crucifixum esse." See our discussion of *duplex peccatum*, *infra*, p. 146ff.

[3] *WA* 4,437.28 (*Gl.* to Ps. 139:10): "Caput i.e. superbia, que est mater erroris, caput heresium omnium." 4,384.16ff (*Schol.* to Ps. 118:163): "...proprium sensum: qui est caput in corpore peccati et princeps aliorum operum carnis... Nam unde rixe, secte, dissensiones, contentiones nisi ex sensu proprio..." Cf. 4,384.33f.

[4] *WA* 3,498.11 (*Schol.* to Ps. 73:23): "...causa incredulitatis et initium omnium malorum."

[5] *WA* 4,379.25ff.

[6] *WA* 4,363.29ff (*Schol.* to Ps. 118:122): "Spiritus enim concupiscit adversus carnem et econtra. Inde fit ut omnis fidelis anima gemat, quod caro suggerit superbos motus, semper nititur statuere idolum zeli (id est proprii sensus) in loco sancto in spiritu..." See 4,418.4ff.

[7] *WA* 4,214.26ff (*Schol.* to Ps. 106:9): "...Ista superbia impedit intellectum,

fact that in the sins of the flesh there is no substance capable of supporting man: "non est ibi substantia."[1] It is not surprising in light of these statements that Luther can conclude that pride is the attempt to be "either equal with or superior to God."[2]

Faith and hope are the very reverse of one's own prideful understanding. They do not presume to possess the power to create saving objects and conditions, but rather recognize and confess what we can now describe with precision as the soteriologically 'de-substantial' character of self and world.[3]

Faith is able to compare temporal with eternal and carnal with spiritual things, recognizing the misery to which the one leads and the glory which the other makes possible.[4] Faith and hope not only direct

---

affectum et memoriam in proficiendo. Facit enim hominem putare et videri sibi satis assecutum luminis et ardoris quoad intellectum et affectum, et perseverentie securitatisque quoad memoriam." 3,603.19ff (*Schol.* to Ps. 78:7): "...Quod peccata non tantum bona opera et affectus velut populum comederunt, sed etiam proposita, intentiones, instituta, directiones, electiones, quibus aliquis vitam suam ordinare et regulare intendit, in oblivionem egerint." Cf. 4,383.31ff.

[1] *WA* 3,419.2ff (*Schol.* to Ps. 68:2): "Et caro nostra vere est limus de limo facta, limus permanens, limus rursum futura. Iniquitas autem divitiarum aque, quia sicut aque fluunt et non manent, ita divitie similiter: limus autem etiam post hanc vitam in terra est. Igitur Christus infixus est in nostro limo, id est concupiscentiis carnis nostre, que ad profundum ducit et abyssum. Et proprie peccatum carnis profundo comparatur. Quia inter omnia maxime excecat et bestiam facit omnino. Ideo non est ibi substantia."

[2] *WA* 3,498.6f (*Schol.* to Ps. 73:5): "Quia qui superbit, deo vel equalis vel superior esse nititur."

[3] The descriptive phrase which we introduce here—the 'soteriologically de-substantial' character of human life—will be approached from other perspectives throughout the remainder of our study. It defines the consequences of sin in the context of Luther's definition of *substantia*. See *supra*, 105ff. Here we emphasize that the 'de-substantial character' of which we speak is *soteriological*, and it is not to be construed as a philosophical statement in the realm of ontology. It has reference to the absence of resources, *post peccatum Adae*, requisite to a salutary standing before God and in the face of sin and death. Secondly, the *substantia* here involved concerns a "substaculum seu subsidentia" in which one can affectively and intellectively support his life, and it is not to be interpreted as an ethical judgment in the realm of morality. Here philosophical and ethical presuppositions and consequences are not simply muffled; they are completely beside the point. We put our point so strongly not in order to suggest that Luther fails to speak of 'reality' or that there are not major ethical implications involved here, but to underscore the fundamentally theological nature of his concern in this period: *homo peccator coram deo*. Cf. 3,301.32f: "...omnino nos nihil in nobis salutis habemus."

[4] *WA* 4,272.32ff (*Schol.* to Ps. 115:10): "*Ego autem humiliatus sum nimis.* Hic totam literam et sapientiam carnis destruit et deiicit, quia per fidem eruditur, quod omnis gloria carnis sit flos foeni. Fides enim facit temporalia comparari cum eternis et carnalia cum spiritualibus. Tunc videt, quanta sit miseria spiritualibus carere

the soul to a place "above the earth," establishing the 'feet of the soul' firmly in heaven,[1] and "constituting" one before God,[2] but they also make manifest the absence of soteriological resources in the generations of man.

In regard to the latter, Luther writes that it is only through faith that memory is fastened to the works of God. This is an attachment which occurs only within the recognition of the absence of resources requisite to salvation in oneself and in one's world: "all this cannot happen unless one first despairs of himself and the world and places hope in the Lord." For it is only as the heart sheds its "hope in the generations of man" and stands resource-less and naked before God that it is able to receive the works and words of God in faith and hope.[3]

Because this life is recognized as soteriologically de-substantial, and because the substantiating "good things" are understood as not yet present in visible victory, the faithful live in the tribulation of evil and in the hope for what is still to be. Paradoxically, faith and hope

---

et temporalibus abundare. Ideo dicit: ex fide nunc intelligo, quod vehementer nihil fui et miser, cum extra fidem in me fuerim, etiam si rex, dives, potens sim etc." Cf. 4,150.23ff (*Schol.* to Ps. 101:4), where *excessus mentis* means *agnoscere, sentire* and *lugere* the "vanitas mundi et hominis," achieved by "quilibet fidelis atque populus dei." Here, Luther concludes, is a view of life "in conspectu dei": "Tunc... mensurat et estimat dies, sicut sunt coram deo, ubi sunt omnes nihil et velut iam preteriti." See further the parallel of *excessus mentis* and *humiliatio coram deo* at 3, 171.19ff.

[1] *WA* 3,227.20ff (*Schol.* to Ps. 39:2 3): "...sunt ['pedes Christi'] affective virtues cuiuslibet sancti, in quo Christus habitat. Et tales sunt pedes Christi tropologici, fundati supra petram fidei, ut iam nullis affectionum ventis in temporalibus rebus moveantur, sed spe coelestium stant solidi. Et horum etiam dirigit gressus et illorum in os mittit Canticum. Et sic credo istum versum [ps. 39:4] dici a Christo pro suis et fere ad literam. Quia communiter petra pro Christo et fide accipitur, supra quam non nisi sanctorum anime statuuntur et pedes spirituales." 3,199.37ff (*Gl.* to Ps. 35:6): "...Misericordia tua non dignus est nisi qui credit et sperat. In fide et spe enim est misericordia tua in hominibus. Ideo per spem est in coelo, per fidem sursum in aere super terram."

[2] *WA* 4,149.32f (*Schol.* to Ps. 101:5): "Constituitur autem coram domino per intellectum fidei et affectus intensionem, sicut econtra coram mundo etc." 3,185. 17 (*Gl.* to Ps. 33:6): "*Accedite* per veram fidem intellectu et affectu *ad eum*..." Cf. 4,107.30ff.

[3] *WA* 3,566.32ff (*Schol.* to Ps. 77:7): "Impossible enim est, qui opera Christi in corde figit et vera credit verba eius, quin promptus fiat mandata eius exquirere. Et econtra: impossibile est, quod is exquirat, qui operibus et verbis eius non credit ac non figit in memoriam. Figitur enim per fidem memoria operum domini. Sed hec omnia non potest facere, nisi prius de se et mundo desperet et in domino spem ponat. Tunc enim potest opera eius et verba figere in cor, postquam evulserit spem seculi et nudus in Domino ceperit sperare. Quare primum est, ut sit pauper spiritu etc."

are the proper correlates not only of "having" and "delight and peace in conscience," but also—and just as strongly so!—of "not having" and "crying."[1]

The 'place' where the faithful live is not yet present *in re*, only *in fide* and *spe*. This is the case not only because of the nature of faith and hope, but also because of the nature of that for which they hope. Thus, one awaits what he can neither create nor possess in this life, and yet he awaits it as one whose very waiting is a 'substantiating' form of having. He journeys to a destination which he can neither comprehend nor attain in this life, and yet he journeys as one whose very journeying is a 'substantiating' form of arrival. And he lives in the recognition of the soteriological non-possibilities of man and the world, and yet such recognition is a 'substantiating' form of divine presence.

Faith and hope, therefore, stand in opposition to pride and one's own understanding on two counts. First, they recognize and confess that man possesses no resources for the establishment of a saving relation with God. Human life cannot be substantiated by the realities present to man in the world. The immediate correlate of this recognition of the soteriologically de-substantial character of self and world is the awareness that it is only faith and hope in the words, works and promises of God, which can form the 'objective context' in which man subsists and flourishes before God and in the face of sin and death.

9. LAW AND GOSPEL

We receive a further and final clarification of the decisive importance of the objective context, and we receive added support for our conviction that the existentialist approach cannot carry the full weight of Luther's thought in the *Dictata*, when we turn to the relationship between law *(lex vetus, lex Mosi)* and gospel *(lex nova, Evangelium)*.

---

[1] *WA* 4,147.23ff (*Schol.* to Ps. 101:3): "Quia enim bona nostra nondum in re habemus, sed in fide et spe, ideo necesse est in tribulationibus esse et malis. Si enim hic essent in vita ista, mala non haberemus. Nunc autem ista bona non habemus et illa adhuc speramus. Non restat, nisi ut mala ista habeamus. In hiis autem ne deficiamus, clamamus ad dominum, ut non deserat nos in tribulatione." 3,344.32 (*Schol.* to Ps. 59:8): "...Qui extra tribulationem est, extra statum et spem salutis est." 4,403.4f (*Schol* to Ps. 121:4): "...Etiam est Ecclesia testimonium et non reale quid, quia non exhibit se talem, qualia promissa sunt in ea et de ea, sed solum testimonium dat." See our discussion of *clamare*, *infra*, 152ff, 174ff.

At first sight, our argument appears to be misplaced, for Luther speaks as if the old law were an object capable of engendering and supporting *both* a carnal and a spiritual affection and understanding. He speaks of the old law as "precisely a firmament resting between the waters of the letter and the waters of the Spirit, since it can be led to both."[1] And he argues that the "spiritual law" and the gospel are "identical."[2] Thus, we are apparently presented with one object *(lex vetus)*, which offers two opposed possibilities of understanding *(ad literam, in spiritu)*, one of which *(lex spiritualis)* is identical with the gospel.

This raises two questions. The first concerns the identity of the law spiritually understood with the gospel. If the old law can establish an objective context identical with that of the gospel, then are we not confronted with a serious threat to the integrity and distinctiveness of law and gospel? This leads to a second question, which concerns the double interpretation to which the old law apparently lends itself. Is the 'object' (in this case the old law) really the 'subject', i.e. does it reserve the originating and preserving power which our analysis has attributed to it, or is the human subject the 'subject' in the sense that this power (in this case the qualification of the old law as either carnal or spiritual) is within the resources of one's own affective and intellective powers?

The issue we are here raising can be summarized in another way. Are we dealing with two diametrically opposed 'objects' (law and gospel), which retain the power to establish and sustain two diametrically opposed 'contexts', in which two diametrically opposed affections and understandings may arise; or are we dealing with two diametrically opposed affections and understandings which are possibilities contingent upon the anthropological resources of man, whether he is in confrontation with the old law or the new law, in the Synagogue or in the Church?[3]

---

[1] *WA* 4,174.32f (*Schol.* to Ps. 103:2-3): "Lex vetus recte est firmamentum medians inter aquas litere et spiritus, quia ad utrunque potest duci."

[2] *WA* 4,134.13ff (*Schol.* to Ps. 100:2): "Unde hic videtur elucere vera differentia psalterii et cithare in significato. Quia cithara veterem legem testem future exprimit: ideo sursum sonat, quasi vocans eam de coelis. Psalterium autem novam per veterem testificatam: quia inde deorsum sonat, quasi vocata ab inferiori et terra. Ideo ps. 98 [:5] pulchre: 'Psallite domino in cithara, in cithara et voce psalmi.' Quomodo in cithara psalli potest, cum hoc sit psalterii officium? Sed vult in cithara spirituali, que est idem, quod psalterium. Quia lex spiritualis et evangelium idem sunt."

[3] M. A. H. Stomps clearly decides for the latter, and he indicates the 'a-objective'

We find evidence to argue that not only is the old law spiritually understood not identical with the gospel, but also that Luther ultimately does not consider the old law to be the empowering 'object' of a "spiritual understanding" even on the level of possibility.

In scattered *scholia*, we find that Luther strongly distinguishes the old law and the gospel and the situations they create. The gospel is correlated with understanding[1] and spiritual benefits:[2] the ministry of mercy and the Spirit.[3] On the other hand, the old law is paralleled with "sense only,"[4] malediction,[5] death,[6] and corporeal benefits:[7] the inability to administer mercy.[8]

The situation cannot be so simply summarized, however, for the specification of the nature of the double interpretation to which the

---

extremes to which the existentialist interpretation of Luther can go, as he writes: "Der Mensch ist (Wesen) gerichtet auf seine Möglichkeiten. Sein Sein ist Wählen, Gehen von Entschluß zu Entschluß. Die Gerechtigkeit ist: dieses Hin-sein-auf auch wirklich sein, den Weg gehen. Der Glaube ist die 'Form', ist die Weise, in der der Mensch sich seiner Möglichkeiten bemächtigt." "Die eigentliche Seinsweise des Menschen ist eine Möglichkeit des Sünders als solchen, sie ist nur von der Sünde aus und in der Sünde." *Die Anthropologie Martin Luthers: Eine philosophische Untersuchung* (Frankfurt a/M, 1935), 125, 29.

[1] *WA* 4,285.10ff (*Gl.* to Ps. 118:34): "*Da mihi intellectum*, quia lex Evangelii solo intellectu percipitur, quia solum invisibilia promittit, lex autem Mosi sensum tantummodo ducebat..." Cf. 4,134.37ff (*Schol.* to Ps. 100:2): "Ideo citharisant et non intelligunt. Sed non econtra psallere potest quis et non intelligere vere, quia Evangelium sciri sine intellectu non potest et fide."

[2] *WA* 4,447.33f (*Gl.* to Ps. 143:9): "Canticum vetus est confessio de beneficiis corporalibus, sed novum de spiritualibus. Hoc Ecclesia, illud Synagoga cantat."

[3] *WA* 4,159.17ff (*Schol.* to Ps. 101:15): "...Ibi [in veteri lege] Moses et prophete receperunt quidem spiritum, sed administrare aliis non nisi literam potuerunt. Sicut Apostolus 2 Corin. 3 [6] disputat: 'Qui fecit nos idoneos ministros novi testamenti, non litere, sed spiritus.' Et sic sensus est: tunc non tantum accipient misericordiam, sed etiam miserebuntur ipsi aliis et misericordiam aliis ministrabunt et spiritum, per quod differt a veteri lege." See 4,397.20f, where "cognitio peccati tantum" can be given "per legem Mosis et prophetas."

[4] See *supra*, note 1.

[5] *WA* 4,309.15ff (*Schol.* to Ps. 118:12): "Precipis et das gratiam implendi, que precipis. Das legem, simul et plentitudinem eius. Non sic Moses: non enim dedit benedictionem talis legislator, sed maledictionem. Lex enim iram operatur et maledicit non implentes." Cf. 3,641.29ff.

[6] *WA* 3,591.25f (*Schol.* to Ps. 77:50-51): "...Iudei vere iumenta, conclusi sunt in morte, in litera, in mortua synagoga et exire non possunt."

[7] See *supra*, note 2.

[8] *WA* 4,160.5ff (*Schol.* to Ps. 101:14): "...Moses et Aaron cum suis omnibus successoribus ministri sacrificiorum et tabernaculi non poterant misereri terre, sed tantum denunciabant et indicabant misericordiam futuram." See *supra*, note 3.

law lends itself is still to be accomplished. In this regard, we call attention to two *scholia* which introduce distinctions which will put us in a position to make a definitive statement.

First, in a comment on psalm 101, Luther treats the difference between the "people who carnally understand the law" and the "people who spiritually understand the law." This is done in terms of the former succumbing to the "titillation" of the flesh which the "promises of the letter" encourage, while the latter enter the "restoration" of the spirit made possible by the "promises of the Spirit." The one people rejects what the other affirms, desires and enjoys. Here one 'object' *(lex vetus)* presents two empowering objects—promises of the letter and promises of the Spirit—with corresponding affective and intellective reactions and states: titillation of the flesh and restoration of the spirit.[1]

A second *scholion* comes from psalm 103, where Luther explicates the difference between the old law and the new law and distinguishes two ways of looking at the old law: "as the reality and not a sign" and "as a sign and not the reality."[2] The explication is as follows. The *inspectus* of the old law "as a sign and not the reality" is a spiritual understanding of the law, which, Luther concludes, is "nothing else than crucifixion of the flesh" *(crucifixio carnis)*. It teaches that the desires of the flesh are to be killed. The new law, over against this view of the old law spiritually understood, is described as the "salvation and liberation of the spirit." Thus the resulting correlations: *lex vetus spiritualiter intellecta*, *destructio veteris hominis*, *iudicium*, *ira*, *dura*, on the one hand, and *lex nova*, *constructio novi hominis*, *iustitia*, *miseri-*

---

[1] *WA* 4,159.7ff (*Schol.* to Ps. 101:10-12): "...Est differentia...populi spiritualiter et populi carnaliter legem intelligentis. Quoniam qui comedunt verba legis secundum superficiem litere, videntur sibi lautitias et delicias comedere et eos, qui hec fastidiunt et potius spiritualiter intelligunt, exprobrant et inimicantur eis. Nam litere promissa titillant carnem, sed promissa spiritus spiritum recreant. Et mutuo sibi cinerem obiiciunt alterum alteri. Nam spiritus cinerem affirmat ea, quibus caro deliciatur. Caro contra cinerem estimat, quibus spiritus reficitur."

[2] *WA* 4,174.13ff (*Schol.* to Ps. 103:2-3): "Si legem inspicias ut signum et non rem, pellis est et sine carne, si autem inspicias ut rem et non signum, caro est et non pellis. Sed tamen caro in illa pelle fuit." 4,306.9ff (*Schol.* to Ps. 118:1): "...Lex Mosi non est mala nec maculata in se, sed quia scribe, qui eam non cum spiritu intelligebant et docebant, faciunt eam maculatam. Nam lex Mosi habet utrunque, scilicet literam significantem et spiritum significatum per literam. Et omnes qui eam susceperunt ut significantem et figuram futurorum, bene beati sunt et fuerunt." Cf. 4,306.16ff.

cordia, *dulcis*, on the other.[1] And they are not 'identical,' but "come together as friends."[2]

In these *scholia*, two important distinctions are present. The first concerns the old law, which is presented not as one object with two possible understandings but as manifesting two objects which empower and sustain two diametrically opposed affective and intellective states. The second distinction concerns the relationship between the old law and the new law, which is described as a 'friendly convening' of the old law spiritually understood, which judges and destroys the old man, and the new law, which graces and constructs the new man.

It is clear that when Luther speaks of the old law spiritually understood he means "crucifixion of the flesh." Further, when he distinguishes the old law as manifesting two opposed objects and affective and intellective states, he is not exalting the old law, even the old law spiritually understood, to identity with the new law. He is, rather, attempting to create in the midst of the Old Testament people the saving 'objective context' which is the peculiar and inalienable property of the gospel.

This leads us to a question which will take our argument a step further. While the law spiritually understood is not identical with the gospel—*amice conveniunt!*—is it possible that the gospel is identical with the law spiritually understood? This is not meant in the sense that friendly convening is destroyed—this confirms their distinctiveness—but in the sense that the affective and intellective state engendered by the law spiritually understood is incorporated into the gospel as a necessary and simultaneous correlate to the peculiar liberation and salvation which the gospel alone makes possible.[3] We find that this is precisely the case.

First, while there are no clear statements that the old law spiritually

---

[1] *WA* 4,174.17ff (*Schol.* to Ps. 103:2-3): "Unde notandum, quod lex vetus spiritualiter intellecta non est nisi crucifixio carnis. Quia pellis ideo vocatur, quod sit vacua carne et doceat carnem evacuandam suis concupiscentiis pinguibus et crassis. Ideo non nisi Ihesum crucifixum prenunciat. Sed lex nova est salus et liberatio spiritus. Et sic veteri conveniunt omnia, que ad destructionem veteris hominis pertinent, nove autem omnia, que ad constructionem novi hominis. Ideo illa iudicium, hec iustitia, illa ira, hec misericordia, illa dura, hec dulcis."

[2] *WA* 4,176.27ff (*Schol.* to Ps. 103:3): "Et iste due penne singulorum iunguntur, quia vetus et nova lex conveniunt, sicut homo vetus occisus et homo novus suscitatus. Vetus lex hominem veterem monstrat mortuum, nova vivum novum exhibet. Et sic amice conveniunt..."

[3] Ebeling writes: "...Die Linien vom AT zum NT laufen über das Kreuz und verlaufen darum, bildlich gesprochen, kreuzweise. *So* macht Christus aus dem Gesetz das Evangelium." *ZThK* (1951), 213.

understood grants liberation and salvation, we find that Luther frequently describes the gospel as not only the source of liberation and salvation, but as "castigating us according to the flesh,"[1] as one with the "word of Christ crucified," which damns and destroys the old man and raises up the new man,[2] and as manifesting sins and judging the old man.[3] The gospel, in short, is "our adversary."[4]

Further, Luther describes the prophet who speaks of the "blessed who are undefiled in the way" (ps. 118:1), as seeing and understanding the law of Moses with "spiritual eyes." But what he sees and understands is not the law of Moses but the "law of faith" *(lex fidei)*, the "gospel of grace" *(Evangelium gratiae)* and the "promised invisible things" *(promissa invisibilia)* which are hidden concealed in the law of Moses.[5] He who so sees and understands is already "outside the letter" and "outside the Synagogue."[6] When the words of the old law are

---

[1] *WA* 4,230.20 (*Schol.* to Ps. 109:3): "...Evangelium castigat nos secundum carnem."

[2] *WA* 4,253.2ff (*Schol.* to Ps. 111:6): "...Verbum crucis Christi et Evangelium positum est, ut omnia ea damnet, que sunt veteris hominis, et destruat, et omnia erigat et salvet, que sunt novi hominis, docens carnem iudicare et crucifigere et spiritum salvare et suscitare."

[3] *WA* 4,310.15ff (*Schol.* to Ps. 118:13): "Sic enim Evangelium iudicat, id est arguit peccata, ut vitentur, et castigat veterem hominem, ut proficiat iustitia interioris. Et que ad ista duo pertinent in Evangelio, sunt iudicia, quia damnant peccata et carnem peccati."

[4] *WA* 3,574.8ff (*Schol.* to Ps. 77:18): "Quidquid audimus, quod nobis placet, suspectum esse debet. Et econtra: quidquid audimus, quod nos offendit atque durum est, suscipiendum est. Quia sic Evangelium habet nomen et verbum dei, quod sit adversarius noster." Cf. the discussion of the gospel as "virga ferrea" in the *scholia* on psalm 2.WA 55,II.37.22ff.

[5] *WA* 4,305.19ff (*Schol.* to Ps. 118:1): "Igitur propheta intuitus oculis spiritualibus legem Mosi, videns in ea latere et clausam esse legem fidei, evangelium gratie et promissa invisibilia, sicut sub cortice nucleum aut sub terra thezaurum..." See 4,376.10ff (*Schol.* to Ps. 118:148): "Fidelis populus spiritualia querit, que sunt in fide et evangelio nobis donata maxima, ergo ut eloquia eius (in quibus omne bonum nobis contulit) non tantum audiat, sed etiam meditetur et per incrementum sibi incorporet. Mira est enim hec petitio, non nisi verba peti a deo, non res, sed signa rerum. Quis enim pro verbis tam anxie unquam clamavit? Sed quia in verbis per fidem, abscondite sunt res non apparentes, ideo habens verba per fidem habet omnia, licet abscondite. Et ita patet, quod iste versus petit literaliter, non futuram Ecclesiam nec eius bona, sed presentem et eius bona; *que non sunt nisi ipsum evangelium gratie*, quod est signum et verbum sperandarum rerum et non apparentium. Et tali cibo nos alit Christus." Emphasis mine. 3,457.15f (*Schol.* to Ps. 70:15): "...Spiritus seu Evangelium seu lex spiritualiter intellecta..."

[6] *WA* 3,400.1ff (*Schol.* to Ps. 67:17): "Dicit: 'si habueritis fidem sicut granum sinapis et dixeritis monti huic: tollere et mittere in mare: fiet [Matt. 17:20f].' Hoc sic fit: quando Mosem aut prophetas fide aspicio, tunc cessant stare in litera;

spiritually understood, it is not the old law but the "testimonies of future things," testimonies of "Christ to come," which form the 'object' engendering the "delight" and "serenity" of the conscience of the Old Testament people.[1] The law is a word of Moses "to us" *(ad nos)*, remaining outward and speaking of visible things and the shadows of future things; the gospel is a word of God "into us" *(in nos)*, penetrating within and speaking of inward, spiritual and true things.[2]

The 'identity' of the gospel and the law spiritually understood *from the side of the gospel* raises the question of contemporizing the objective context of the gospel amidst the Old Testament people. This is a problem foreign to Tauler, who can invoke the soteriological resources of the ground of the soul and the transhistorical nature of the Spirit of God to account for a saving presence of God not only with the Old Testament people, but, indeed, with all who live *ante adventum Christi in carnem*. If, however, one considers human life, *post peccatum Adae*, to be soteriologically de-substantial and so emphasizes the distinctiveness and historical nature of the gospel that he cannot identify a spiritual understanding of the law with the gospel *from the side of the law*, then the contemporization of God's saving presence *ante adventum Christi in carnem* becomes something more than a peripheral issue.

Luther's solution is reached through his understanding of the testimonial, promissorial framework of God's saving presence and the three-fold character of the advent of Christ.

In both the old law and the gospel—*prae* and *post adventum Christi in carnem*—the faithful live in orientation to the testimonies of God.

---

sed mihi sunt iam extra literam in spiritu, extra synagogam per totum mundum. Quia tales montes per mysticam intelligentiam, que est fides, transeunt de litera et angusta synagoga in spiritum et totum mundum."

[1] *WA* 4,310.29ff (*Schol.* to Ps. 118:14): "'Testimonia' porro dicuntur, quia testantur de futuris bonis; non sunt exhibitiones presentium, sed testimonia futurorum, ideoque faciunt fidem esse substantiam futurorum, non apparentium. Sic antiquis nondum apparuit gratia dei, sed prophetabatur. Et nobis nondum apparet quid erimus, sed testimonia habemus super iis. Vel 'testimonia' dicuntur veteris legis verba spiritualiter intellecta, que testantur nihil nisi solum Christum futurum, sicut nove legis testantur gloriam futuram. In utrisque autem, immo in via eorum est delectatio, quia exercitatio in illis conscientia serenat etc. Quare...totus psalmus [118] est nihil aliud nisi petitio, ut reveletur lex spiritualis, ut auferatur litera, proferatur spiritus, tollatur velamen et appareat facies, veniat Christus et transeat Moses."

[2] *WA* 4,9.28ff (*Schol.* to Ps. 84:9): "*In me.* In hoc tangitur differentia evangelii et legis. Quia lex est verbum Mosi ad nos, evangelium autem verbum dei in nos. Quia illud foris manet, de figuris loquitur et umbris futurorum visibilibus; istud autem intus accedit et de internis, spiritualibus et veris loquitur." Cf. 3,457.1ff.

By 'testimonies', Luther means witnesses to good things which are future, not exhibitions of present things.[1] These testimonies *make* faith the "substance of future things." The grace of God did not yet appear to the faithful in the Old Testament, but it was present in the form of prophecy. And what the faithful in the present will be has not yet appeared, but it is present in the form of testimonies. Thus, they too live "as Abraham," believing the future things that are promised as Abraham believed the promises of God.[2] Both people are directed to God's Word. And both share the same delight in the paths they walk; their practical engagement in the testimonies of God brightens and makes their conscience serene.[3]

The two people, then, live in faithful and hopeful orientation to testimonies of God. These testimonies are different insofar as they concern "Christ who will come" for the one people, and "glory that will be" for the other. But they are identical insofar as they are promissorial in nature, received in the awareness of the soteriologically desubstantial nature of self and world, Christologically conditioned, and constitutive of the same affective and intellective state: faith which 'substantiates' and makes conscience serene, hope which sustains all things, in the present.

The last two require a final word. How does Christology condition the testimonies of God and account for the saving presence of God not only to the faithful *post adventum Christi in carnem*, but also *ante adventum Christi in carnem?*

When Luther speaks of the advent of Christ, he means a three-fold reality. The "face of Christ" is *triplex*. One concerns his first advent,

---

[1] The following remarks have reference to *WA* 4,310.29ff, quoted *supra*, p. 127, note 1.

[2] *WA* 4,322.20ff (*Schol.* to Ps. 118:31): "Scimus enim que fiunt et facta sunt, credimus que futura promittuntur, ut Abraham credidit deo promittenti. Et qui sic adheret testimoniis et promissis dei, non confunditur: quia implebitur promissum, quod credidit, ut sit ei gloria credidisse."

[3] As concerns the orientation of the *populus fidelis* before the advent of Christ *in carnem*, see 4,149.11ff (*Schol.* to Ps. 101:5): "Quare totus psalmus [101] est querela fidelis populi vel cuiuslibet anime gementis de vetustate sua et lege peccati ad novitatem gratie que est in Christo, quem advenire petit." In regard to the orientation of the *populus fidelis* after Christ's advent *in carnem*, see 4,360.6ff (*Schol.* to Ps. 118:111): "Promissa enim dei cor letificant eorum qui credunt et sperant in ipsa. Igitur iterim exultamus in fide et spe futurorum, que nobis promisit deus: ideo autem exultamus quia certi sumus, quod non mentitur, sed faciet quod promisit, et auferet a nobis omne malum corporis et anime, conferet autem omne bonum et hoc sine fine." And in regard to both people, see 4,373.6f (*Schol.* to Ps. 118:143): "Spes enim promissionis omnia sustinere potest. Ergo verbo dei omnes sustentamur." Cf. 4,271.24ff.

when he is the incarnate Son of God, the "face of the Father." The second concerns his "spiritual advent," without which the first advent is not at all beneficial *(nihil prodest)*. This advent concerns the "acknowledgement of his face through faith, in which all good things are present." And, thirdly, there is the final advent, when his face will be fully visible.[1]

It is in Luther's understanding of the spiritual advent of Christ that he is enabled to contemporize the objective context of the gospel among the Old Testament people, placing faith and "all good things" in their midst. This is accomplished without an appeal to significant soteriological resources in the will and understanding of man *post peccatum Adae* and without the destruction of the historical integrity of the law and the gospel. We can summarize and deepen these points with the aid of the following diagram:

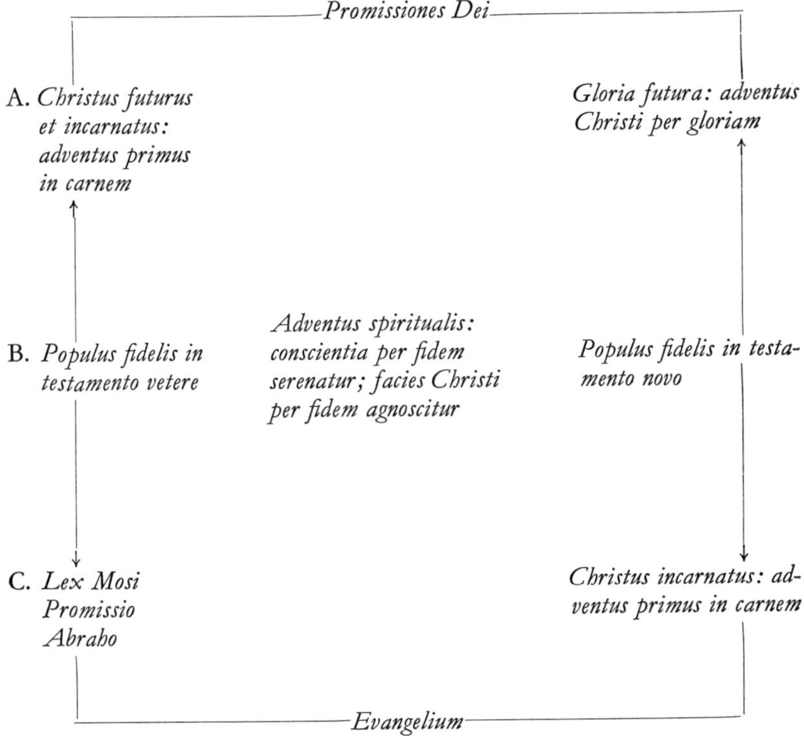

[1] *WA* 4,147.10ff (*Schol.* to Ps. 101:2): "...Facies Christi est triplex. Primo in adventu eius primo, quando incarnatus est filius dei, qui est facies patris. Et sic sensus est ex persona humane nature in electis... Secundo in adventu spirituali,

In this diagram A is the promised future, C the remembered past, and B the existential present. The diagram makes it clear that both people live 'between' remembered past and promised future works of God—within an 'objective context.' The Old Testament people remember the law of Moses and the promise to Abraham. And these remembered events do not direct them to themselves and their present visible 'good.' One remembers only what is not present, and one hopes only for what is still to come. Thus, they are directed to the future advent of Christ *in carnem*. The objective situation is similar with the New Testament people. They remember Christ's advent *in carnem*, and, again, this remembered event does not direct them to themselves and their present visible 'good,' but to hope in the future advent of Christ *per gloriam*.

Thus, behind and before both people stand the *opera Dei*. Remembering what is past and hoping for what is still to come, both people live in a 'soteriological vacuum.' Anthropological resources cannot 'fill' it; if they could there would be no reason to remember what is past and to hope for what is still to come. What does 'fill' it? *Adventus spiritualis!*

Both people find their conscience serene "through faith;" through faith the "face of Christ" is recognized. Here they find a *substaculum vitae*, 'ground' on which they can stand in the present confident that they will not fall into the abyss of sin and death. This existential 'subsistence' and 'flourishing' *in the present* is made possible by the objective context in which they live. Without this context, i.e. without the remembered past and the promised future works of God, there would be no 'substantiating' presence of God, no *adventus spiritualis*.

It is, then, in and between memory and hope, both negating the location of soteriological resources in man's own present life, that the faithful people in both testaments live.

The gospel embraces all these things for Luther.

10. THE DUALISM SOUGHT IN THE *DICTATA*

The question of 'ontological' presuppositions in the *Dictata* has proven to be a very complex question and has taken us into many areas of Luther's thought. We found evidence to suggest the influence

---

sine quo primus nihil prodest. Et ita est faciem eius per fidem agnoscere, in quo omnia bona sunt... Tercio in adventu secundo et extremo ubi facies eius plene videbitur." Cf. 4,305.31ff.

of Neoplatonism, but we cannot agree that such influence is decisive. We have found the existentialist approach much more fruitful, although here, too, we have raised serious questions about its ability to deal with the full range of Luther's thought in the *Dictata*. Our effort to construct an 'objective context,' in which the existential possibility of faith arises, is both a criticism of its inadequacy and an adoption of its relevance.

Should a defensible clarification of the 'dualism' in the *Dictata* be forthcoming and the fundamental theological and philosophical elements of Luther's 'world-view' made manifest, the following motifs must be taken into account: the concern for the unity of the soul and the predilection for speaking of man *coram Deo* in terms of the active correlation of *intellectus* and *affectus*; the soteriologically de-substantial character of this life; the 'substantiating' power of *fides* and *spes*; and the centrality of a comprehensive objective framework.

A major weakness of both the neoplatonic and the existentialist theses, and in large measure accountable for their failure to reach such a defensible solution, is the assumption that Luther's overarching concern is to distinguish and oppose irreconcilable 'entities,' whether they be body and soul, God and the world, or *Existenzmöglichkeiten*. We find that the reverse is rather the case: Luther is primarily concerned not to distinguish and oppose irreconcilable entities, but to reconcile distinct and opposed entities. He seeks neither the 'both-and' nor the 'either-or,'[1] but the *simul*. Let us follow one of the more revealing aspects of this quest.

We call attention to three passages in the *scholia* to psalm 118, each of which emphasizes the incompleteness of the present life and the impossibility of 'resting' here. In the first passage, Luther adopts and theologically applies to the present life of the *fideles* a concept of movement *(motus)* which is drawn from both theological and philosophical sources. He writes:

---

[1] Representative of the 'either-or' interpretation of the dualism in the *Dictata* is Schwarz's statement: "Entweder ist der Mensch unter der Herrschaft der caro im amor mundi entflammt und im amor dei erkaltet, oder er wird durch den heiligen Geist vom amor dei entzündet und ist dem amor mundi abgestorben. Mit der Liebe zum einen ist immer die Ablehnung des anderen gepaart: ...Es ist nicht möglich, die himmlischen Güter in einem höheren Grade und daneben die irdischen Güter in einem geringeren Grade zu lieben." *Fides, Spes und Caritas beim jungen Luther*, 218-19. We agree with the exclusion of the gradualistic 'both-and,' but is an unconditional 'either-or' Luther's serious alternative? We think not; the 'either-or' is used to destroy the 'both-and' and becomes his point of departure for the *simul*. Cf. *infra*, 135.

> Although I am not perfect, I am nevertheless in the work I did and I do. For who, indeed, is perfect or thinks he has apprehended? Therefore, what you have done is still to be perfected. As Ecclesiastes [1:9] says: 'What is what was? That which is still to be done.' And it is written in Ecclesiasticus [18:6]: 'When man has reached the end, then will he begin.' Movement is not to have done sufficiently and to rest, but, according to philosophy,[1] it is an imperfect act, always partly acquired and partly to be acquired. It is always between contraries *(semper in medio contrariorum)*, consisting simultaneously *(simul)* in a point of departure and a point of destination. Were it only at the one or at the other, it would not be a movement. This present life is a certain movement and passage, i.e. a journey, a Galilee, a migration from this world to a future world which is eternal. Therefore, we have a share in that future world in conscience,[2] but we also share in the tribulations of the flesh. Thus we are constantly moved between the exterior evils of sins and the interior goods of merits, as in a point of departure and a point of destination. But further into this elsewhere.[3]

Before turning to the "elsewhere," we call attention to the fact that Luther interprets the "semper partim acquisitus et partim acquirendus" of "philosophy" as "semper in medio contrariorum et simul in termino a quo et ad quem consistens." The present life of the *fideles* is *always in the middle of opposites*, *simultaneously* in its point of departure and its point of destination. In its theological application to the *vita fidei*, the philosophical concept of movement receives a quite different form.

Let us push further. The "elsewhere" to which Luther referred above is the following statement in which the *semper motus* concept is made theologically fruitful in application to the relationship of *spiritus*

---

[1] The philosophy Luther has in mind is Aristotelian. Cf. W. D. Ross, *Aristotle: A Complete Exposition of his Works and Thought* (Cleveland, 1962), 83f.

[2] Note *WA* 3,616.10f (*Schol.* to Ps. 80:6): "...testimonium futurorum et testimonium conscientie, et quod sumus filii regni."

[3] *WA* 4,362.32-363.5 (*Schol.* to Ps. 118:121): "Licet non perfecerim, sum tamen in opere, feci et facio. Quis enim perfectus est aut se apprehendisse putat? Igitur que fecisti, perficienda sunt. Ut Ecclesiastes: 'Quid est quod fuit? id quod faciendum.' 'Homo enim cum consummaverit, tunc incipiet.' Non enim fecisse satis est et quiescere, sed secundum philosophiam motus est actus imperfectus, semper partim acquisitus et partim acquirendus, semper in medio contrariorum et simul in termino a quo et ad quem consistens. Quod si in uno fuerit tantum, iam nec motus est. Vita autem presens est motus quidam et phase, id est transitus et Gallilea, id est migratio ex hoc mundo ad futuram, que est quies eterna. Ergo partim illam habemus in conscientia, partim tribulationes in carne. Et sic inter mala (exteriora) peccatorum et bona (interiora) meritorum assidue movemur velut in termino a quo et ad quem. Sed hec latius alibi tractanda."

and *caro* and the nature of righteousness, i.e. in the areas of theological anthropology and soteriology.

> Who will boast that he is a pure spirit, now without flesh, the adversary of the spirit, even if he presently finds in himself no part in or temptation to luxury, avarice or other manifest iniquities? If flesh is with you and you are in the flesh, certainly pride is with you and you are in it, and it remains until your body becomes wholly spiritual. Therefore, we always sin *(semper peccamus)* and are always unclean. And should we say that we have no sin, we are liars, for we deny that we have flesh in the face of the fact that wherever flesh is it has with it those evils, and thus fights against the spirit. Since one and the same man is spirit and flesh, it is certain that it is man's guilt that flesh is so evil and does evil things. Thus, as I said above, we who are righteous are always in movement, always to be made righteous *(semper iustificandi)*. Hence it follows that all righteousness for the present moment is sin to that which is to be added in the following moment. Saint Bernard rightly says: 'When you begin to be disinclined toward becoming better, you cease to be good. For there is no standing still in the way of God; that delay is sin.' Thus, he who is confident that he is just in the present moment and stops has lost his righteousness, just as movement is lost when one stops. The point to which we have come in the present moment is a point of departure in the succeeding moment. The point of departure is sin, from which we are always to be going, and the point of destination is righteousness, to which we are always to be going. Thus, I was right when I said above that preceding righteousness is always iniquity to the righteousness that follows, just as the letter to the spirit and emptiness to fullness.[1]

---

[1] *WA* 4,364.5ff (*Schol.* to Ps. 118:122): "Quis enim gloriabitur se esse purum spiritum et non habere adhuc carnem adversariam spiritui, etiam si iam nec luxurie nec avaritie aut aliarum manifestarum nequitiarum pars aut tentatio in ipso sit? Si enim caro est tibi et in carne es, certe superbia ista quoque tecum est et tu in illa, usque dum corpus istud fiat totum spirituale. Semper ergo peccamus, semper immundi sumus. Et si dixerimus, quod peccatum non habemus, mendaces sumus, quia negamus nos habere carnem, cum tamen caro ubicunque sit, secum ista mala habet, ut spiritum impugnet. Et quia spiritus et caro unus homo est, sine dubio culpa hominis est, quod caro tam mala est et male agit. Quare, ut supra dixi, semper sumus in motu, semper iustificandi, qui iusti sumus. Nam hinc venit, ut omnis iustitia pro presenti instanti sit peccatum ad eam, que in sequenti instanti addenda est. Quia vere dicit B. Bernardus: 'Ubi incipis nolle fieri melior, desinis esse bonus. Quia non est status in via dei: ipsa mora peccatum est.' Quare qui in presenti instanti se iustum confidit et stat, iam iustitiam perdidit, sicut in motu similiter patet; terminus, qui in isto instanti est ad quem, ipse in sequenti instanti est terminus a quo. Terminus autem a quo est peccatum, a quo semper eundum est. Et terminus ad quem est iustitia, quo semper eundum est. Quare recte dixi, quod semper precedens iustitia est iniquitas ad sequentem, et velut litera ad spiritum, vanitas ad plenitudinem, ut supra."

Before commenting on this passage, we cite a final commentary from the *scholion* on 118:28. Here Luther concludes a description of all who are progressing, seeking and expecting perfection, the historical examples being those who, under the law, expected the revelation of the Spirit, and the Apostles before the coming of the Spirit. He writes:

> As we said above, the stage in which we are is as a letter of that to which we go: the end of the first step and the beginning of the next. Just as Christ is the end of the Synagogue and the beginning of the Church, so is every power, every act, all knowledge and understanding [an end and a beginning]. But disgust creeps into this movement; the step we have reached begins to be distasteful and the one not yet attained is incapable of coming to our aid. So the soul begins to sleep from weariness with the letter and the delay of the Spirit. In this interval *(intermedio)* nothing is more efficacious than the Word of God, which strengthens us in the present step and excites us to the future... For the Word of God, more than anything else, has moving power *(vim motivam)*. It is not only an illuminating, but also a heating, fire. 'The Word of God is living, more penetrating than any two-edged sword' [Heb. 4:12]. Therefore, in all moments of disgust, remember *(recurre ad memoriam)* the Word of God, and you will be confirmed in your resolution.[1]

In these three passages, a *motus* concept, drawn from philosophical and monastic (Bernard) sources and denying an immanent perfection or completion of the life of man and of the world, is taken over by Luther and made theologically fruitful in his description of the *vita fidei*. We direct our final comments in this chapter to the theological consequences of this denial, which forms the major 'ontological' presupposition of Luther's thought in the *Dictata*.

1. The denial of a *terminus ad quem* in this present life, when theologically (soteriologically) intensified and applied to the *vita fidei*, influences the argument for the full persistence of prideful flesh and its evils, a persistence expressed not only in the passages cited here, but

---

[1] *WA* 4,321.26ff (*Schol.* to Ps. 118:28): "...Ut diximus supra, gradus in quo sumus, est velut litera eius, ad quem imus: qui est finis primi et initium futuri. Sicut Christus finis Synagoge et initium Ecclesie, ita omnis virtus, omnis actus, omnis scientia et intelligentia. Sed tedium obrepit in iis; quia habitus gradus incipit fastidiri, et nondum habitus non potest subvenire. Et ita dormitat anima pre tedio litere et dilatione spiritus. In quo intermedio nihil efficacius quam verbum dei, quod confirmat in gradu presenti et excitat ad futurum... Quia verbum dei super omnia habet vim motivam: est enim ignis non tantum lucens, sed et ardens, et 'sermo dei vivus est, penetrabilior omni gladio ancipiti': igitur in omni tedio recurre ad memoriam verbi et confirmaberis in proposito tuo."

throughout the *Dictata* whenever Luther uses the adverbs, *semper* and *nondum*, as descriptive qualifications of the *vita fidei*. The faithful always sin and are always to be judged and accused *in conspectu dei*.[1] They always confess their utter *paupertas*, their not having and their needing.[2] They are always in tribulation and always invoke God's assistance;[3] they are always beginning again,[4] always on the way and in desire.[5] They are "not yet" wholly spirit, new, soul, heaven, of Christ and of God; something from the letter, the old man, the flesh, the earth, the world and the Devil remains present.[6] They understand and speak of themselves as if they were in the Synagogue.[7] They live, as *fideles*, in the full recognition of the abiding soteriologically unfulfilled nature of this life.

The *semper* and *nondum* lay the foundation for a *simul*. He who is *always* in sin and *always* "not yet" righteous can only be righteous as one who is simultaneously sinful. He cannot be 'partly righteous and partly sinful,' nor can he be 'either righteous or sinful.' He must be righteous and sinful simultaneously. Through the *semper*, Luther discovers that opposition (either-or) must *remain* in man's reconciliation and union *(simul)* with God.[8]

---

[1] *WA* 3,291.14f (*Schol.* to Ps. 50:6-7): "...semper nos accusandum et iudicandum in conspectu dei."

[2] *WA* 3,442.32ff (*Gl.* to Ps. 69:5): "Pauper est, qui non habet. Egenus, qui etiam eo indiget, quod non habet. Sancti autem dei, quantumcunque profecerint, semper sese confitentur non habere et egere, i.e. pauperes et egenos, ideo digni et apti sunt adiuvari a deo."

[3] *WA* 4,88.10 (*Schol.* to Ps. 92:3-4): "Cum ergo semper sit invocandus deus, ergo semper in tribulatione essendum est."

[4] *WA* 4,140.2ff (*Schol.* to Ps. 100:8): "Et ideo in isto versu [ps. 100:8: "in matutino interficiebam omnes peccatores terre: ut disperderem de civitate Domini omnes operantes iniquitatem"] optime instituitur vita proficientis, ut scilicet discat, qui vitia vult vincere et disperdere, semper in matutino sit [4,139.31: "matutinum morale est initium fidei"], semper inchoet, semper nihil se fecisse putet et cogitet..." 4,401.31: "...semper de novo incipiunt."

[5] *WA* 4,283.11ff (*Gl.* to Ps. 118:20): "*Concupivit...anima mea*, caro enim contrarie concupiscit, *desyderare iustificationes tuas*, quia in hac vita non attingimus perfecte, ideo semper in via, semper in desiderio esse oportet..."

[6] *WA* 4,320.17ff (*Schol.* to Ps. 118:25): "Unicuique restat aliquid de litera, ut non sit totus spiritus, de veteri homine, ut nondum sit totus novus, de carne, de terra, de mundo, de diabolo, ne sit totus anima, totus celum, totus Christi, totus Dei." Cf. 4,328.20ff, 349.15ff.

[7] *WA* 4,400.2f (*Schol.* to Ps. 121:2): "...omnis proficiens ita sentire et loqui debet ac si in synagoga esset."

[8] In his interpretation of the *scholion* on 115:1 (see our discussion *infra*, 162ff), Leif Grane emphasizes the importance of Luther's *semper* motif in regard to the scholastic (specifically, nominalist) *dispositio ad gratiam*: "...Das Leben auf dieser Erde ist in allen seinen Stadien Vorbereitung, die das nächste Stadium nicht voll-

2. The denial of an immanent soteriological goal, indeed, of any salutary stopping-place in this life, influences the establishment of faith and hope as the forms in which man is 'substantiated' in this life. Thus, we find faith and hope frequently correlated with salvation "in hac vita."[1] A major point of this correlation is the suspension of the possibility of achieving the *visio dei*—final eschatological rest—in this life.[2] If there is no realization of righteousness in this life, if this life is soteriologically *res*-less and substance-less, then the substance of the faithful people must be received from outside their own resources and possibilities. So, Luther writes, "the testimonies of future things make faith to be the substance of what is [still] to be."[3] "Hope in the promise [of God] can support all things; therefore, we are all sustained by the Word of God."[4] "I believed, i.e. I had faith, and this is my whole

---

gültig verdient. Damit ist der entscheidende Unterschied zwischen dem vorbereitenden Stadium und dem Stand der Gnade, der für die scholastische Lehre von *dispositio ad gratiam* so wichtig ist, im Grunde aufgehoben worden." *Contra Gabrielem: Luthers Auseinandersetzung mit Gabriel Biel in der Disputatio contra scholasticam theologiam 1517* (Gyldendal, 1962), 276. This is certainly correct as far as it goes. The really significant aspect of the *semper* motif, however, is not fully exploited when it is directed solely against the *praeparatio (facere quod in se est)* of scholastic theology in general and the nominalism of Gabriel Biel in particular. This exclusive focus leaves the impression that Luther simply *intensifies* the "mora est peccatum" motif of Bernard and monastic piety. It is when the *semper* motif of the *Dictata* is recognized as laying the foundation for the *simul iustus et peccator* of Luther's Reformation theology that the gulf between Luther and his scholastic predecessors, not only in regard to the *dispositio ad gratiam* but throughout the areas of anthropology and soteriology, becomes fully manifest.

[1] *WA* 3,200.5ff (*Gl.* to Ps. 35:8): "*Filii autem hominum* forte filii viri ut ps. 4 [:3]; Hebr. Adam, quamdiu sunt in hac vita: *in tegumine* fide *alarum tuarum* protectionum tuarum, que sunt gratie spiritus sancti *sperabunt*, quia hic per spem salvi sumus." 3,604.36 (*Gl.* to Ps. 79:4): "Ita nunc salvi sumus in spe, tunc autem in re." 3,389.33f (*Gl.* to Ps. 67:28): "Per fidem enim deum hic confitemur, per spem in celo habitamus, per charitatem ad omnes dilatamur." 4,409.17f (*Gl.* to Ps. 124:8): "Nunc enim nomen domini tantum habemus, sed in futuro rem revelatam per speciem. Quia hic in fide vivimus." Faith and hope confirm and underscore the historicity of this life: "...*Et tu* intende *domine* verus Deus in teipso *deus virtutum* angelorum coelestium per claram cognitionem *deus Israel* fidelium per fidem." 3, 327.1f (*Gl.* to Ps. 58:6)

[2] *WA* 4,65.1ff (*Schol.* to Ps. 90:1): "Nolite velle immediate in deo habitare. Nolite abiicere protectionem eius. Quoniam in haec vita non facie ad faciem est. Non in deo habitare potestis, sed in protectione eius, in umbraculo eius erit vobis mansio [4,62.11: "umbra fidei"]. Et in hanc sententiam omnia istius verba sonant, immo tota Scriptura prophetarum antiquorum." 3,148.17f (*Gl.* to Ps. 26:4): "*Ut videam* hic per fidem et in futuro per speciem." 3,150.35f (*Gl.* to Ps. 26:13): "...In hac vita credimus bona domini, in futura autem videbimus." Cf. 3,469.1ff, 607.4ff, 608.26ff.

[3] *WA* 4,310.30f. Cf. *supra*, p. 127, note 1.

[4] *WA* 4,373.6f (*Schol.* to Ps. 118:142): "Spes enim promissionis omnia sustinere potest. Ergo verbo dei omnes sustentamur."

possession, which is substance, i.e. the possession of things hoped for, not the substance of things present [Heb. 11:1]."[1]

3. Finally, the denial of an immanent goal for the *vita fidei*, which goes so far as to argue that every present moment is a point of departure which is "iniquity" and "sin" to the succeeding moment, undermines the interpretation of the *vita fidei* within the traditional framework of *fides informis*, *infusa* and *formata*. For in this framework, one may be conceived as being *often* at the beginning of the order of salvation (viz., the sacrament of penance), but he is never *always* in a beginning which is iniquity and sin. The logic and order which the traditional framework introduces into the mystery of salvation gives way in Luther's thought to a picture of the *vita fidei* as a hearing and believing, a trusting and going, with no "support" except the Word of God. Thus, there is the emergence in the *Dictata* of a correlation between faith, hearing and the name of God, which forms the objective context in which the *vita fidei* arises, is sustained and persists in this life.[2]

We bring our conclusions together. Luther's theological interpretation of the *motus*-character of the present life of the *fideles* has the immediate consequence of denying any 'habitation' of righteousness in this life.[3] What persists and abides in this life is iniquity and sin: unlikeness and opposition to God. If man is to withstand the power of sin and death, he can do so only as he stands on 'ground' more solid than that which is available to him from his own resources. What is soteriologically de-substantial cannot 'substantiate' life before God and in the face of sin and death.

---

[1] *WA* 4,271.24ff (*Schol.* to Ps. 115:10): "Intentio psalmi est docere tantum spiritualia bona in Christo expectare, et promissa in lege de spiritu et fide intelligenda esse, non de re temporali: contra insipientiam carnalium Iudeorum, qui fidem respuunt et rem expectant. Rem inquam temporalium, nam fides habet rem eternam. Dicit ergo: *Credidi*, id est fidem habui, et hec tota mea possessio, que est substantia, id est possessio rerum sperandarum, non autem substantia rerum presentium." Cf. 4,272.22ff.

[2] *WA* 4,368.8ff (*Schol.* to Ps. 118:132): "Diligunt enim nomen domini et hoc solo vivunt contenti. Quod proprie pertinet ad Ecclesiam militantem: nam hec nondum rem, speciem, substantiam dei videt, sed tantum nomen eius audit et ex auditu in fide diligit, ubi vani homines vel suum nomen, immo speciem et rem suam diligunt." See 4,403.20ff, quoted *supra*, p. 97, note 2.

[3] This is the anthropological point of Luther's "pecca fortiter": "Esto peccator et pecca fortiter, sed fortius fide et gaude in Christo, qui victor est peccati, mortis et mundi. *Peccandum est, quamdiu hic sumus; vita haec non est habitatio iustitiae*, sed expectamus...coelos novos et terram novam, in quibus iustitia habitat." *Luthers Werke in Auswahl*, 6, *Luthers Briefe*, 56, 1ff (= *WA Br* 2,372.84ff). Emphasis mine.

The present life does not surrender its soteriologically de-substantial nature: not being God is what being man means. This life can be neither 'partly righteous and partly sinful' nor 'either righteous or sinful.' These alternatives negate not only the seriousness of its sinfulness, but also its very humanity. The present life of the *fideles*, therefore, must be sinful and righteous in such a way that (1) the radical opposition between the righteousness of God and the sinfulness of man, (2) the distinction between divine and human nature and activity, and (3) the miraculous reality of God's presence to man in faith and hope, are clearly preserved and set forth.

Realities which are radically opposed to one another require the full opposition of the other to manifest themselves. One cannot understand darkness without knowing what light is. And one cannot speak of and understand the righteousness of God without the immediate reference to the sinfulness of man. For the sake of the reality of God's righteousness and for the sake of the preservation of the integrity-giving distinction between divine and human nature—for God's sake and for man's sake—the either-or must become a *simul*.[1]

The important thing about the dualism in the *Dictata* is that it is a dualism in search of a 'reconciled dualism,' a dualism in which opposites coexist simultaneously. Righteous in faith and hope, sinful in faith and hope—simultaneously righteous and sinful in faith and hope: this is the reconciled dualism which is coming to expression in the *Dictata*. In subsequent chapters, we will enrich this conclusion.[2]

---

[1] Kjell ove Nilsson's interpretation of the *simul* is reached through the application of the *communicatio idiomatum* of Chalcedonian Christology to Luther's theological thought. "Göttliches Handeln und menschliche Werke dürfen niemals vermischt oder identifiziert werden, und doch gehen sie ständig ineinander über —*ein stetes simul*." "Das ist das Zentrum in [Luther's] Anthropologie und Christologie, in Ekklesiologie und Ethik." *Simul. Das Miteinander von Göttlichem und Menschlichem in Luthers Theologie. Forschungen zur Kirchen- und Dogmengeschichte*, 17 (Göttingen, 1966), 29. In the sphere of soteriology, this *simul* does not carry the weight of Luther's thought in the *Dictata*. It preserves and to a defensible extent clarifies the distinction in union between divine and human nature, but it is hardly appropriate for understanding the radical opposition in union between the righteousness of God and the sinfulness of man. *Communicatio idiomatum* cannot bear the full weight of *simul iustus et peccator*, and it cannot, therefore, serve as the clarifying paradigm of Luther's anthropology.

[2] See our discussion *infra*, 152ff, 178ff, 184ff.

CHAPTER NINE

THE ISSUE OF A NATURAL 'COVENANT'

1. CHRIST AND THE *SYNTERESIS*

In two early sermons (1510-12), Luther describes the will of man as possessing freedom which can determine his salvation. Man has the "possibility" and the "power" to perform acts on which his salvation depends.[1] In a later sermon, *De propria sapientia et voluntate* (December, 1514), which will be the subject of this section, we encounter a similar attribution of significant moral and soteriological resources to human nature *post peccatum Adae*. But here, as we will see, ambiguity shrouds this attribution. We call attention to Luther's understanding of the *synteresis*[2] *voluntatis et rationis*.

The *synteresis* is described in this sermon as remaining continuously in the will and inextinguishably in reason. Its presence is manifest, on the one hand, in the will's inalienable desire to be saved, to live well and happily and avoid damnation, and, on the other hand, in reason's entreaty of the highest things, i.e. what is true, right and just.[3] More

---

[1] In a sermon on Matt. 7:12, Luther describes the "talentum nobis datum" as "nostra possibilitas, teutonice unser vermögen," and he makes it quite clear that the right exercise of this possibility and power is conditional for "salus": "Qui videt nudum et non vestit si potest, non salvabitur." *Luthers Werke in Auswahl*, 5, 22.9ff, 24.8ff (= *WA* 4,591.31ff; 593.18ff). In a sermon on John 3:16, there is a lengthy portrait of man as a "microcosmus," whose "liberum arbitrium" "solum sufficere posset ad salutem." *Ibid.*, 31.11ff. My dating of these sermons in the period 1510-12 follows Vogelsang's research, *ibid.*, 19f.

[2] *Synteresis* has alternative spellings in the edited texts. It appears as *syntheresis* in the *Dictata*, but in this sermon as *synteresis*. In the texts of Gerson, it was consistently *synderesis*. We preserve the edited form in the quoted texts. In our discussion, the form *synteresis* is used.

[3] After Alexander of Hales, who emphasized the distinction in every act of conscience between an inherent and inerrant drive *(synteresis, scintilla conscientiae)* in man to God and the human misuse of this drive (the application in a particular act of conscience), the late medieval tradition was divided over the location of this natural orientation to God. Bonaventure, Henry of Ghent and Gerson located it in the will or affective powers; Albertus, Thomas and Scotus placed it in reason or the intellective powers. Cf. Willy Bremi, *Was ist das Gewissen? Seine Beschreibung, seine metaphysische und religiöse Deutung, seine Geschichte* (Zürich, 1934), 103ff. Hirsch, *Lutherstudien*, I, 16ff. In this sermon, Luther speaks of a double *synteresis*—*synteresis voluntatis et rationis*. This indicates that he draws upon and even brings these two

specifically, the *synteresis* is the conservation, remnant, residue and highest part of nature preserved by God after the corruption of human nature in Adam. It remains as a "tinder" and "seed"—the "material" which is to be "resuscitated" and "restored" through grace.

Luther stresses the importance of its presence. Had God not preserved it, man would have become a Sodom.[1] Or, as he concludes in the *Dictata* in early 1515, and in obvious reference to the *synteresis*, if there are no vestiges of God *(vestigia dei)* "in our wings" (our *affectiones* and *meditationes*), then we will "crawl upon the earth" *(reptabimus in terra)*.[2]

Thus, we find Luther arguing in this sermon that, although the "whole will" abandons the love of what is good, and the "whole reason" is completely incongruous *(omnino difformis)* with the wisdom of God, there is a fundamental congruity *(conformis)* between the will and wisdom of God and the *synteresis* of man's will and reason.[3] Because of this *synteresis* there is a "residue of health" in all men with which the Physician can work and because of which one need not despair of his illness as "incurable." The *synteresis* is the connecting link between the work of Christ and the illumination of reason, and between the work of the Spirit and the will's achievement of health.[4]

---

late medieval traditions together. Thus, Bremi's suggestion that it is through Gerson that Luther encounters and interprets the *synteresis* *(Was ist das Gewissen?*, 108), must be qualified in light of this sermon. See our discussion of *synteresis* in Luther's lectures on Romans, *infra*, p. 186ff.

[1] *WA* 1,32.1ff: "Nam ista synteresis in voluntate humana in perpetuum manet, quod velit salvari, bene beateque vivere, nolit et odiat damnari, sicut et rationis synteresis inextinguibiliter deprecatur ad optima, ad vera, recta, iusta. Haec enim synteresis est conservatio, reliquiae, residuum, superstes portio naturae in corruptione et vitio perditae ac velut fomes, semen et materia resuscitandae et restaurandae eius per gratiam... Nisi Dominus reliquisset nobis semen, quasi Sodoma fuissemus, i.e. moraliter loquendo, nisi synteresin et reliquias naturae conservasset, tota periisset." There is an early reference to the *synteresis* as "lux" in Luther's notes on Augustine's *De trinitate* and *De civitate dei*. *WA* 9,18.15f.

[2] *WA* 4,176.9ff (*Schol.* to Ps. 103:3). See 4,190.32, where "reptilia" are considered to be the unrighteous *(iniusti)*. On the use of the *pennae* imagery, see Gerson, *De myst. theol. pract.*, *cons.* 11,205.127ff.

[3] *WA* 1,36.11ff: "Illud autem, quod dictum est de voluntate hominum quod sit conformis voluntati Dei, intelligendum est de synteresi voluntatis seu superstite portione, quae naturalier vult bonum. Nam de tota voluntate loquendo aeque ipsa deficit in amando bono, sicut ratio in intelligendo recto et vera. Sicut ergo synteresis rationis etiam conformis est sapientiae Dei, licet tota ratio omnino difformis sit ei, ita synteresis voluntatis est conformis voluntati dei: nam cum utrique ponantur invisibilia et abscondita, tam ratio non ea capit quam voluntas ea non amat, licet per synteresin inclinentur et apta sint ea nosse et amare."

[4] *Ibid.*, 36.37ff: "Imo pro illuminatione rationis incarnatum est verbum, sapien-

Human nature, therefore, because of the *synteresis*, remains capable of "revivification," if only no obstacle is placed to grace.[1] Indeed, right or errant willing apparently not only initiates but determines salvation and reprobation. Luther concludes:

> That part of the will [the *synteresis*] is firmly rooted, so that even in those who are damned, the singular cause *(sola causa)* of the whole infernal penalty in their rejection of him [sc. Christ] and their willing, with intense vehemence, a contrary [form of] salvation.[2]

These strong statements in support of the salutary resources and possibilities of the *synteresis* do not escape a certain ambiguity, as is already indicated by Luther's insistence upon the defection and incongruity of *tota voluntas* and *tota ratio* from what is good and true. If one is going to speak of the *synteresis* "of the will" and "of the reason," it would seem that the defection and incongruity of the "whole will" and "whole reason" would have serious repercussions on the parts.

But this is only the beginning of the difficulties we find in this sermon. There is the statement that all experience concupiscence to be completely invincible and incapable of removal by man's own resources and plans.[3] It is argued that it is "in the wings of Christ" that

---

tia Patris, et pro sananda voluntate missus est Spiritus, sic ut ille lucem rationi, hic ignem voluntati conferret, ac sic intelligeret et amaret invisibilia et supra se existentia, quae per synteresin apta est intelligere ac amare, sed impediente rationis et voluntatis defectu non diligit nec intelligit. Ideo semper gemendum et orandum. Simile est cum medicina aegroti, quia aegrotus adhuc utique habet synteresin sanitatis, quam medici vocant vires naturae, quia sunt apti et inclinati agere ea quae sani agunt, sed non possunt agere. Si enim non esset residuum sanitatis aliquod, desperata esset aegritudo et incurabilis."

[1] *Ibid.*, 32.14ff: "Resuscitabilis itaque est natura, nisi ponatur obex et gratiae resistatur, quod faciunt impii, qui freti sua synteresi et prae voluntate ac sapientia propria nolunt restaurari, sed sani sibi videntur." Bernhard Lohse underestimates the soteriological potency of the *synteresis* for Luther in this sermon, when he concludes that the conformity between the *synteresis rationis* and the *sapientia Dei* exists "nur in der ohnmächtigen Verzweiflung über die Sünde." *Ratio und Fides. Eine Untersuchung über die ratio in der Theologie Luthers* (Göttingen, 1958), 31.

[2] *WA* 1,32.16ff: "Igitur adeo radicaliter ista portio voluntatis inest, ut etiam in damnatis sola sit causa totius pene inferni, quod nolunt eum et volunt contrariam salutem inaestimabili vehementia." See the statement that the will is "naturaliter inclinata ad bonum" and the understanding "ad verum" in Luther's comments on Lombard (1509-10). *Luthers Werke in Auswahl*, 5, 14.31ff (*WA* 9,79.16ff). We agree with Leif Grane's conclusion that, in the commentary on Lombard, Luther considers the will to be good in itself, oriented by its nature to the good, and sinful only as it freely succumbs to the constantly present threat of concupiscence: sin is *actus voluntarius*. *Contra Gabrielem*, 276f.

[3] *WA* 1,35.34ff: "Per legem cognitio peccati [Rom. 3:20]. Nam si cognoscatur, quod nullis consiliis, nullis auxiliis nostris concupiscentia ex nobis possit auferri, et haec contra legem est, quae dicit 'non concupisces', et experimur omnes invin-

salvation is to be obtained, since "we are utterly unable to be saved by our own righteousness."[1] Further, hope, the antidote to despair, is directed to salvation in Christ, not to the resources of the *synteresis voluntatis et rationis*.[2] Finally, there is the apparent suspicion on Luther's part that the resources of the *synteresis* do not automatically react to the emergence of one's own opinion as the *medium* to a salutary goal. For we find him urging that one ought to detest such an event, ought to bewail his misery, and ought to petition assistance.[3]

In light of these ambiguities, if not conscious qualifications of the efficacy of the *synteresis*, the following questions can be raised. Does the placement of hope in the "wings of Christ" entail the suspension of the "vestiges of God" in our wings as significant soteriological resources? Does the description of salvation as taking refuge under the wings of Christ through hope suggest an alternative to a restoration and resuscitation of nature as the form of salvation? Is natural conformity with the will and wisdom of God *per synteresim* to be considered a serious and necessary foundation for historical conformity with God? Is the conflict between the divine and human wills such that what discongruity at the point of "means to the end" really involves is a basic disagreement over the end itself?

In regard to the last question, we call attention to Luther's statement: "all want to be saved and please God [conformity with respect to the end]; but they dissent from that by which God is to be pleased [absence of conformity with respect to the means]."[4] To say, as Luther does here, that all will to be saved and please God, and yet all dissent

---

cibilem esse concupiscentiam penitus, quid restat, nisi ut sapientia carnis cesset et cedat, desperet in semetipsa, pereat et humiliata aliunde quaerat auxilium, quod sibi praestare nequit."

[1] *Ibid.*, 31:3ff: "Sic enim et ego semper praedico de Christo, gallina nostra, efficitur mihi errans et falsum dictum 'Vult dominus esse gallina nostra ad salutem, sed nos nolumus' [Matt. 23:37]. Hoc est enim, quod dixi, quod nos nostris iustitiis prorsus salvari non possumus, sed sub alas huius gallinae nostrae oportet nos confugere, ut quod minus in nobis est de eius plenitudine accipiamus. Sic enim Malach. 4 [2], 'Et orietur vobis timentibus nomen meum Sol iustitiae et salus in pennis eius.' Et psalm. 90 [4], 'Scapulis suis obumbrabit tibi, et sub pennis eius sperabis.' Et psalm. 62 [8-9], 'Et in velamento alarum tuarum sperabo, me suscepit dextera tua."

[2] Cf. *supra*, note 1.

[3] *WA* 1,35.9f: "Quoties nos proprio sensu percipimus moveri ad statuendam propriam opinionem, cum gemitu destestari nos ipsos debemus et nostram deflere miseriam." Cf. *ibid.*, 36.27ff, *supra*, p. 140, note 4.

[4] *WA* 1,30.31f: "Tota conflictatio est de mediis ad finem: de fine consentiunt omnes. Omnes volunt salvari et Deo placere, sed dissentiunt in eo, in quo placendum est." See *infra*, 190-91.

from that by which God is to be pleased, is not tidy reasoning. What the establishment of "one's own opinion" as the *medium salutis* would seem to entail is the establishment of a concept of salvation *(finis)* which is quite different from that understanding of salvation which is pleasing to God. There is a logical contradiction on Luther's part here, which suggests his awareness of a deeper-lying soteriological contradiction within the nature of man.

We emphasize that the issues we have raised with the interpretation of this sermon do not concern the existence or non-existence of a natural tendency toward what one assumes to be a salutary goal. The question which begs to be answered is whether such a tendency, granting its existence, plays as prominent a soteriological role in Luther's theological thought as the *Seelengrund* and *synteresis* play for the theological thought of Tauler and Gerson respectively. This question will be our Virgil as we resume our journey through the *Dictata* (sections 2-5 and Chapter X) and explore the conclusions Luther draws in the lectures on Romans and in his marginal notes on Tauler's Sermons and on Gabriel Biel's *Sentences* commentary (Chapter XI).

Further, by introducing the descriptive phrases, 'natural conformity' and 'historical conformity' with God, we indicate our intention of extending the issues raised by the *synteresis voluntatis et rationis* not only into the area of anthropology and natural 'covenant' (sections 2-5), but also into the area of Luther's historical covenant theology (chapter X), as this becomes manifest in his remarks about the *meritum de congruo* and *facere quod in se est* in the *Dictata*. In this undertaking, we will draw freely from the insights we have received in the first chapter of our study.

As we proceed, we will work with the same hypothesis employed in our studies of Tauler and Gerson, viz., that the attribution of a significant soteriological role to anthropological resources available to man *post peccatum Adae* is not of minor significance to the form in which the order of salvation and the union with God in this life is understood. The issues which appear on the level of anthropology are mirrors in which the full range of a theologian's thought can be seen.

What we have said here is applicable not only to the medieval mystical traditions, as we have encountered them in Tauler and Gerson, but to the scholastic traditions as well. The assumptions that God and man are bound as first Cause and secondary cause and that human nature is naturally and inalienably directed to God as its proper end (final Cause), are not unrelated to Thomas' conviction that God is a debtor to His system of salvation (the Church and her means of grace).[1] And the assumption that man can *ex puris naturalibus* and with God's blessing love God above all things is not unrelated to the nominalist conviction that God is a debtor to those who do the best that is in their power.[2] Nor are these convictions on the level of man's

[1] After arguing that merit is possible only "secundum praesuppositionem divinae ordinationis," Thomas draws the conclusion: "Dicendum quod quia actio nostra non habet rationem meriti nisi ex praesuppositione divinae ordinationis, non sequitur quod Deus efficiatur simpliciter debitor nobis, sed sibi ipsi, inquantum debitum est ut sua ordinatio impleatur." *STh* (Ottawa ed.) I-II[ae], q. 114, art. 1, 1391a. He argues further that God moves man's will and what God, not man, intends is infallibly achieved, concluding: "Et tunc habet necessitatem ad id quod ordinatur a deo, non quidem coactionis, sed infallibilitatis, quia intentio dei deficere non potest..." *Ibid.*, q. 112, art. 3, 1376[a]. Behind these statements is not only the philosophical cause-effect schema which Thomas appropriates from Aristotle, and which, on the one hand, makes it quite clear that God holds the initiative in salvation (cf. *ibid.*, q. 112, art. 1, 1374[a]) and, on the other hand, establishes an ontologically fixed relation between God (first Cause) and creatures (secondary causes). *Ibid.*, q. 114, art. 8, 1397[a]. Also present is the basic assumption that nature is inalienably oriented to God as the principle and end of natural good: "Natura... diligit deum super omnia, prout est principium et finis naturalis boni..." *Ibid.*, q. 109, art. 3, 1355[a]. "Diligere autem Deum super omnia est quiddam connaturale homini; et etiam cuilibet creaturae non solum rationali, sed irrationali et etiam inanimatae, secundum modum amoris qui unicuique creaturae competere potest." *Ibid.*, q. 109, art. 3, 1354*b*. Cf. the persuasive argument of W. Pannenberg that Thomas entangles God in His own system: "...Intention und Ausführung [können] im göttlichen Wollen nicht streng gesondert werden." The "Gegenüber" of God and man is thus seriously threatened. *Die Prädestinationslehre des Duns Skotus* (Göttingen, 1954), 40, 86-88, 42f, 54. See also the important monograph by Ernst Wolf, "Zur Frage des Naturrechts bei Thomas von Aquin und bei Luther," *Peregrinatio. Studien zur reformatorischen Theologie und zum Kirchenproblem* (München, 1962), 198f.

[2] Grane argues that Scotus, Occam and Biel (illogically) juxtapose an Augustinian doctrine of God with an Aristotelian estimate of the efficacy of man's natural powers. *Contra Gabrielem*, 218; cf. 214. Oberman writes that with Biel "man's moral ascent meets God's gracious descent." *The Harvest of Medieval Theology*, 153. See further Oberman's discussion of Biel's "almost Thomist" position on natural law. *Ibid.*, 109. Paul Vignaux concludes in his study of Luther and Occam that, "impuissante à meriter l'acceptation au salut, la nature selon Ockham n'apparaît nullement inacceptable à Dieu, telle qu'elle est, bonne en soi." "Sur Luther et Ockham," *FS*, 32 (1950), in *W. Ockham (1349-1949): Aufsätze zu seiner Philosophie und Theologie* (Münster, 1950), 26-27. Finally, one should not overlook the important little study by Heinrich Appel, in which the interrelation between the *synteresis*, *bonum morale* and the reception of divine grace is summarized as follows: "Die Scholastiker lehren, daß der Mensch kraft der synteresis fähig sei, aus eigenen Kräften das Gute zu thun... Im Grunde genommen ist das bonum morale die Vorstufe zum bonum meritorium. Das bonum morale soll nur dann zum meritorium werden können, wenn Gottes Gnade hinzutritt, aber Gottes

natural condition and relation to God disconnected with the *de facto* form in which the life of faith is understood by Thomas and Biel, viz., as a progressive enhancement of human nature through loving activity *(fides infusa caritate formata)* which is empowered by the impartation of a supernatural *forma accidentalis* to the soul *(gratia infusa/gratum faciens)*.[1]

2. NATURAL 'COVENANT' IN THE *DICTATA*: A REAL ISSUE?

There are sufficient passages in the *Dictata* which so emphasize the inability of man, *post peccatum Adae*, to initiate and preserve a saving relation with God that it may appear quite superfluous to raise the issue of a natural 'covenant' in which resources requisite to such initiation and preservation are ascribed to the reason and will of man. Not only do we find general statements which describe human life as an unconcerned sleeping and dreaming,[2] transient as the hay in the fields and "incapable of [receiving] eternal mercy,"[3] but also statements which emphasize man's inability even to recognize his need for redemption. He is as dust, yet until the Spirit brings him to the acknowledgement *(agnitio)* of this situation his plight remains unknown to him.[4] Before the gospel comes and makes it manifest, he is unaware that he is "under the wrath of God;"[5] only "through faith and the Spirit" are the wrath of God and the sins of man known.[6] In short,

---

Gnade, wird weiter gelehrt, fehlt keinem, der das bonum morale thut, soviel in seinen Kräften steht." *Die Lehre der Scholastiker von der Synteresis* (Rostock, 1891), 56. For Luther's break with this nominalist assumption and the consequences it entails for the crystallization of his theology, see our discussion *infra*, 159ff, 184ff.

[1] See Reinhold Seeberg, *Lehrbuch der Dogmengeschichte*, II (Erlangen, 1898), 103f. In regard to Biel and nominalism, see especially Paul Vignaux who concludes that, *de potentia Dei ordinata*, "le nominalisme demeure dans la perspective de l'habitus." *Luther, commentateur des Sentences. Études de philosophie médiévale*, XXI (Paris, 1935), 79, n. 3; cf. 66, 71f.

[2] *WA* 4,54.24 (*Schol.* to Ps. 89:5): "...vere somnium est vita hominum."

[3] *WA* 4,165,4f (*Gl.* to Ps. 102:15): "...*Homo*, inquantum homo et nondum filius Dei, *sicut faenum*, quare non est capax eterne misericordie, sed transitorie tantummodo et foenee, sicut ipse fenum est..." Cf. 4,446.11ff.

[4] *WA* 4,171.22ff (*Gl.* to Ps. 103:29): "...Mystice: aufert spiritum eorum et dat spiritum suum, quando peccatores convertit et deficere facit. Tunc in pulverem suum revertuntur, i.e. in agnitionem sui, quod sint pulvis. Et ita renovantur et creantur in novam creaturam." Cf. 4,383.7ff.

[5] *WA* 4,50.27f (*Gl.* to Ps. 89:1): "Ignoravit enim omnis homo se esse sub ira Dei, donec evangelium veniret et eam manifestaret."

[6] *WA* 4,60.4ff (*Schol.* to Ps. 89:11): "*Quoniam quis novit potestatem ire tue et pre timore tuo iram tuam dinumerare?* q.d. nullus scit, quanta sit fortitudo ire tue, quam

"damnation of the flesh" and the "justification of the soul" are possible only through God's power.[1]

As we have seen in section 1, however, Luther's remarks about the *synteresis voluntatis et rationis*, occurring at a time when he is in the middle of the *Dictata* (December, 1514), make our question a legitimate and important one. This is especially true when these remarks are considered together with his espousal of an apparently strong *meritum de congruo* and *facere quod in se est*, crucial cornerstones in the Pelagian covenant theology of late medieval nominalism. We must, therefore, turn to the question of the nature of the *synteresis* in the *Dictata*. But first, let us prepare the way.

3. *DUPLEX PECCATUM* AND *DUPLEX CONFESSIO*

Before we take up the issue of the *synteresis*, introductory remarks are in order concerning Luther's understanding of the two-fold character of sin and of confession. We call attention especially to the importance of *agnitio* in one's *becoming* a sinner. For it is precisely within the context of this problem—how man becomes an acknowledged sinner—that the question of the soteriological significance of the *synteresis* must be answered.

In the *scholia* to psalm 50, we find the following statement.

> First, all men are in sins and sin before God, i.e. all men are truly sinners. Secondly, God declared this very fact through the prophets, and finally He gave it confirmation in the suffering of Christ. For it is because of the sins of man that God made Him suffer and die. Thirdly, God is not justified in Himself, but in His words and in us. Fourthly, it is when we acknowledge *(agnoscimus)* ourselves to be sinners before God—for such we are—that we become sinners.[2]

---

nullus resistere, nullus fugere, nullus flectere potest, nisi tu eis revelaveris, quod fit per fidem et spiritum." Cf. 4,388.30ff, 233.10ff.

[1] *WA* 4,115.20ff (*Gl.* to Ps. 96:8): "Ex iudiciis tuis patet, quod es altissimus. Quia animam iustificare et carnem damnare coram deo non potest nisi altissimus, qui potestatem huius rei habet. Quis enim salvabit, quem ille non salvabit? Quis damnabit, quem ille non damnat?"

[2] *WA* 3,287.32-288.7 (*Schol.* to Ps. 50:6): "Primo. Omnes homines sunt in peccatis coram deo et peccant, i.e. sunt peccatores vere. Secundo. Hoc ipsum deus per prophetas testatus est et tandem per passionem Christi idem probavit; quia propter peccata hominum fecit eum pati et mori. Tertio. Deus in seipso non iustificatur, sed in suis sermonibus et in nobis. Quarto. Tunc fimus peccatores, quando tales nos esse agnoscimus, quia tales coram deo sumus."

Here Luther speaks of sin in a two-fold sense. All men are *peccatores vere*, a fact declared and witnessed in the Old and New Testaments —not a 'natural' fact. But all men do not acknowledge their sinfulness; all are not 'acknowledged sinners' before God.

In the *scholion* on psalm 1:1, it is argued that the unacknowledged and unconfessed sinner sins doubly *(duplex peccatum)*, for he not only walks in the "way of sinners" and is impious through his conscious and free *(deliberate, voluntarie)* consent to it, but he goes still a step further and becomes "idolatrous." He defends himself against correction and rebuke, excuses his sinful condition, establishes his own iniquity against God and His righteousness and refuses to make confession and give glory to God.[1] In terms of our earlier discussion, he creates by and for himself the 'objective context' in which salvation is to be found; he defines *what* salvation is and the *means* to it.[2]

Over against this situation, the confession of sin and the judgment of oneself as sinful not only justify and verify God, but they also justify and make the one who so confesses and judges truthful. For he acknowledges himself to be as God declares him to be, and he is thus in conformity and harmony with God.[3]

If the refusal to become a sinner by refusing to acknowledge and confess one's sinfulness and, indeed, even defending oneself in it

---

[1] *WA* 55,II.2.3-3.10 (*Schol.* to Ps. 1:1): "Impietas enim contra Deum est et contra cultum eius, qui est pietas. Quod autem addit 'consilium', notat voluntatis vitium, quia de industria et voluntarie, deliberate et consilio impii agunt, non ex ignorantia... *Et in via peccatorum non stetit.* 'Via peccatorum' est ipsa vita impiorum de qua iam dictum est, in quam 'abeunt', qui fiunt impii. Sed hic secundus gradus est peior, qui facit primum peccatum duplex, et iam non sunt 'impii', sed quod plus est, 'peccatores'. 'Peccatum' autem in Scriptura frequentius pro idolatria capitur. Hoc est autem duplex peccatum: stare, defendere, resistere corrigenti et revocanti, 'nolle acquiescere', sicut Saul 1 Reg. 16 [I Kings 15:20f], 'declinare cor in verba malitie ad excusandas excusationes in peccatis', seipsum iustificare, postquam peccavit, ac sic suam iniquitatem statuere contra Deum et iustitiam eius, i.e. negare Deum et idolum fingere sibi, suarum manuum opus, negare confessionem et gloriam Deo, sicut fecerunt Iudei tunc et usque nunc contra Christum. Ideo iam non tantum 'impii' in simplici peccato, sed et 'peccatores' in duplici." See Luther's *Adnotationes Quincuplici Psalterio adscriptae* (Faber Stapulensis), *WA* 4, 467.7ff.

[2] See *supra*, p. 118ff.

[3] *WA* 3,289.31ff (*Schol.* to Ps. 50:7): "Qui sese iustificat, Deum condemnat, qui illum peccatorem esse affirmat per omnes scripturas, maxime ps. 13 [3f] ut apostolus allegat Ro. 3 [10f]. Qui sese iudicat et confitetur peccatum deum iustificat et verificat; quia dicit id de se, quod deus dicit de eo. Et ita iam conformis deo est et verax et iustus, sicut deus, cum quo concordat. Quia eadem dicunt." 3,291.27f (*Schol.* to Ps. 50:7): "...accusare seipsum sit iustificare deum et per consequens seipsum."

makes one 'doubly' sinful before God, then he who becomes a sinner through the confession of his sinfulness is 'doubly' graced before God. Two passages from the *scholia* to psalm 95, where we find a consideration of *duplex confessio* in the detailed context of Luther's anthropology, make this instructively clear. He writes first:

> In the soul is [the power of] understanding and will. The former is adorned by confession, the latter by beauty, the one through light, faith and understanding, the other through heat, love and affection. Thus, confession is that light of the mind by which we know what we are in ourselves and what we have from God. The acknowledgement of these is true two-fold confession: confession of our misery, sins and evils and of the mercy, grace and goodness of God. And that is the full adornment of the intellect, reason and the speculative powers. Through this adornment man is unable to deny God the things that are His and to attribute to himself what are not his own. Therefore, it is most properly called 'confession,' for what belongs to each is confessed and attributed to each. But 'beauty' is the good will, the appetitive power, adorned with all the practical virtues, by which one loves in himself the things of God and hates what are his own in accordance with what prior confession has shown him. But all these things are only in God's sight—there, to this end, he is illumined.[1]

A few lines later in these same *scholia*, Luther picks up the terms, *confessio* and *pulchritudo*, once again. He now stresses their identity *(idem)* and the simultaneity *(simul)* of confessed sin and righteousness before God. This identity expresses the correlative, reciprocal relationship between *intellectus (confessio)* and *affectus (pulchritudo)*, and this simultaneity manifests the 'reconciled dualism' after which Luther quests in the *Dictata*.[2] *Confessio* and *pulchritudo*, confessed sin and righteousness, are now brought together as Luther summarizes:

---

[1] *WA* 4,109.16ff (*Schol.* to Ps. 95:6): "In anima autem est intelligentia et voluntas; ista per confessionem, hec per pulchritudinem ornatur; ista per lucem, hec per calorem; ista per fidem, hec per amorem; ista per intellectum, hec per affectum. Ergo confessio est ipsa lux mentis, qua cognoscimus nos, quid simus in nobis et quid deus in nobis, quid ex nobis, quid ex deo habemus. Agnitio autem ista utriusque rei est ipsa vera duplex confessio, scilicet miserie nostre et misericordie dei, peccati nostri et gratie dei, malitie nostre et bonitatis dei. Et iste est totus ornatus intellectus, rationis, speculative virtutis; per hanc enim fit, ut homo non possit negare deo que dei sunt, nec potest sibi attribuere que sua non sunt. Ideo propriissime dicitur 'confessio', quia confitetur et tribuit unicuique quod suum est. Sed 'pulchritudo' est bona voluntas, totus ornatus practice virtutis, vis appetitive: quo amat in se que dei sunt et odit que sua sunt, sicut confessio prior ostenderat. Sed hec omnia non nisi in conspectu dei sunt; ibi enim ad hoc illuminatur."

[2] Cf. *supra*, p. 111ff, 130ff.

> In another way, confession and beauty are understood as identical *(idem)*... For by the same grace with which the soul is adorned, it is at the same time *(simul)* confessed that we are nothing and have everything from God. And so our confession is the extent to which we are nothing, and our beauty is the extent to which we have received [from God]. Acknowledge, therefore, that you are nothing and you have confession. Acknowledge the mercy of God and you will be beautiful. Be filth to yourself and you will be beautiful to God. Be infirm to yourself and you will be strong to God. Be a sinner to yourself and you will be righteous before God.[1]

In these passages it is clear that knowledge of sin, i.e. the achievement of the status of an acknowledged sinner, is contingent upon special divine activity, which illumines the intellective powers and correlatively warms the affective powers. Further, the achievement of this recognition—the 'understanding' and 'affection' of sinfulness—is not only the reconciliation of the 'dualism' of *homo peccator* and *homo iustus* but also the occasion for its establishment and permanence *(simul!)*. Or put another way, the confession of sin and the achievement of beauty and righteousness are correlative, simultaneous and abiding *in conspectu dei*.

4. *SYNTERESIS* IN THE *DICTATA*: TWO QUALIFICATIONS

As we have seen, the problem which sinfulness poses is the inability to recognize and confess that one is sinful. The *vere peccatores* are the unacknowledged sinners; the acknowledged sinners are 'simultaneously' also not sinners, for by 'becoming' sinners they have become righteous.

Does the *synteresis voluntatis et rationis* play a crucial role in one's becoming a sinner? As a residue of health and the orientation of reason to what is true and the will to what is good, does it provide a foundation for the initiation of the order of salvation?[2] In this section,

[1] *WA* 4,110.11ff (*Schol.* to Ps. 95:6): "Potest et aliter intelligi, quod confessio et pulchritudo idem sit... Quia eadem gratia, qua ornatur anima, simul confitetur nos esse nihil et ex deo habere omnia. Et ita inquantum nihil sumus, confessio nostra est, inquantum accepimus, pulchritudo nostra est. Agnosce ergo, quod nihil es, et habes confessionem, et agnosce misericordiam dei et pulcher eris. Tibi esto fedus, et eris deo pulcher. Tibi esto infirmus, et eris deo fortis. Tibi esto peccator, et eris deo iustus."

[2] The following statement suggests that the reaction to sin is both natural and automatic: "Quando enim anima peccaverit, mox incipit strepitus et murmur syntheresis, que valde clamorosa vox est in auribus dei." *WA* 3,617.36f (*Schol.* to Ps. 80:8). See our discussion of *clamare*, *infra*, 152ff, 174ff.

we will specify two qualifications which Luther makes in regard to the soteriological efficacy of the *synteresis*. These will make possible an answer to these questions, as we consider the operation of the *synteresis* in conjunction with Luther's understanding of *clamare* (section 5). The important point to which we will be working is the following. The fact that the *synteresis* may be designated an agent through which man cries to God in the face of sin is not Luther's major concern with it. What concerns him, as the discussion of *duplex peccatum* has shown, is the way in which one reaches the point that he is able to recognize and acknowledge his sinfulness. For it is only in such recognition that crying to God occurs. We will argue from a variety of perspectives throughout the remainder of our study that it is the *intellectus* and *affectus* of faith and hope, and not the insight of a synteretically endowed and directed conscience, heart, soul, spirit or mind, which makes this possible.

Writing in 1513, Luther contrasts the righteous man's awareness of divine presence with the life of the impious, who conducts himself as if God's eyes were shut to his activities. He then argues that the impious are nonetheless "interrogated" by God, who warns them by "beating on the *synteresis*." The conclusion is drawn that no one is so evil that he fails to sense the "murmur of reason and the *synteresis*," in accordance with the Aristotelian dictum: "reason always calls out to the highest things."[1]

Aristotelian reason *or* a special "beating" of God: does Luther consider the *synteresis* to be a natural and uninterrupted awareness of and orientation to the highest things in accordance with the Aristotelian definition of *ratio*, or is the awareness of the things which convict one of his evil before God historically contingent upon special divine activity? The statement immediately following answers:

> Although as far as the impious are concerned, God seems to be blind, they are nonetheless unable to deny that they sense themselves to be accused by conscience and censured by the *synteresis*, which ask: 'Why do you do evil?' He who, therefore, does not yet everywhere and always fear and think ahead to God's reaction [to what he does] is one for whom the eyes of the Lord have no regard. To him, God sleeps

[1] *WA* 55,II.113.1ff (*Schol.* to Ps. 10:5): "Quia iusti semper agunt (in timore), ac si Dominus eos videat. Impii autem secure ambulant, quasi Deus clausis, palpebris eos non videat, cum tamen etiam sic eos 'interroget' et pulset in syntheresi monendo iuxta illud Apoc. 3[20]: 'Ego sto ad ostium pulsans' etc. Quia nullus est tam malus, quin sentiat rationis murmur et syntheresim iuxta illud: 'Ratio semper deprecatur ad optima'." See Aristotle, *Ethica*, I,13,1102*b*.14f; *infra*, 207.

—the very God who nevertheless is incapable of sleeping, since 'the eyes of the Lord are upon the righteous' [1 Pet. 3:12], and, 'behold, He who watches over Israel will neither slumber nor sleep' [ps. 121:4]. His eyes are open when He makes us have open eyes and to be vigilant. They are shut, however, to him whom He permits to sleep and to fall, or when He allows us to know nothing about Him.[1]

In this passage we find the first of two qualifications of the operation of the *synteresis*. The *synteresis* is not presented as a 'natural' operation in the sense of being universal and automatic, contingent upon anthropological resources possessed by all men and mobilized or immobilized as one wills. The universal presence of the *synteresis* is not denied; a particular, soteriological operation is stringently qualified inasmuch as it is possible for man to know utterly nothing about God. The effectiveness of the *synteresis* depends upon special divine activity.

In early 1514, a second qualification of the *synteresis* is manifest. In the *scholia* to psalm 41, Luther argues that "a *synteresis* and desire of good" exist "inextinguishably" in man, although they are impeded in many. This resource is paralleled with the "desire" to depart "from the Synagogue into the Church and from Egypt and sins into grace," suggesting that the *synteresis* has not only moral *(desyderium boni)*, but also soteriological *(desyderium exire de peccatis in gratiam)* dimensions. Yet one notes the conclusions: "God certainly heeds this desire, and especially does He hear it favorably *after Christ has made Himself a mediator for it*."[2]

Although this Christological interjection is hardly indicative of a Christological exclusivity, it does introduce a second significant qualification of the soteriological potential of the *synteresis*. Further, bearing in mind Luther's parallel of the *synteresis* and *desyderium boni* with the

[1] *WA* 55,II.113.9ff (*Schol.* to Ps. 10:5): "...Etsi coram impiis Deus videatur non videre, non tamen possunt negare, quin sentiant se argui conscientia et queri a syntheresi, cur male faciant. Qui ergo nondum ubique et semper Deum timet et providet, hunc nondum respiciunt oculi Domini, quia dormit ei Deus, qui tamen dormire non potest. 'Oculi enim Domini super iustos.' 'Ecce non dormitabit neque dormiet, qui custodit Israel.' Aperti sunt oculi eius, quando facit nos oculos habere apertos et vigilare; 'palpebre' autem sunt ei, quando dormitare et stertere sinit aut permittit nos nihil de eo cogitare."

[2] *WA* 3,238.9ff (*Schol.* to Ps. 41:8): "...Intentio psalmi est ad literam de egressu Synagoge in Ecclesiam, de Aegypto et peccatis in gratiam, et de desyderio sic euntium. Et tale desyderium naturale quidem est in humana natura, quia syntheresis et desyderium boni est inextinguibile in homine, licet impediatur in multis. Et pro tali syntheresi et in persona eius factus est psalmus iste; quod desyderium utique Deus audit et precipue etiam exaudit, postquam Christus pro eo se mediatorem fecit." Emphasis mine.

Synagogue, his comment, following on the heels of this parallel, suggests that christological qualification may, indeed, be *en route* to Christological exclusivity as concerns the location of resources requisite to salvation. He writes:

> The Synagogue was then in the Spirit but not with much depth. Now, however, it is nothing. For then it had something of grace and a little light, but hidden in mystery.[1]

These two qualifications, one making the efficacy of the *synteresis* in the order of salvation strictly dependent upon divine stimulation, the other exalting Christological mediation, are significant. They add additional weight to the importance of the Christological concerns in the December, 1514 sermon, *De propria sapientia et voluntate*. Still, what we have said thus far concerns primarily tendencies in Luther's interpretation of the *synteresis*. Only as we turn to his understanding of *clamare* do we make the decisive step toward the clarification of the issue of a natural 'covenant' in the *Dictata*, and toward the confirmation of our conviction that Luther considers the *synteresis*, in itself, to be soteriologically inefficacious in the fullest possible sense of the word.

5. *CLAMOR* AND *SPES*: THE ABSENCE OF A NATURAL 'COVENANT'

In this section, we will consider *clamare* in conjunction with its materially parallel terms: *petere*, *expectare*, *implorare*, *invocare*, *murmurare*, *desiderare*, *lugere*, and *gemere*. Each of these verbs can be associated, directly or indirectly, with the operation of the *synteresis*. Our argument will be two-fold. First, we will argue that *clamare* concerns a reaction to the recognition and acknowledgement of one's sinfulness and soteriological impotence in the face of the oppressiveness of sin and death. In personal awareness that one is oppressed by sins, *clamare* is the pronouncement of a *non in homine* upon all possible resources requisite to salvation.

Secondly, *clamare* concerns a corresponding and existentially simultaneous reaction to the recognition of soteriological resources in the promises, words and works of God: *desyderium Christi*! In this sense, and we emphasize this point, *clamare* is the immediate correlate of *spes*, which directs the one who cannot 'subsist' in himself to a 'substance'

[1] *WA* 3,239.23f (*Schol.* to Ps. 41:8): "Synagoga autem in spiritu modicus tunc erat. Sed nunc nihil: quia tunc habuit aliquid et modicum lumen et gratiae, sed occultum in mysterio."

outside himself: *substantia rerum sperandarum, substantia rerum futurarum.* To state our position succinctly: one cries for what he does not have, but only as he is fully aware that he does not have it does he cry for it, and only as it is recognized and acknowledged as being somewhere other than with him is it clear to him that he does not have it. It is within such a unifying 'objective context,' where one sees both the misery in himself and what he lacks and needs to overcome this misery, that *clamare* is to be understood.

Several passages are important in this regard. In the *scholia* to psalm 80, Luther places the historical deliverance from Egypt in the service of understanding the spiritual deliverance of the faithful from the oppression of sins. Of particular concern to us is the point at which "crying to God" or the "invocation of God" occurs.

First, Luther writes, God warns us and causes us to be mindful of the misery in which we are prior to our deliverance. In this awareness of tribulation and the full weight of the burden of sins, an invocation and crying to God "through the *synteresis*" occurs, an action understood through the parable of the prodigal son, whose crying occurs in the midst of his awareness that he is damned.[1]

In the *scholia* to psalm 78, Luther comments on the rapidity and ease with which one falls from his high purposes and schemes, and cites specifically the way in which the grand plans one erects are crumbled by the "people of the flesh." For the flesh both depresses one's cognitive senses and weighs down the affective powers, bringing desolation and operational immobilization. In the wake of this attack, one is an utter pauper. And it is precisely at this point—when all strength is demolished—that one "implores" the assistance of the Lord. For it is only now that he "petitions" divine vengeance upon the flesh and the divine possession of what remains in his desolate condition. Here he asks for the ability to do penance and petitions God to take over and support that "residue of former goods," which remains in the affective *synteresis*.[2]

---

[1] *WA* 3,617.19ff (*Schol.* to Ps. 80:8): "*In tribulatione invocasti me et liberavi te: et exaudivi in abscondito tempestatis* [vs. 8]. Hoc in Aegypto factum est. Sed nunc multo magis in spiritu. Monet enim nos et memores facit miserie nostre, in qua fuimus ante neomeniam istam, ut perpetuo cogitemus penitere et torcular calcare salutis. Cum enim dixisset 'divertit ab oneribus etc.', iam rationem assignat: quoniam in tali tuo labore et tribulatione invocasti me etc. Hec invocatio potest vel ea intelligi, quando adhuc in peccatis per syntheresim clamat ad deum, sicut filius prodigus a longe agens agnoscitur." Cf. further in reference to the parable of the prodigal son, 4,206.12f. See 3,548.38ff.

[2] *WA* 3,603.24ff (*Schol.* to Ps. 78:7): "Experientia autem docet nos, quam cito

It is a frequently expressed conclusion in Luther's thought that only as one is oppressed by sins, "senses" himself driven by the Devil and coerced by his sinful members into uninterrupted *(semper)* sinfulness,[1] and "acknowledges" his infirmity and proneness to evil, does he "cry," "mourn" and "groan" to God.[2] He cries with the voice and desire of the heart "out of the depths *(de profundis)*," i.e. "out of a multitude of sins and intense miseries," that God redeem him.[3]

Luther may or may not specify the *synteresis* as the agent of such crying. When he does so specify it, it is as a *synteresis* illumined and aroused by special divine grace and in full awareness of the powerlessness of the whole creature in the face of sin and death. For it is *out of* "a multitude of sins" that one cries, not out of a position of strength—not even a residue of strength.

But we have seen only half of the picture. If, from his level, man cries *out of* a God-awakened recognition of his utter soteriological impotence, what are the 'objective' correlates *from* and *for* which he cries on the level of God's graciousness? We approach this question through another question: who are the crying and groaning people? Does the psalmist speak for mankind?

It is clear that Luther considers all men to cry and groan in this life: *clamor* and *gemitus* are not only the *proprietates fidei*.[4] However, and

---

et facile a propositis et regulis prestitutis labamur. Multa proponimus et grandes structuras erigimus in intellectu. Sed iste gentes carnis desolantur ea omnia cito. Caro enim deprimit sensum multa cogitantem (quo ad intellectum) et aggravat animam (quo ad affectum), ne opera producat, id est comedit Iacob et locum eius desolatur. Inde sequitur, quod pauperes facti sumus nimis, et quod adiutorium domini imploremus contra illa. // Tunc petitur, ut vindicta illorum nota fiat in carne, et relique mortificatorum possideantur a domino, id est ut penitentiam opere faciamus et residuum preteritorum bonorum, quod in affectu remansit syntheresico, a domino suscipiatur et possideatur."

[1] *WA* 3,535.31ff (*Schol.* to Ps. 76:2): "...Filii Israel in Aegypto clamaverunt ad dominum oppressi dura servitute. Ita peccator oppressus peccatis, sentiens se cogi a diabolo et membris peccati ad peccandum semper, clamat intus et murmurat gravi conscientie voce."

[2] *WA* 4,154.10ff (*Schol.* to Ps. 101:6): "...A voce gemitus adhesit (adhesisse agnoscit) os carni sue, quia videt et sentit sese infirmum ad bonum et pronum ad malum." 4,154.18ff (*Schol.* to Ps. 101:6): "Talem autem sese invenit omnis recte compunctus, quia vehementer sese infirmum invenit ad bonum et pronum ad malum. Ideo gemit et luget. Quod non faciunt, qui ita anxii et lugentes non sunt, id est qui suam infirmitatem non agnoscunt nec pronitatem ad malum percipiunt, sed sibi fortes et boni satis videntur."

[3] *WA* 4,418.23-419.1 (*Gl.* to Ps. 129:1-2): "*De profundis* de multis peccatis et miseriis interioribus *clamavi* voce et desiderio cordis *ad te domine; domine exaudi*, ut redimas me de profundis, *vocem meam* cordis, que vere est mea."

[4] On the other hand, the crying and groaning with which Luther is primarily

this is the important point of distinction, while all men groan and cry, they do not all do so out of the same recognition nor from and for the same 'objects.'

The Jews, heretics and prideful cry to the Lord, but they are not heard since they do not cry from the law of the Lord *(lex Domini)* and from the law of faith *(lex fidei)*, but rather from their own law *(lex sua)*, the law which their sins construct *(lex peccatorum)*.[1] The ungrateful and forgetful of God "murmur," but they do not do so because they seek future or spiritual things nor because they have faith in God, but because the temporal and present things which they desire are absent.[2] It is in the absence of present, visible things—not in the recognition and acknowledgement of the burden of sins—and in the desire for temporal goods and pleasures—not in the hope for spiritual things—that these people cry and murmur.

The situation with the *populus fidelis* is the very reverse. They have heard of the power, wisdom and strength of God, and, seeing the infirmity of their own strength and the condemnation of their own righteousness, wisdom and power, they acknowledge their unrighteousness, foolishness and impotence before God.[3] The faithful people cry not on their own but upon divine initiative;[4] and they cry not to those

---

concerned are certainly the *proprietates fidei*. In this connection, he writes that could we see the magnitude of our sins and God's wrath against us—a 'sighting' made possible in faith—then we would cry and groan: "Quia si et nos iram dei et magnitudinem peccatorum videre possemus, tunc etiam sic gemeremus et doleremus..." *WA* 3,211.34f (*Gl.* to Ps. 37:1). And he can insist that one should groan at least over his inability to groan: "...geme saltem quod gemere non potes." 3,431.10 (*Schol.* to Ps. 68:17)

[1] *WA* 4,322.6ff (*Schol.* to Ps. 118:29): "Qui clamant ad Dominum, nec exaudivit eos ps. 17 [42]. Quare? Quia non de lege Domini clamant, non de lege fidei, sed de lege sua et lege peccatorum."

[2] *WA* 4,198.35ff (*Gl.* to Ps. 105:7): "Quia cum presentia et temporalia tantummodo saperent, futura vel spirit[u]alia sperare non poterant; ideo absentibus temporalibus semper murmurabant nec crediderunt Deo." See 4,150.1ff.

[3] *WA* 4,204.22ff (*Schol.* to Ps. 105:2): "*Quis loquetur potentias domini?* Quia dominus factus est nobis virtus et sapientia et potentia, ideo ipse solus a nobis predicandus est, et nostra potencia infirmanda et sapientia infatuanda atque bonitas seu iustitia nostra condemnanda. Sed ...pauci hoc volunt... Sed suam iustitiam, sapientiam, potentiam iactant et querunt, et in hoc ipso faciunt iniquitatem et non iudicium. Quod faciunt solum illi, quia suam iustitiam, sapientiam, potentiam condemnant, agnoscentes iniustitiam, insipientiam, impotentiam suam coram deo. Et sic resurgunt pii in iudico, sed impii non sic..."

[4] *WA* 4,206.37f (*Gl.* to Ps. 106:6): "Sic deus misericorditer visitat eos, qui dissimulant penitere per flagellum aliquod et tunc clamant et se in errore esse cognoscunt."

who give carnal salvation, but to the "father and saviour of the spirit."[1] They cry because they know that God has *promised* to hear their crying.[2]

The faithful man cries out of, from and for what every man should cry out of, from and for, but as an unacknowledged sinner cannot. The psalmist, therefore, does not speak for all men. He speaks for the *populus fidelis* in the Synagogue and in the Church. Luther is quite explicit in this regard.

The faithful in the Old Testament cry "with the whole heart," with "all their powers" and with "great desire." Such is not done by all; only he who has the "most perfect *desire for Christ*," for truth, righteousness and eternal salvation cries in this way.[3] Moreover, the foundation of this crying is neither a potential nor an actual act of merit, for the cry is *before* the emergence of the day of grace, i.e. before the time of Christ (first Advent) and of merit. Indeed, the cry comes even before the time of crying. It is a cry founded upon and emergent from sheer hope in the "words" and "promises" of God.[4]

In a *scholion* on psalm 118:146—"I cried to you, 'save me [O Lord],' in order that I might keep your commandments"—Luther makes it clear that the situation of the faithful people in the Church is no less

---

[1] *WA* 4,300.27f (*Gl.* to Ps. 118:146): "*Clamavi ad te* patrem et salvatorem spirituum, non ad potestates huius mundi, qui salvat carnaliter."

[2] *WA* 4,21.29f (*Gl.* to Ps. 85:7): "'Exaudisti', i.e. quia preordinasti exaudire seu promisisti, ergo clamavi."

[3] *WA* 4,373.34-373.4 (*Schol.* to Ps. 118:145): "Ipsa enim est, que hic dicit: 'Clamavi in toto corde', id est omnibus viribus et magno desiderio te vocavi. Quantus est iste ardor, qui non vocare tantum, sed clamare cogit et clamare toto corde! Qui enim ore vocat, aliquid facit, sed magis qui vocando clamat, maxime autem qui tota voce et pulmone clamat. Sed multo amplius est cor quam vox. Ergo toto corde clamare non cuiuscunque est, sed perfectissime Christum desiderantis. At nunc multi nec sibilant quidem, sed est silentium in corde, quia nullum desiderium Christi, veritatis, iustitie, salutis eterne. Magnus autem clamor in lucra, honores, voluptates..." Cf. 4,373.15f, 4,149,11f. Emphasis mine.

[4] *WA* 4,301.20ff (*Schol.* to Ps. 118:147): "...Quilibet gratiam petens necesse est, ut veniat in immaturitate, q.d. licet nondum sit tempus clamandi et salvandi et forte vanum ante lucem surgere, eo quod indignus sit exaudiri, qui nondum est in gratia; tamen nimius ardor et desiderium gratie et misericordie cogit me prevenire, maxime quia in verba tua speravi: promisisti enim petentibus gratiam, licet sint indigni." See 4,334.22ff, where *promissiones*, not the "virtus meritorum meorum" form the foundation of the *petitio*. Cf. 4,344.24ff: "ex promissione et misericordia" and not "ex operibus" is the singular way to salvation. See still further 4,390.22f, 393,1f, where *petere*, *orare* and *clamare* are the very antitheses of *meritum*. This conjunction of *clamare* with human activity rather than with human nature, i.e. its application to the issue of man's historical relation to God rather than to the issue of a possible natural 'covenant', anticipates our next chapter. See *infra*, p. 159ff, 197ff.

under a "not yet." "Always crying for salvation" is the *abiding* posture of the faithful people in every age. Luther writes:

> 'I seek my salvation so that I may serve you.' In this way, [the psalmist] confesses that he is an infirm and miserable servant of the law of sin. This confession is made by every humble man whether he is one who is well advanced or one who is only beginning. The prideful man, however, refuses to make such a confession, for he considers himself to be saved and without sin. Thus, he does not cry for salvation so that he may keep God's commandments. He thinks that he has kept them, and hence he rests in undisturbed security. Our situation is different. We are indeed always saved in regard to those things which we have attained and experienced as beginners. But in regard to those things which are still before us and to which we must extend ourselves by going further, we are not yet saved but rather infirm, captive and miserable. In regard to these things salvation is something for which we are always to be crying *(semper clamandum)*. For the people who cry here were not without salvation, light and grace. But they did not yet have the promised future [salvation] which they knew was still to be attained, still to be sought and desired. This future [salvation] was present with them enclosed in their faith in what was still to be revealed. In such a way we are all between grace received and grace still to be received. And thus our situation is always one of grace for grace and progression, in ourselves, from clarity into clarity.[1]

What is the significance of Luther's understanding of *clamare*? Two things can be said. First, *clamare* expresses that character of the *vita fidei* which we found to result from Luther's denial of an immanent and final *terminus ad quem* in this life.[2] Specifically, *clamare* is the existential form of the recognition and acknowledgement that there is no anthropological structure and resource which can establish a saving relationship with God, and, further, no residence of grace in the faith-

---

[1] *WA* 4,374.36ff (*Schol.* to Ps. 118:146): "Ad hoc quero salvus esse, ut serviam tibi. Ac per hoc utique se confitetur infirmum, miserum, captivum et sub lege peccati esse. Quod et omnis humilis facit, non tantum incipiens, sed et proficiens. Superbus autem hoc negat, quia sibi salvus et sine peccato videtur: Unde neque clamat salvari, ut custodiat mandata tua, quia custodisse se putat et secure sibi tacet. Nos autem non sic, sed semper sumus salvi quidem ad ea, que habemus et peregimus incipiendo. Sed ad ea, que ante nos sunt et in que extendi habemus proficiendo, nondum salvi sumus, sed infirmi, captivi, miseri. Ideo et ibi clamandum est semper pro salute. Nam et iste populus, qui hic clamat, non erat sine salute et luce et gratia. Sed futuram nondum habuit, promissam, ad quam tenebatur habendam, querendam, desiderandam. Tenebatur enim clausus in fide revelanda. Ita omnes sumus in medio gratie habite et habende, ut sic semper sit gratia pro gratia et profectus in nobis de claritate in claritatem."

[2] See *supra*, 130ff.

ful which would prevent their being always—at every step of their 'progression'—*clamantes.*

Secondly, the existence of any form of a natural 'covenant,' to which one might turn with hope in the face of sin and death, is altogether denied by the confession made by *clamare.* Not only must the *synteresis* be illumined and aroused by special (historical) divine activity, but it must be possessed and taken over by God. In itself, the *synteresis* is as soteriologically de-substantial as the creature. It is for this reason that, in the *clamare* passages cited here which concern that *for which* and *from which* one cries, there is no mention of the *synteresis.* The promises and testimonies of God form the foundation for man's crying to God: a God-awakened *desyderium Christi,* not a natural *desyderium boni et veri.* Only faith and hope, which by definition look to the promises of God and not to the resources of human nature, 'substantiate' human life before God and in the face of sin and death. Summarized as succinctly as possible, the correlation made manifest by *clamare* is not a desire for what is good and true through the *synteresis* of the will and reason, but the desire for Christ through the affection of hope and the understanding of faith.

CHAPTER TEN

HOMINI FACIENTI QUOD IN SE EST, DEUS INFALLIBILITER DAT GRATIAM?

1. THE PROBLEM

The *sola gratia* appears repeatedly in the *Dictata*, and in explicit denial of the influence of man's activity and merits upon the will of God. We read that only God's mercy, "anticipating and moving *gratis*, without merit," turns man to Christ[1] and that mercy and truth "precede and prepare righteousness."[2] The blessings of God are "purely of mercy and not merited."[3] Our spiritual goods are "unowed."[4] Indeed, the grace of God operates "without us and ahead of us."[5] For just as Christ is conceived by the Holy Spirit, so, *tropologice*, every faithful person is "justified and reborn by no human work, but by the grace of God alone and the activity of the Holy Spirit."[6]

In spite of these eloquent statements, the issue of a highly refined Pelagian *facere quod in se est* and *meritum de congruo* is something more than a strawman. Not only does one find the systematic content of these *termini technici* of nominalist covenant theology in the *Dictata*,

[1] *WA* 4,446.31ff (*Gl.* to Ps. 143:2): "Non enim protegit nisi liberatum, nec liberat nisi susceptum, nec suscipit nisi ad se confugientem. Non confugit autem ad eum, nisi misericordia eius preventus et motus gratis sine merito. Igitur quia miseretur, nos cum fiducia ad eum confugiamus."

[2] *WA* 4,38.38ff (*Gl.* to Ps. 88:15): "Quod ipsi parantur in sedem tuam iustitia et iudicio, et quod in eos advenit, non habent ex operibus et meritis suis precedentibus, sed misericordia et veritas precedit et preparat iustitiam." Cf. 4,309.6ff, 35ff.

[3] *WA* 4,212.8f (*Schol.* to Ps. 106:8): "...beneficia dei in nobis sunt pure misericordie et non merita."

[4] *WA* 4,133.14ff (*Schol.* to Ps. 100:1): "Ergo bona spiritualia, immo quecunque, tribue misericordie Dei et lauda Dominum in hiis. Mala autem corporalia huiusque vite molestias temporales tibi imputa ut propria et debita: illa autem indebita et mere gratis data."

[5] *WA* 3,389.12f (*Gl.* to Ps. 67:29): "...*Deus...operatus es* antequam cooperemur *in nobis* etiam sine nobis et ante nos."

[6] *WA* 3,468.17f (*Schol.* to Ps. 71:6): "Sicut enim Christus de spiritu sancto conceptus est: ita quilibet fidelis nullo opere humano, sed sola gratia dei et operatione spiritus sancti iustificatur et renascitur." Note the placement of *promissio* and *meritum* in diametrical opposition: "...*Vivifica me* per gratie augmentum *secundum verbum tuum* secundum regulam Evangelii tui, vel secundum promissum, non secundum meritum." 4,284.2ff (*Gl.* to Ps. 118:25). Cf. 4,288.10ff; 304.5ff.

but one also finds that these terms are explicitly employed to define the relationship between human preparation and God's granting grace.[1] This fact makes it impossible to dismiss this issue by simply concluding that "mournful waiting and praying" are the only forms of preparation for the advents of Christ;[2] that preparation for grace is only "the direction of [one's] mind, heart and conduct to the Advent [of Christ];"[3] that preparation for grace is "already the work of grace;"[4] or that man's disposition for grace is "nothing other than God's 'Disposition'."[5]

In order to bring the full complexity of the problem before the reader, we call attention to four strong statements, two relatively early (Summer, 1514), in which the systematic content of nominalist covenant theology is evident, and two quite late (Autumn, 1515), in which the *termini technici* themselves become manifest.

In the *scholion* on psalm 50:7—"Behold, I am conceived in iniquities"—Luther underscores the sinfulness of all men before God and the residence of righteousness with God alone. To emphasize further these points, it is argued that the faith and grace by which we are righteous in the present would have no efficacy apart from God's covenant *(nisi pactum Dei faceret)*. We are saved, therefore, solely on the basis of God's having covenanted with us to the effect that whosoever believes and is baptised is saved (Mark 16:16)—a covenant to which God is true and faithful.

Thus, we are always sinful before God, and God alone exercises the power of righteousness in accordance with the covenant He has made with us. But, Luther concludes, highlighting the issue before us, he who thinks that he is without sin and does not confess his sin is not justified by God in His covenant. Why? Because the unbelief of man *incapacitates* God so that He is unable to save him *(eo quod non possit Deus)*.[6]

---

[1] Cf. *infra*, 162ff, 174ff.

[2] Vogelsang, *Die Anfänge von Luthers Christologie*, 71.

[3] Rudolf Hermann, *Luthers These 'Gerecht und Sünder zugleich'* (1930), in photomechanical reprint (Gütersloh, 1960), 204, n. 4; cf. 141, n. 1.

[4] Werner Jetter, *Die Taufe beim jungen Luther* (Tübingen, 1954), 279.

[5] Link, *Das Ringen Luthers*, 55.

[6] *WA* 3,288.39ff: "Ergo verum est, quod tibi sum peccator et peccavi, ut tu solus gloriosus sis in iustitia et iustificeris solus, quando omnes sumus peccatores. Et verum est. Quia adeo nos coram deo sumus iniusti et indigni, ut quecunque facere possemus, nihil coram eo sint. Immo et fides et gratia, quibus hodie iustificamur, non iustificarent nos ex seipsis, nisi pactum dei faceret. Ex eo enim precise, quia testamentum et pactum nobiscum fecit, ut qui crediderit et baptisatus fuerit,

A second early passage is a marginal gloss on psalm 66:5—"since you judge the people in equity." Commenting on the justness of the judgment of Christ *(iudicium Christi in equitate est)*, Luther contrasts the saving and reprobating policies of God formerly and now, in the present, according to the spirit. Formerly, God saved the Jews bodily and without discrimination—the good and the evil, the faithful and the unfaithful, alike. Now, in the time of Christ, only those who have willed to believe are saved, and only those who have refused to believe are reprobated.

This change in policy is contingent upon the relocation of salvation and reprobation from the corporeal to the spiritual sphere:

> The reason for this is that He now saves with regard to the spirit, for He is not able simultaneously to make common cause with evil and good, as He was well able to do formerly in the letter and flesh.[1]

In these *scholia*, are salvation and reprobation made contingent upon human choice? Is the relationship between the confession of one's sin, the decision to believe and divine acceptance of the one who believes a relation of antecedent and consequent, the former demanding, even legally requiring, the latter? When these *scholia* are considered in the context of Luther's two early sermons (1510-12) and the December, 1514 sermon, *De propria sapientia et voluntate*,[2] there are certainly sufficient anthropological grounds for a very positive answer to these questions. Although the *termini technici* are absent, Luther is assuming a highly refined version of a Pelagian *facere quod in se est* and *meritum*

---

salvus sit, salvi sumus. [Mark 16:16]. In hoc autem pacto deus est verax et fidelis et sicut promissit, servat. Quare verum est nos esse in peccatis coram illo semper, ut scilicet ipse in pacto suo et testamento, quod nobiscum pepigit, iustificator sit. Unde litera Hebr. sic 'Tibi soli peccavi, propterea iustificabis in verbo tuo,' i.e. pacto tuo. Qui ergo non peccat nec peccatum confitetur, hunc non iustificat deus in pacto: quia 'qui non credit etc' [Mark 16:16], *eo quod non possit deus*." Cf. 3,437. 23: "...non potest deus eos salvare contra eorum voluntatem."

[1] *WA* 3,383.27ff: "Iudicium Christi in equitate est, quod Iudeos, quia Domino volunt omnia, ut dicitur, in sacco vendere sine electione et reprobatione, non omnes suscepit indifferenter, sicut olim in figura, quando omnes secundum carnem indifferenter salvavit tam bonos quam malos, tam credulos quam incredulos, tam patientes quam murmuratores, sed tantum eos qui credere voluerunt. Similiter quod non omnes gentes reprobavit sicut olim in figura, sed tantum eas, que credere noluerunt. Et sic sine iniquitate, i.e. sine acceptione personarum regnat, ut quicunque crediderit, salvetur et quicunque non crediderit, condemnetur. Sed hec est equitas, quia omnibus est equus et idem... Et ratio est, quia nunc salvat secundum spiritum, quod non potest malis simul et bonis communicari, olim autem in litera et carne, quod bene potuit utrisque communicari."

[2] See *supra*, 139ff.

de congruo. Has the situation changed in Autumn, 1515? Let us push further, taking two later *scholia*, which appear to be of an identical nature, into consideration.

Commenting on psalm 118:168—"I have kept your commandments; for all my ways are in your sight"—Luther concludes that there is a difference between commandments and testimonies. The former concern what we promise to do, and, although we fail often, God believes and accepts those who promise to do these things. Testimonies, on the other hand, have reference to the things which God promises to do, and we accept them by believing and hoping and loving them.[1]

It is emphasized by Luther that the commandments have priority *(prius)* to the testimonies, for he who is not actively obedient to the commandments does not acknowledge or care for the promises of God. The commandments prepare the soul for the promises of God, and without the commandments there is no realization of hope, for hope requires "some merits."[2] We note, however, that on the very next page of the *Dictata*, in the exposition of 118:169—"O Lord, let my cry come before you"—Luther places *oratio*, *deprecatio* and *petitio* in uncompromising opposition to meritorious activity: "Non oratione, sed operatione fit meritum."[3] A specification of the *faciens* of the faithful people is being drawn from Luther's understanding of the theological significance of *clamare*.[4]

Finally, we call attention to the lengthy *scholion* on psalm 115:1—"Not from ourselves, O Lord, not from ourselves." In his exposition, Luther explicitly espouses a *meritum de congruo* and *facere quod in se est*.

---

[1] *WA* 4,389.19ff: "Differentiam ponit inter 'mandata' et 'testimonia'...quod 'mandata' sunt, que nos promittimus implere, et promissionibus iis deus credit et acceptat, licet fallamus eum sepius... 'Testimonia' autem sunt, que deus promittit et nos credimus et acceptamus credendo, sperando, amando. Ipse autem non fallit, sicut nos ipsum fallimus..."

[2] *WA* 4,389.36ff: "Et nota, quod prius 'mandata' quam testimonia' dicit. Quoniam qui non opere prius obedierit mandatis, neque promissa agnoscit aut curat, quia mandata preparant animam ad spem promissorum, et sine mandatis non fit spes, que merita aliqua prerequirit." Note, however, that love of the *mandata dei* gains soteriological significance only when it is embraced by the "expectation" *(expectare)* and "desire" *(desiderium)* for Christ. 4,303.21ff.

[3] *WA* 4.390.22ff: "Quod autem petit dari, significat gratiam esse, non meritum. Non enim sunt debita, que petuntur, sed gratia donanda. Non oratione, sed operatione fit meritum." Note also that when Luther now writes that God is unable to save the "nolentes", he clearly has reference to the situation of man *coram lege dei* and not *coram promissionibus dei*. Cf. 4.370.12ff.

[4] See our discussion of *clamare*, *infra*, 174ff.

Luther begins his commentary with the insistence that the advent of Christ in the flesh is based on the sheer mercy of a God who promises, and is in no way contingent upon either the merits or demerits of human nature. However, it was "fitting" that there be a disposition to and preparation for His reception, as was in fact done through the lineage of Christ (i.e. the house of David) in the whole of the Old Testament.[1]

God's mercy, therefore, underlies the promise of His Son and God's truthfulness the fact that He came. Luther cites Micah 7:20—"What you swore to our fathers in olden days, truth to Jacob and mercy to Abraham, you will give [us]"—in order to illustrate the location of the initiative with God alone. All is done in accordance with God's "swearing", not as we have merited.[2]

Following this strong statement on divine promise and fidelity, Luther returns to a consideration of the *praeparatio* for the spiritual and future advents of Christ. He writes that God has required nothing except our preparation, so that we may be capable of receiving His gifts. It is just as if an earthly prince or king should promise a thief or murderer a hundred gulden only on condition that he be prepared to expect *(expectare)* him at an appointed place and time. Clearly the king is a 'debtor' to this man on the basis of his gratuitous promise and mercy. But it is equally clear that neither the merit nor the demerit of the recipient occasions the promise.[3]

This parable exemplifies man's situation before the spiritual *(per gratiam)* and future *(per gloriam)* advents of Christ. Neither advent is conditioned by human merit; both are based solely upon the promise of a merciful God. For in reference to the spiritual advent, we have

---

[1] *WA* 4,261.25ff: "*Non nobis domine, non nobis.* Sicut adventus Christi in carnem ex mera misericordia dei promittentis datus, nec meritis humane nature donatus, nec demeritis negatus: nihilominus tamen preparationem et dispositionem oportuit fieri ad eum suscipiendum, sicut factum est in toto vetere testamento per lineam Christi."

[2] *WA* 4,261.29ff: "Nam quod promisit deus filium suum, fuit misericordia, quod autem exhibuit, fuit veritas et fidelitas eius, sicut Miche [7:20] ultimo: 'dabis veritatem Iacob et misericordiam Abraam: sicut iurasti patribus nostris a diebus antiquis,' non ait 'sicut meruimus,' sed 'sicut iurasti.' Unde quod deus fecit se debitorem nobis, ex promissione est miserentis, non ex dignitate nature humane merentis."

[3] *WA* 4,261.34ff: "Nihil enim nisi preparationem requisivit, ut essemus capaces doni illius, sicut si princeps vel rex terre suo latroni aut homicide promitteret centum floreni, tantummodo ut ille tempore et loco statuto eum expectaret paratus. Hic patet, quod rex ille debitor esset ex gratuita promissione sua et misericordia sine merito illius, nec demerito illius negaret, quod promisit."

God's promise: "Petition and it will be given you, seek and you will find, knock and it will be opened to you" (Matt. 7:7-8).[1]

It is precisely at this point—"he who *petitions*, receives"—that Luther expresses agreement with those *doctores ecclesiae* who say that God infallibly gives His grace to one who does what is in his power. Such preparation, it is argued, is not "from worthiness" *(de condigno)*, for grace is a gift too incomparable to human nature that the latter can presume worthiness of it. Preparation for grace, rather, is from a "fittingness" *(de congruo)* made possible by the promise of God and His covenant of mercy.[2]

The identical situation is depicted in regard to the future advent of Christ. Titus 2:12f—"...that we may live justly and soberly and piously in this age, expecting *(expectantes)* what is a blessed hope"—reveals the promise of God for this advent. And, again, a *de condigno* preparation and reception is denied, while a "bene congrue" is presented. For while all is given *gratis*, i.e. only on the basis of the promise of God's mercy, God wishes that we be prepared to the extent that we are able.[3]

Thus, Luther concludes, just as the law was a preparation of the Old Testament people for the reception of the first advent, so our doing as much as is in us disposes us to the grace of the spiritual advent. And in like manner, the whole time of grace is a preparation for future glory and the final advent. In regard to all three advents, God commands us to be vigilant and prepared to expect *(expectare)* Him.[4]

---

[1] *WA* 4,261.39-262.3: "Ita et spiritualis adventus est per gratiam et futurus per gloriam, quia non ex meritis nostris, sed ex mera promissione miserentis dei. Promisit enim pro spirituali adventu sic: 'Petite et accipietis, querite et invenietis, pulsate et aperietur vobis. Omnis enim qui petit, accipit etc.'"

[2] *WA* 4,262.4ff: "Hinc recte dicunt doctores, quod homini facienti quod in se est, deus infallibiliter dat gratiam, et licet non de condigno sese possit ad gratiam preparare, quia est incomparabilis, tamen bene de congruo propter promissionem istam dei et pactum misericordie."

[3] *WA* 4,262.7ff: "Sic pro adventu futuro promisit, 'ut iuste et sobrie et pie vivamus in hoc seculo, expectantes beatam spem' [Titus 2:12f]. Quia quantumvis sancte hic vixerimus, vix est dispositio et preparatio ad futuram gloriam, que revelabitur in nobis, adeo ut Apostolus dicat: 'Non sunt condigne passiones huius temporis etc' [Rom. 8:18]. Sed bene congrue. Ideo omnia tribuit gratis et ex promissione tantum misericordie sue, licet ad hoc nos velit esse paratos quantum in nobis est."

[4] *WA* 4,262.13ff: "Unde sicut lex figura fuit et preparatio populi ad Christum suscipiendum, ita nostra factio quantum in nobis est, disponit nos ad gratiam. Atque totum tempus gratie preparatio est ad futuram gloriam et adventum secundum. Idcirco iubet nos vigilare, paratos esse et expectare eum etc."

The two later, as the two earlier, passages which we have summarized in this section appear to be solidly within the sphere of nominalist covenant theology. Indeed, Luther seems to wave the nominalist banner rather boldly: "facienti quod in se est, deus infallibiliter dat gratiam." Heiko Oberman draws what would seem to be the obvious conclusion: so far as the *meritum de congruo* and *facere quod in se est* between the human will and divine grace are concerned, Luther is still *within the nominalist fold* until 1515-16.[1]

Our more comprehensive approach to Luther's thought in the preceding chapters places us in a position (1) to specify the theological motifs which converge to make the *facere quod in se est*, as this is understood in nominalism, simply untenable for Luther, and (2) to suggest why the phrase, 'bene congrue,' remains important to him once the nominalist content is dismissed.

We emphasize the importance of approaching this problem with attention directed to the *de facto*, historical situation of man before God. One cannot come to grips with it by simply pointing to the frequency with which Luther invokes a *sola gratia*. For in nominalist thought, as Oberman has made clear,[2] the *sola gratia* is no stranger within the sphere of the *potentia absoluta* of God. And in this context, it is by no means exclusive of a soteriologically significant *facere quod in se est* and *meritum de congruo* in the area of the *potentia ordinata* of God—the historical order of salvation which God has mercifully established (doctrine of predestination) in His eternal freedom.

To be effective, therefore, our argumentation will focus on Luther's *qualification of the historical situation* of man before God. Generally, we will have special regard to the way in which the promissorial nature of God's presence and the soteriologically de-substantial character of human life converge to create a new understanding of 'congruency'

[1] Oberman concludes: "There is...good reason to believe that Luther at the end of 1509 has become independent of the nominalistic tradition as regards the relation of faith and reason while retaining till 1515-16 the doctrine of the *facere quod in se est* in its application to the relation of will and grace." "Facientibus quod in se est Deus non denegat gratiam: Robert Holcot, O.P. and the Beginnings of Luther's Theology," *HTR*, 55 (1962), 333. It is unquestionably clear that in his 1516 *Quaestio de viribus et voluntate hominis sine gratia disputata*, Luther is explicitly critical of the *meritum de congruo* and the *facere quod in se est*: "Homo, Dei gratia exclusa, praecepta eius servare nequaquam potest neque se, vel de congruo vel de condigno, ad gratiam praeparare, verum necessario sub peccato manet." And: "Homo quando facit quod in se est, peccat, cum nec velle aut cogitare ex seipso possit." *WA* 1,147.10ff; 148.14f.

[2] Oberman, *HTR* (1962), 327.

between the will of man and the grace of God. Specifically, we will focus attention on (1) the unnominalistic treatment of *bonitas* as an exclusive property of God (section 2), (2) the location of all soteriological resources in the first and spiritual advents of Christ (section 3), and (3) the reinterpretation of *praeparatio* through *clamare* and *expectare* (section 4). As we have seen, *expectare* was directly present in the *scholion* on psalm 115:1, and indirectly relevant to the interpretation of the *scholion* on 118:168. And we have seen that Luther places *deprecatio* (and its parallels) in uncompromising opposition to *meritum*.[1] What does it mean, for Luther, that man 'expects' and 'cries out' to God? When we have answered this question, the untenability of the nominalist *facere quod in se est* for Luther will be manifest.

2. *BONITAS:* A *PROPRIUM DEI*

A major constituent of the nominalist understanding of the *facere quod in se est* and the *meritum de congruo* is the conviction that human acts can achieve *bonitas* simply by the exercise of man's natural powers *(ex puris naturalibus)*. This *bonitas* is the crucible in which the salutary effects of the *gratia gratum faciens* are received and fomented. To borrow Oberman's analogy:

> ...Grace, the seed of acceptability, has to be planted in fertile earth, that is, the *bonitas* of the act. As regards making the earth fertile *(bonus)*, free will is the horseman, grace the horse.[2]

Leif Grane stresses a similar point in an analysis of Biel's concern to argue against Gregory of Rimini that man can perform morally good acts which are conformed to God *quoad substantiam actus*, i.e. good in themselves and of the same 'substance' as those good acts which are done in a state of grace *(quoad intentionem praecipientis)*. Grane concludes:

---

[1] Cf. *supra*, p. 162, notes 2 and 3.

[2] Oberman, *The Harvest of Medieval Theology*, 163. Biel summarizes: "Anima obicis remotione ac bono motu in deum ex arbitrii libertate elicito primam gratiam mereri potest de congruo. Probatur quia actum facientis quod in se est deus acceptat ad tribuendum gratiam primam, non ex debito iusticie, sed ex sua liberalitate, sed anima removendo obicem, cessando ab actu et consensu peccati et *eliciendo bonum motum in deum* tanquam in suum principium et finem facit quod in se est. Ergo actum remotionis obicis et *bonum motum in deum* acceptat deus de sua liberalitate ad infundendum gratiam." II *Sent.*, d. 27, q. I, *art.* 2, *concl.* 4 (K), cited *ibid.*, 172, note 80. Emphasis mine.

> [Biel's] interest in what man can do naturally and apart from grace (viz. *bonum naturale*) originates in a concern to show that man possesses the possibility of preparing himself for the reception of grace.[1]

With Luther, *bonitas* is consistently absent from discussions of the *meritum de congruo*, and it is never treated in reference to man in a soteriologically significant way. Why is this the case? Because Luther is clear that the only *bonum* admissible within the sphere of salvation is the *bonitas Dei*. He is most emphatic in this regard.

In matters concerning salvation, precisely as in His 'cosmological' activity, God creates *ex nihilo*: "total dejection and depression" are the 'materials' with which He works.[2] God is by definition a giver only: "this is to be God—not to receive goods, but to give them."[3] It is His *proprium* to give benefits "above the power, knowledge and will of man."[4] "Goodness," in distinction from what is "just," is the ability to give "good things for evil,"[5] and it is a property which God alone possesses: God is the benefactor of the "unmerited and unworthy."[6]

For Luther, Christ and the gospel manifest this property of God.[7] Thus, "beauty," i.e. everything in a person which makes him *in-*

---

[1] Grane, *Contra Gabrielem*, 214. cf. 220.

[2] *WA* 4,256.17ff (*Schol.* to Ps. 112:7): "Hec est natura veri creatoris, ex nihilo omnia facere. Idcirco nullum suscitat, nisi qui sit non suscitatus, sed iacens et deiectus. Nec erigit ullum nisi depressum, ita ut, nisi sit nihil erectionis et suscitationis in ipso, sed tota deiectio et depressio, non suscitat nec erigit." Worthy of a separate study in itself is Luther's strong doctrine of providence in the *Dictata*. One of the most conscious criticisms of Aristotle is precisely at this point. See 4,459.28ff, 79.9ff, 61.13ff.

[3] *WA* 4,269.25f (*Schol.* to Ps. 115:12): "Hoc est esse deum: non accipere bona, sed dare, ergo pro malis bona retribuere."

[4] *WA* 4,213.24f (*Schol.* to Ps. 106:8): "Hoc est dei proprium, ut supra virtutem, cognitionem et voluntatem nostram nobis faciat misericordias."

[5] *WA* 4,427.39ff (*Gl.* to Ps. 135:1): "Non enim bonus est, quia reddit bona pro bonis, quod est esse iustum, sed dat pro malis bona. Sicut misericors est, non qui sunt beati, sed qui sunt miseri."

[6] *WA* 4,278.7ff (*Schol.* to Ps. 117:1): "Bonitas enim est, quando quis benefacit immeritis et indignis. Qui enim sunt meriti, iis non benefit, sed iuste fit et redditur bonum pro bono et debitum est eis reddi. Qui autem digni sunt, iis quidem non redditur tanquam meritis, sed tanquam iuste debitum velut superioribus et equalibus. Deus autem indignis et immeritis, insuper et multum demeritis benefecit per Christum incarnatum, quia et per hoc ostendit se esse non fictum, sed verum et viventem deum, quod *nihil boni et meriti a nobis suscepit*, sed omnino gratis tribuit." Emphasis mine.

[7] *WA* 4,289.10ff (*Gl.* to Ps. 118:65): "*Bonitatem fecisti*, i.e. filium in carnem misisti, *cum servo tuo* populo tuo fideli *domine: secundum verbum tuum* promissum tuum, quia 'fecisti', inquit, non 'reddidisti iustitiam'... *Bonitatem* i.e. Christum seu Evangelium Christi." Cf. 4,450.7f.

trinsically worthy of honor and glory, belongs to "Christ alone."[1] Here only, Luther argues, do we men find "our goodness,"[2] in Christ, the "object, cause and fount of faith and the source of our glory and beauty."[3]

Bonitas, therefore, cannot be a property of man *extra Christum* and *extra fidem*; it is present only with the "new man."[4] In Autumn, 1514, Luther emphasizes that men not only disregard the commandments of God "quoad substantiam facti vel operum"—the source of the *bonitas* foundational to the *facere quod in se est* and *meritum de congruo* in nominalist theology—but, what is much more, even ignore them as far as the quality or quantity of the work is concerned.[5] Indeed, it is the very distinguishing mark of the *presumentes*—those presuming "equality with God"—to think that they are what characterizes God alone: "good in themselves."[6]

3. THE *SCHOLIA* ON PSALM 84: THE INVOCATION OF THE *EXTRA NOS*

The central importance of the *scholia* on psalm 84 for understanding the rich, theological complexity of Luther's interpretation of the *iusti-*

[1] *WA* 4,252.10ff (*Schol.* to Ps. 111:3): "'Decor' autem est omne ornamentum in persona, propter quod honoratur et glorificatur. Idcirco ubi gloria est sine decore, vana est. Sed in solo Christo est decor. Idcirco extra Christum omnis gloria est vana."

[2] *WA* 4,336.29ff (*Schol.* to Ps. 118:65): "Igitur Christi adventus est bonitas nostra; quia penas, que sunt mala nostra, abstulit a conscientia primum, deinde etiam auferet a corpore, et sic perfecte erit bonitas nostra. Item 'bonitas'...quia redditur non pro bono quod esset 'Iustum', sed pro malo nobis et iniustitiis nostris."

[3] *WA* 4,242.6ff (*Schol.* to Ps. 110:3): "...ipsa humanitas Christi...est 'gloria et decor.' 'Gloria', quia in multis fidelibus clarificata et revelata, 'decor' autem quo ad se in suis dotibus. Nam secundum hanc ipse est obiectum fidei et causa et fons et caput glorie et decoris nostri, per ipsum enim, id est fidem in ipsum nos clarificamur et decori efficimur, sicut omne concretum per suum abstractum."

[4] *WA* 4,337.17f (*Schol.* to Ps. 118:66): "Bonitas dicitur ad ea, que pertinent ad spiritum et novum hominem..."

[5] *WA* 3,430.1ff (*Schol.* to Ps. 68:17): "...tandem omissiones preceptorum dei, non tantum quoad substantiam facti vel operum, sed multo magis etiam quoad qualitatem vel quantitatem. Quia diligere deum et proximum et cetera, quoties offendisti?" See 4,202.9f. See the development of this motif in the lectures on Romans, *infra*, 206ff.

[6] *WA* 4,210.20ff (*Schol.* to Ps. 106:1): "Duo autem sunt genera hominum, qui non confitentur Domino, quoniam bonus. Primum est desperantium, qui bene credunt, quod potest et novit salvare, sed non credunt, quod etiam velit, metientes divinam voluntatem ad modum sue voluntatis. Alterum est presumentium, qui sese bonos existimant et sibi sufficere, quasi non egeant bonitate divina. Et hii quidem ad equalitatem dei presumunt ascendere, quia volunt esse, quod est deus, scilicet boni in seipsis."

tia dei passiva has been instructively demonstrated in Regin Prenter's study of the differences between Luther's treatment of this psalm and that of Augustine.[1] What strikes us in these *scholia* as being of equal significance with and intimately related to the departure from Augustine in Luther's new understanding of the righteousness of God are Luther's introductory and concluding references to Aristotle,[2] which compose a misguided defense of Aristotle.[3]

We find a long gloss on the first paragraph of the *scholia*, which attacks those who abuse Aristotle. And the concluding remarks of the exposition return again to a 'defense' of the Philosopher. Here we find a polemical context which embraces the *scholia* not only literally, but, as we will argue, materially as well.

What is at issue in these attacks on a sound Aristotelian principle in the midst of a 'defense' of Aristotle is the invocation of a *non in homine* in reference to both the origin and preservation of the 'goods' constitutive of the Christian. We orient our discussion to the interpretation of verse 12: "Truth has arisen in the earth and righteousness looks down from heaven."

Luther develops a consideration of the "truth by which we are truthful."[4] He writes with regard to the reconciliation of righteousness and peace in Christ[5] and the peace with God made possible for man through it. Prior to Christ's coming, there was no peace, only impiety and consequent confusion. For however great one's righteousness may have been through the fulfilment of the law, it was not embraced by peace, at least not the peace of God.[6]

---

[1] See Prenter's conclusion, *supra*, p. 45.

[2] Heinrich Bornkamm recognizes, but does not develop, the importance of Luther's attack on the Aristotelian understanding of righteousness. "Die befreiende Wirkung von Luthers neuem Verständnis der iustitia dei erweist sich auch daran, daß er nun in einer Fülle rasch herausströmender Äußerungen seit den späteren Teilen der Psalmenvorlesung den Gerechtigkeitsbegriff in die Mitte einer lebhaften Auseinandersetzung mit Aristoteles und der Jurisprudenz rückt... An der iustitia dei ist ihm aufgegangen, daß das Gerechtsein dem Gerechthandeln vorausgehen muß." "Iustitia Dei in der Scholastik und bei Luther," *ARG*, 39 (1942), 40-41. There is a two-way street here. The attack on the Aristotelian "Gerechtigkeitsbegriff" can be viewed as an integral part of, and not just consequential to, the new understanding of the *iustitia dei.*

[3] Cf. *infra*, p. 172, note 2.

[4] *WA* 4,15.22ff.

[5] *WA* 4,16.30: "Iustitia et pax osculate sunt, quia idem Christus est utrunque."

[6] *WA* 4,16.20ff: "Sic nunc iustitia nostra Christus est et pax nostra, quam deus nobis dedit. Et per illam nos iustificavit, et ita pacem habemus. Ante ipsum enim non fuit pax, quia nec iustitia nobis, sed impietas, et ideo turbatio... Nam quan-

In the reconciliation of peace and righteousness in Christ, Luther sees the establishment of "truth in the earth" *(veritas in terra)*, i.e. the historical fulfilment of the promises of God to be merciful by sending His Son. This truth in the earth is the *foundation* for man's justification, for the coming to him of righteousness "from heaven" *(iustitia de coelo)*.

What is meant when truth is manifest *within* the earth, but is not *from* the earth, and righteousness looks down from heaven and does not reside on earth?

Luther rewards our patience with a step by step explanation. He points out that God is first true to His promises, and from the exhibition of His fidelity here, we are now to become righteous before Him. We cannot, therefore, come before Him already righteous and demand His fidelity on the basis of meritorious activity, for it is from His, not our own, fidelity that we obtain righteousness. The fact that He is faithful is the incontrovertible touchstone. For it is clear that Christ's coming and His being born "on the earth" was based on the promise of God alone *(sola promissio)* and not on human merits. And since it is through the advent of Christ that we are righteous, it simply cannot be the case that we were first righteous and meritorious, having this as a foundation upon which God should be expected to demonstrate His fidelity by sending His Son. Were this true, Luther exclaims, then God's fidelity will come from heaven and our righteousness will look up from the earth demanding it—a view which exceeds the boundaries of perversity![1]

Continuing and heightening this motif, Luther raises the question why the psalmist speaks of the "origination" of truth within the earth and the "looking down" of righteousness from heaven. His initial answer is that the advent of Christ *(veritas)*, while promised and exhibited to all, is not received by all. Therefore, all are not justified by it, as John 1:11 makes clear for him.

---

tamcunque iustitiam habuerimus ex lege: pax non osculabatur eam, saltem pax dei."

[1] *WA* 4.17.17ff: "Sed nunc sic est, quod prius est deum veracem esse in promissis, et ex illa exhibita nos demum iustos fieri: prius mittat misericordiam et veritatem, et sic iustificabimur. Non autem eum preveniemus iustificati atque eius veritatem meritis expostulemus, sed ex eius veritate iustitiam consequamur. Igitur quia veritas de terra orta est, hinc habemus, quod iustitia de coelo prospicit super nos. Quia quod Christus venit et natus est, promissio sola fuit et non meritum. Et per hoc ipsum iam iustificamur, scilicet per adventum eius. Et non sic, quod prius iusti fuerimus et meriti, et per hoc deus verax sit, quia miserit eum. Alioquin veritas de coelo orietur et iustitia de terra suspiciet: quod est perversissimum." This statement is continued *infra*, p. 171, note 1.

Shifting the tack of his analysis somewhat, Luther focuses on the implications of the psalmist's statement that righteousness "looks down from heaven." He concludes that the psalmist speaks in this way to indicate that the righteousness of Christ is not from us *(ex nobis)*. The 'from heaven' correlates with a 'not from man.' And the psalmist marshals the words 'looks down' in order to indicate that righteousness *remains* in heaven *(in coelo manet)* and has "regard" *(respicere)* to us so that we may become "heavenly."

Summarized, the situation is as follows. Christ comes to the earth so that we may be raised to heaven. He comes to us where we are *(ubi sumus)* so that He might lead us to where He is. His coming is based on God's promise, and it is because of this promise that truth—the advent of Christ as the exhibition of the fidelity of God to His promises—has arisen on the earth. That we now come to Him, however, is achieved by His righteousness which is and remains in heaven. Through fidelity to the promises He made, God comes to us; through righteousness we come to Him:

> This is a marvelous mixture! There it is clear that those who have rejected a residence in heaven are not righteous. For righteousness has not arisen from the earth, but remains in heaven, and from there looks down upon us, electing and giving itself only to those who are chosen.[1]

These comments, together with the other *scholia* considered in this section, indicate that Luther is bringing together the objective context of the gospel, in its historical and existential dimensions,[2] and the discovery of the soteriologically de-substantial nature of human life. The two comments on Aristotle, which provide the *termini* of the *scholia*, and which captured our interest in Luther's interpretation of

---

[1] *WA* 4,17.27ff: "Sed cur dicit 'orta est,' et 'ibi prospexit?' Credo, quia adventus Christi omnibus communis est, sed non susceptio eius in omnibus est. Ad omnes venit, sed non ab omnibus suscipitur, ut Iohan. I [11]: 'In propria venit et sui eum non receperunt.' Ideo dicit: quo ad veritatem de terra ortus est. Quia omnibus promissus, omnibus exhibitus, sed non omnes inde iustificati. Ideo iustitia prospicit de coelo. Quod 'de coelo' ait, non ex nobis esse significat iustitiam Christi. Quod autem 'prospicit' significat eam in coelo manere et nos respicere, ut efficiamur coelestes. Ideo enim venit Christus in terram, ut nos exaltaret in coelum. Venit ad nos ubi sumus, ut duceret ad se ubi est ipse. Sed quod ad nos venit, promissio fecit. Ideo de terra oritur veritas. Quia promissum fuit, ut ad nos veniret. Et sic expleta est veritas. Sed quod nos ad eum venimus, iustitia facit eius. que est in coelo. Et sic per veritatem ipse ad nos, per iustitiam ipsi ad eum. Et inde mira mixtura. Qui ergo noluerunt esse in coelo, non sunt iustificati. Quia non iustitia de terra orta est, sed manet in coelo et prospicit de coelo eligens et electis tantum sese tribuens."

[2] See *supra*, p. 129ff; *infra*, 174.

psalm 84, are instructive in this regard. They suggest that it is the 'embrace' of these two systematic motifs—the objective context of the gospel and the soteriologically de-substantial nature of human life—which forms the framework in which the embrace of peace and righteousness in Christ is discovered. Both comments take their cue from verse 14: "righteousness will precede him and place his feet on the way." We present both in their full contexts before elaborating further this suggestion. First, Luther writes:

> 'Righteousness will precede him.' Or better stated: 'He who is first righteous will do righteous works, and he will not be righteous because he first worked.' This is to say that righteousness will not be from his works, but his works from righteousness—which is directed against the Jews and the prideful who walk in advance of righteousness. For these people think that by first working and doing, they seize righteousness. Therefore, they do not place their feet on the path but perversely place the path under their feet, and want what they do to be righteousness. And they do this even against Aristotle, saying, 'By doing righteous works the righteous are made!' Rather should it be said: 'From being righteous, righteous works are done.' And this is clear from all that we have learned from nature; for as nature teaches, something is not hot because it gives warmth, but, being hot, it gives warmth.[1]

The second comment, employing the same logic from natural analogies, reiterates Luther's attack with even greater precision:

> It is not right to say that a flame is warm because it gives heat, but rather must we say that it warms because it *is* heat, so that heat precedes the flame and causes the flame, 'setting the steps of the flame on the way.' Thus, righteousness precedes—it 'is' before it 'works'—and sets one on the way. I do not have vision because I see, but rather I see because I have vision. Hence, Aristotle is not to be understood as saying that someone is able to do righteous works when he is not yet righteous.[2] He is not able to do this even with a perfect habit. There-

---

[1] *WA* 4,3.26ff (*Gl.* to Ps. 84:1): "'Iustitia ante eum ambulabit.' Melius sic: id est operabitur iusta, quia iustus primum. Et non erit iustus, quia operetur primum. Hoc est: non ex operibus erit eius iustitia, sed opera eius erunt ex iustitia; quod est contra Iudeos et superbos, qui ante iustitiam ambulant. Quia prius operari et agere et sic iustitiam apprehendere se putant. Et ideo non ponunt in via gressus suos, sed potius viam in gressus suos perverse, volentes hanc esse iustitiam, quod operantur. Et hoc etiam contra Aristotelem est dicentem 'operando iusta iusti efficiuntur': sed sic: existendo iusti iusta operantur. Et hoc omnis natura docet; quia non calefaciendo aliquid calefit, sed calefactum calefacit."

[2] For Aristotle, natural virtues like sight and hearing are not acquired, but are already present before they are activated: "we had them before we used them." With moral virtues, however, the situation is the very reverse: "moral virtue comes about as a habit;" "we are adapted by nature to receive them, and are made

> fore, one should be righteous in the will *(iustus in voluntate)* and proceed thence to the work. This is said against the prideful, who want righteousness to be credited to them from what they do. They do not see that righteousness must first be credited to them so that they may work righteously. This righteousness which comes from works and is credited to works is human righteousness *(iustitia humana)*. But the other righteousness which is before every work is the righteousness of God *(iustitia Dei)*. Just as original sin is before every evil work we do, so original righteousness was before every good work we do, in the place of which the righteousness of Christ is given before every meritorious work.[1]

What is witnessed in these comments is the application of the denial of a natural 'covenant' between God and man to the form of man's historical relation with God. Righteousness *precedes* good works *and the will for* good works. This is the insight systematically and Christocentrically belabored throughout the *scholia* on psalm 84. The location of truth, mercy and peace in the advent of Christ *in terram* and of righteousness *in coelo* is the twin form of the recognition of the soteriologically de-substantial nature of human life. A *non in homine* is the anthropological correlate of the *in adventu Christi*. Because the truth which is manifest upon the earth is exclusively *ex adventu Christi* and not *ex homine*, a natural 'covenant,' in which residues of health—*syn-*

---

perfect by habit;" among the "virtues we get by first exercising them" are moral virtues. *Ethica* II,I,1103^{a}.14-1103*b*.2. What Luther does in his 'defense' of Aristotle is to apply to moral virtues (righteousness) what Aristotle says about natural virtues, or put otherwise, Luther interprets his own understanding of righteousness in analogy with Aristotle's understanding of *natural* virtues. Why this total reversal occurs is a question worthy of pursuit, and historically would have to be pursued in regard to 15th and 16th century disputes over the interpretation of Aristotle. Systematically, one may suggest that Luther's, defense by misinterpretation'—and a misinterpretation which does no less than stand Aristotle on his head—may not be so 'misguided' after all but a sardonic statement of the extent of their differences in the understanding of righteousness in this life.

[1] *WA* 4,19.18ff (*Schol.* to Ps. 84:14): "Sicut ergo non valet dicere: ignis calescit, quia calefacit, sed quia calescit seu calidus est, ideo calefacit, et ita calor ante ignem ambulat et ponit in via, id est operatione gressus. Sic iustitia ante ambulat (id est operatur prius quam ipse) ct ponit in via gressus suos. Non enim habeo visum, quia video, sed quia habeo visum, ideo video. Unde nec Aristoteles sic intelligendus est, quod quis iusta operari possit nondum iustus. Sed non potest perfecto habitu. Oportet enim esse iustum in voluntate et sic in opus procedere. Contra autem superbi, qui ex eo quod operantur, volunt sibi imputari iustitiam et non prius imputari sibi iustitiam, ut operentur. Et hec est iustitia humana, que ex operibus fit et imputatur. Sed illa est iustitia Dei, que est ante omne opus. Sicut peccatum originale est ante omne opus nostrum malum; sic fuisset iustitia originalis ante omne opus nostrum bonum. Cuius loco nobis nunc iustitia Christi datur ante omne opus meritorium."

teresis voluntatis et rationis or the *gemuete* and *grunt der selen*—are serious antidotes to despair and resources for initiating one's standing before God and in the face of sin and death, is dismissed. And, as the precedence of righteousness to righteous works and the residence of righteousness with God's electing Will "in heaven" make clear, the denial of a natural 'covenant' is correlative with the dismissal of a historical covenant in which the rational *and* volitional activity of man may obligate God to dispense His grace.

This highlights Luther's fundamental differences not only with the Pelagian covenant theology of nominalism, but also with Tauler and Gerson. Because of Luther's awareness of the *historical* character of the gospel *(veritas in terra)* and of the uniqueness of the objective context which it alone establishes, the reconciliation of peace and righteousness, theologically and existentially, is Christocentric and fidelic rather than theocentric and 'synderetic' (Gerson) or 'gemuetlich' (Tauler). Luther does not speak of the exaltation of the highest powers of the soul to a form of generic similitude with God (Gerson), nor of the absorption of the ground of the soul in the uncreated Ground (Tauler). He speaks of Christ's coming to men "where they are," and the effective presence *(effective, spiritualiter)* of righteousness, peace, mercy and salvation in and through faith in Christ.[1]

4. *CLAMARE: CONGRUENTIA CORAM DEO*

The *scholia* to psalm 84 are not the only occasion on which Luther applies his dismissal of a natural 'covenant' to an understanding of man's historical relation with God. In a *scholion* on psalm 118:17 —"Return to your servant; enliven me that I may keep your words"— this application is most explicit.

Luther first argues unhesitatingly for a *meritum de congruo*, and in the context of what appears to be the traditional understanding of faith as *informis* and *infusa*. The petition that God "return", it is argued, is based on the *meritum de congruo* of those who have served the law *liter-*

[1] *WA* 4,19.32ff (*Schol.* to Ps. 84:14): "Nam quecunque de adventu primo in carnem dicuntur, simul de adventu spirituali intelliguntur. Immo adventus in carnem ordinatur et fit propter istum spiritualem; alioquin nihil profuisset. Unde et ista verba 'misericordia et veritas' non possunt de Christo dici nisi propter adventum secundum; quare iste principaliter intenditur. Quid enim prodesset deum hominem fieri, nisi idipsum credendo salvaremur? Quocirca Christus non dicitur iustitia, pax, misericordia, salus nostra in persona sua nisi effective. Sed fides Christi, qua iustificamur, pacificamur, per quam in nobis regnat." Cf. 4,3.17ff.

aliter, the latter being best understood, we think, as equivalent to a fulfilment of the law *quoad substantiam actus*. Such service, Luther argues further, by no means establishes a *meritum de condigno*. It is based on a congruous or fitting disposition, not on an achieved status of worthiness. For service to the law *literaliter* was a disposition to and training for Christ, just as now faith in Christ is a disposition to and training for glory. It is a *meritum de congruo* on the basis of God's covenant and promise and the faith of the people—a faith which was to be committed to "another faith."[1]

When one reads further, however, he finds alternative interpretations of this verse which introduce every major constituent of Luther's attack on and rejection of a natural 'covenant.' Here we find a denial of human *bonitas*; the emphasis that it is fitting and exclusively characteristic of God to return good, not for good, but for evil; the assertion that we "always sin" and are "always beginning anew;" the insistence that God holds the initiative for any 'retribution' He will make; and the statement that one must be brought to the "recognition," "hope" and "love" for the return of *bona* before he is aroused to keep the commandments.[2] Similar qualifying points are present in Luther's interpretations of the parallels to *retribue*, *vivifica*[3] and *revela*.[4]

In light of this concatenation of motifs, which we have found Luther developing throughout the *Dictata*, and his compression of them into one paragraph which stands in juxtaposition to a statement which supports a *meritum de congruo* and *facere quod in se est*, we can conclude that here is an application of the consequences of the dismissal of a natural 'covenant' to a historical covenant in which the

---

[1] *WA* 4,312.38ff: "Petit autem retribui, quia ii qui legem literaliter servabant, licet non de condigno mererentur, tamen quia erat dispositio et pedagogus in Christo, sicut fides Christi ad gloriam: ideo de congruo fuit meritum ex pacto et promissione dei et fide, que erat in aliam fidem traducenda."

[2] *WA* 4,313.12ff (*Schol.* to Ps. 118:17): "Denique preter hec adhuc aliis modis potest intelligi: primo secundum b. Augustinum: Retribue, scilicet tua bona pro meis malis. Quia per Adam omnes amisimus bona et habemus multa mala. Est autem hoc decens et proprium deitatis, ut reddat bonum pro malis, et non bonum pro bono, ne egere nostris bonis videatur... Secundo moraliter pro quolibet retribue, scilicet gratiam pro culpa actuali, quia semper amittimus, semper peccamus, semper morimur: ideo semper opus habemus, ut retribuat et semper incipiamus a novo. Tercio retribue, id est fac ut retribuas, ut meritum habeam, cui premium fiat et retributio in patria. Quia sic potest exponi anagogice. Quarto fac me retributionem agnoscere et sperare et amare: quia hoc miro modo inflammat ad custodiendum mandata."

[3] *WA* 4,314.1ff.

[4] *WA* 4,314.6ff.

moral *activity* of man significantly conditions the gracious activity of God. The alternative interpretations may be considered either as consciously polemical or as simply clarifying the first interpretation. In either case, it is clear that Luther does not here support a concept of merit and a *congrue* disposition to God in the sense in which nominalism understands them.

A final perspective on this issue is forthcoming when we return once again to the very important term, *clamare*. For just as the *clamare* proved decisive in the rejection of a natural 'covenant,' so we find *scholia* in which it is also the instrument through which the *coup de grâce* can be administered to a Pelagian historical covenant.

Commenting on psalm 118:41—"Let your mercy come upon me, O Lord; save your servant according to your word"—Luther points out that the petition for and the expectation of *(petere* and *expectare)*—sister terms of *clamare*—the advent of Christ (first advent) and the grace of Christ *(adventus spiritualis)* is without human merit. For were this not the case then Christ's coming would be a matter of paying a debt to us. Indeed, He would not come in accordance with God's Word and the sheer promise of mercy, but on the basis of man's own righteousness and in accordance with man's own merit.

The situation is such, Luther concludes, that *moraliter* as well as *literaliter*, the coming of Christ is on the same basis. Just as the human race received Christ not on the basis of its own righteousness but on the basis of God's mercy "to the extent that it had disposed itself *congrue*," so each one receives the grace of God *gratis* "to the extent that he disposes himself *congrue*." Grace, however, is not given on the basis of one's preparation, but on the basis of God's covenant, for God promises to come through this preparation *(per apparatum)*, "*if* He is expected *(expectetur)* and called upon *(invocetur)*."[1]

We call attention to three important points in this *scholion*. First, the *congrue* is employed with no mention of *meritum*. As *bonitas* disappears

---

[1] *WA* 4,329.26ff (*Schol.* to Ps. 118:41): "...petitur adventus et gratia Christi. Et 'veniat' inquit, quia expecto, licet sine merito: quia non tantum veniret tunc, sed redderetur potius debitum. Nec tunc esset 'secundum eloquium tuum' et nudam promissionem misericordie. Ac sic nec esset 'misericordia tua' nec 'veniret' nec 'secundum eloquium tuum', sed esset 'iustitia mea' et 'reddenda secundum meritum meum'. Sic etiam moraliter fit, quia sicut humanum genus recepit Christum non ut iustitiam suam, sed ut misericordiam dei, quantumlibet congrue sese disponebat: ita quilibet gratiam eius gratis accipit, quantumlibet sese congrue disponat. Non enim ex meo paratu, sed ex divino pacto datur, qui promisit per hunc apparatum se venturum, si expectetur et invocetur."

from the discussion of *congrue*, so too does *meritum*![1] Secondly, the interpretive framework for *congrue* is formed by the terms, *expectare* and *invocare*. And, finally, it is in the context of these terms that the conditional "if" is to be understood. A *congrue* relation or disposition to God is one in which man stands *expecting* and *invoking* God's presence.

As we have seen in our previous chapter, he who expects and calls upon God is not one who stands in a position of strength but rather one who has been brought to the recognition and acknowledgement of his utter soteriological impotence. If *praeparatio* means *expectare* and *invocare*, and this composes a *congrue* disposition to God, then by a *congrue* disposition Luther does not mean *bonum morale* or the fulfilment of the commandments of God *quoad substantiam actus*. He means simple expectation on the basis of God's promise and in full recognition and confession of one's utter *discongruity* with God and the things of God. What correlates and 'congrues' from man's side with the *bonitas* and *gratia Dei* are not good works and merits, but sinful works and unrighteousness!

A second *scholion* from psalm 118:147—"I came too soon and I cried; for I hoped above hope in your words"—confirms this situation, as it becomes clear that it is the marriage of *clamare* and *spes*, i.e. the recognition and confession of the soteriologically de-substantial nature of human life in the context of the recognition of the 'substantiating' power of God's promises, that defines *praeparatio* for the *adventus Christi*. Luther writes:

> How is he [the psalmist] able to anticipate God by crying? But he does not simply anticipate Him; he comes even when the time is not yet ripe.[2] For it was not yet day, and the time of grace was not yet present. This was an untimely season. Indeed, it was extremely 'early in the morning' at exactly that time when the night of the law was coming to an end and the breaking of the light of the new law was barely detectable. Therefore, [we hear him saying]: 'Although I am still in a time unfitted for crying, a time when the Spirit is not yet given nor grace and the gospel revealed, still I cry and for this reason: I have your promises. In your words I have hoped above hope. God promised Christ and His grace. Therefore, I come early, even before Christ and

---

[1] Earlier, *expectatio* and *meritum* were tightly bound together: "...expectatio mea, i.e. id quod expecto seu praemium patientie mee." 3.353.4f. (*Gl.* 61:6)

[2] *WA* 4,139.31f: "Matutinum morale est *initium fidei*, oriens quodcunque propositum bonum in anima." Emphasis mine. The *scholion* on psalm 118:147 applies to the faithful people in every age. Cf. 4,375.31ff, beginning, "Moraliter *nos omnes semper* prevenimus immature..." Emphasis mine.

His grace are given and manifest, and I come as one unworthy of both. Still you are faithful to what you have promised. I do not rise up and cry because you are a debtor to me, or because I have merited or am worthy of so great a gift.[1] Were this the case, I would not approach you unexpectedly, but I would step forward as one with a legal claim, demanding what was rightfully owed me. I come rather because I have hoped in your words. It is the mercy of your promise that motivates and emboldens me to petition before merits are present and thus unseasonably!'[2]

5. THE SIMULTANEITY OF OPPOSITES

One encounters a series of explicit *simul* statements in the *Dictata* which bring together conditions of the *vita fidei* which would seem to be irreconcilable, understandable perhaps if they were considered in an antecedent-consequent sequence,[3] but hardly capable of being "simultaneously" together. The believer lives in present, visible evils and sees and hopes for invisible goods.[4] He praises God for his sal-

---

[1] This is stressed elsewhere also. *WA* 4,419.14: "...non quia meruit aut dignus sit." 4,426,8f: "*Omnia quaecunque voluit* non coactus aut alicuius merito preventus nec vi prohibitus, *dominus fecit in caelo...et in terra...*" Oberman stresses a distinction between merit in the weak *(mereri - meritum de congruo)* and in the strong *(promereri - meritum de condigno)* sense. "Das tridentinische Rechtfertigungsdekret im Lichte spätmittelalterlicher Theologie," *ZThK*, 61 (1964), 251ff. To the extent that Luther's repeated distinction *(aut)* between *mereri* and *dignus* can be interpreted in parallel with Oberman's distinction, Luther explicitly excludes both forms of merit from the *ordo salutis* in the *Dictata*. Cf. Vogelsang, *Die Anfänge von Luthers Christologie*, 72f.

[2] *WA* 4,375.16ff: "Quomodo potest prevenire deum clamando? Sed non simpliciter prevenit, immo 'in immaturitate'. Nam nondum erat dies et tempus gratie, sed adhuc immaturum et valde mane, quando iam fere incipiebat nox legis finiri et prope erat ortus nove legis. Ideo licet sim in tempore nondum apto ad clamandum, nondum datus spiritus, qui clamet, non revelata gratia et evangelio: nihilominus clamo, et hoc, quia promissa tua habeo. 'In verba tua supersperavi.' Promisisti enim Christum et gratiam eius: ideo prevenio quidem ante datam et exhibitam, sed utcunque indignus sim, tu tamen verax es, qui promisisti. Neque ideo prevenio et clamo, quia debitor mihi sis, aut ego meruerim aut dignus tanto munere (quia tunc non prevenirem, sed legitime venirem debita poscens), sed quia speravi in verba tua. Misericordia tua promittentis fecit me audacem, ut ante merita et intempestive peterem." Cf. 4,375.31ff.

[3] Luther can speak in this way. 3,345.29f: "Quia nemo per fidem iustificatur nisi prius per humilitatem sese iniustum confiteatur. Hec autem est humilitas." 4,343.31f: "...sicut homines literaliter humiliantur, antequam exaltentur, ita tu hoc spiritualiter et vere...facis..." Note, however, in the *scholion* on psalm 60, the emergence of a "simul": "Non potest deus laudari, iustificari, glorificari, magnificari, admirari, etc nisi *simul et prius* nos vituperemur, accusemur et confundamur et econtra." 3,292.1f. Emphasis mine.

[4] *WA* 3,455.13ff (*Schol.* to Ps. 70:14): "...non tantum in bonis te laudabo, ubi

vation and "simultaneously" groans over the sinfulness, evils and perils in which he remains.[1] He is to bless God and sing of His mercy "simultaneous" with his singing of and blessing God's judgment of him as he suffers injuries, evils and damnation.[2] His descension into humility is "simultaneous" with his ascension in power.[3] His being righteous is "identical" with his confession of sins.[4] Self-denial, confusion and defilement are the only bed-fellows with Christ's honor and beauty in him.[5] Two 'forms,' two 'forms' even diametrically opposed, coexist simultaneously.

This understanding of the simultaneity and congruity of opposites is a motif in opposition to the theological application of the Aristotelian principle that two forms cannot coexist simultaneously. It was the application of this principle that operated in a determinative way to shape Tauler's and Gerson's understanding of the union with God. For Gerson, it is the generic similitude of human and divine 'spirit' that makes possible man's union with God. For Tauler, it is the *weseliche gelicheit* of human and divine 'spirit' that makes possible the *weseliche einikeit* between God and man. *Mutatis mutandis*, for both Tauler and Gerson the *unio mystica* is the point of maximum similitude

est materia totius laudis; sed etiam in malis, in quibus nulla videtur materia laudis, nisi iis qui spe vivunt et in malis presentibus et visibilibus simul invisibilia vident et sperant."

[1] *WA* 3,644.34ff (*Schol.* to Ps. 83:4): "Simul quidem laudare oportet deum et gemere peccata nostra; laudare quia salvi facti sumus, gemere quia peccavimus et in malis sumus huius vite et periculis. Possunt enim hec simul fieri, ut deum laudemus et amemus et delectemur in eo, et tamen nos vituperemus, odiamus et tristemur in nobis."

[2] *WA* 4,131.33f (*Schol.* to Ps. 100:1): "Sed si vere credis, quod indignus sis bonorum et dignus malorum (utrunque enim simul necesse est esse), iam vere cantas misericordiam et iudicium." 4,132.39: "laudans quia misericordiam simul habet cum iudicio."

[3] *WA* 4,178.35f (*Schol.* to Ps. 113:9): "Non enim ascendunt virtutes, nisi nostre infirmitates etiam descendant. Simul fit ascensus et descensus, id est incrementum virtutum et humilitatis."

[4] *WA* 3,409.30ff (*Schol.* to Ps. 67:32): "...quia confiteor me nigram, ideo formosa sum. Quia qui peccat, iustificat deum in sermonibus eius et ita dat gloriam deo, per quod iam ipse quoque iustus est. Quia 'confessio et pulchritudo in conspectu eius' [ps. 96:6]. 'Dixi: confitebor. Et tu remisisti etc.' [ps. 32:5] Ergo confiteri peccatum et esse iustum idem sunt." Cf. 4,239.1f.

[5] *WA* 4,172.35ff (*Schol.* to Ps. 113:1): "...tropologice, quando nos confessionem huiusmodi et laudem et honorem ei exhibemus: tunc enim iam in nobis etiam talis est, qualis in persona est. Et fides eius est tunc confessio et decor, quem ipse spiritualiter induit. Quia per fidem eum confitemur et honoramus atque decoramus. Sed hoc non fit, nisi nos negemus, confundamus, et defoedemus. Non enim simul illum decorabimus et nos, non simul illum confitebimur et nos, sed nos abnegantes eum confitebimur et nos polluentes eum decorabimus."

with God.[1] For Luther, man's union with God *in via* both presupposes and confirms the *maximum dissimilarity* between man and God: he who is 'unlike' God is one with God.[2]

Luther's statement on *humilitas* and *gratia* in the *scholia* on psalm 95 is instructive in this regard, and it is a fitting conclusion to our study of natural and historical 'covenants' in the *Dictata*. For here it is clear that humility and grace do not relate as antecedent demanding consequent, but as 'inseparables' like John the Baptist and Jesus Christ. And, further, it is clear that only he who recognizes and confesses his dissimilitude with God is in a salutary relation with God, for it is only in darkness that light is received.

> How does light arise now before the righteous [ps. 97:11], when one is not able to be righteous except as light has already arisen? We answer as follows. Light does not arise except with those who are in darkness. For those who are already in the light, light cannot arise, since it is the nature of light that it does not arise with itself, but only in and with darkness. Thus, those who see themselves as being in darkness and unworthy are already righteous, because they give to themselves what is their own, and to God what is His own. Thus, light arises with them. This means simply that they have confessed that they are in darkness and that light is of God. *Therefore, we read that it is to the humble that God gives his grace* [I Peter 5:5]. And from this it follows that before all

[1] To the extent that Tauler and Gerson are representative of the late medieval mystical traditions, we cannot agree with Rühl that the non-Aristotelian, opposites-reconciling *Denkmethode* is the positive point of contact between Luther and mysticism. See *supra*, p. 7. Tauler and Gerson certainly 'reconcile' opposites, but they do so only by removing their opposition: God and man are reconciled by becoming 'like' one another (Gerson) or simply one another (Tauler). Luther, however, reconciles opposites by establishing and maintaining their *distinctiveness and opposition in union*. The *Denkmethode* of Tauler and Gerson is not non-Aristotelian to the extent that the sound Aristotelian axiom that two distinct forms cannot coexist simultaneously is fundamental to their thought. Similar problems are present in Josef Quint's conclusion that the "adäquateste Denk- wie Aussageform" of the speculative mystics is a "Paradoxie" which strives "unvereinbare Gegensätze durch die Verbindung von Position und Negation in scharf antithetischer Aussage zur coincidentia oppositorum zu zwingen." "Mystik und Sprache", *Altdeutsche und altniederländische Mystik*, 150. Earlier in this article, Quint stresses the centrality of the "Gleichheitsprinzip" for these same mystics! Cf. *supra*, p. 23, note 1.

[2] In this regard, one should not overlook Luther's fascination with the way in which opposites come together in Jesus Christ (*stultitia* and *sapientia*, *descensus* and *ascensus*, *infirmitas* and *potentia*, *mors* and *vita*, *iudicium dei* and *misericordia dei*, etc.) and in the believer who is conformed with Christ. Cf. 3,458,2ff, 431.40ff, 246.19ff, 160.6ff, 440.29ff, 426,34ff; 4,87.20ff, 119.29ff, 243,6ff, 173.21ff. See James S. Preus, "Old Testament *Promissio* and Luther's New Hermeneutic", *HTR*, 60 (1967), 147, 160f.

> things we should be humiliated, so that we may receive light and grace, and indeed, that we may preserve light and grace. Humility and grace simply will not be separated, although one precedes the other as John the Baptist precedes Christ, quickly following one upon the heels of the other. Thus, it follows that as long as confession *remains* in the heart, so long does beauty remain, and as long as humility *remains*, so long does grace remain.[1]

Axel Gyllenkrok, expressing his conviction that Luther views *humilitas* strictly as a "presupposition" and not "one aspect" of faith,[2] interprets this passage in terms of *necessary* antecedent and consequent.[3] He thus fails to see that John the Baptist *(confessio peccati, humilitas)* "precedes" Christ *(gratia, adventus spiritualis)* not as a precondition which causes His coming, but as the expectation which abides as the only receptacle of Christ's presence with the faithful. John the Baptist and Christ belong together and 'fit' together.[4] As the "vox clamantis," John the Baptist is God's *opus alienum* which ever remains the singular and simultaneous correlate of God's *opus proprium*: "Iohannes 'vox clamantis,' id est EVANGELIUM!"[5]

---

[1] *WA* 4,111.28ff: "Quomodo enim oritur [lux] iam iusto, cum iustus non sit nisi iam orta luce? Respondetur: quod lux non oritur nisi iis, qui in tenebris sunt. Qui autem iam in luce sunt, non potest illis oriri, cum sit natura lucis non ante semetipsam oriri nec nisi in tenebris oriri. Igitur qui sibi tenebre videntur et indigni, iam sunt iusti, quia dant sibi quod suum est, et deo quod suum est; ideo illis oritur. Et est nihil aliud, nisi quod confitentur se in tenebris esse et lucem dei esse; ideo humilibus deus dat suam gratiam. Quare ante omnia humiliandum est, ut lucem et gratiam suscipiamus, immo et conservemus. Nolunt enim separari humilitas et gratia, licet una precedat aliam, sicut Iohannes Baptista Christum, sed mox in pede se sequuntur. Igitur quam diu confessio in corde manet, tam diu et pulchritudo, quam diu humilitas, tam diu et gratia." Emphasis mine. See further the *scholion* on psalm 91:3—"veritas per noctem." *WA* 4,84.18ff.

[2] Gyllenkrok, Axel, *Rechtfertigung und Heiligung in der frühen evangelischen Theologie Luthers* (Uppsala, 1952), 45f.

[3] *Ibid.*, 47: "Für ihn [Luther] ist es ganz klar, daß die Demut, auch wenn man Gnade und Demut nicht von einander trennen kann, doch vor der Gnade kommen muß, wie der Täufer vor Christus. Die Demut ist ja die Aufgabe, die erfüllt werden muß! Igitur quam diu humilitas, tam diu et gratia." Adolf Hamel interprets this passage as an "Ineinander von temporal-konditionaler Priorität und grundsätzlicher Gleichzeitigkeit." Despite the latter phrase, Hamel persists in viewing *humilitas* as pre-Reformation "Zweckhaftigkeit": "Denn es bleibt...noch im Rahmen der zweckhaften accusatio sui..." *Der junge Luther und Augustin. Ihre Beziehungen in der Rechtfertigungslehre nach Luthers ersten Vorlesungen 1509-1518 untersucht*, Teil I (Gütersloh, 1934), 149, 190, 191, n. 1. This interpretation is simply untenable.

[4] It is not the case that Christ *must* be present with the humble, but rather that He *can* only be present with the humble: "Cum isto [the prideful man]... non potest esse Christus, quia solum cum humilibus esse potest." *WA* 4,138.1f.

[5] *Sermo in die S. Thomae* (1516), *Luthers Werke im Auswahl*, 5, 421.23ff, 422.19ff

6. CONCLUSION

Luther uses the terms *facere quod in se est* and *meritum de congruo*, together with a strong Augustinian doctrine of grace, in such a way that he appears to be well within the *potentia ordinata—potentia absoluta* framework of nominalist theology. In the *Dictata*, these *termini technici* of nominalist covenant theology are a live option for understanding the relationship between human preparation *(humilitas)* and the spiritual advent of Christ *(gratia)*.

Several qualifications of man's historical situation before God, however, clearly indicate that the nominalist understanding of the *facere quod in se est* and *meritum de congruo* is not Luther's answer to the nature of this relationship. Not only is the entrance of man's moral *bonitas*—the fulfilment of the law *quoad substantiam actus*—bracketed out of the order of salvation, but it is unequivocally stated that the only soteriologically significant resource and activity are to be found solely in the first and second advents of Christ.

Further, Luther's placement of *praeparatio* within the context of *expectare* and *clamare* indicates a reinterpretation of what a *congrue* disposition or relation to God involves. In this context, *praeparatio* has no refined Pelagian overtones. It is a God-awakened awareness that all that man is and does remains completely powerless in the face of sin and death, and thoroughly ineffective before God. He who cries confesses by his very crying that he does not have and cannot attain that for which he cries. He who hopes and expects confesses by his very expectation and hope that it is only in God's fidelity to His promises that he can receive what he expects and hopes. Crying, expectation and hope point both to the absence—the soteriologically de-substantial nature of human life—and the reality—the promises of God, 'outside' man's power—of that for which one cries, expects and hopes.

God does not find his 'likeness' among men. He dwells with the one who has surrendered all attempts to be 'like' Him and lives in the recognition and confession of Godlessness. As darkness is the receptacle of light, so humility is the receptacle of grace. And as John the Baptist 'precedes' Christ, so humility 'precedes' God's gracious presence with man in Christ. This is not as antecedent and consequent, but as expectation and fulfilment, the former *needing*, not demanding,

(= *WA* I,113.4ff; 34f). Emphasis mine. See our discussion of law and gospel, *supra*, 121ff.

the latter to empower and justify its presence. Thus, beauty and grace can remain only as confession and humility *remain*: there is a simultaneity and congruity of opposites. And this is the sense in which "humilibus deus dat suam gratiam."

CHAPTER ELEVEN

HOMO SPIRITUALIS

1. "CHRISTUS ENIM NON NISI IN PECCATORIBUS HABITAT"[1]

The above caption is taken from a letter written by Luther on April 8, 1516 to his friend Georg Spenlein. This letter contains a noteworthy autobiographical comment which is not only strikingly appropriate in light of our interpretation of the *Dictata*, but also because it suggests that Luther has reached clarity on an issue of singular importance. He writes:

> For many in our time presumption is a raging temptation, especially with those who zealously strive to be righteous and good by their own powers. Oblivious to the righteousness of God, which is given freely and most abundantly to us in Christ, they try to perform good works with their own resources in an effort to reach the point where they are confident of standing before God on the basis of good deeds and merits. This is impossible! You were once among us in this opinion, indeed in this error, and so was I. But now I also fight against it, although I have not yet conquered it.[2]

In our previous chapters, we have witnessed both this error to which Luther was party and the beginning of his fight against it. For in two early sermons, we have seen Luther's former conviction that

---

[1] *WA Br* 1,35.29. The conclusion drawn from this statement is: "Igitur non nisi in illo [Christus], per fiducialem desperationem tui et operum tuorum, pacem invenies..." *Ibid.*, 33f.

[2] *Ibid.*, 17ff: "Fervet enim nostra aetate tentatio praesumptionis in multis, et iis praecipue, qui iusti et boni esse omnibus viribus student; ignorantes iustitiam Dei, quae in Christo est nobis effusissime et gratis donata, quaerunt in se ipsis tam diu operari bene, donec habeant fiduciam standi coram Deo, veluti virtutibus et meritis ornati, quod est impossibile fieri. Fuisti tu apud nos in hac opinione, imo errore; fui et ego, sed et nunc quoque pugno contra istum errorem, sed nondum expugnavi." Note the similar confession made in early 1516 in a criticism of the discussion of man's election in terms of "necessitas consequentiae" and "contingens consequentis". For Luther, this is just a subterfuge for Pelagianism. "Hec tantum vacua verba sunt, presertim cum hoc 'consequentis contingere' velint intelligere aut saltem occasionem intelligendi dant, quod nostra arbitrio fiat vel non fiat salus. Sic enim ego aliquando intellexi." *WA* 56,382.24ff. It is noteworthy that as late as 1532, Luther confesses that he is *still fighting* to overcome the desire to earn salvation and to stand before God with "glawben inn diesen einigen Mittler [Christus]." *WA* 36, 372.25-35

man possesses the "possibilitas," the "vermögen," to either win or lose his salvation.[1] In the December, 1514 sermon, *De propria sapientia et voluntate*, he could still speak of the *synteresis voluntatis et rationis* as an antidote to despair, and even make damnation "solely" *(sola causa!)* contingent upon the rejection of what it teaches.

In this same sermon, however, we also observed statements which located hope in Christ, attested the failure of the "whole will" in the love of what is good and the discongruity of the "whole reason" with the wisdom of God, and called attention to the invincibility of concupiscence.[2] In the *Dictata*, we found evidence to intensify these statements. Here we noted the strong providential and Christological qualifications of the operation of the *synteresis*. We witnessed the way in which the concepts of *promissio* and *testamentum Dei*, *fides* and *spes*, *clamare* and *expectare* interrelated to attest the soteriologically de-substantial nature of all anthropological resources. Man does not find grounds for hope in himself and his world; he must "despair of self and world."[3] Man and God were related as darkness and light are related, not as light and Light are related. And humiliational activity and grace were related as John the Baptist and Jesus Christ are related, i.e. not as antecedent and consequent, the former demanding and necessitating the latter, but as expectation and fulfilment are related, i.e. the former needing the latter to empower and justify it.[4]

In our final chapter, we witness further Luther's efforts to define man's situation before God and in the face of sin and death. As we proceed, the following will be our concern. We will turn first to two statements on man's petition for the "highest things." The first is from the notes on Tauler's sermons (1515-16), the second from the interlinear glosses on chapter eight of the lectures on Romans[5] (Spring, 1515-Autumn, 1516).[6] These passages will orient our discussion of the development of the *synteresis* concept in the lectures on

[1] See *supra*, 139f.
[2] See *supra*, p. 141f.
[3] See *supra*, p. 120.
[4] See *supra*, p. 180ff.
[5] Ficker points out that portions of this eighth chapter were written "gleichzeitig" with the notes on Tauler's Sermons. *WA* 56,376, n. 22. This makes this chapter especially important to us, and we will have occasion to point out the parallels with the notes on Tauler's Sermons.
[6] The lectures on Romans run through three semesters, beginning in the Spring of 1515 and concluding in Autumn, 1516. Luther was working on the *scholia* to 3:5 in October, 1515, and by February, 1516 was concluding the *scholia* to chapter 8. Our dating follows Ficker's research. *WA* 56, XXIX.

Romans, which, together with passages from the notes on Tauler's Sermons, will make manifest the impossibility of seeking *iustitia coram Deo* in and by the *vires hominis*.

After this section, we will turn once again to these same sources, this time extending our consideration to include Luther's comments on Gabriel Biel's *Sentences* commentary (1515-Summer, 1516).[1] Here we will specify the way in which the dismissal of the *vires hominis* from a significant role in the order of salvation is interwoven with the dismissal of the *actiones* and *merita hominis* from such a role also. We so distinguish these two—*vires hominis* and *actiones* and *merita hominis*—not only for clarity's sake, but also because it is a mistaken evaluation of the former which Luther considers to be the presupposition—the "fundamentum"—of the optimistic estimate of the efficacy of the latter before God.

2. *IUSTITIA CORAM DEO* AND THE *VIRES HOMINIS*

In a comment on Tauler's sermon on Mark 7:31f, Luther makes his only reference to the *synteresis* in his notes on Tauler's Sermons. His comment is in response to Tauler's discussion of the presence of the eternal Word in man, and man's inability to hear it, since "the devil has whispered in his ear." For now man has heard so much about temporal things from this Enemy that he is deaf and dumb to what is innermost to himself: "he does not recognize himself."[2] Luther comments as follows:

---

[1] Degering dates the notes on Biel's *Sentences* Commentary broadly, from the beginning of 1515 to the summer of 1516—practically identical with the period of the lectures on Romans. *Luthers Randbemerkungen zu Gabriel Biels Collectorium und zu dessen Sacri canonis missae expositio, Lyon, 1514*, ed. Hermann Degering, *Festgabe der Kommission zur Herausgabe der Werke Martin Luthers zur Feier des 450. Geburtstages Luthers* (Weimar, 1933), xii. Grane, however, argues on grounds of content for Autumn, 1516, the period directly preceding the *Disputatio contra scholasticam theologiam* (1517); this is because he finds Luther to be finally clear and specific against the *facere quod in se est* here. Since we find evidence for a clear and specific stand against the *facere quod in se est*, whether in the form of a *meritum de congruo* (Oberman, Gyllenkrok) or a *fides humilitate formata* (Bizer) (see *infra*, p. 215, note 2), we find no reason on this score to choose as late a date as Grane. Between Summer, 1515 and Winter, 1516, i.e. the period of the *scholia* on the *Dictata* from psalm 108 and following and the development in the lectures on Romans from chapter 4 to 8, Luther is in good position to make a critical stand against the *facere quod in se est*.

[2] Vetter, 191.10ff: "...und wissent doch das das ewig wort uns also unsprechlichen nach und inwendig ist in unserem grunde das der mensche im selber und sine eigene nature noch sin gedank noch alles das man genemmen oder gesagen

> [Tauler] speaks in regard to the 'foundation.' For if the Word of God which made everything (i.e. the Lord) is closer to those things than they are to themselves, how much more intimate is this Word to the most noble of [created] things, i.e. to the soul, than the soul is to itself! And for this reason, everyone senses that his *synteresis* calls out to the highest things. And no one is able to express in words to another [this utterance of] the *synteresis*, especially the affective *synteresis*.[1]

In itself this is a very positive statement on the *synteresis*,[2] and, for reasons that will become clearer as we proceed further, it should be dated in close proximity with the December, 1514 sermon, *De propria sapientia et voluntate*, probably in January or February, 1515. For at this time Luther was not yet explicitly critical of the *synteresis*; indeed, as we have called attention to several times, he could speak of it as a serious antidote to despair.

When we turn to his interlinear gloss on Romans 8:26-27, however, we find words which form such a literal parallel with the above statement from the notes on Tauler's Sermons, that we are led to suggest that Luther here consciously dismisses the *synteresis* from the order of salvation. Indeed, he literally 'reads it out':

> *In a like way the Holy Spirit helps* [by] making us petition and groan deeply *our infirmity*... our impotence and impossibility. *For what* as regards the object of our prayer *we should pray for* as regards the affect or manner in which our petition is made *we do not know*... But *the* Holy

---

mag oder verston mag, das enist alles nút als nach noch inwendig als das ewig wort in dem menschen ist, und spricht ane alle underlos in dem menschen, und der mensche enhoert dis alles nút von grosser toupheit die den menschen besessen hat. Wes schult ist dis? Das sag ich úch. Da ist neiswas dem menschen fúr die oren gevallen, das hat im die oren verstophet, das er dis minnekliche wort nút gehoeren enmag, und ist von dem also verblent das er och stum ist worden, das er sich selber nút enbekent. Und wolt er von siner inwendikeit sprechen, er koende es nicht getuon und enweis wo er dar an ist, und er erkent sin eigen wise nút. Dis ist die sache. Der vijent der hat sin gerúne mit im gehabet, und dem hat er geloset, und dannan ab ist er toub und stum worden. Wels ist dis schedelich gerúne des vijendes? Das ist alle die unordenunge die dir in lúchtet und in sprichet, es si mit minnen oder mit meinungen der creaturen oder es si die Welt und was der anhaft: gut oder ere, frúnt oder moge und din eigen nature und was dir in bildet minne oder gunst der creaturen: mit allem disem hat er sin gerúne, wan er ist alle zit bi dem menschen."

[1] *WA* 9,103.22ff: "Ex fundamento loquitur. Quia si verbum dei, quod fecit (i.e. dominus) omnia, intimior est rebus caeteris quam ipse sibi, quanto magis intimior est rerum nobilissimae scilicet animae quam ipsa sibi. Et hinc venit, quod syntheresin suam quilibet sentit ad optima deprecari. Sed et [n]ullus potest alteri eam verbis tradere, maxime affectivam syntheresin."

[2] Hirsch considers it Luther's last strictly positive statement, in strong parallel with Tauler's *Seelengrund. Lutherstudien*, I, 109.

> *Spirit asks* makes us ask *for us with unutterable groanings* which can be expressed in words by no man; nor is anyone able to sense them except God—this is not the same for everyone.[1] But God alone *who searches the hearts* [of men], the innermost place, which is closer to us than we to ourselves *knows* acknowledges, senses and approves *what the* Holy *Spirit desires*, and to Him these groanings are not incommunicable. Therefore, I say the Spirit knows *because He asks* makes us ask *for the saints in accordance with God* i.e. for those things which are pleasing to God according to the will of God.[2]

The *subject* of these incommunicable groanings is specified as the Holy Spirit, and *what* is cried for is what is known by the Spirit. In the *Dictata*, Luther had spoken of the divine possession of the *reliquae mortuorum*; after the desolation in which sin leaves man, he is hopeless unless God takes over and supports what remains of him.[3] Now this possession is expressed by the Spirit's assumption of the role of crying to God in and through man. The absence of the *synteresis* from the discussion strongly suggests that Luther suspends it as a significant *soteriological* resource.

In the *scholia* on 8:26-27, there is no mention of Tauler's "fundamentum" or the *synteresis*, a fact that is all the more interesting since it is precisely at this point that Tauler is mentioned in the lectures on Romans.[4] The leitmotif which pervades these *scholia*, and which we will encounter often in this chapter, takes its cue from Isaiah 55:8-9:

---

[1] In his lectures, Luther gave the following interpretation of these words, "non similiter omnibus." They mean "non omnibus simpliciter quia deo sunt cogniti." *WA* 56,82. n. 15. This makes it clear that he is not carving out a special group of *sancti*.

[2] *WA* 56,82.7-83.4: "*Similiter autem spiritus* sanctus *adiuvat* sc. profunde gemere et petere faciens *infirmitatem nostram*... impotentiam, impossibilitatem nostram: *nam quid* quoad id, quod petitur *oremus sicut oportet* quoad affectum seu modum, quo petitur *nescimus...sed ipse spiritus* sanctus *postulat* postulare facit *pro nobis gemitibus inenarrabilibus*, qui nulli hominum enarrari verbis possunt nec ullus sentire potest nisi Deus — non similiter omnibus. Sed solus scil. Deus *Qui autem scrutatur corda:* intima, etiam plus quam ipsi nos *scit* agnoscit, sentit et approbat *quid desyderet* huic enim non sunt inenarrabiles *spiritus* sanctus: ideo, inquam, scit, *quia secundum deum* i.e. que Deo placita sunt secundum voluntatem Dei *postulat* postulare facit *pro sanctis*." Cf. Luther's later statement: "Fides nostra est infirma et tamen est potens, quia es ist ein klein geistlin im hertzen, das heist gemitus inenarrabilis und Spiritus Sanctus da zu, der es versteht. Die thun es." *Luthers Werke in Auswahl*, 8, *Tischreden* (Berlin, 1950), no. 425 (1532), 53 (= *WA Tischreden* I, 184.16ff.).

[3] See our discussion *supra*, p. 152ff, where it was clear that *clamare* is a confession of soteriological impotence which embraces all man's powers.

[4] See *WA* 56,378.13f. Here it is not an anthropological "fundamentum" that interests Luther, but Tauler's concern for *sufferentia*: "De ista patientia Dei et sufferentia vide Taulerum, qui pre caeteris hanc materiam preclare ad lucem dedit in lingua teutonica."

"My thoughts are not your thoughts nor are my ways your ways." Luther emphasizes this verse in his description of the peculiar nature of God's saving work with men, in which all man's plans and works are destroyed before God's own is granted.[1] He writes in this regard:

> By this most holy plan, He *makes us capable* of His gifts and works. Only when our own plans have ceased and our works have stopped, and we are purely passive in relation to God, both inwardly and in our outward activity, are we capable [of receiving] His works and plans. This is what He means when He says: 'My thoughts are not your thoughts nor are my ways your ways.' Thus, at the point when everything starts to work against our desires and prayers, those unutterable groanings begin. And at this point 'the Spirit helps our infirmities.' For without the help of the Spirit, it would be impossible for us to stand up under this activity of God, in which He hears and fulfils what we pray for.[2]

With this background and orientation, we will follow Luther's statements on the *synteresis*, turning first to the development in the lectures on Romans and then to the notes on Tauler's Sermons. Four *scholia* from the lectures on Romans initiate our discussion.[3]

First, in the *scholia* to Romans 1:19-20—"the invisible things of Him are clearly seen from the creation of the world"—we find the following statement:

---

[1] *WA* 56,375.18ff: "...Natura dei est, prius destruere et annihilare, quicquid in nobis est, antequam sua donet..." The historical paradigm for this operation is God's own proper work: Jesus Christ. "Sic enim egit in opere suo proprio, quod est primum et exemplar omnium operum suorum, i.e. in Christo. Quem tunc, quando voluit glorificare et in regnum statuere, sicut omnium discipulorum piissima cogitatio ferventer optabat et expectabat, maxime contrarie fecit mori, confundi et ad inferos descendere." *WA* 56,377.4ff. On the *contraria* theme in regard to the person and work of Christ, see further 55,II,72,24; 73.13f.

[2] *WA* 56,375.21-376.6: "Eo enim consilio suo piissimo facit nos capaces donorum suorum et operum suorum. Capaces autem tunc sumus operum et consiliorum eius, quando nostra consilia cessant et opera quiescunt et efficimur pure passivi respectu Dei, tam quoad interiores quam exteriores actus. Hoc est, quod ait: 'Cogitationes meae non cogitationes vestrae neque viae meae viae vestrae.' Hic ergo cum omnia iam desperata sunt et contra vota precesque nostras omnia incipiunt fieri, incipiunt gemitus illi inenarrabiles. Hic 'spiritus adiuvat infirmitates nostras'. Quia sine spiritu adiuvante impossibile foret nos sustinere hanc operationem Dei, qua nos exaudit et facit, quod petimus." Emphasis mine. See 56,378. 14f: "Sic, Sic 'Nescimus, sicut oportet, orare'. Ideo necessarius est spiritus nobis, qui adiuvet infirmitates nostras. Quis enim crederet haec verba esse tam profunda!"

[3] The four passages are: the *scholia* to Rom. 1:19-20, 56,177.14ff, Rom. 3:10, 56,236.31-237.8, Rom. 4:7, 56,275.17ff, and Rom. 8:3, 56,355.28-356.6. The excellent chapter by Lennart Pinomaa, "Das Verschwinden der anthropozentrischen Synteresis," analyzes each of these passages. *Der existenzielle Charakter der Theologie Luthers. Das Hervorbrechen der Theologie der Anfechtung und ihre Bedeutung für das*

> They [the Gentiles] knew, therefore, that it is characteristic of divine nature or of Him who is God, to be powerful, invisible, righteous, immortal and good. Therefore, they knew the invisible things of God and His eternal strength and divinity. This major [premise] of the practical syllogism, this theological *synteresis*, is in every man and is incapable of being obscured. But in the minor [term] they erred by drawing the conclusion that this [idol], i.e. Jupiter or another idol similar to him, is this [divine] nature. Here the error began and it fostered idolatry. And thus each wished to subject [divine nature] to his own particular desire.[1]

This statement is a scholastic presentation of the pastoral explication of the *synteresis* in the December, 1514 sermon, *De propria sapientia et voluntate*.[2] By associating the theological *synteresis* with the major premise of a practical syllogism, Luther expresses man's general awareness of divine nature. In terms of the earlier sermon, this is

---

Lutherverständnis. Annales Academiae Scientiarum Finnicae, XLVII[1] (Helsinki, 1940), 37ff. The weakness of Pinomaa's treatment lies in his failure to see (1) that the *synteresis*, as we will show, does not simply "disappear," but is *delimited* to the sphere *coram nobis*, to *particularis et legalis iustitia*, and (2) that the removal of the *synteresis*—not from man but from the order of salvation—does not simply indicate a part of Luther's "theologische Weg von Anthropozentrizität zur Theozentrizität" (*ibid.*, 53), in conjunction with a view of the "totale Verderbnis des Menschen" (*ibid.*, 51), but lays the groundwork for the consideration of *man as man*, and not as an organ whose only significance lies in the realization of the potentialities of a hidden, divine 'residue.' In this sense, it is a very positive anthropological judgment. In regard to this second point, we have difficulties with Grane's insistence that "alles [ist] pervertiert." *Contra Gabrielem*, 325. Our description, the 'soteriologically de-substantial' nature of human life, is intended to counter just such imprecision.

[1] *WA* 56,177.11ff: "Cognoverunt ergo, quod divinitatis sive eius, qui est Deus, sit esse potentem, invisibilem, iustum, immortalem, bonum; ergo cognoverunt invisibilia dei sempiternamque virtutem eius et divinitatem. Hec maior syllogismi practici, hec syntheresis theologica est inobscurabilis in omnibus. Sed in minore errabant dicendo et statuendo: Hic autem i.e. Iupiter vel alius huic simulacro similis est huiusmodi etc. Hic error incepit et fecit idolatriam, dum quisque studio suo subsumere voluit." We call attention to Luther's later (1532) statement on the "syllogism" which functions in the Psalms: "David...ist poeta und orator ex Mose worden und kann die lieblichsten Psälmlin daraus machen. Nam totum psalterium nihil aliud est quam syllogismi ex primo praecepto. Minor, die heißt fides; maior heißt verbum dei; conclusio, die ist factum et executio. Maior: Deus respicit miseros; minor: Ego sum miser; Conclusio: Ergo Deus me quoque respiciet. De minore dubitat homo." *TR* I, Nr. 369, 160.4ff. Cited by Heinrich Bornkamm, *Luther und das Alte Testament* (Tübingen, 1948), 141.

[2] This syllogism is traditional. In the classical form given it by Albertus Magnus, it proceeds as follows: "1. Obersatz: synteretisch erfaßte Allgemeinwahrheit; 2. Untersatz: das Urteil der Vernunft; 3. Schlußsatz: der Akt der Conscientia." Willy Bremi, *Was ist das Gewissen?*, 106. See further Pinomaa, *Der existenzielle Charakter der Theologie Luthers*, 47, and Hirsch, *Lutherstudien*, I, 28ff. Luther's 1514 sermon, *De propria sapientia et voluntate*, is discussed *supra*, 139ff.

parallel with man's conformity with God insofar as a salutary goal is concerned. The statement that there is error in regard to the minor term—the conclusion drawn in light of the major premise—parallels what the earlier sermon described as discongruity with God as far as the means to a salutary goal were concerned.

Let us move a few months and *scholia* further to Luther's comments on Romans 3:10—"there is none righteous." He writes in reference to a statement attributed to Seneca.

> ...That saying of Seneca is full of pride and every sin: 'Should I know that men would not know it and the gods would overlook it, still I would not sin.' Now in the first place, it is impossible for man to have this will from himself, since he is always inclined toward evil and only through the grace of God is he able to be excited to good. Therefore he who presumes that he is able to do so much is one who does not yet know himself. Certainly I admit that he can do and will some good things with that frame of mind, but not all things. For we are not so completely inclined to evil that a portion does not still remain which is inclined toward good, as is evident in the *synteresis*. Secondly, even if he says that he would not sin although he knew the gods would overlook it and men would not know it, is he bold enough to say that he would choose to do good even if he knew the gods and men would not care? If he so dares, he is prideful in the same measure as he is bold; for he would not escape, at least not in himself, a boastful glory in which he is self-satisfied. For man is not able to seek anything except what is his own and to love himself above all things *(se super omnia diligere)*. This is the sum of all his faults. Hence such men seek themselves in [their] good and virtuous acts.[1]

In this passage, the *synteresis* makes possible the performance of "some good things." As far as the achievement of an unselfish and unprideful life *before God* is concerned, however, it is absolutely inef-

---

[1] *WA* 56,236.31-237.8: "Unde superbiae et omni peccato plenum verbum est illud Senece: 'Si scirem homines non cognituros et deos ignoturos, adhuc peccare nollem.' Primo, quod non sit possibile hominem ex seipso hanc voluntatem habere, cum sit semper ad malum inclinatus, adeo ut non nisi per gratiam dei possit erigi ad bonum. Igitur nondum seipsum cognovit, qui tantum de se praesumpsit. Verum quidem esse fateor, quod aliqua bona eo animo possit facere et velle, sed non omnia, quia non sic inclinati sumus ad malum omnino, quin reliqua fit nobis portio, quae ad bonum sit affecta, ut patet in syntheresi. Secundo, etiamsi nolle se dicit peccare, ubi deos ignoscere et homines ignorare sciret, utrum etiam audet dicere se velle bonum facere, etiamsi sciret deos id non curare neque homines? Si audet, superbus est eodem modo, quia omnino non effugeret gloriam et iactantiam, saltem apud seipsum, in qua sibi placeret. Quia homo non potest, nisi que sua sunt, querere et se super omnia diligere. Que est summa omnium vitiorum. Unde et in bonis et virtutibus tales querunt seipsos..."

fective. Even in his particular good acts and virtuous deeds, man seeks himself.

We detect a shift in accent in this passage,[1] which weakens the assumption that the *synteresis* is conformed with God at the point of knowing and willing the right end or general ethical axiom which conforms with what God desires for man. It may direct one to *particular good acts*, but even these, before God, are acts of prideful self-satisfaction. Why does this shift in accent begin to occur, and where does it culminate?

Again, we must move further in time and commentary to the *scholia* on Romans 4:7. Here we find an attack on the assumption that man can, from his own powers, love God above all things and perform the works of the law "quoad substantiam facti"—according to the substance of the act. Luther writes:

> It is sheer delusion when it is said that man can, from his own powers *(ex viribus suis)*, love God above all things and perform the works of the law according to the substance of the act but not according to the intention of the Lawgiver (the latter is denied since he is not in a state of grace). O fools, O pig-theologians![2]

What is behind this delusion which Luther considers tantamount to saying that man can fulfil the law without grace? When we read a few lines further, we find that it is *precisely the synteresis*—this "small motion to good"—which grounds this exaggerated and perverse assumption.

> All these monstrosities came from the fact that they[3] did not know

[1] There is a parallel to this on the level of activity in this same chapter. Luther attempts both to maintain preparatory good works and yet to bracket them from the "via Dei," i.e. from righteousness before God. "Alioquin studiosissime fieri eiusmodi debent et omni fervore exerceri, eo scil. fine, ut per ipsa tanquam preparatoria tandem apti et capaces fieri possimus iustitiae Dei, non ut sint iustitia, sed ut querant iustitia. Ac per hoc iam non sunt iustitia nostra, dum nos ipsa non pro iustitia nobis imputamus. Parare enim illis omnibus oportet viam Domini venturi in nobis. Non autem sunt via Domini. Hec est enim iustitia Dei, quam presens Dominus post illa in nobis efficit salus." *WA* 56,233.26ff. And later in the same chapter, the *sola gratia* is invoked for the historical order: "Immo nec opera precedentia nec sequentia iustificant, quanto minus opera legis! Precedentia quidem, quia preparant ad iustitiam; sequentia vero, quia requirunt iam factam iustificationem. Non enim iusta operando iusti efficimur, sed iusti essendo iusta operamur. Ergo sola gratia iustificat." *WA* 56,255.15ff.

[2] *WA* 56,274.11ff: "Quocirca mera deliria sunt, que dicuntur, quod homo ex viribus suis possit deum diligere super omnia et facere opera precepti secundum substantiam facti, sed non ad intentionem praecipientis, quia non in gratia. O stulti, O Sawtheologen!"

[3] Ficker cites Scotus, II *Sent. dist.* 39, q. 2, n. 5, and Biel II *Sent. dist.* 39, q. un., art. 2, conclu. 1.

> either what sin or its remission were. For they reduced sin, as they did righteousness, to a certain very small motion of the soul. [They conclude] that because the will has that *synteresis* it is, although feebly, 'inclined to good.' And, further, they dream that this little motion toward God (which man is naturally able to make) is an act of loving God above all things! But look at this man who is completely filled with sinful desires (and these are not obstructed by that tiny little motion to good!). The law commands him to empty himself so that he may be wholly brought to God. Therefore Isaiah [41:23] ridicules them, chiding, 'Do good or evil—if you can!'[1]

Here it is clear that Luther considers an *exaggerated* view of the powers of the *synteresis* to underlie the claim that man can love God above all things. For Luther's opponents, man's natural *ability* grounds salutary *activity* before God. Only as it is clear that man possesses no soteriological resources for initiating his saving relationship with God is it possible to overcome the conclusions drawn in the *facere quod in se est.*

Faced with an exaggeration of the powers of the *synteresis*, Luther makes a decision which climaxes the development we have been following. He *delimits* the the efficacy of the *synteresis*—man's natural inclination to good—to the sphere of "particular and legal righteousness," i.e. to that righteousness which goes bond before and between men but not before God. Two passages witness this decision. The first is the following comment on Romans 3:9:

> Hence it is clear that when the Apostle said above [Rom. 2:14] that 'the Gentiles by nature perform the works of the law,' he meant to say that they were righteous in particular and legal righteousness but not in the universal and infinite, eternal and utterly divine righteousness which is given to us only in Christ.[2]

---

[1] *WA* 56,275.17ff: "Haec portenta omnia ex eo venerunt, quod peccatum, quid esset, ignoraverunt, nec quid remissio. Quia peccatum artaverunt usque ad minutissimum quendam motum animi sicut et iustitiam. Ita enim, quia voluntas habens istam syntheresim, qua, licet infirmiter, 'inclinatur ad bonum.' Et huius parvulum motum in deum (quem naturaliter potest) illi somniant esse actum diligendi deum super omnia! Sed inspice totum hominem plenum concupiscentiis (non obstante isto motu parvissimo). Hunc lex vacuum esse iubet, ut totus in deum feratur. Ideo Isa. 41, irridens eos dicit: 'Bene quoque aut male, si potestis, facite.'"

[2] *WA* 56,234.13ff: "Unde patet, quod illud, quod supra dixit: 'Gentes, que naturaliter faciunt, que legis sunt', non voluerit per hoc iustos asserere, nisi particulari et legali iustitia, sed non universali, que est infinita, eterna et prorsus divina, que non nisi in Christo nobis datur." See 56,204.8ff, where the "cogitationes" of conscience can excuse us "before ourselves" ("coram nobis facile sit excusari nos"), but those plans that defend us ("defendentes cogitationes") "before God" come "non nisi a Christo et in Christo." See further the statement from

The second passage is a corollary to his comments on Romans 8:3. Here we find the following statement in which the position outlined in the December, 1514 sermon, attributing to the *synteresis voluntatis et rationis* a conformity with God as far as a salutary 'goal' was concerned, is reversed. Now Luther writes that man knows and wills what is good in particular cases, viz., those which are good for himself. He possesses neither knowledge of nor a will toward good in a general, universal sense, i.e. before God and fellowman.

> It is said that human nature knows and wills good in a general and universal sense, but errs and does not will good in particular cases. It would be better to say [the reverse]: human nature knows and wills good in particular cases but in a universal sense neither knows nor wills good. And this is its own good, or what is good, honorable and useful for itself, but not, however, what is such before God and with others. Therefore, it is more in particular good, indeed, it is only in that good which is good for the individual, that human nature knows and wills what is good. And this harmonizes with Holy Scripture, which describes man as curved in upon himself so that not only corporeal but also spiritual goods are turned to himself, and he seeks himself in all things. Now this curvedness is natural; it is a natural fault and a natural evil. Therefore, he does not receive help from his natural powers, but must seek it from another more powerful Help, which is not in himself. This is Love...[1]

At best the *synteresis* is an awareness of and motion toward the particular and legal righteousness which goes bond among men; at worst, i.e. when the whole man, with all his resources, dreams that he can establish a saving relation with God, it is a motion toward a particular good which is good only for oneself, irrespective of God and fellowman. In neither case does it function *within the order of*

---

the *scholia* to psalm 111: "Auditio mala est duplex similiter bona, scilicet interior conscientie, que est vermis et murmur syntheresis, vel gaudium et susurrus spiritus sancti." *WA* 4,253.23f.

[1] *WA* 56,355.28ff: "Quod dicitur humanam naturam in genere et universali nosse et velle bonum, sed in particulari errare et nolle; melius diceretur in particulari nosse et velle bonum, sed in universali non nosse neque velle. Ratio, quia non novit nisi bonum suum, seu quod sibi bonum est et honestum et utile, non autem, quod deo et aliis. Ideo magis particulare, immo individuum tantummodo bonum novit et vult. Et hoc consonat Scripturae, quae hominem describit incurvatum in se adeo, ut non tantum corporalia, sed et spiritualia bona sibi inflectat et se in omnibus querat. Quae curvitas est nunc naturalis, naturale vitium et naturale malum. Ideo ex naturae viribus non habet adiutorium, sed ab extrinseco aliquo potentiore opus habet auxilio, quod est Charitas [i.e. Spiritus Sanctus] sine qua semper peccat contra legem..."

salvation in a positive and significant way. The righteousness which is effective here is given "only in Christ," and only with the 'outside' help of the Holy Spirit does man seek that which is "good" "before God and with others."

What we have witnessed in these statements in the lectures on Romans is paralleled in the notes on Tauler's Sermons. As we saw at the beginning of this chapter, these notes contain a very positive statement on the orientation of the affective *synteresis* to the "highest things." When we read further, however, taking into account two of Luther's comments which *immediately* follow this statement, two significant factors come to the fore: historical Christology and faith.

The first comment is written in response to Tauler's lamentation that a number of people meditate on Christ's passion with a blind, unfeeling devotion which fails to issue into an active reformation of their lives: "they all remain just as they are."[1] In Tauler's order of salvation, it should be remembered, this is a part of the stage of preparation, when devout, spiritual meditation on the suffering of the historical Christ helps one assemble all the powers of his soul and bring them into the ground of the soul, thus achieving that pure disposition to God which precedes God's birth in the soul. This is not the ultimate stage. For the ultimate stage involves the removal of all historical pictures, indeed, the suspension of God's *potentia ordinata* completely. Here it is not the passion of Christ but *weselich* life in and with God that is sought.

Glossing the phrase, "devout meditation on the holy [suffering of Christ],"[2] Luther writes: "to remember the suffering of Christ

---

[1] Vetter, 199.20ff: "Alsus solt du mit gedultigem lidende und mit aller demuetkeit dich in sin liden erbilden und dich dar in trucken. Nu entuont dis die lúte nicht; aber ein ieklichs gedenket wol an das heilige liden unsers herren in einer verloeschener blinder rower minne, also das der gedank in der uebunge nút enwúrket das er sins gemaches oder hofart oder eren oder liplicher genuegden ir sinne dar umbe enberen welle, denne si blibent alles als si sint."

[2] Note Luther's later praise of Tauler's placement of Christ against our "little works" and self-fashioned plans for life. "Quicunque omisso Christo in Ecclesia docent suas operatiunculas, a se repertos vivendi modos, ut hodie sunt magni harum perditionum gurgites, sicut et Iohannes Taulerius saepius et egregie monet..." *Operationes in psalmos*, *WA* 5,353.38f. This is hardly surprising since Luther read no one who emphasized more than Tauler the centrality of the life of Christ as *the* pattern for the lives of the faithful. The difference, however, is that Tauler speaks of an imitation of Christ as preparation for a stage where historical Christology, as God's *potentia ordinata* in general, is suspended and *weselich* union with God—God's birth in the soul—attained. For Luther, "in solo deo" means "passionem Christi in memoria habere," and "theologia propria" speak s"de spirituali nativitate verbi incarnati." Cf. *infra*, p. 196, notes 1 and 2.

spiritually is 'life;' to remember it literally produces nothing."[1]

To appreciate the full significance of this statement, we must recall what we have learned about *memoria* in the *Dictata*. There we argued that 'to remember' or 'be mindful' means intellectively and affectively to locate one's life in a 'place'—*substaculum seu subsidentia*—where one can stand with the 'feet' of his soul confident that he will not fall into the abyss of sin and death. When Luther writes that the remembrance of Christ's passion *is* "life," he means to say that it is this historical event which forms the 'place' where such 'subsistence' is possible. Or stated more comprehensively, it means that soteriological resources reside with the three-fold *adventus Christi*.[2]

But if this is the case, where is faith? For we also argued in our study of the *Dictata* that it is the *intellectus* and *affectus fidei* whch enables man to live in God's 'substantiating' past, present and future works. Let us read the comment immediately following, which takes us still a step further.

> ...Will: i.e. the affects. Certainly it is not evil to have knowledge and good things..., but to be so influenced by them that one trusts *(confidere)* and takes exceeding pleasure in them and places every possible affection in them, this is pride and the destruction of the soul... Therefore the affects should be naked, stripped of all our wisdom and righteousness, and one should rest on God alone and regard himself as nothing.[3]

'Naked affection,' a 'stripped' will, the consideration of oneself as 'nothing,' and 'resting on God alone': as far as the drama of salvation is concerned, historical Christology and the soteriologically desubstantial nature of human life, not the affective *synteresis*, play the

---

[1] *WA* 9,103.28f: "Nota: passionem Christi habere in memoria literaliter nihil prodest; spiritualiter vita est." See the popular statement in the lectures on Hebrews (1517-18): "Igitur qui vult salubriter ascendere ad amorem et cognitionem Dei, dimittat regulas humanas et methaphisicas de divinitate cognoscenda et in Christi humanitate se ipsum primum exerceat." *WA* 57,99.5f.

[2] In response to Tauler's understanding of the birth of God in the soul, Luther writes: "Loquitur [Tauler] enim de nativitate spirituali verbi increati. Theologia autem propria de spirituali nativitate verbi incarnati habet unum necessarium et optimam partem. Haec non sollicita est et turbatur erga plurima et contra peccata crescit et pugnat ad virtutem sollicita, quaerit, ubi illa victrix viciorum triumphat." *WA* 9,98.22ff. See our discussion *supra*, p. 173f, 105ff, 110f, 129.

[3] *WA* 9,103.31ff: "*Kinder ich sage eüch in dem willen* [Vetter, 384.14f]: i.e. affectus; q.d. non est malum habere scientiam et bona..., sed affici illis, confidere et complacere ac omnino affectum in illis habere quemcumque: hoc superbum est et perditio animae... Ideo oportet affectum esse nudum et exutum ab omni sapientia et iustitia nostra et in solo deo niti et se nihil reputare."

essential roles. In this recession of the *synteresis* and the entrance of the passion of Christ *in memoriam*, we can answer the question that was left dangling above: where is faith? Luther's very next comment answers succinctly: "homo spiritualis nititur fide."[1]

3. *IUSTITIA CORAM DEO* AND THE *ACTIONES* AND *MERITA HOMINIS*

1. *Luther and Tauler*

In the previous section, we argued that the *synteresis* becomes delimited in its significance to the sphere "before men" and has no role to play in man's achievement of a saving relation with God. It has potential ethical, but not soteriological significance—a distinction overlooked by Hirsch.[2] The exaggeration of its powers, manifest in

---

[1] *WA* 9,103.40f. See the statement in the lectures on Hebrews: "...Sola enim incredulitas separat a deo sicut sola fides coniungit..." *WA* 57,19.4f. See further, 57,147.20f, 139.13ff, 142.26ff, 151.13ff, 171.3ff, 159.15f. In a fragment from the work for the publication of the *Dictata*, Luther places the "lumen fidei" in explicit contradistinction to the *synteresis* in his interpretation of psalm 4:7: "signatum est super nos lumen vultus tui." "Multi hunc versum exposuerunt de synteresi, quae vocatur scintilla rationis inextinguibilis. Bona intelligentia. Sed quid ad textum?... lumen fidei intelligendum hic est..." *Unbekannte Fragmente aus Luthers zweiter Psalmenvorlesung 1518*, ed. Erich Vogelsang (Berlin, 1940), 54.26-55.5. Our study of the *synteresis* in the lectures on Romans leads us to agree with Schwarz against Vogelsang on the earlier date for these fragments. *Fides, Spes und Caritas beim jungen Luther*, 154. One of Vogelsang's reasons for dating these fragments in 1518 is the distinction between *fides* and *synteresis* in this passage. *Unbekannte Fragmente...*, 18, 30. We think it quite clear that such distinction is already most explicit in the period 1515-16. Further, Hirsch stresses the "bona intelligentia" in this passage (against Pinomaa) in defense of his conviction that Luther preserves the *synteresis*. *Lutherstudien*, I, 116. The issue, however, is not whether Luther preserves or dismisses the *synteresis*, as Hirsch and Pinomaa argue, but the *capacity* in which it is preserved or dismissed. See *infra*, note 2; p. 198, note 1. In regard to *fides* and the *synteresis*, see Luther's interpretation of psalm 4:7 in the *Dictata*, where *fides* and "lumen vultus [Dei]" are firmly linked. *WA* 55,II,80.29f. Compare this with Gerson, who interprets the *intelligentia simplex* as the "lumen" of psalm 4:7. *Supra*, p. 60. Finally, we call attention to the statement on psalm 4:7 in the *Operationes in psalmos*: "Quo fit, ut hic versus [4:7] nequeat intelligi de naturali ratione synderesi, sicut multorum habet opinio dicentium, principia prima in moralibus esse per se nota sicut in speculabilibus. Falsa sunt haec. Fides est primum principium omnium bonorum operum..." *WA* 5,119.12ff.

[2] Hirsch argues against Pinomaa that Luther does not drop the term *synteresis* because it is 'Pelagian' but because it is "nicht biblisch;" the term, but not the content it bears is removed: "Das grundlegende ethisch-religiöse Verständnis des Wesens des Menschen, ist bei der Befreiung von der scholastischen Denkform ja gerade erhalten geblieben." *Lutherstudien*, I, 121. Hirsch, further, finds this content preserved in Luther's understanding of natural reason (which bears the

the conclusion that it can empower acts of loving God above all things, was dismissed as a perversion. The good which man can know and do *ex puris naturalibus*, as we pointed out, is at best effective only in the legal and particular 'righteousness' that goes bond among men;[1] at worst, it is the subjection of temporal and spiritual goods to one's own selfish purposes.[2]

---

reality of the *synteresis rationalis*) and natural conscience (which bears the reality of the *synteresis affectualis*). *Ibid.*, 125f. We make no effort to evaluate the later Luther. But as far as the period 1513-16 is concerned, Luther comes to the conclusion that what ethical possibilities human nature may possess have no significance in the initiation and preservation of man's religious situation before God. Before God and in the face of sin and death, man is soteriologically 'de-substantial'. See further our comments on Karl Holl, *infra*, note 2.

[1] On the basis of this "at best" aspect of the *synteresis*, which we do not find to be negated by the "at worst" aspect, Nilsson's conclusion, drawn from Luther's later writings, can be seen as being already implicit in the development we have traced in the *Dictata*, the lectures on Romans and the notes on Tauler's Sermons. "Für den homo theologicus und in bezug auf das Gottesverhältnis bedeutet der Sündenfall eine Wesensänderung [but only as *soteriological* Wesensänderung!!] und eine totale Verderbnis, aber für den homo politicus ist der Verlust partiell, und die imago Dei ist weiterhin coram hominibus imstande, in einigem Umfang das dominium auszuüben, das Gott dem Menschen geschenkt hat." *Simul*, 108.

[2] At this point, we find Karl Holl's interpretation of Luther's "Religion" as "Gewissensreligion" which rests "im Bewußtsein des Sollens" imprecise. "Was verstand Luther unter Religion?", *Gesammelte Aufsätze zur Kirchengeschichte*, I, *Luther* (Tübingen, 1932), 35f. In a larger summary, Holl writes: "[Die Religion] beruht ihm [Luther] vielmehr auf einer für sich bestehenden Beziehung, auf einem *Sollen*, auf einer ursprünglichen, schon in der Tatsache, d.h. dem *Geschenk* des Lebens an sich begründeten und durch die Gabe des Christus vertieften *Verpflichtung*; einer Verpflichtung, die unverändert bleibt, mögen die sonstigen Bedingungen des Daseins sich gestalten, wie sie wollen." "Die Kulturbedeutung der Reformation", *Ibid.*, 470. Such a positive connection ("das Bewußtsein des Sollens") between man *ex puris naturalibus* ("das Geschenk des Lebens an sich") and the faithful man is not evident in the period 1513-16. Such a connection could exist only for the confessed, acknowledged sinner who is *simul* the faithful man, already united with Christ. The conscience of the unconfessed sinner can be utterly without a transcendent reference and self-censure. Cf. *supra*, 146ff, 149ff. The customary criticism of Holl fails to stress this important point. Ole Modalsli and Regin Prenter hasten to attack Holl's understanding of the relationship between "iustum reputare" and "iustum efficere" as one of "means" and "end", thus making justification a prelude to the full realization of man's moral possibilities. *Das Gericht nach den Werken: Ein Beitrag zu Luthers Lehre vom Gesetz* (Göttingen, 1963), 27ff. *Spiritus Creator*, trans. John M. Jensen (Phil., 1953), 41, 97. Neither point out that it is the definition of Luther's "Religion" as "Gewissensreligion" that forms the important anthropological presupposition for Holl's concern to have the order of salvation culminate in the realization of man's moral possibilities. Our criticism of Holl at this point is not intended to limit or question the genuine ethical thrust of Luther's theology. It seeks to make clear that when one lets ethical consciousness precede and ethical responsibility succeed justification by faith, as Holl does, then Luther's doctrine of sin is seriously abridged and his

A second conclusion we reached was that faith and not a natural, anthropological resource is exclusively and comprehensively definitive of man before God. This second conclusion is the correlate of the first.

These conclusions are solidly prepared in the *Dictata*, where three motifs evidence the suffocation of the *synteresis* as a significant soteriological resource. These are: (1) the necessity of special divine grace to awaken the *synteresis*; (2) the discovery of the soteriologically desubstantial nature of the *whole* creature (manifest especially in the concept, *clamare*); and (3) the location of all soteriological resources outside of man in the three-fold advent of Christ.[1] As God had been considered to take possession of the *reliquiae mortuorum* in the *Dictata*, so in the lectures on Romans the Holy Spirit is the agent of the groaning in and through and for man, as the creation is led to seek what it does not and cannot attain from itself. And in the notes on Tauler's Sermons, it is the man who regards himself as nothing, stripped of his own will, remembering the passion of Christ and supported by God alone, who is "homo spiritualis."

We venture further. If, as we have argued, a natural, creational 'covenant,' which attributes soteriologically significant resources to the soul of man (the *Seelengrund* or the *synteresis*), is logically foundational to a Pelagian historical covenant, which attributes soteriologically significant activity to the will of man *(facere quod in se est)*, then Luther's delimitation of the efficacy of the *synteresis* should lead to the dismissal of a *facere quod in se est* which would in any significant way obligate God to dispense His grace.

We begin by calling attention to a lengthy comment Luther makes on Tauler's discussion of sufferance and the birth of God in the soul. The Tauler passage on which he comments is the following.

> In Job [17:12] we read, 'post tenebras spero lucem,' after the darkness we hope for the light. Hold yourself together [when you are in darkness]! Do not run away! Bear your suffering to the end and seek nothing else! Some men flee when they find themselves in this inner poverty; they always seek something else by which they might escape this suppression. This is an utterly disastrous evasion! Or they lament, question the Teacher and become more and more confused. [Unlike them] you should suffer this anguish, free from every doubt that after the darkness comes bright day, [blazing] sunlight. So be on your guard, just as if it were a question of your life [or death]! Persevere so

---

doctrine of justification is subtly 'secularized'. *Luther secularizes man, not man's justification before God.*

[1] See *supra*, p. 149ff, 168ff.

> that you do not go to ruin on something else. For, truly, when you stand this storm, the birth [of God] is close at hand, and God will be born in you. Take me at my word, when I say that no such anguish arises in man except as God wants to bring forth a new birth in him.[1]

The major portion of Luther's response to this concatenation of imperatives is as follows:

> Although we might know that God does not work in us without first destroying us and what is our own (i.e. through a cross and suffering), still we are so foolish as to desire that the sufferings we undergo are only those which we choose or which we have read about or seen in the lives of others. Thus, we dictate to God the extent and form [of these sufferings], and are prepared to teach Him what He may do and how far He may go when he deals with us. We do not [in other words] stand in sheer faith *(in mera fide)*. [Now God deals with us only on His own terms.] He will either have nothing to do with us at all, or He will work in us as in those who have no knowledge [of His way of salvation]. What He works He works in those who do not understand it, so that there may be [only] saving faith and a naked will. A craftsman does not work with his material according to the form which the material has and *de facto* exhibits. Nor does he work with his material according to the form which it can receive in addition to its original form. For, then, it would simply receive an accidental form *(forma accidentalis)*.[2] No, the craftsman immediately destroys that substantial form *(formam substantialem)* so that he may introduce another form which is utterly contrary *(omnino diversam)* to the prior form [of his material]. So is it with God who says: 'as clay in the hands of the potter, so you arc in my hands' [Jer. 18:6]. He immediately shatters our purpose *(propositum)*, hope and design *(intentionem)*. He disperses our plan *(consilium)* with a work that is the very reverse of it *(contrario opere)*. He reproves all the schemes of the people so that He may introduce His plan. And His plan satisfies with incomparably greater abundance than would have been the case had He been subservient to our own. Yet when this happens, disbelieving and distrusting children, seeing that

---

[1] Vetter, 172.7ff: "Job: 'post tenebras spero lucem, nach dem vinsternisse hoffen wir des liechtes.' Blibe allein bi dir selber und enlouf nút us und lide dich us und ensuche nút ein anders! So louffent etliche menschen als si in disem inwendigen armuete stont, und suchent iemer út anders, das si des gestrenges dar mit engont. Das ist als schedelich. Oder si gont klagen oder lerer fragen und werdent me verirret. Blibe bi disem ane allen zwivel; nach dem vinsternisse kumet der liechte tag, der sunnen schin. Huet dich als dines libes das du uf nút anders enslahest, wan warte. In der worheit, blibest du do bi, die geburt die ist nach und sol in dir geborn werden. Und wissist uf mich das niemer enkein getrenge in den menschen uf gestot, Got enwelle nach dem ein núwe geburt in im ernúwen."

[2] This is an implicit criticism of the *habitus gratiae*, the infused *forma accidentalis animae*, traditional in Thomism and nominalism. Luther works with a new understanding of substance and accident. See our discussion *supra*, p. 105ff.

what is completely the reverse *(penitus contrarium)* of their own understanding is happening, do not hold on to the plan of God but think that it is all from the Devil! So they retreat to the plan of the impious and believe that their plan and design are from God and that what runs counter to them is from the Devil. In spite of [their interpretation we know that] what opposes *(contra)* our every design is from the Devil and what is the very reverse *(contraria)* [of our every design] is from God, as [Matthew 5:25] says: 'Agree with your adversary on the way.' Thus, as [Tauler] says here, the whole of salvation is resignation of will in all things, whether spiritual or temporal—and naked faith *(nuda fides)* in God.[1]

What is the major thrust of these comments? Here Luther sets himself against the intrusion into the sphere of salvation of all that man can plan and execute: his *propositum*, *voluntas*, *spes*, *intentio*, *consilium*, *cogitatio* and the meritorious value he attributes to them.[2] The plans of man are not only irrelevant, but inimical to the *consilium Dei*. So God destroys them. He destroys man's 'substantial form!' But if man loses his substantial form, how can he 'be'?

---

[1] *WA* 9,102.10ff: "Et si sciamus, quod deus non agat in nobis, nisi prius nos et nostra destruat (i.e. per crucem et passiones), tamen adeo stulti sumus, ut eas velimus tantum suscipere passiones quas nos elegimus vel quas in aliis factas vidimus vel legimus. Et ita deo statuimus modum et ipsum docere parati sumus, quid et quantum nos erudiat. Et non nudi stamus in mera fide, cum tamen deus velit vel non agere in nobis vel ignorantibus et nobis et id quod agit non intelligentibus agere, ut sic salva sit fides et nuda voluntas. Sicut Artifex non agit in materiam secundum formam quam ipsa habet, ostendit et exhibet de facto nec secundum eam, quam ipsa posset exquirere extrinsecus sua priore salva: haec enim fieret accidentalis forma. Sed directe illam substantialem formam destruit, ut aliam introducat omnino diversam a priore. Sic deus qui dicit, 'Sicut lutum in manu figuli ita vos in manu mea,' directe agit contra nostrum propositum, spem et intentionem et omne consilium nostrum contrario opere dissipat et omnes cogitationes populorum reprobat, ut suum consilium inducat, quod tamen abundantius nostro consilio satisfacit incomparabiliter, quam si nostro obsecutus fuisset. Tunc quando hoc fit, increduli et filii diffidentiae videntes penitus contrarium suo sensui fieri non sustinent consilium dei, immo a diabolo putant hoc esse. Et ita abeunt in consilium impiorum eo, quod suum consilium et intentionem ex deo esse credant et omnem contrariam ex diabolo: cum tamen contra omnis nostra intentio ex diabolo et contraria ex deo sicut dicit, 'Esto consentiens adversario tuo in via.' Igitur tota salus est resignatio voluntatis in omnibus ut hic docet sive in spiritualibus sive temporalibus. Et nuda fides in deum." See the *scholion* on Romans 8:26, which makes reference to Isaiah 64:8: "Qui spiritum non habent, fugiunt et nolunt opera Dei fieri, sed seipsos formare." *WA* 56,376.28f.

[2] Luther is explicit against the meritorious value which men attribute to their plans and schemes: "Sic invenias aliquos qui audierunt de aliquo sancto, quod hoc vel hoc passus est: tunc sibi devotionem et promptum animum figunt ad sustinendum similia. Et hic iam sese bonos et iustos arbitrantur et nonnunquam vel quaerunt etiam, ut sibi ista vel aliqua eorum irrogentur vel, si sic praecogitata veniunt, sustinent et magnum meritum se fecisse confidunt." *WA* 9,102.37ff.

Without our study of Luther's understanding of *substantia* in the *Dictata*, we, like the secondary literature to date, would have to ignore this important statement. With the understanding of *substantia* and of Luther's conviction that human life is soteriologically de-substantial which we gained there, we have a perspective from which we can present a clarification of its import.

By 'substance,' Luther means a 'solid place' where one can place the 'feet of his soul' (*affectus* and *intellectus*), confident that he will not sink into the abyss of sin and death. What constitutes and defines man is not what he quidditatively is but what he looks for and expects; where he is *in affectu et intellectu* 'substantiates' him. As Luther stresses in the *scholion* on Romans 8:19—"for the expectation of the creature..."—it is not speculation about *quidditates* and *qualitates*, but the "expectation of the creature" that Paul introduces as the clue to understanding the creature.[1]

What God destroys when he destroys man's 'substantial form,' then, is the perverse 'objective context'—his 'plan' for his life—which man himself creates and in which he attempts to live before God and to which he even attempts to subject and measure God's dealing with him. And when God destroys this 'form' what emerges? What is the 'residue'? Precisely the recognition of the soteriologically de-substantial nature of one's life—the 'multitude of sins' out of which one can only cry for what he does not possess. For now he sees that he has no resources for standing before God; he recognizes that before sin and death all his good deeds and meritorious acts, all the most refined and sophisticated plans which go bond among men, are simply 'fluff.' His own 'context' of salvation, the *termini a quo* and *ad quem* which he has fashioned to orient and support his life—e.g. a 'small motion to good in the soul' *(terminus a quo)* and 'loving God above all things *ex puris naturalibus*' *(terminus ad quem)*—cannot support his 'feet' before God. His idols must be replaced with words and promises —God's plan. And faith in these words and promises—memory of the

[1] *WA* 56,371.1ff: "Aliter Apostolus de rebus philosophatur et sapit quam philosophi et metaphysici. Quia philosophi oculum ita in presentiam rerum immergunt, ut solum quidditates et qualitates earum speculentur, Apostolus autem oculus nostros revocat ab intuitu rerum presentium, ab essentia et accidentibus earum, et dirigit in eas, secundum quod futurae sunt. Non enim dicit 'essentia' vel 'operatio' creaturae seu 'actio' et 'passio' et 'motus', sed novo et miro vocabulo et theologico dicit 'expectatio creaturae', ut eoipso, cum animus audit creaturam expectare, non ipsam creaturam amplius, sed quid creatura expectet, intendat et quaerat." Cf. 56,371.28ff, 372.22ff. See our discussion of *substantia*, *supra*, p. 105ff.

past manifest works of God and hope in the promised future works of God—must build for him a new 'context,' *penitus eontrarium* to his own, if he is to have a place where he can stand before God.

This is not Tauler's understanding. His concept of 'will-lessness' is a concept of a means employed to achieve the full emergence of man's own substantial form—the *Seelengrund* which becomes *weselich* one with God. Tauler does not see the fulfilment of the *vita fidei* within an objective context of remembered past and hoped for future works of God, but as the suspension of all historical works of God for the sake of a trans-historical attainment of the being of God.

Has Luther overlooked this radical difference? Has genuine appreciation for Tauler's stress on *resignatio voluntatis* led him to be totally uncritical? The two statements—"homo spiritualis nititur fide" and "nuda fides in Deum"—should have put us on our guard. Let us look at another comment on Tauler to see how explicitly critical non-explicit criticism can be.

In a Christmas sermon on Isaiah 9:6, Tauler specifies the conditions and nature of man's becoming one with God. He speaks of the necessity of an "entrance" *(ingang)* into the "ground," i.e. an assemblage of all the powers of the soul and their subjection to the highest power, the ground of the soul. From this activity follows a "departure" *(uzgang)* from all one's desires; a pure disposition to God is attained.[1] And this forms the final preparatory stage for the birth of God in the soul.[2] If you have emptied yourself, then God must fill

[1] Vetter, 9.26ff: "...alle die krefte versamment sint, sinnelichen und guenlichen und bewegelichen krefte, in die obersten, in den grunt, dis ist der ingang. Denne sol do geschehen ein uzgang, jo ein úbergang usser ime selber und úber in, do súllent wir verloeugenen allen eigenschaft wellens und begerens und wúrckens, denne do sol bliben ein blos luter meinen Gottes, und des sinen nút eigens in dekeiner wise zu sinde oder zu werdende oder zu gewinnende, denne allein zu sinde und ime stat zu gebende uf daz hoehste und uf daz nehste, das er sins werkes und sinre geburt in dir bekummen múge und von dir des ungehindert werde. Wan wenne zwei súllent eins werden, so mus sich daz eine halten lidende und daz ander wúrckende..."

[2] Tauler's words, "ingang" and "uzgang," find latin equivalents in Luther's use of the words, "exire" and "introire." Note that the "exire" has exclusive reference to God's initiating activity which brings about our "entrance" into ourselves ("introire"), and that this entrance is not into a ground of the soul, but into the recognition and confession that we are "mendaces," "iniusti" and "infirmi." For Luther, "introire" means *becoming a sinner*. (See *supra*, 146ff.) "Quia sicut solus Deus verax et iustus et potens in seipso, vult etiam extra se i.e. in nobis esse talis, ut sic glorificetur... Ita vult, quod sicut solus (omnis) homo est mendax, iniustus, infirmus extra se (i.e. coram Deo), ut etiam talis fiat et intra se, i.e. ut confiteatur et agnoscat se talem, qualis est. Et ita Deus per suum exire nos facit ad

the empty place: "so much out, so much in."[1]

Luther's comments register strong agreement with the emphasis Tauler places on resignation and sufferance in divine things.[2] When he comments on the "uzgang" motif, he writes that this is an "excessus mentis et affectus": the departure of every affect from all created things so that one is stripped of his affection for temporal things; and, correlatively, a departure of every thought of knowledge and wisdom so that peace and quiet reign in the soul.[3]

How far does Luther go with Tauler? We must look more closely at what Tauler means by resignation and Luther by *excessus mentis et affectus* to answer this question.

From our earlier study of Tauler, it is clear that resignation and the achievement of a pure disposition to God are activities for which man is as much responsible as God: "so much out, so much in." The line between human and divine activity, like that between human and divine being, is most tenuous. Further, the the goal of the pure disposition to God is the stage in which the ground of the soul is freed from all historical, temporal realities. Here all historical 'pictures', including the passion of Christ, the Word of God, the sacraments and human activity are suspended. The point of the "uzgang" is that point where nothing of one's own remains ("des sinen nút eigens in dekeiner wise").[4] The activity of man is suspended, as God's *potentia ordinata* is

---

nos ipsos introire et per sui cognitionem infert nobis et nostri cognitionem [viz., as "mendaces ac iniusti"]." *WA* 56,229.15ff.

[1] See *supra*, p. 32.

[2] *WA* 9,97.12ff: "Nota, quod divina pati magis quam agere oportet, immo et sensus et intellectus est naturaliter etiam virtus passiva. Et Apostolus: 'Velle mihi adjacet, perficere non invenio' [Rom. 7:18] i.e. nos materia sumus pura, deus formae factor, omnia enim in nobis operatur deus."

[3] *WA* 9,97.18ff: "Est excessus de quo hic loquitur mentis, immo affectus et per omnium affectum i.e. timoris, spei, odii, amoris, gaudii, tristitiae erga quamcumque creaturam, expoliationem et denudationem qua... plurimorum nuditas vel vacuitas...qui et omnem exuit; omnium intellectum i.e. scientiae, sapientiae...ut sit ibi quies et pax omnimodo." The comment is incomplete (...), but Luther's point is clear.

[4] See *supra*, p. 203, n. 1. Note the following statement by Tauler: "Als nu dise uswendigen groben gebresten ab geschorn sint, so blibent doch in dem grunde der neiglicheit die bilde der vorgegangener gewonheit; die sol der mensche vertriben mit den minneklichen bilden unsers herren Jhesu Christi und sol recht einen val mit dem anderen us slahen und sol die als innerlichen mit grosser andacht in sich ze grunde trucken und ziehen, *das alle ungelicheit in im verwerde und verloesche*." Vetter, 237.29ff. Emphasis mine. Luther's comment on this passage is: "Nos autem debemus transferri a claritate quidem in claritatem, *sed tamen in eandem formam*." *WA* 9,104.5f. Emphasis mine.

suspended, when the distinction between divine and human *wesen* is suspended.

From our study of Luther, it is clear that a "departure" of *affectus* and *intellectus* from temporal things does not expose a ground of the soul, nor remove (a) the distinction between the soul and its Creator and (b) the radical opposition between the acknowledged sinner and the righteous man. The very reverse is the case: the total absence of soteriological resources in the nature and activity of man is made manifest. For here all plans which man can fashion through the interaction of his own powers and the objects present to him in the world are shown to be incapable of 'substantiating' him before God and in the face of sin and death. A 'vacuum' emerges, and Luther agrees with Tauler and Augustine that its persistence is simply not possible.[1] But how is it filled for Luther? It is not filled with a *Seelengrund* in substantive unity with the uncreated Ground, but with "sheer" and "naked" faith in God alone, i.e. in the "plan" of God, i.e. in the "passion of Christ."

Faith is "sheer" and "naked" because the *intellectus* and *affectus fidei* are located in a 'context' where no visible things can be present. They are empowered and sustained by other 'objects': the Son of God-incarnate-crucified-dead-and-resurrected-for-our-salvation according to the *Dictata*;[2] "the passion of Christ in memory" according to the notes on Tauler's Sermons. The *intellectus* and *affectus fidei* discern and live in the real miracle of God's historical "plan," his 'covenant' with man, not in nature, but in the three-fold advent of Christ.

Quite the reverse of Tauler, Luther suspends the activity of man within the *ordo salutis* and concomitantly exalts the soteriological uniqueness and sufficiency of the incarnation when the distinction and opposition between divine and human *wesen* is fully *established.*

2. *Luther and the 'Scholastics'*

When we turn form the mystical to the scholastic traditions, the dismissal of the *facere quod in se est* and the presentation of the objective context of faith and hope in the plan or works of God are also manifest, although now expressed in the 'language of the school.' In this section, we will demonstrate this by examining conclusions Luther

[1] *WA* 9,98.4f: "Vacuum naturale non est possibile, multo minus spirituale est possibile." Tauler appeals to Augustine in the passage on which Luther here comments.

[2] Cf. *supra*, p. 112ff.

draws in the lectures on Romans and his notes on Biel's *Sentences* commentary.

First, let us orient ourselves before we proceed. In our study of the *Dictata*, we found that several motifs converged to undermine a Pelagian understanding of the historical order of salvation, especially as this was formulated in the *facere quod in se est* of nominalism. These factors were: (1) the insistence that the *bonitas Dei* is the only *bonitas* admissible within the order of salvation;[1] (2) the understanding of the *adventus Christi* as the establishment of saving *veritas* in the earth and thus as the sole basis on which *iustitia* has saving regard to man 'from heaven;' and (3) the interpretation of *congrue* apart from the concept of merit and within the context of *expectare* and *clamare*.[2] It is possible to add a fourth to these, although it did not function for Luther in a major way as did the three here mentioned. This is the acknowledgement that man does not fulfil the law *quoad substantiam actus*.[3]

This last point now becomes a major target of attack in the lectures on Romans and the notes on Biel's *Sentences* commentary. This is resultant from Luther's awareness of the interconnection between the conviction that man can love God above all things *ex puris naturalibus* and the assumption that the small motion to good with which man is naturally endowed *(synteresis)* legitimates this optimistic view. Luther sees the mediating link between the exaggeration of the effectiveness of the *synteresis* and the alleged attainment of a love of God above all things to be the further assumption that man fulfils the law *quoad substantiam actus*. The fact that man does his very best and keeps the commandments of God to the extent that he is able outside a state of

---

[1] Luther writes in the lectures on Romans: "Ubi ergo nunc est iustitia nostra? Ubi sunt opera bona? Ubi sunt libertas arbitrii, contingentia rerum? Nempe sic predicandum est, hoc est recte predicare, hoc est 'prudentiam carnis' iugulare. Siquidem hucusque Apostolus precidit ei manus et pedes et linguam, hic autem iugulat penitus et occidit eam. Quia nunc videt, quod in se nihil est, sed tantum in deo totum suum bonum." *WA* 56,382.16ff.

[2] Cf. *supra*, p. 166ff. "Praeparatio" is interpreted through *clamare* and in the context of God's merciful promise in the *Operationes in psalmos* (1519-21). Commenting on psalm 10:7, Luther writes: "...paratus et promptus es exaudire, ut etiam antequam clament, sola desyderia cordis audias, immo impatientior tu es morae, ut audias, quam illi, ut clament, optasque clamare, ut locum habeas exaudiendi, adeo praevenit et parata est voluntas tua exaudiendi desyderium eorum clamandi. Sic Isa. lxv [65:24]: 'Eritque antequam clament, ego exaudiam, adhuc loquentibus illis (id est nondum finito clamore aut sermone) audiam.' 'Tunc invocabis et dominus exaudiet, clamabis, et dicet: 'ecce adsum,' quia misericors sum, dominus, deus tuus.' [Isa. 58:9]." *WA* 5,351.9f.

[3] Cf. *supra*, p. 168.

grace, indicates for Luther's opponents both a natural ability which makes it possible and a culmination in an act pleasing to and rewarded by God. Luther will now attack each of these three points. Seen from an anthropological perspective and concern, it is the removal of the exaggerated view of the powers of the *synteresis* which forms the logically first step in this attack. As Luther will point out, Biel has the wrong "fundamentum."

In chapter 8 of the lectures on Romans, we find this evaluation expressed frequently. The very point of Paul's letter to the Romans, Luther argues, is to attack those who, "trusting in their own natural powers," thought that no other aid was necessary to righteousness and good works than knowledge of the law.[1] The opening words of the comment on this chapter bring together Luther's criticism and his alternative. He writes in response to verses 1-4, where Paul states that what the law, weakened by the flesh, could not do, God has done by sending His Son.

> Where is free will now? Where are those who endeavor to maintain that we are able to perform an act in which we love God above all things from our natural powers? If I said that the commands of the law are impossible for us to fulfil, that would be sufficient [reason for them] to curse me! But now the Apostle is the one who says that it was impossible for the law to condemn sin, and even that infirmity [which comes] through the flesh. This is what I said frequently before; it is simply not possible to fulfil the law from ourselves. And it is of no value to say that we are able to fulfil the law according to the substance of the act but not according to the intention of the Lawgiver, as if the ability and will to fulfil the law were truly within our power, but not the manner which God wishes, viz., within a state of grace. In this view grace is certainly useful but it is not necessary, nor [are we considered] to incur the corruption of our nature through the sin of Adam, but rather we are [considered to be] sound in our natural powers. So we smell the stench of philosophy, as if reason could always call out to the highest things! And we chatter so much about the law of nature.[2]

---

[1] *WA* 56,360.18f: "Quia contra eos potissimum disputat, qui in naturae propriis viribus confidentes nullum aliud auxilium necessarium ad iustitiam et bona opera putabant quam cognitionem legis..." It is those who argue that "voluntas posse elicere actum dilectionis dei super omnia ex puris naturalibus" whom Paul attacks. 56,359.12f. Cf. the *scholion* on Romans 1:1: "Deus enim nos non per domesticam, sed per extraneam iustitiam et sapientiam vult salvare, non que veniat et nascatur ex nobis, sed que aliunde veniat in nos, non que in terra nostra oritur, sed que de celo venit. Igitur omnino externa et aliena iustitia oportet erudiri. Quare primum oportet propriam et domesticam evelli." 56,158.10ff.

[2] *WA* 56,355.3ff: "Ubi nunc est liberum arbitrium? Ubi sunt, qui ex naturalibus

This critical reference to reason's entreaty of the highest things, repeated a second time in this chapter,[1] is an explicit dismissal of the *synteresis rationis* and *voluntatis* as a significant, natural, soteriological resource. And with the removal of its exaggerated significance within the order of salvation, the *facere quod in se est*, as far as Luther is concerned, loses its anthropological foundation.

> How can he love whom he does not know? How can he know Him who by the fault of the first sin is in darkness and chains in his intellective and affective powers? Therefore, unless faith illumines and Love sets him free, man is not able to will, have or do anything good. All he does is evil, even when he does what is good.[2]

In the notes on Biel's *Sentences* commentary, the situation is just as explicit. When Biel draws the conclusion that "one is able to love and enjoy God above all things from his natural powers," Luther comments: "grace is denied, and he argues absurdly, presupposing a healthy will."[3] The same judgment falls when Biel argues from the assumptions (1) that "to love God above all things is a dictate of right reason," and (2) that "the will is able by its own natural power to conform to every dictate of right reason," that the conclusion follows: the will of man can love God "above all things." Luther responds:

> And consequently [the will] is not infirm and in need of God's grace. And all these statements proceed from the foolish foundation of free

---

nos posse elicere actum diligendi Deum super omnia (affirmare conantur)? Ego si dicerem impossibilia nobis precepta, maledicerer. Nunc Apostolus dicit impossibile fuisse legi peccatum damnare, immo ipsam infirmitatem per carnem. Hoc est, quod supra sepius dixi, simpliciter esse impossibile legem implere ex nobis, et non valere, quod dicitur, quia preceptum secundum substantiam facti, sed non ad intentionem legislatoris possimus implere quasi scil. ex nobis quidem velle et posse sit, sed non modo, quo vult Deus, sc. in gratia. Ac per hoc utilis quidem, sed non necessaria est gratia. Nec per peccatum Adae vitium naturae incurrimus, sed integri in naturalibus sumus. Ita olet philosophia in anhelitu nostro, quasi ratio ad optima semper deprecetur, et de lege naturae multa fabulamur."

[1] *WA* 56,355.15ff: "Verum est sane, quod lex naturae omnibus nota est et quod ratio ad optima deprecatur. Sed quae? Non secundum deum, sed secundum nos, i.e. male bona deprecatur. Quia se et sua in omnibus querit, non autem Deum, quod sola fides in charitate facit."

[2] *WA* 56,355.22ff: "Quomodo diligeret, quem non novit? Quomodo nosset, qui vitio peccati primi in tenebris et vinculis quoad intellectum et affectum est? Igitur nisi fides illucescat et Charitas liberet, non potest homo quicquam boni aut velle aut habere vel operari, sed malum tantum, tunc etiam, quando bonum operatur." See our discussion of *bonitas*, *supra*, 166ff.

[3] Degering, *Festgabe*, 15. Biel: "Ergo pari ratione potest diligere deum ex suis naturalibus super omnia et frui eo." Luther: "Negatur gratia et insulse arguit, sanam voluntatem praesupponens."

> will. As if free will is able from itself to move in either a good or evil direction, when it is [in fact] prone only to evil! Even if it turns against this proneness, it does so at least unwillingly, and in this [act] it does not love divine things. For love goes together with delight just as fear with punishment.[1]

And, finally, when Biel concludes, with a flourish of quotations from Scripture, that *secundum legem ordinatam*, the *facere quod in se est* is a sufficient disposition for the reception of grace, Luther retorts:

> As if these words [from Scripture] want to maintain that it is within our own power, grace excluded, to seek and turn [to God], whereas psalm 13[:2] says, 'man is not understanding, not requiring God, etc..' Therefore, those words do not support [his] point.[2]

Biel's point is beside the point for Luther because Luther is convinced that all that man can think and do is beside the point before God and in the face of sin and death.

4. FAITH AND HOPE: AGREEMENT WITH THE 'ADVERSARY'

In Luther's notes on Tauler's Sermons, we have seen that man's union with God in this life involves agreement with a 'consilium,' a plan, which is the very reverse of man's own natural way of charting

---

[1] *Ibid.*, 14-15. Biel: "Viatoris voluntas humana ex suis naturalibus potest diligere deum super omnia. Probatio omni dictamini rationis rectae voluntas ex suis naturalibus se potest conformare: sed diligere deum super omnia est dictamen rationis rectae; ergo illi se potest voluntas ex suis naturalibus conformare: et per consequens deum super omnia diligere." Luther: "Et per consequens non est infirma nec eget gratia dei. Omnia ista ex stulto fundamento procedunt liberi arbitrii, quasi li. arb. possit ex se ipso in utrumque oppositorum, cum solum ad malum sit pronum. Aut si contra pronitatem se erigit, manet saltem invita, ut per hoc nec amet diva. Amor enim delectationem habet sicut timor poenam."

[2] *Ibid.*, 16. Biel: "Probatur: quia secundum legem ordinatam cuilibet facienti quod in se est: et per hoc sufficienter disposito ad gratiae susceptionem: deus infundit gratiam secundum illud prophetae, 'Convertimini ad me et ego convertar ad vos' Zach. I [:3], et illud Jaco IV [:8], 'Approp[inqu]ate Deo et appropinquabit vobis,' scilicet per gratiam. Et illud Luc. XI [:9], 'Quaerite et invenietis, pul. et ape. vobis.' Et Hiere. XXIX [:13], 'Cum quaesieritis me in toto corde vestro; inveniar a vobis.' Et in psal. XXI [:27], 'Qui requirent eum, vivent corda eorum.' Vivimus autem per gratiam. Hinc Chrysost. lib. I. de compunctione cordis. Non inquit personarum acceptor est deus." Luther: "Quasi illa dicta id velint, quod nostrae virtutis sit seclusa gratia quaerere, converti, cum dicat ps. 13 [:2], 'Non est intelligens, non est requirens deum etc.' Omnia ergo ista non sunt ad propositum."

and living his life before God. God has His own unique plan for salvation, and salvation is consenting to this 'Adversary'. It means confessing oneself to be nothing and resting on God alone—on the passion of Christ—through sheer, naked faith.

This interpretation finds a parallel in the *scholia* on chapter 8 of the lectures on Romans, as the phrase "conformitas voluntatis dei" comes into the foreground.

The first thing to be noticed here is that Luther attacks precisely *the effort to break the 'contraria' character* of the *consilium Dei* and to subject God to conformity with man's own will and desire, i.e. to make God's plan conform with man's. When God's "strange work" *(opus alienum)* comes upon men, and it is discovered to be the complete reverse of their own will and plan, they refuse to be in agreement with God.

> They want to be as God and have their plans not beneath God's but on His level *(iuxta Deum)*, completely conformed [to His] and perfect. This is as possible, indeed so little possible, as that clay, which by its own nature is adapted to become a pitcher or some sort of container, can in its present form be like the form or idea of the craftsman, who knows what it will be, and in accordance with [his plan] intends to form the clay.[1]

What these people cannot and will not accept is the otherness and contrariety of God's plan for their lives: they refuse to consent to their 'Adversary.' And further *(duplex peccatum)*, they attempt to remove the opposition between themselves and God by insisting that the plan of God not only conform to, but indeed become *identical* with, their own.

> Is this not to curse God that one regards God in his heart as his adversary and enemy and wills and thinks what is contrary [to Him], and with all his powers tries to establish what is contrary to God, and even attempts to destroy God and His will and change them into his own will, i.e. to change them into nothing?[2]

---

[1] *WA* 56,376.19ff: "Ipsi vero sicut Deus esse volunt et cogitationes suas non esse infra, sed iuxta Deum, omnino conformes scil. atque perfectas, quod tam est possibile, immo minus possibile, quam quod lutum, quod natura sua aptum est ad urceum vel quodlibet vas, sua praesenti forma simile sit formae seu Ideae artis, que est in figulo, quam in lutum intendit formare. Stulti autem potius et superbi sunt eiusmodi et ignorantes Deum et seipsos."

[2] *WA* 56,369.15ff: "An non est hoc maledicere, in corde cogitare Deum adversarium inimicum, contrarium sentire et velle atque totis viribus, si posset, contrarium statuere, immo Deum et voluntatem eius perire et mutari in voluntatem suam i.e. in nihilum?"

On the other hand, the faithful people, the people who have received the "prudence of the Spirit," love the will of God and, conformed to it, they rejoice in it.[1] What is the greatest horror for others—God's judgment—becomes the highest joy for them, for they will for themselves what God wills for them.[2] They are reconciled to what is their *very opposite*, to what stands in unyielding opposition to all their willing and thinking. In this regard, Luther writes:

> All these people say secretly in their heart: 'God acts like a tyrannt; he is no Father, but an adversary.' And this is quite true! But they do not know that one must agree with this adversary and [by this agreement] He becomes his friend and father—otherwise this never happens. For He will not agree with us, and He will not change [so that He conforms to our plans], in order that we may be His friends and children.[3]

This point, further, is obliquely made in Luther's concluding discussion of predestination in chapter 8 of the lectures on Romans. Predestination—the placement of the 'plan' for man's life in God's hands—is the diametrical opposite of man's plan—salvation in accordance with what goes bond among men, viz., that one should receive as much as he rightfully merits. Luther writes:

> Thus, although these words [the teaching of God's predestination], which contain the most perfect and solid food, may not yet give those [who are turning from the 'prudence of the flesh' to the 'prudence of the spirit'] direct pleasure, for the present they are nevertheless words of comfort and consolation through an *antiperistasis*, i.e. through a situation in which contraries are juxtaposed.[4] And they are such because there are no words which are more effective in terrifying and humiliating the pride of man and destroying his preconceived notions about merits.[5]

---

[1] *WA* 56,364.35-365.1: "Qui vero 'prudentiam spiritus' habent, voluntatem Dei diligunt et ei conformes congratulantur."

[2] *WA* 56,365.4f: "Ita quod aliis est summus horror [viz., iudicium extremum], ipsis est summum gaudium eo, quod volunt perfecta voluntate idem, quod Deus vult." See 56,365.19f: "...per conformitatem voluntatis Dei quietatur conscientia."

[3] *WA* 56,368.25ff: "Omnes itaque eiusmodi occulte in corde dicunt: tyrannice agit Deus, non est Pater, sed adversarius, quod et verum est. Sed nesciunt illi, quod adversario huic consentiendum est et sic fiet amicus et pater et alias nunquam. Non enim Ipse nobis consentiet et mutabitur, ut nos amici eius simus et filii."

[4] In regard to the phrase, "per antiperistasim," Ficker directs the reader to chapter 8 of Aristotle's *Physica*. In this chapter, we find nothing to indicate that Luther is using the phrase in an Aristotelian sense. Indeed, we find the words: "...contraries annihilate or obstruct one another." VIII, 8, 262^{a}.11f.

[5] *WA* 56,387.2ff: "Igitur etsi iis non directe adhuc sint dulcia ista verba per-

Gerson had spoken of strength through an "antiperistasis spiritualis." But for him this "antiperistasis" strengthens precisely because it drives one to the "safe place of contemplation," i.e. to a region where opposition can be escaped.[1] Inasmuch as the faithful man, for Luther, is *semper incipiens a novo*—and that means *semper peccans* before God—opposition remains as the *abiding* context of peace and union with God.[2]

Now we must ask precisely what it means for man to live in conformity with God's will and plan for his salvation. If all that man can think, desire, plan and execute has no place before God, what empowers this conformity?

In our study of the *Dictata*, we argued that it is only faith and hope which 'substantiate' man's life before God and in the face of sin and death. Or, as it was summarized in the notes on Tauler's Sermons, "nuda fides in Deum" constitutes the spiritual man. In the lectures on Romans, the answer is no different. Commenting on Romans 8:24f —"For we are saved by hope; but hope that is seen is not hope"— Luther writes:

> Although this manner of speaking is grammatically figurative, when it is theologically grasped, it is most to the point. For it expresses the most intense affection. This is because hope, which comes from the desire for something which is loved, always intensifies love when the beloved object is not yet present. Thus, what is hoped for and the one who hopes become as one through intense hope, as St. Augustine says, 'the soul is more where it loves than where it lives.'[3] And as it is commonly said, 'my flame is here,' and as the poet says, 'Amyntas is my fire.' Also Aristotle says in the third chapter of his *De Anima* that the understanding and what is understood, sensation and what is sensed,

---

fectissimi et solidissimi cibi, interim tamen per antiperistasim i.e. contrarii circumstantiam sunt eis mitia et consolatoria. Sic scil. quia nulla sunt verba efficatiora ad terrendum, humiliandum et superbam presumptionem de meritis destruendum quam ista."

[1] *De myst. theol. pract., cons.* 9, 189.123ff: "Sic enim 'columba' rationalis non habens 'ubi pes' desiderii 'requiescat', revertitur ad archam contemplationis, sic eadem archa crescentibus aquis tribulationum amplius sublevatur, sic 'ascendunt' tribulati 'in superiora domus' sue spiritualis, ut 'Iudith' et 'Petrus', dum vel obprobrium aliquod, vel parentum mortem, vel patrie afflictionem, vel rerum inopiam accipiunt. Hec est antiperistasis quedam spiritualis, que contrarium fortificat..." Gerson is in agreement with Aristotle. Sce *supra*, p. 212, note 4.

[2] Cf. *supra*, p. 130ff.

[3] Exactly from whom Luther takes this statement is not clear. Ficker argues that it is Tauler, but Bernard and Hugh of St. Victor are also cited as possibilities. Cf. *WA* 56,374.n.10.

> and, generally, the activity of a power and its object become one.[1] Thus, love conveys the one who loves to his beloved. And so hope brings [the one who hopes] to what he hopes for, but what he hopes for is not apparent.[2]

Luther can express the situation with exclusive reference to faith, as he does in the marginal gloss on 8:16, as he draws together "credere," "habere" and the "testimonium Dei":

> *The* Holy *Spirit* given to us *gives testimony* by empowering trust in God *to our spirit that we are sons of God.* We are and we have as much as we believe. And he who believes and trusts that he is a son of God, is a son of God, for Mark 11[:24] says: 'whatever, praying, you should seek, believe that you will receive it, and it is yours.' And Matthew 9 [:29] says: 'according to your faith it is yours.'[3]

And, finally, Luther can bring faith and hope together with the activity of the Holy Spirit to summarize man's 'sonship with God' in this life:

> For he who trusts with a strong faith and hope that he is a son of God, is a son of God; and this is possible for each only through the Spirit.[4]

[1] *De Anima*, III, 1, 425*b*.27f: "The activity of the sensible object and that of the percipient sense is one and the same activity, and yet the distinction between their being remains." "The actualities of the sensible object and of the sensitive faculty are *one* actuality in spite of the difference between their modes of being..." *Ibid.*, III, 2, 426ª.15f. Note here the emphasis on distinction and difference within unity. These are natural analogies which Luther can make theologically fruitful.

[2] *WA* 56,374.6ff: "Ista locutio [Rom. 8:24f] grammatice licet sit figurativa, theologice tamen est propriissima et propter expressionem intensissimi affectus posita. Quia spes, que fit ex amatae rei desiderio, semper amorem dilatione auget. Ideo fit, ut ex re sperata et sperante per intensam spem velut unum fiat, secundum illud B. Augustini: 'Anima plus est, ubi amat, quam ubi animat.' Sic et vulgo dicitur: 'Hic meus ardor.' Et poeta: 'Meus ignis Amynta.' Et Aristotoles 3. de anima dicit, quod ex intellectu et intelligibili, ex sensu et sensibili fit unum et universaliter ex potentia et obiecto suo. Sic amor transfert amantem in amatum. Ergo spes transfert in speratum, sed speratum non apparet." Cf. 56,374.17f: "...anima facta est spes et speratum simul, quia in eo versatur, quod non videt, i.e. in spe."

[3] *WA* 56,78.13-79.5: "*Ipse enim spiritus* sanctus datus nobis *testimonium reddit* confortando fiduciam in Deum *spiritui nostro quod sumus filii Dei.* Tantum enim sumus et habemus, quantum credimus. Qui ergo plena fide credit et confidit se esse filium Dei, est filius Dei, quia Marci: 'Quicquid orantes petieritis, credite, quia accipietis, et fiet vobis,' Mar. XI. Matt. 9: 'secundum fidem vestram fiat vobis'." In the lectures on Hebrews, Luther offers the summary: "Ex hiis enim tribus fit unum: fide, verbo, corde. Fides est glutinum seu copula, verbum et cor sunt extrema, sed per fidem unus spiritus, sicut vir et mulier 'una caro'." *WA* 57,156.20f. See the parallels of *credere* and *habere supra*, p. 108.

[4] *WA* 56,79.15f: "Quia qui confidit forti fide et spe se esse filium Dei, ipse est filius Dei, quod sine Spiritu nemo potest."

The conformity with God achieved in faith and hope is neither the *weselich* union of Tauler nor the generic similitude of Gerson. We are "brothers" and "coheirs" with Christ by adoption through grace, not substantively one with God the Father.[1] And by the same faith in which the righteousness of God lives in us, sin also lives in us: conformity with God is simultaneously disconformity with God.[2] Two 'forms' and two 'plans,' two forms and plans which are diametrically opposed, coexist simultaneously: *simul iustus et peccator*.[3]

5. CONCLUSION

Our study has sought to make two points especially clear. First, Luther's statement which initiated this enterprise, "homo spiritualis nititur fide," is not only a perfect summary of his Reformation discovery, as this is approached from the perspective of anthropology, but it is also expressive of a chasm between his theological thought and that of Tauler and Gerson, which is quite incapable of being bridged. Luther certainly profited from both, especially from the *resignatio* motif of Tauler[4] and from the correlative, reciprocal nature

[1] *WA* 56,79.6f: "*coheredes...Christi*: quia fratres eius per gratiam qui filius Dei est per naturam." 56,78.24f: "...non ex natura, ut Christus solus, et semine neque ex meritis (ut Iudei presumebant), sed ex gratia adoptionis filii Dei sunt." See also 56,369.2ff: "Nec enim ea diligere possumus, que Deus diligit, nisi habeamus amorem et voluntatem et spiritum ipsius. Quia si debet esse conformitas in diligendis, oportet et conformitas esse in affectu dilectionis. Et ii vocantur deiformes homines et filii Dei, quia spiritu Dei aguntur." This is not Gerson's *conformitas*, which accents the generic similitude *(homogeneitas)* of human and divine spirit, not the guidance of the Holy Spirit which empowers faith and hope.

[2] *WA* 56,231.6ff: "Etsi nos nullum peccatum in nobis agnoscamus, credere tamen oportet quod sumus peccatores. Unde Apostolus: 'Nihil mihi conscius sum, sed non in hoc iustificatus sum' [I Cor. 4:4]. Quia sicut per fidem iustitia dei vivit in nobis, ita per eandem et peccatum vivit in nobis, i.e. sola fide credendum est nos esse peccatores, quia non est nobis manifestum, immo sepius non videmur nobis conscii. Ideo iudicio Dei standum et sermonibus eius credendum quibus nos iniustos dicit, quia ipse mentiri non potest. Ac ita necesse est, licet non appareat; 'fides enim est argumentum non apparentium' [Heb. 11:1] et solis verbis Dei contenta est."

[3] *WA* 56,272.16ff: "Nunquid ergo perfecte iustus? Non, sed simul peccator et iustus; peccator re vera, sed iustus ex reputatione et promissione dei certa, quod liberet ab illo, donec perfecte sanet. Ac per hoc sanus perfecte est in spe, in re autem peccator, sed initium habens iustitiae, ut amplius querat semper, semper iniustum se sciens." Note how the "simul" and "semper" converge here. See *supra*, p. 135ff. Later (Sept., 1538), Luther writes: "Quomodo concordant sanctum esse et orare pro peccato? Mira profecto res est. Es ist warlich ein fein ding. Reim da, wer reimen kan. Duo contraria in uno subiecto et in eodem puncto temporis." *WA* 39/1, 507.20ff.

[4] The *resignatio* motif is very strong also in Staupitz, as Ernst Wolf has pointed

of *affectus* and *intellectus* in Gerson. But when these parts are seen within the whole of each man's thought, Luther is saying something which is quite different. As a statement expressing the exclusive location of *all* soteriological resources outside man, "homo spiritualis nititur fide" is the very antithesis of Tauler's concern to promote the *Seelengrund* and Gerson's concern to enhance the soteriological possibilities of the *synteresis*.

A second major point we have endeavored to contribute to the literature on Luther's relation to Tauler and Gerson is that, while the latter consider man's union with God in this life to be the attainment of maximum similitude with God, Luther understands man's union with God to be *simultaneously* the full recognition of man's unlikeness and opposition to God.[1] He who recognizes and acknowledges his unlikeness and opposition to God is the one who is conformed and united with Him, and vice-versa, and *simul*.[2]

We have argued that there is an interrelation between these two points. Tauler's conviction that the *Seelengrund* is a reality which was once eternally one with God, and which, *post peccatum Adae*, remains a reality from which God neither can nor desires to separate Himself, is clearly connected in a formative way with his defense of a *weselich* union with God in this life. Gerson's consideration of the *synteresis* as

out. "Johannes von Staupitz und die theologischen Anfänge Luthers," *Luther Jahrbuch* (1929), 56f. Wolf concludes, however, that for Luther *resignatio* "Wirklichkeit ist, nicht fromme und zweckhafte Übung, wie in der Mystik und auch bei Staupitz." *Ibid.*, 75-76.

[1] Later (July, 1533), Luther writes: "Christiana vita non est hypocritarum; speculantur nescio quas uniones cum sponso Christo. Non sensi istos gustus, quos ipsi fingunt. Anima sponsa et Christus sponsus confluunt etc. Sed fabulae sunt. Est hypocrisis illa; Christiana vita est hec: ante omnia apprehendere verbum; hec unio cum deo, illud quotidianum exerceri et augeri, quia diabolus, mundus, caro veniet et tentabit." Scheel, *Dokumente zu Luthers Entwicklung (bis 1519)*, II (Tübingen, 1929), 105.

[2] For this reason, we find Bornkamm's arguments against Ernst Bizer most persuasive. According to Bizer, Luther, in the period of the *Dictata* and the lectures on Romans, "predigt zunächst nicht Glaubens-, sondern Demutsgerechtigkeit." "Der Begriff der formalen Gerechtigkeit ist nicht überwunden; die Demut *ist* eine formale Gerechtigkeit, und es ist die Demut, nicht einfach der Glaube, die hier den Menschen rechtfertigt." *Fides ex auditu: Eine Untersuchung über die Entdeckung der Gerechtigkeit Gottes durch Martin Luther* (Neukirchen, 1961), 31, 51; cf. 29f. Bornkamm replies by insisting upon the "Zusammengehörigkeit von humilitas und fides": "Man kann nicht eine davon, das Bekennen der Sünde, herausgreifen und an der *humilis* fides das Hauptwort beiseite schieben. Sondern das alles ist Glaube, der sich auf die Barmherzigkeit Gottes in Christus richtet." "Zur Frage der Iustitia Dei beim jungen Luther," II, *ARG*, 53 (1962), 24, 20. Cf. *ibid.*, I, *ARG*, 52 (1961), 23f.

a basically pure part and power of a soul *de facto* ordained to return to its origin in the divine Mind, is unquestionably connected in a formative way with his understanding of man's union with God as a generic likeness *(homogeneitas)* in and through which intellective and affective communion between two 'likes' occurs.

Luther's realization that all anthropological resources and possibilities—substantive, accidental and existential—are utterly powerless before God and in the face of sin and death, reflects a very different understanding of the order of salvation and man's union with God in this life.

The *intellectus* and *affectus* of faith and hope, i.e. orientation to and trust in the remembered past works of God *(adventus Christi in carnem)* and the promised future works of God *(adventus Christi per gloriam)*, 'substantiate' *(adventus Christi spiritualis)* man's present life before God and in the face of sin and death: "homo spiritualis nititur fide."

BIBLIOGRAPHY

Primary Sources

Aristotle, *The Basic Works of Aristotle*, ed. Richard McKeon (New York, 1941).
Augustine, *De spiritu et anima*, *PL*, 40 (Paris, 1887).
Bernard of Clairvaux, *De diligendo deo*, *PL*, 182 (Paris, 1879).
Bonaventura, *S. Bonaventurae opera omnia*, II (Quaracchi, 1885).
——,*Itinerarium mentis in deum* in *Bonaventura. Itinerarium mentis in deum. De reductione artium ad theologiam* (München, 1961).
Eckhart, Meister, *Meister Eckhart. Die deutschen und lateinischen Werke. Die deutschen Werke*, ed. Josef Quint, I (Stuttgart, 1958).
Gerson, Jean, *Oeuvres complètes*, ed Palémon Glorieux (Paris, 1960-).
——,*Epistola prima ad fratrem bartholomaeum*, in *Essai sur la critique de Ruysbroeck par Gerson*, ed. André Combes (Paris, 1945), 616ff.
——,*Ioannis Carlerii de Gerson. De mystica theologia*, ed. André Combes (Lugano [1958]).
Luther, Martin, *D. Martin Luthers Werke. Kritische Gesamtausgabe* (Weimar, 1883-).
——,*Luthers Werke in Auswahl*, 5, *Der junge Luther*, ed. Erich Vogelsang (Berlin, 1955).
——,*Luthers Werke in Auswahl*, 6, *Luthers Briefe*, ed. Hanns Rückert, 2. Aufl. (Berlin, 1955).
——,*Luthers Werke in Auswahl*, 8, *Tischreden*, ed. Otto Clemen (Berlin, 1950).
——,*Luthers Randbemerkungen zu Gabriel Biels Collectorium in quattour libros sententiarum und zu dessen Sacri canonis missae expositio Lyon 1514*, ed. Hermann Degering, *Festgabe der Kommission zur Herausgabe der Werke Martin Luthers zur Feier des 450. Geburtstages Luthers* (Weimar, 1933).
——,*Unbekannte Fragmente aus Luthers zweiter Psalmenvorlesung 1518*, ed. Erich Vogelsang (Berlin, 1940).
——,Scheel, Otto, *Dokumente zu Luthers Entwicklung (bis 1519)*, II (Tübingen, 1929).
Occam, William of, *Gulielmi Ockham, Expositionis in Libros Artis Logicae Prooemium et Expositio in Librum Porphrii de Praedicabilibus*, ed. Ernest A. Moody (St. Bonaventure, N.Y., 1965).
Tauler, Johannes, *Die Predigten Taulers*, ed. Ferdinand Vetter (Berlin, 1910).
——,*Johannes Tauler Predigten*, ed. Walter Lehmann, I, II (Jena, 1923).
——,*Johannes Tauler Predigten*, ed. Georg Hoffmann (Freiburg, 1961).
Thomas Aquinas, *Summa Theologiae* (Ottawa, 1941).
——,*S. Thomae Aquinatis, Scriptum super sententiis magistri Petri Lombardi*, ed. M. F. Moos, O.P. (Paris, 1933).

Secondary Sources

Appel, Heinrich, *Die Lehre der Scholastiker von der Syntheresis* (Rostock, 1891).
——,"Die Syntheresis in der mittelalterlichen Mystik," *ZKG*, XIII (1892), 535ff.
Bernhart, Joseph, *Bernhardische und Eckhartische Mystik in ihren Beziehungen und Gegensätzen* (Kempton, 1912).
——,*Die philosophische Mystik des Mittelalters von ihren antiken Ursprüngen bis zur Renaissance* (München, 1922).
Bettoni, Effrem, *Duns Scotus: The Basic Principles of His Philosophy* (Washington, 1961).

Bizer, Ernst, *Fides ex auditu: Eine Untersuchung über die Entdeckung der Gerechtigkeit Gottes durch Martin Luther* (Neukirchen, 1961).

Boehner, Philotheus, *Collected Articles on Ockham*, ed. E. M. Buytaert (St. Bonaventure, N.Y., 1958).

Bornkamm, Heinrich, "Iustitia Dei in der Scholastik und bei Luther," *ARG*, 39 (1942), 1ff.

——,"Zur Frage der Iustitia Dei beim jungen Luther," I, *ARG*, 52 (1961), 16ff.

——,"Zur Frage der Iustitia Dei beim jungen Luther," II, *ARG*, 53 (1962), 1ff.

Brandenburg, Albert, *Gericht und Evangelium: zur Worttheologie in Luthers erster Psalmenvorlesung* (Paderborn, 1960).

Bremi, Willy, *Was ist das Gewissen? Seine Beschreibung, seine metaphysische und religiöse Deutung, seine Geschichte* (Zürich, 1934).

Champollion, Claire, "La place des termes 'gemuete' et 'grunt' dans le vocabulaire de Tauler," *La mystique rhénane* (Paris, 1963), 180ff.

Combes, André, *Essai sur la critique de Ruysbroeck par Gerson*, III (Paris, 1959).

——,*Jean Gerson commentateur dionysien: Les Notulae super quaedam verba Dionysii de Caelesti Hierarchia* (Paris, 1940).

——,*La théologie mystique de Gerson: Profil de son évolution* (Socii Editores Pontificii, 1963).

Connolly, James L., *John Gerson: Reformer and Mystik* (Louvain, 1928).

Copleston, Frederick, *A History of Philosophy*, III², *Late Mediaeval and Renaissance Philosophy* (New York, 1963).

Dinkler, Erich, *Die Anthropologie Augustins* (Stuttgart, 1934).

Dress, Walter, *Die Theologie Gersons: Eine Untersuchung zur Verbindung von Nominalismus und Mystik im Spätmittelalter* (Gütersloh, 1931).

Ebeling, Gerhard, "Die Anfänge von Luthers Hermeneutik," *ZThK*, 48 (1951), 172ff.

Ficker, Johannes, "Zu den Bemerkungen Luthers in Taulers Sermones (Augsburg, 1508)," *ThStK* (1936), 46ff.

Forest, Aimé, "Das Erlebnis des consensus voluntatis beim Hl. Bernhard," in *Bernhard von Clairvaux. Mönch und Mystiker. Internationaler Bernhard-Kongress Mainz 1953*, ed. Joseph Lortz (Wiesbaden, 1955), 120ff.

Gerrish, B. A., *Grace and Reason: A Study in the Theology of Luther* (Oxford, 1962).

Gilson, Etienne, *History of Christian Philosophy in the Middle Ages* (New York, 1955).

——,*Philosophie et incarnation selon Saint Augustin* (Montreal, 1947).

——,*The Mystical Theology of Saint Bernard*, trans. A. H. C. Downes (London, 1940).

Grabmann, Martin, *Mittelalterliches Geistesleben. Abhandlungen zur Geschichte der Scholastik und Mystik* (München, 1926).

Grane, Leif, *Contra Gabrielem. Luthers Auseinandersetzung mit Gabriel Biel in der Disputatio contra scholasticam theologiam* (Gyldendal, 1962).

Grunewald, Käte, *Studien zu Johannes Taulers Frömmigkeit* (Leipzig, 1930).

Gyllenkrok, Axel, *Rechtfertigung und Heiligung in der frühen evangelischen Theologie Luthers* (Uppsala, 1952).

Hahn, Fritz, "Faber Stapulensis und Luther," *ZKG*, 57 (1938), 357ff.

Hägglund, Bengt, "Luther's Doctrine of Justification in Late Medieval Theology," *Lutheran World*, 8 (1961).

Hamel, Adolf, *Der junge Luther und Augustin. Ihre Beziehungen in der Rechtfertigungslehre nach Luthers ersten Vorlesungen 1509-1518 untersucht*, Teil I (Gütersloh, 1934).

Hendrikx, Ephraem, *Augustins Verhältnis zur Mystik* (Theol. Diss. Würzburg, 1936), in *Zum Augustin-Gespräch der Gegenwart. Wege der Forschung*, V (Darmstadt, 1962).

Hering, Hermann, *Die Mystik Luthers in Zusammenhange seiner Theologie und ihrem*

Verhältniss zur älteren Mystik (Leipzig, 1879).
Hermann, Rudolf, *Luthers These 'Gerecht und Sünder zugleich'* (1930), in photomechanical reprint (Gütersloh, 1960).
Hirsch, Emmanuel, *Lutherstudien*, I (Gütersloh, 1954).
Hiss, Walter, *Die Anthropologie Bernhards von Clairvaux* (Berlin, 1964).
Hoffmann, P. Adolf, "Sacramentale Heilswege bei Tauler," in *Johannes Tauler. Ein Deutscher Mystiker. Gedenkschrift zum 600. Todestag*, ed. E. Filthaut O.P. (Essen, 1961).
Holl, Karl, *Gesammelte Aufsätze zur Kirchengeschichte*, I, *Luther* (Tübingen, 1932).
Hunzinger, A. W., *Lutherstudien*, I, *Luthers Neoplatonismus in der Psalmenvorlesung von 1513-1516* (Leipzig, 1906).
Jetter, Werner, *Die Taufe beim jungen Luther* (Tübingen, 1954).
Kihm, Sr. M. Engratis, "Die Drei-Wege-Lehre bei Tauler" in *Johannes Tauler. Ein Deutscher Mystiker. Gedenkschrift zum 600. Todestag*, ed. E. Filthaut O.P. (Essen, 1961).
Kropatscheck, Friedrich, *Die natürlichen Kräfte des Menschen in Luthers vorreformatorischer Theologie* (Greifswald, 1898).
Link, Wilhelm, *Das Ringen Luthers um die Freiheit der Theologie von der Philosophie* (München, 1955).
Lohse, Bernhard, *Ratio und Fides. Eine Untersuchung über die ratio in der Theologie Luthers* (Göttingen, 1964).
Metzger, G. K., *Gelebter Glaube. Die Formierung reformatorischen Denkens in Luthers erster Psalmenvorlesung dargestellt am Begriff des Affekts* (Göttingen, 1964).
Moeller, Bernd, "Tauler und Luther," in *La mystique rhénane* (Paris, 1963), 157ff.
Modalsli, Ole, *Das Gericht nach den Werken. Ein Beitrag zu Luthers Lehre vom Gesetz* (Göttingen, 1963).
Müller, A. V., *Luther und Tauler auf ihren theologischen Zusammenhang neu untersucht* (Bern, 1918).
Müller, Hans M., *Erfahrung und Glaube bei Luther* (Leipzig, 1929).
Mulligan, Robert W., "*Ratio Superior* and *Ratio Inferior:* the Historical Background," *The New Scholasticism*, 29 (1955), 1ff.
Nilsson, Kjell Ove, *Simul. Das Miteinander von Göttlichem und Menschlichem in Luthers Theologie. Forschungen zur Kirchen- und Dogmengeschichte*, 17 (Göttingen, 1966).
Oberman, Heiko Augustinus, "Facientibus quod in se est Deus non denegat gratiam: Robert Holcot, O.P. and the Beginnings of Luther's Theology," *HTR*, 55 (1962), 317ff.
——, "'Iustitia Christi' and 'Iustitia Dei': Luther and the Scholastic Doctrines of Justification," *HTR*, 59 (1966), 1ff.
——, "Simul gemitus et raptus: Luther und die Mystik," in *Kirche, Mystik, Heiligung und das Natürliche bei Luther. Vorträge des Dritten Internationalen Kongresses für Lutherforschung* (Göttingen, 1967), 20ff.
——, *The Harvest of Medieval Theology: Gabriel Biel and Late Medieval Nominalism* (Cambridge, Mass., 1963).
——, "Das tridentinische Rechtfertigungsdekret im Lichte spätmittelalterlicher Theologie," *ZThK* (1964), 251ff.
Pannenberg, Wolfhart, *Die Prädestinationslehre des Duns Skotus* (Göttingen, 1954).
Pinomaa, Lennart, *Der existenzielle Charakter der Theologie Luthers. Das Hervorbrechen der Theologie der Anfechtung und ihre Bedeutung für das Lutherverständnis, Annales Academiae Scientiarum Finnicae*, XLVII[1] (Helsinki, 1940).
Pourrat, P., *Christian Spirituality in the Middle Ages*, II (Westminster, Md., 1953).
Prenter, Regin, *Der barmherzige Richter: Iustitia dei passiva in Luthers Dictata super psalterium 1513-1515* (København, 1961).

——, *Spiritus Creator*, trans. John M. Jensen (Philadelphia, 1963).
Preus, James S., "Old Testament *Promissio* and Luther's New Hermeneutic," *HTR*, 60 (April, 1967), 145ff.
Quint, Josef, "Mystik und Sprache. Ihr Verhältnis zueinander, insbesondere in der spekulativen Mystik Meister Eckeharts," *Altdeutsche und altniederländische Mystik. Wege der Forschung*, XXIII, ed. Kurt Ruh (Darmstadt, 1964), 113ff.
Quiring, Horst, "Luther und die Mystik," *ZSTh*, 13 (1936), 150-174, 179-240.
Reypens, P. L., "Der 'goldene Pfennig' bei Tauler und Ruusbroeck," *Altdeutsche und altniederländische Mystik. Wege der Forschung*, XXIII, ed. Kurt Ruh (Darmstadt, 1964), 353ff.
Rühl, Artur, *Der Einfluss der Mystik auf Denken und Entwicklung des jungen Luthers* (Oberhessen, 1960).
Ruhland, Friedrich, *Luther und die Brautmystik nach Luthers Schrifttum bis 1521* (Gießen, 1938).
Saarnivaara, U., *Luther Discovers the Gospel* (St. Louis, 1951).
Scheel, Otto, "Taulers Mystik und Luthers reformatorische Entdeckung," *Festgabe für Julius Kaftan* (Tübingen, 1920), 198ff.
Schmaus, Michael, *Die psychologische Trinitätslehre des hl. Augustinus. Münsterische Beiträge zur Theologie*, 11 (Münster, 1927).
Schwarz, Reinhard, *Fides, Spes und Caritas beim jungen Luther unter besonderer Berücksichtigung der mittelalterlichen Tradition* (Berlin, 1962).
Seeberg, Reinhold, *Die religiösen Grundgedanken des jungen Luthers und ihr Verhältnis zu dem Ockamismus und der deutschen Mystik* (Berlin, 1931).
——, *Lehrbuch der Dogmengeschichte*, II (Erlangen, 1898).
Söhngen, Gottlieb, "Der Aufbau der augustinischen Gedachtnislehre," *Die Einheit in der Theologie. Gesammelte Abhandlungen, Aufsätze, Vorträge* (München, 1952), 63ff.
Steinbüchel, Theodor, *Mensch und Gott in Frömmigkeit und Ethos der deutschen Mystik* (Düsseldorf, 1952).
Stelzenberger, Johann, *Die Mystik des Johannes Gerson. Breslauer Studium zur historischen Theologie*, X (Breslau, 1928).
Stomps, M. A. H., *Die Anthropologie Martin Luthers: Eine philosophische Untersuchung* (Frankfurt a/M, 1935).
Tarvainen, Olavi, "Der Gedanke der conformitas Christi in Luthers Theologie," *ZSTh*, XXII (1953), 26ff.
Thimme, Wilhelm, "Die 'Deutsche Theologie' und Luthers 'Freiheit eines Christenmenschen.' Ein Vergleich," *ZThK*, 3 (1932), 193ff.
Vignaux, Paul, *Luther, commentateur des Sentences. Études de philosophie médiévale*, XXI (Paris, 1935).
——, "Sur Luther et Ockham," *FS*, 32 (1950) in *Wilhelm Ockham (1349-1949): Aufsätze zu seiner Philosophie und Theologie* (Münster, 1950), 21ff.
——, *Philosophy in the Middle Ages: An Introduction*, trans. E. C. Hall (Cleveland, 1962).
Vogelsang, Erich, *Die Anfänge von Luthers Christologie nach der ersten Psalmenvorlesung* (Berlin, 1929).
——, "Die Unio Mystica bei Luther," *ARG*, 35 (1939), 63ff.
——, "Luther und die Mystik," *Luther Jahrbuch* (1937), 32ff.
——, "Zur Datierung der frühesten Lutherpredigten," *ZKG*, 50 (1931), 112ff.
Von Walter, Johannes, *Mystik und Rechtfertigung beim jungen Luther* (Gütersloh, 1937).
Weier, Reinhold, "Der Einfluss des Nicolaus Cusanus auf das Denken Luthers," *Das Cusanus-Jubiläum. Mitteilungen und Forschungsbeiträge der Cusanus-Gesellschaft*, 4 (Mainz, 1964), 214ff.

——,*Das Thema vom verborgenen Gott von Nikolaus von Kues zu Martin Luther. Buchreihe der Cusanus-Gesellschaft*, II (Münster Westf., 1967).
Weilner, Ignaz, *Johannes Taulers Bekehrungsweg: Die Erfahrungsgrundlagen seiner Mystik* (Regensburg, 1961).
Wentzlaff-Eggebert, F. W., *Deutsche Mystik zwischen Mittelalter und Neuzeit. Einheit und Wandlung ihrer Erscheinungsformen* (Berlin, 1944).
Wolf, Ernst, "Johannes von Staupitz und die theologischen Anfänge Luthers," *Luther Jahrbuch* (1929), 43ff.
——,"Zur Frage des Naturrechts bei Thomas von Aquin und bei Luther," *Peregrinatio. Studien zur reformatorischen Theologie und zum Kirchenproblem* (München, 1954), 183ff.
Wyser, Paul, "Der Seelengrund in Taulers Predigten," *Lebendiges Mittelalter. Festgabe für Wolfgang Stammler* (Freiburg, 1958), 204ff.
Zellinger, Eduard, *Cusanus-Konkordanz. Unter Zugrundelegung der philosophischen und der bedeutendsten theologischen Werke* (München, 1960).

INDEX OF NAMES

INDEX OF SUBJECTS